294.356 Bst
Bstan-dzin-rgya-mtsho
In praise of great
compassion

3 4028 10291 2871
HARRIS COUNTY PUBLIC LIBRARY

$29.95
on1124466342

W9-CNC-397

DISCARD

Advance Praise for
In Praise of Great Compassion

"Another insightful volume in an important series, *In Praise of Great Compassion* is a deep and wonderful book that offers crucial lessons for our time—and for all time."
—Daniel Gilbert, Edgar Pierce Professor of Psychology, Harvard University

"*In Praise of Great Compassion* is a welcome arrival that illuminates the interface between two Buddhist traditions, Mahāyāna and Theravāda, through the common ground of compassion. These valuable teachings are a gift and a powerful message to the world."
—Ajahn Sundara, Amaravati Monastery

"His Holiness the Dalai Lama, together with Bhikṣuṇī Thubten Chodron, lucidly present the Buddha's teachings to a wider readership. The inclusion of different Buddhist traditions' practices on the important topic of great compassion is especially welcome, and I am delighted to see a chapter on Chinese Buddhism and its introduction to the Seven Round Compassion Contemplation, as well as the Four Great Vows. These are powerful practices not only to develop compassion but also to eliminate one's own karmic obstacles. May all beings benefit from this latest volume of the valuable Dharma series, the *Library of Wisdom and Compassion*."
—Bhikṣu Jian Hu, abbot of Sunnyvale Zen Center

THE LIBRARY OF WISDOM AND COMPASSION

The Library of Wisdom and Compassion is a special multivolume series in which His Holiness the Dalai Lama shares the Buddha's teachings on the complete path to full awakening that he himself has practiced his entire life. The topics are arranged especially for people not born in Buddhist cultures and are peppered with the Dalai Lama's unique outlook. Assisted by his long-term disciple, the American nun Thubten Chodron, the Dalai Lama sets the context for practicing the Buddha's teachings in modern times and then unveils the path of wisdom and compassion that leads to a meaningful life, a sense of personal fulfillment, and full awakening. This series is an important bridge from introductory to profound topics for those seeking an in-depth explanation from a contemporary perspective.

Volumes:

1. *Approaching the Buddhist Path*
2. *The Foundation of Buddhist Practice*
3. *Saṃsāra, Nirvāṇa, and Buddha Nature*
4. *Following in the Buddha's Footsteps*
5. *In Praise of Great Compassion*

More volumes to come!

THE LIBRARY OF WISDOM AND COMPASSION • VOLUME 5

In Praise of Great Compassion

Bhikṣu Tenzin Gyatso,
the Fourteenth Dalai Lama

and

Bhikṣuṇī Thubten Chodron

Wisdom

Wisdom Publications
199 Elm Street
Somerville, MA 02144 USA
wisdomexperience.org

© 2020 Dalai Lama and Thubten Chodron
All rights reserved.

No part of this book may be reproduced in any form or by any means, electronic or mechanical, including photography, recording, or by any information storage and retrieval system or technologies now known or later developed, without permission in writing from the publisher.

Library of Congress Cataloging-in-Publication Data
Names: Bstan-'dzin-rgya-mtsho, Dalai Lama XIV, 1935– author. | Thubten Chodron, 1950– author.
Title: In praise of great compassion / Bhiksu Tenzin Gyatso, the fouteenth Dalai Lama and Bhiksuni Thubten Chodron.
Description: Somerville, MA, USA: Wisdom Publications, 2020. | Series: The library of wisdom and compassion; 5 | Includes bibliographical references and index.
Identifiers: LCCN 2020001758 (print) | LCCN 2020001759 (ebook) | ISBN 9781614296829 | ISBN 9781614296836 (ebook)
Subjects: LCSH: Compassion—Religious aspects—Buddhism. | Joy—Religious aspects—Buddhism. | Love—Religious aspects—Buddhism. | Bodhicitta (Buddhism) | Buddhism—China—Tibet Autonomous Region—Doctrines.
Classification: LCC BQ4360 .B883 2020 (print) | LCC BQ4360 (ebook) | DDC 294.3/5677—dc23
LC record available at https://lccn.loc.gov/2020001758
LC ebook record available at https://lccn.loc.gov/2020001759

ISBN 978-1-61429-682-9 ebook ISBN 978-161429-683-6

24 23 22 21 20
5 4 3 2 1

Cover photo by Gen Heywood. Cover and interior design by Gopa & Ted 2.

Printed on acid-free paper that meets the guidelines for permanence and durability of the Production Guidelines for Book Longevity of the Council on Library Resources.

Printed in the United States of America.

Publisher's Acknowledgment

The publisher gratefully acknowledges the generous help of the Hershey Foundation in sponsoring the production of this book.

Contents

Preface

THE *LIBRARY OF WISDOM AND COMPASSION*, of which this volume is the fifth in the series, will be, when completed, His Holiness the Dalai Lama's major English-language text on the path to awakening. Before delving into this volume, a review of previously covered topics is helpful; you may want to read previous volumes for more on ideas and concepts mentioned in this volume or to provide background so that you will know where topics explained in this volume fit in the overall scheme of the path. The first volume, *Approaching the Buddhist Path,* explores the Buddhist view of life, mind, and emotions. It provides historical background, introduces us to a systematic approach to the spiritual path, and discusses how to apply Buddhist ideas to contemporary issues.

The second volume, *The Foundation of Buddhist Practice*, discusses gaining nondeceptive knowledge, the nature of mind, and the rebirth process. Chapters on how to be a sincere Dharma student, how to create a healthy relationship with spiritual mentors, and how to structure a meditation session follow. We then consider the essence of a meaningful life and the law of karma and its effects, which has to do with the ethical dimension of our actions. If we use our lives wisely and make wise ethical decisions, our deaths will be free from regret and fear. Having fortunate rebirths in the future, we will have conducive circumstances to continue our spiritual practice.

Volume 3, *Saṃsāra, Nirvāṇa, and Buddha Nature*, explores the four truths that constitute the Buddha's first teaching and encompass a study of, first, our present situation within cyclic existence (*saṃsāra*), the cycle of constantly recurring difficulties (*duḥkha*) under the influence of ignorance, mental afflictions, and polluted karma; second, the origins of this unsatisfactory situation, the afflictions that exist in our mind; third, the possibility of release—the cessations of saṃsāra and its cause, the peaceful state of nirvāṇa; and fourth, the path of practice and transformation leading to that state. Liberation and full awakening are possible because each of us has the potential to become a fully awakened buddha. Although this buddha nature may temporarily be covered by defilements, it never disappears and the obscurations covering it are adventitious and can be removed.

Volume 4, *Following in the Buddha's Footsteps*, begins with a discussion of taking refuge, the process of entrusting our spiritual guidance to the Three Jewels—the Buddha, Dharma, and Saṅgha. This follows naturally from volume 3, because the last two truths—true cessation and true paths—are the Dharma Jewel, which when actualized in our own mindstream protects us from all misery. The true path encompasses the methods to practice in order to overcome these defilements: the three higher trainings of ethical conduct, concentration, and wisdom. This includes practical instructions on how to live ethically, how to develop meditative concentration, and how to generate wisdom through the practice of the four establishments of mindfulness—mindfulness of the body, feelings, mind, and phenomena—and the thirty-seven harmonies with awakening.

This leads us to the present volume, *In Praise of Great Compassion*.

Overview of In Praise of Great Compassion

In volumes 3 and 4, we delved into the four truths; the first two truths concern saṃsāra and its causes, the last two liberation and the path that brings it about. The emphasis was on our situation as an individual and taking responsibility for it: our mind is the creator of both duḥkha and peace, of saṃsāra and nirvāṇa, so rather than blame others or adopt a victim mentality, we are encouraged to be conscientious regarding our actions, tame our afflictions, and cultivate ethical conduct, concentration, and wisdom to free ourselves from saṃsāra.

This does not mean that we are isolated individuals in a cold universe. Rather, the buddhas and bodhisattvas, who have accomplished what we aim to achieve, are always ready to teach and guide us. In addition, we are embedded in a universe with other sentient beings, all of whom have been kind to us in one way or another and in one rebirth or another. It is only suiting that we repay their kindness, and the best way to do this is to subdue our afflictions and cultivate our good qualities so that we can increase our ability to benefit them temporarily while we're in saṃsāra, and ultimately, by leading them to supreme awakening. *In Praise of Great Compassion* is about opening our hearts to others and generating and strengthening our determination to benefit sentient beings.

To do this, we begin with cultivating a positive attitude toward others by contemplating the four immeasurables—immeasurable love, immeasurable compassion, immeasurable empathic joy, and immeasurable equanimity—as taught and practiced in both the Pāli and Sanskrit traditions. The method to do this is the topic of the first chapter. Bodhicitta, the aspiration to attain full awakening in order to benefit all sentient beings most effectively, is based on the four immeasurables and on knowledge that attaining liberation and awakening is possible; this is explained in chapter 2. The Sanskrit tradition has two ways of developing the altruistic intention of bodhicitta—the seven cause-and-effect instructions and equalizing and exchanging self and others—which are described in chapters 3 and 4.

Chapter 5 discusses the difference between the self-centered attitude and self-grasping ignorance as well as other topics that pertain to cultivating bodhicitta and becoming a bodhisattva, and chapter 6 explains Candrakīrti's famous homage to great compassion at the beginning of his *Supplement to the "Middle Way"* (*Madhyamakāvatāra*). With all this as background, in chapter 7 we are ready to generate aspiring and engaging bodhicitta. Aspiring bodhicitta wishes to attain full awakening for the benefit of all beings, and engaging bodhicitta commits to practice the path that leads to supreme awakening by adopting the bodhisattva ethical code.

Love, compassion, bodhicitta, and the bodhisattva ethical codes in Chinese Buddhism are explained in chapter 8, showing how bodhicitta is emphasized in East Asian Buddhist traditions. Many people do not know that the Pāli tradition also presents bodhicitta, its cultivation, and the perfections; these are discussed in chapter 9. Chapter 10 describes the very practical techniques of mind training that help us to generate bodhicitta and maintain an attitude of kindness and compassion no matter what comes our way. Each chapter contains reflections that you are encouraged to contemplate. The reflections not only review some of the major points but also give you a chance to put these teachings into practice and transform your mind.

A glossary, section on recommended reading, and index can be found at the end of the book. The next volume in the series will continue by setting forth the ten perfections as practiced in both the Pāli and Sanskrit traditions.

How This Book Came About

The prefaces of the preceding volumes of the *Library of Wisdom and Compassion* told the story of the conception and development of this series, so here I will mention only a few things that pertain to this volume in particular.

You will notice that the volume contains many citations from Śāntideva's *Engaging in the Bodhisattvas' Deeds* (*Bodhicaryāvatāra*). His Holiness has often stated that this is one of his favorite texts, which explains why he has frequently taught it during public teachings in India. The experience of sitting in a crowd of thousands of people who have gathered together to learn about great compassion and bodhicitta from a teacher such as His Holiness is indescribable, especially considering that most large events in our world are sports events, political rallies, concerts, and conferences where people's motivations range widely.

His Holiness also frequently teaches mind-training texts such as "The Thirty-Seven Practices of Bodhisattvas" and "The Eight Verses of Mind Training"—short texts that emphasize bodhicitta—in non-Buddhist countries and in India and Asia as preludes to Buddhist tantric empowerments. Another of his favorite texts to teach is Kamalaśīla's *Middle Stages of Meditation* (*Bhāvanākrama II*), which discusses the seven cause-and-effect instructions, and various texts on the stages of the path (*lam rim*) that emphasize bodhicitta. It happens not infrequently that His Holiness is moved to tears when teaching one of these texts or when giving the ceremonies for aspiring and engaging bodhicitta.[1]

Please Note

Although this series is coauthored, the vast majority of the material is His Holiness's teachings. I researched and wrote the parts about the Pāli tradition, wrote some other passages, and composed the reflections. For ease of reading, most honorifics have been omitted, but that does not diminish the great respect we have for the most excellent sages, practitioners, and learned adepts. Foreign terms are given in italics parenthetically at their first usage. Unless otherwise noted with "P" or "T," indicating Pāli or Tibetan, respectively, italicized terms are Sanskrit or the term is the same in Sanskrit and Pāli. When two italicized terms are listed, the first is Sanskrit, the second Pāli. For consistency, Sanskrit spelling is used for Sanskrit and Pāli terms in common usage (nirvāṇa, Dharma, arhat, and so forth), except in citations from Pāli scriptures. The term *śrāvaka* encompasses solitary realizers, unless there is reason to specifically differentiate them, as is done, for example, in chapter 5. To maintain the flow of a passage, it is not always possible to gloss all new terms on their first usage, so a glossary is provided at the end of the book. "Sūtra" often refers to Sūtrayāna and "Tantra" to Tantrayāna—the Sūtra Vehicle and Tantra Vehicle, respectively. When these two words are not capitalized, they refer to two types of scriptures: sūtras and tantras. Mahāyāna here refers principally to the bodhisattva path as explained in the Sanskrit tradition. In general, the meaning of all philosophical terms accords with the presentation of the Prāsaṅgika Madhyamaka tenet system. Unless otherwise noted, the personal pronoun "I" refers to His Holiness.

Appreciation

My deepest respect goes to Śākyamuni Buddha and all the buddhas, bodhisattvas, and arhats who embody the Dharma and with compassion teach us unawakened beings. I also bow to all the realized lineage masters of all Buddhist traditions through whose kindness the Dharma still exists in our world.

This series appears in many volumes, so I will express appreciation to those involved in each individual volume. This volume, the fifth in the *Library of Wisdom and Compassion*, has depended on the abilities and efforts of His Holiness's translators—Geshe Lhakdor, Geshe Dorji Damdul, and Mr. Tenzin Tsepak. I am grateful to Geshe Dorji Damdul, Geshe Dadul Namgyal, and Bhikṣuṇī Sangye Khadro for checking the manuscript, and to Samdhong Rinpoche for clarifying important points. I also thank Bhikkhu Bodhi for his clear teachings on the Pāli tradition and for generously answering my many questions. He also kindly looked over the sections of the book on the Pāli tradition before publication. The staff at the Private

Office of His Holiness kindly facilitated the interviews, and Sravasti Abbey supported me while I worked on this volume. Mary Petrusewicz skillfully edited this book. I thank everyone at Wisdom Publications who contributed to the successful production of this series. All errors are my own.

Bhikṣuṇī Thubten Chodron
Sravasti Abbey

Abbreviations

AN — Aṅguttara Nikāya. Translated by Bhikkhu Bodhi in *The Numerical Discourses of the Buddha* (Boston: Wisdom Publications, 2012).

BCA — *Engaging in the Bodhisattvas' Deeds* (*Bodhicaryāvatāra*) by Śāntideva.

BV — *Commentary on Bodhicitta* (*Bodhicittavivaraṇa*) by Nāgārjuna.

BVA — *Buddhavaṃsa* (*Chronicle of Buddhas*). Translated by I. B. Horner in *The Minor Anthologies of the Pāli Canon*, vol. 3 (London: Pāli Text Society, 2007).

CP — *Cariyāpiṭaka* (*The Basket of Conduct*). Translated by I. B. Horner in *The Minor Anthologies of the Pāli Canon*, vol. 3.

DB — *Birth Stories of the Ten Bodhisattvas* (*Dasabodhisattuppattikathā*) by Hammalawa Saddhatissa (London: Pāli Text Society, 1975).

DN — Dīgha Nikāya. Translated by Maurice Walshe in *The Long Discourses of the Buddha* (Boston: Wisdom Publications, 1995).

ERB — *Exhortation to Resolve on Buddhahood* by Peixiu. Translated by Bhikṣu Dharmamitra in *On Generating the Resolve to Become a Buddha* (Seattle: Kalavinka Press, 2009).

LC — *The Great Treatise on the Stages of the Path* (T. *Lam rim chen mo*) by Tsongkhapa, 3 vols. Translated by Joshua Cutler et al. (Ithaca, NY: Snow Lion Publications, 2000–2004).

LS *Praise to the Supramundane* (*Lokātītastava*) by Nāgārjuna.

MA *Madhyamakālaṃkāra* by Śāntarakṣita. In James Blumenthal, *The Ornament of the Middle Way: A Study of the Madhyamaka Thought of Śāntarakṣita* (Ithaca, NY: Snow Lion Publications, 2004).

MMA *Supplement to "Treatise on the Middle Way"* by Candrakīrti. Translated by Jeffrey Hopkins in *Compassion in Tibetan Buddhism, Tsong-ka-pa* (Ithaca, NY: Snow Lion Publications, 1980).

MMK *Treatise on the Middle Way* (*Mūlamadhyamakakārikā*) by Nāgārjuna.

MN Majjhima Nikāya. Translated by Bhikkhu Ñāṇamoli and Bhikkhu Bodhi in *The Middle-Length Discourses of the Buddha* (Boston: Wisdom Publications, 1995).

P Pāli.

POW *Pearl of Wisdom: Buddhist Prayers and Practices, Book 2*. Edited by Thubten Chodron (Newport, WA: Sravasti Abbey, 2014).

PV *Commentary on the "Compendium of Reliable Cognition"* (*Pramāṇavārttika*) by Dharmakīrti.

RA *Ratnāvalī* by Nāgārjuna. Translated by John Dunne and Sara McClintock in *The Precious Garland: An Epistle to a King* (Boston: Wisdom Publications, 1997).

RGV *Sublime Continuum* (*Ratnagotravibhāga*, *Uttaratantra*) by Maitreya.

SCP *Tale of a Wish-Fulfilling Dream* (*Svapna-cintāmaṇi-parikathā*) by Nāgārjuna. Translated by Geshe Kelsang Wangmo. At http://ibd-buddhism.org/GeshePALSANG/2017DreamTale/DreamTale_Tib-Eng_20171104.pdf.

Sn Suttanipāta. Translated by Bhikkhu Bodhi in *The Suttanipāta* (Somerville, MA: Wisdom Publications, 2017).

SN Saṃyutta Nikāya. Translated by Bhikkhu Bodhi *in The Connected Discourses of the Buddha* (Boston: Wisdom Publications, 2000).

T Tibetan.

TP *A Treatise on the Pāramīs* by Ācariya Dhammapāla. Translated by Bhikkhu Bodhi (Kandy: Buddhist Publication Society, 1978). Also at https://www.accesstoinsight.org/lib/authors/bodhi/wheel409.html.

TTG *Treatise on the Ten Grounds* by Nāgārjuna. Translated by Bhiksu Dharmamitra (Seattle: Kalavinka Press, 2019).

Vism *Visuddhimagga* by Buddhaghosa. Translated by Bhikkhu Ñāṇamoli in *The Path of Purification* (Kandy: Buddhist Publication Society, 1991).

VTBV *Treatise on the "Generating the Bodhi Resolve Sūtra"* by Vasubandhu Bodhisattva. Translated by Bhikṣu Dharmamitra in *Vasubandhu's Treatise on the Bodhisattva Vow* (Seattle: Kalavinka Press, 2009).

WSW *The Wheel of Sharp Weapons* by Dharmarakṣita, in Thubten Chodron, *Good Karma* (Boston: Shambhala Publications, 2016).

Introduction

KINDNESS IS our first experience in life; our mother and those around her immediately extended affection, care, and a warm heart toward us. As we grow up, we continually experience the kindness of others—our teachers, friends, even the people we don't know personally who provide the food, shelter, clothes, and medicine we need to stay alive. The kind hearts of others benefit us, but developing a kind heart ourselves really enriches our life by connecting us to others and enabling us to experience the joy of caring for and loving other sentient beings. In short, a kind heart is essential for our own and others' welfare. For this reason I say, "My religion is kindness." Everyone—even animals and insects—understands kindness and thrives by giving and receiving kindness.

Why should we be kind to others? First, kindness isn't something foreign. Even ants and bees cooperate and take care of one another. They know that to survive they must work together. Animals look after their own kind. Rather than survival of the fittest, survival of the most cooperative enables life to continue. Charles Darwin said in the *Descent of Man*:[2]

> As man advances in civilisation, and small tribes are united into larger communities, the simplest reason would tell each individual that he ought to extend his social instincts and sympathies to all the members of the same nation, though personally unknown to him. This point being once reached, there is only an artificial barrier to prevent his sympathies extending to the men of all nations and races . . . Sympathy beyond the confines of man, that is, humanity to lower animals, seems to be one of the latest

> moral acquisitions . . . This virtue, one of the noblest with which man is endowed, seems to arise incidentally from our sympathies becoming more tender and more widely diffused, until they are extended to all sentient beings.

And Albert Einstein tells us:[3]

> A human being is part of the whole, called by us "Universe," a part limited in time and space. He experiences himself, his thoughts and feelings as something separate from the rest—a kind of optical delusion of consciousness. The striving to free oneself from this delusion is the one issue of true religion. Not to nourish it but to try to overcome it is the way to reach the attainable measure of peace of mind.

Our happiness and well-being are interrelated with those of others. We depend on one another to have the necessities and enjoyments of life; so if others suffer, we too will be affected. Since we depend on others so much, they deserve to be treated well; repaying their kindness only makes sense. Extending ourselves to others with a warm heart, even in small ways, brings so much goodness in our world.

Love and compassion are not foreign to us. Those mental factors are an inextricable part of our minds. Through Buddhist practice, we consciously cultivate and extend our instinctual affinity for kindness and our innate ability to empathize and share with others. As sentient beings' love and compassion increase, so does forgiveness. We become able to communicate better with others, listening to their stories and paying attention to their feelings and needs as well as to our own. This has a ripple effect in society, spreading a feeling of well-being within each person as well as among people, groups, and nations.

Generating love and compassion takes effort; first we must learn how to cultivate these qualities and use them effectively with wisdom. Reading the teachings in this book will give you the tools to go in that direction. Practicing under the guidance of a Buddhist teacher who can model the teachings in his or her own behavior is of great help and inspiration as well.

1 | The Four Immeasurables

FOLLOWERS OF the Pāli tradition cultivate the four brahmavihāras (divine abidings, immeasurables)—immeasurable equanimity, love, compassion, and empathic joy—toward others. In the Mahāyāna these four are expanded and built upon to become the altruistic intention of bodhicitta that seeks to attain buddhahood in order to benefit all sentient beings. Practitioners engage in the practices of the Perfection and Vajra Vehicles motivated by this altruistic intention.

We'll begin by exploring the four immeasurables as explained in the Pāli text *The Path of Purification* (*Visuddhimagga*), by the fifth-century Indian sage Buddhaghosa. His explanation not only accords with Mahāyāna teachings but also gives practitioners of the Mahāyāna some new angles to approach love (*maitrī, mettā*), compassion (*karuṇā*), empathic joy (*muditā*), and equanimity (*upekṣā, upekkhā*). This will be followed by an explanation of the four immeasurables in the Perfection Vehicle (*Pāramitāyāna*) and in the Vajra Vehicle (*Vajrayāna*). All of these explanations are instructions for meditation.

The Four Immeasurables in the Pāli Tradition

Buddhaghosa devotes an entire chapter of *The Path of Purification* to the development of the four immeasurables, which are widely taught and practiced in both the Pāli and Sanskrit traditions. They are called "immeasurable" or "boundless" (*apramāṇa, appamañña*) for several reasons. First, they are directed with a mind free of prejudice or partiality toward an immeasurable number of sentient beings. In addition, they are ideally to be practiced in states of *dhyāna* in which the limited intentions of desire-realm minds have been superseded. Although meditators may have been born in the desire realm, their minds become form-sphere consciousnesses when entering a dhyāna with one of these four as its object. A form-realm consciousness is not limited by the five hindrances (āvaraṇa) that interfere with the cultivation of concentration: sensual desire (*kāmacchanda*), malice (*vyāpāda, byāpāda*), lethargy and sleepiness (*styāna-middha, thīna-middha),* restlessness and regret (*auddhatya-kaukṛtya, uddhacca-kukkucca*), and deluded doubt (*vicikitsā, vicikicchā*). Dhyānic states also are imbued with the five dhyānic factors: investigation (*vitarka, vitakka*), analysis (*vicāra*), joy (*prīti*, pīti), bliss (*sukha*), and one-pointedness (*ekāgratā, ekaggatā*) that render them boundless.[4]

The four immeasurables are also called "brahmavihāras" or "divine abodes," after Brahmā, the deity who is the ruler of one of the dhyānic realms where beings' minds are pure, smooth, and gentle. In the term "brahmavihāra," "brahma" implies pure because these four are free from attachment, anger, and apathy. They are also the best—another implication of the term "brahma"—because they are beneficial attitudes to have toward sentient beings. The four are called "abodes" or "ways of living" because they are peaceful resting places for the mind, in that they are virtuous mental states that help us to live in constructive ways that help ourselves and others.

Practiced in daily life, love, compassion, empathic joy, and equanimity will make our minds and relationships with others warmer and more peaceful. Practiced in meditation, these four can be used to cultivate concentration and attain the dhyānas (meditative stabilizations). Of course the best effects come if we do both, because maintaining a peaceful mind by practicing the four immeasurables between formal meditation sessions increases their power during meditation sessions. Similarly, after abiding single-pointedly in one of the four immeasurables during meditation, a person's mind tends to be permeated with it after the meditation session.

The Three Higher Trainings and the Four Immeasurables

The three higher trainings are encapsulated in the four immeasurables, as illustrated by the *Mettā Sutta*. At the outset of this sūtra, the Buddha spoke of the type of person who practices love. This practice involves the higher training in ethical conduct, because to develop love for others we must first refrain from harming them. The second part of the sūtra details all the beings to extend love toward and explains how to meditate on love so that it leads to states of meditative absorption, which pertains to the higher training in concentration. The end of the sūtra speaks of how this practice can lead to the cultivation of insight and thus to nirvāṇa, which necessitates the higher training in wisdom.

When practiced by someone who has not cultivated wisdom, meditation on the four immeasurables has the potential to lead to rebirth in any of the divine realms of the Brahmā world that correspond to the dhyānas.[5] However, the ultimate aim of meditation on the four brahmavihāras is to attain a pliable, concentrated mind that can penetrate the three characteristics—that is, the impermanence, unsatisfactoriness, and selflessness of things—and serve as a basis for insight.

In many sūtras, the Buddha spoke of practitioners abiding with their hearts imbued with love that extends in all directions. Such practitioners have attained a meditative absorption that is called the "liberation of mind with love" (P. *mettā-cetovimutti*). This mind, which genuinely wishes all beings to have happiness, has temporarily abandoned the five hindrances, especially anger and malice, through the force of single-pointed concentration. The Buddha praises this samādhi because of its ability to prevent anger from arising and banish anger that has arisen. When practitioners have attained the ārya eightfold path and apply this mind of dhyāna to it, they progress through the stages and attain arhatship.[6]

Teachers may present the four immeasurables in slightly different ways—for instance, as a practice to improve our relationships with others, as a practice to heal destructive emotions, or as a practice through which to cultivate serenity.

One way to practice them in our relationships with others in daily life is as follows: Love has the aspect of friendliness toward sentient beings and wishes them to have happiness and its causes. This should be our basic attitude toward any living being we encounter. When we see the suffering of sentient beings, we respond with compassion, abandoning any fear or disgust, and do what we can to be of assistance. When we witness their happiness, success, virtue, and good qualities, our response is empathic joy—the opposite of the jealousy that so often plagues us. After that, we remain balanced and equanimous because our aims for sentient beings have been accomplished. However, sometimes we see others' duḥkha and try to help, but they are not open to removing the causes of their misery. At that time, rather than giving in to frustration or despair, practicing equanimity is best. In that way, the door remains open so that we can help them if an opportunity arises at a later date.

Introduction to the Four Divine Abodes

The Path of Purification says **love** "has the aspect of friendliness as its characteristic. Its function is to promote friendliness. It is manifested as the disappearance of malice and annoyance. Its proximate cause is seeing others as lovable. When it succeeds, it eliminates malice. When it fails, it degenerates into selfish affectionate desire."

Love views one, many, or all beings as lovable and wishes them well. We may begin with one or just a few people. By gradually increasing our ability to love, we will be able to extend love to more and more living beings until it spreads to all beings without exception. It will spread to both those who treat us well and those who disparage or harm us, to those who have good values and those who do not, to those we approve of and those we don't, to those who are well-liked by all and those who are despised. This love does not seek anything for ourselves; the pleasure is in loving. Such love is strong, not fickle according to either our mood or how others treat us. It is ready to help, but does not have an agenda or coerce others to fulfill our expectations.

Many movies, novels, and other art forms deal with romantic and sensual "love." From a Buddhist viewpoint, this emotion should more accurately be called "attachment," as it is generally based on exaggerating someone's good qualities or projecting excellent qualities that aren't present. Attachment also gives way to emotional neediness and possessiveness that lead to making demands or having high expectations of the other. Immeasurable love is free from such complications.

Combining the understanding of selflessness with love demolishes any sense of possession. Love infused with a sense of selflessness knows that ultimately there is no possessor or person to possess. There is no independent soul or essence in a person to love or to be loved. The highest love wishes beings to have the highest happiness and will show others the path to the end of suffering, the path realized and taught by the Buddha.

In *The Path of Purification* Buddhaghosa says **compassion** "has the aspect of allaying suffering for its characteristic. Its function is to find others' suffering unbearable. It manifests as noncruelty and nonviolence. Its proximate cause is seeing helplessness in those overwhelmed by suffering. When it succeeds, it reduces cruelty. When it fails, it produces personal distress." Compassion enables us to look at suffering in all its tortuous varieties without succumbing to despair. From the annoyance of the smallest inconvenience, to extreme physical pain, to unfathomable emotional misery, all beings caught in saṃsāra are susceptible to duḥkha. Instead of reacting by medicating the distress we experience when seeing our own or others' suffering, compassion opens our heart to this universal experience and reaches out either directly or indirectly to others. This compassion isn't limited to those who are evidently suffering, but extends to those who seem happy at this moment yet still live under the control of ignorance, afflictions, and polluted karma.

Immeasurable compassion, like immeasurable love, does not favor some and exclude others. It does not blame others for their own suffering, but realizes that it was caused by a mind overwhelmed by ignorance. In addition, compassion does not blame one person for another person's suffering, but understands that both beings are controlled by karma and thus both are worthy of compassion, whether they are the perpetrator or victim of harm.

Empathic joy delights at the happiness and good fortune of others. Buddhaghosa says empathic joy "is characterized by bringing joy. Its function is to oppose envy, and it manifests as the abandonment of jealousy and boredom. Its proximate cause is seeing others' success. When it succeeds, it reduces jealousy and boredom. When it fails, it produces overexcitement." In contrast to the misery of jealousy—thinking that we, not they, should be happy and have good opportunities—empathic joy is gladness in our own hearts that rejoices at others' well-being. When we consciously cultivate empathic joy, we see so much goodness in the world. Instead of the world seeming bleak and filled with narrow-minded people and corrupt governments, our view will expand to see the goodness in others and the many ways in which people help each other on a daily basis. At present the source of our empathic joy may be limited to our own personal gain and the gain of those we cherish. As our empathic joy expands, we will rejoice in the virtue and success of others.

Buddhaghosa describes **equanimity** as "characterized by promoting the aspect of balance toward beings. Its function is to see equality in beings. It manifests as the subduing of anger and attachment. Its proximate cause is seeing the ownership of karma thus: 'Beings are owners of their karma. Whose (if not theirs) is the choice by which they will become happy, or will be free from suffering, or will not lose the success they have attained?' When it succeeds, equanimity makes anger and attachment subside. When it fails, it produces an unknowing equanimity, which is [worldly indifference and apathy] based on the householder life."

Our lives consist of so many extremes—wealth and poverty, loneliness and belonging, high and low status, praise and blame—and our emotions likewise vacillate with each new object, person, or situation we encounter. Equanimity is steadiness of mind, tranquility in the midst of whatever environment we find ourselves in and whatever treatment we receive. It is not uninterested, apathetic indifference in which we build a wall to protect ourselves from emotional pain. Rather, equanimity is relaxed, receptive, free of fear and clinging. It allows our spiritual practice to stay on track without being buffeted around here and there by exciting new ideas or intense emotions. Without clinging to anything, equanimity gives space to appreciate everything.

Understanding karma fosters equanimity. People meet with results of causes they created. For example, when we encounter misfortune, there's no reason for depression. The situation is a result of actions we ourselves did, and as with everything, it too will pass. When success comes our way, there's no reason for elation, because it is a passing result of our actions. Rather than blame other people, we accept the results of our actions, knowing that if we want a different future, we must act now to create the causes for it.

Practicing equanimity is helpful when dealing with people who insult us or people who are not receptive to our help. In the former case, we remain equanimous in the face of others' insults, knowing that we don't need to take their words personally and that what they say is more a reflection of their unhappiness than it is of anything we did. In the latter case, someone may have responded to our intention to help by telling us to mind our own business. Rather than feeling frustrated or becoming angry, we can choose to remain equanimous and let the other person be, knowing that we can control neither him nor the situation. As related in the *Upakkilesa Sutta* (MN 128), the monks at Kosambī were engaged in vicious disputes that sometimes spilled over into brawls. The Buddha gave them advice, but the monks refused to listen and responded that it was their quarrel. Seeing that these disciples' minds were overwhelmed with anger, resentment, and belligerence, the Buddha went alone to another village where his disciples were more receptive.

Insight into the nature of reality is helpful for the cultivation of equanimity. Suffering ensues from grasping at I and mine. We think, "*I* was criticized," "*My* new car was dented," "His lies destroyed *my* reputation." Grasping at I and mine clearly disturbs the mind, sending it away from equanimity and into flurries of clinging, animosity, and resentment. Understanding that there is no I or mine releases craving and other afflictions, allowing equanimity to arise.

The commentary *The Illuminator of the Supreme Meaning* (*Paramatthajotikā*), attributed to Buddhaghosa, succinctly defines the four immeasurables (2.128):

> Love is the state of desiring to offer happiness and welfare, with the thought "May all beings be happy," and so forth. Compassion is the state of desiring to remove suffering and misfortunate, with the thought "May they be liberated from these sufferings," and so forth. Empathic joy is the state of desiring the continuity of [others'] happiness and welfare, with the thought "You beings are rejoicing; it is good that you are rejoicing; it is very good," and so forth. Equanimity is the state of observing [another's] suffering or happiness and thinking, "These appear because of that individual's own past activities."

The four brahmavihāras are generated in the above order. Each successive one does not override its predecessor; all four permeate and complement one another. Compassion prevents love and empathic joy from forgetting the misery of the world or becoming wrapped up in the pleasant feelings that they bring. Love prevents compassion from becoming partial and keeps it focused on all beings, not just those with manifest gross suffering. Empathic joy prevents compassion from sliding into despair because empathic joy remembers goodness and happiness. Equanimity keeps love, compassion, and empathic joy focused on the ultimate aim of nirvāṇa. It makes them stable so they don't deteriorate into uncontrolled or sentimental emotionalism.

Here we see that the path is not about cultivating isolated virtuous emotions and attitudes. When cultivated together, these virtuous mental states complement, balance, and enhance one another. It is clear that the path to nirvāṇa does not entail doing one practice only, but developing all aspects of our human character.

REFLECTION

Contemplate the gist of each of the brahmavihāras. How do these short explanations expand the usual way you think of love, compassion, empathic joy, and equanimity? Do these summaries pique your interest in having a deeper understanding of the four?

1. **Love** has the aspect of friendliness and its function is to promote friendliness. It makes malice and annoyance disappear. Its proximate cause is seeing others as endearing. When it succeeds, it eliminates malice. When it fails, it degenerates into selfish affectionate desire.

2. **Compassion** has the aspect of allaying suffering. It functions to find others' suffering unbearable and manifests as noncruelty and nonviolence. Its proximate cause is seeing those overwhelmed by suffering as needing help. When it succeeds, it reduces cruelty. When it fails, it produces personal distress.

3. **Empathic joy** delights at the happiness and good fortune of others. It brings joy and functions to oppose envy; it causes jealousy and boredom to subside. Its proximate cause is seeing other beings' success. When it succeeds, it reduces jealousy and boredom. When it fails, it produces giddy excitement.

4. **Equanimity** promotes balance toward beings and functions to see equality in beings. It subdues anger and attachment. Its proximate cause is seeing

that each being is the owner of their karma. When it succeeds, equanimity reduces anger and attachment. When it fails, it produces indifference and apathy.

Meditation on Love

The *Sutta on Love* (*Karaṇīya Mettā Sutta*, Sn 1.8) speaks of immeasurable love in particular and is one of the most well-liked and oft-recited sūtras. Since animosity is the opposite of love and prevents its development, it is essential to reduce anger and ill will. We begin this process by reflecting on the disadvantages of animosity and the benefits of patience and fortitude. This step occurs at the outset, because we "cannot abandon unseen dangers and attain unknown advantages" (Vism 9.2).

Anger and hatred destroy trust and tear apart valued relationships; they destroy the merit created with great effort; they compel us to act in ways we later regret, bringing on guilt and remorse. Fortitude, on the other hand, is like a soothing balm on a wound and a beautiful piece of jewelry that attracts others to us. It protects our virtue and all that is valuable to us in this and future lives.

Initially it is important to cultivate love toward specific people in a definite order. It is recommended not to begin the cultivation of any of the four immeasurables toward someone to whom you are or could be sexually attracted. There is the amusing but unfortunate story of a man who was meditating on love for his wife and, confusing love with sexual attraction, tried to leave his meditation room to get to his wife. However, so blinded was he by lust, he couldn't see the door and so spent all night fighting with the wall! Also, the people we initially cultivate love toward should be alive. Since the deceased are no longer in the form in which we knew them, cultivating love for them is difficult. However, out of concern for our deceased relatives and friends, we can make offerings to the Three Jewels on their behalf and imagine that they rejoice in the merit dedicated for them.

First cultivate love toward yourself. Contemplate repeatedly, "May I be happy and free from suffering. May I be free from animosity, affliction, and anxiety, and live happily." Add whatever other good wishes you would like, such as, "May I be generous and kind," and "May I be free from internal and external obstacles on the path." Focusing on yourself first is important to develop the feeling of what it is like to wish someone well. In the process of doing this, you will realize that being happy and peaceful and avoiding pain are everyone's fundamental wishes.

Some people may wonder if generating love toward themselves is selfish or self-indulgent. Cultivating love toward yourself is not selfish because the goal is to generate love toward all beings, which includes yourself. You are no more or less important than others; you are also worthy of love and kindness. Since many people suffer from self-hatred, this meditation is an excellent counteracting method. While cultivating love for yourself alone does not bring meditative absorption, it does get you going in the right direction. Conversely, following selfishness and self-indulgence is unkind to yourself and causes misery. Self-centeredness, which makes you greedy, easily offended, and vindictive, does not bring you happiness, whereas developing mental tranquility that is free from afflictions does.

Having generated love for yourself, extend love to others by contemplating, "Just as I want to be happy and never experience suffering, so too do other beings." The next person to send love to should be someone you respect and for whom you have positive feelings. It is recommended to consider the qualities of your spiritual mentor, preceptor, or another teacher and recall the help you have received from them. With awareness of his or her kindness, cultivate love by contemplating, "May he be happy and free from suffering. May he be free from animosity, affliction, and anxiety and live happily." By recalling the inspiring example of this person's virtuous conduct and learning, it is possible to attain meditative absorption on love with respect to him.

Continue to extend love more broadly. Doing this involves breaking down the barrier in your mind that puts people into narrow categories and believes stereotypes. Now cultivate love toward a very dear friend, thinking in the same way as above. Generating love for a dear friend is done after generating it for a respected person because focusing on a dear person can easily make attachment arise under the guise of love, whereas this doesn't happen toward a person you respect and appreciate.

When the mind is malleable, turn your attention to a neutral person and, seeing her as a dear friend, generate love. When your mind is compliant with this, go on to develop love for a hostile person, seeing him as neutral. A hostile person is not someone who is hostile toward you—although he may feel that way—but someone for whom you have hostile feelings. Those fortunate few who do not see others as harmful or threatening and who do not get upset with uncooperative people can skip generating love toward hostile people.

REFLECTION

1. Cultivate love for yourself by reflecting again and again, "May I be happy and free from suffering. May I be free from animosity, anxiety, and live happily." Add whatever other good wishes you would like, such as "May I be generous and kind" and "May I be free from internal and external obstacles on the path." Do this slowly so you feel the change in your attitude for yourself.
2. Contemplate in the same way, wishing the same good circumstances for someone you respect.
3. Contemplate in the same way, wishing the same good circumstances for a friend.
4. Contemplate in the same way, wishing the same good circumstances for a neutral person—for example, a stranger you see at the store.
5. Contemplate in the same way, wishing the same good circumstances for someone you usually feel hostile toward. Imagine that person being happy and because of that their actions and speech change.
6. Rest your mind in the feeling of wishing everyone happiness and imagining them as being happy.

Counteracting Animosity and Anger

Many of us find it difficult to wish happiness and well-being to those who have harmed us, because our mind is chained by resentment and grudge-holding. We may wish to retaliate for the harm we received or hope the government does it for us, through imprisonment, capital punishment, or military strikes. If we see ourselves as civilized, we may simply wish that those who harmed us encounter misfortune that will teach them a lesson or give them a taste of their own medicine. If you cannot get past these negative feelings, return to generating love toward one of the previous persons, and when the mind is drenched in that feeling, then return to the difficult person.

If animosity persists, apply an antidote, such as the ones offered below. If one doesn't release the anger, try another. Practice these antidotes repeatedly over time; don't expect that simply changing your thought once will change it forever.

Reflecting on the disadvantages of anger is a worthy antidote. The Buddha said (MN 128.6.):

> "He abused me, he struck me,
> he defeated me, he robbed me"—
> In those who harbor thoughts like these
> hatred will never be allayed.
>
> For in this world hatred is never
> allayed by further acts of hate.
> It is allayed by nonhatred (compassion)—
> That is the fixed and ageless law.

Bhikkhu Anuruddha explains how he lives in harmony with other bhikkhus (MN 128.12):

> I think thus: "It is a gain for me, it is a great gain for me that I am living with such companions in the holy life." I maintain physical acts of love toward these venerable ones both openly and privately. I maintain verbal acts of love toward them both openly and privately. I maintain mental acts of love toward them both openly and privately. I consider: "Why should I not set aside what I wish to do and do what these venerable ones wish to do?" Then I

> set aside what I wish to do and do what these venerable ones wish to do. We are different in body, but one in mind.

Imagine practicing like Anuruddha does with your family, colleagues, and community members.

The Buddha detailed seven disadvantages of anger in *Sutta on the Wretchedness of Anger* (AN 7.64) by describing what someone wishes for his enemy and showing that anger accomplishes his enemy's wishes. For example, an enemy may wish us to be ugly, to have an unfortunate rebirth, to experience pain, or to lack prosperity, wealth, a good reputation, and harmonious relationships. We accomplish all these things for him, through our own anger, without him harming us at all.

1. Even if we have bathed in fragrant water, wear stylish clothes, and are adorned with luxurious jewelry, we become ugly when angry.
2. Even if we are lying on a comfortable bed snuggled in luxurious blankets, we are in pain when we're angry.
3. We may have prosperity, but when we ruminate with angry thoughts, we make bad decisions that destroy our prosperity.
4. We may have wealth, but a mind bound by anger cannot enjoy it. Although we may work hard to procure wealth, it is dissipated in fines due to unwise actions motivated by anger.
5. We may have a good reputation, but lose it by falling prey to anger.
6. We may want friends and good family relations, but dreading our temper, others stay away from us.
7. Although we wish for a peaceful death and a fortunate rebirth, anger fuels destructive physical, verbal, and mental actions, creating the causes for the opposite.

REFLECTION

Contemplate the seven disadvantages of anger one by one. For each:

1. Imagine relaxing with a peaceful mind untainted by anger.
2. Then think of a person and situation you are upset and angry about and watch your comfort instantly evaporate.

3. Recognize that it is your attitude that brings the pain. The unpleasant situation is not happening to you now, but because the mind clings to an image of the past, you are miserable in the present.

Contemplating these helps us realize that letting our mind dwell in anger and malice is self-sabotaging. External enemies do not make us miserable; our anger already does an excellent job of that.

Hearing others' disturbing speech often triggers anger to arise in the mind. If we remember the above seven disadvantages of anger and apply the following advice the Buddha gave, we'll be able to release animosity and replace it with love (MN 21.11).

> There are these five courses of speech that others may use when they address you: their speech may be timely or untimely, true or untrue, gentle or harsh, connected with good or with harm, spoken with a mind of love or with inner hate . . . Herein, monastics, you should train thus: "Our minds will remain unaffected, and we shall utter no evil words; we shall abide compassionate for their welfare, with a mind of love, without inner hate. We shall abide pervading that person with a mind imbued with love, and starting with him, we shall abide pervading the all-encompassing world with a mind imbued with love, abundant, exalted, immeasurable, without animosity and without malice." That is how you should train.

The love the Buddha speaks of here is love at the state of dhyāna. Such love will carry over when the person leaves the dhyāna state and returns to an everyday state of mind. Even if we have not attained dhyāna yet, training our mind to approach all beings with such a loving attitude will overwhelm any discomfort, suspicion, and malice that our mind harbors and imbue it with a sense of ease and affection toward all.

Contemplating the simile of the saw can free the mind from malice (MN 21.20):

> Monastics, even if bandits were to sever you savagely limb by limb with a two-handled saw, he who gave rise to a mind of hate toward them would not be carrying out my teaching.

Rather than responding with hate, the Buddha recommended responding as in the previous quotation. For those who have strong faith and confidence in the Buddha's teachings and want to adhere to and embody them, thinking as above is effective in releasing enmity.

Reflecting on the person's good qualities is also helpful to bring the mind back to a more balanced perspective. For example, the person who spoke harshly is not physically violent and often helps others to meet a deadline at work. Another person may be ill mannered when driving, but refined when greeting strangers. Recalling the person's good qualities when he is in a congenial situation enables us to dispel our rigid and critical attitude of him. It is best to do this type of reflection often, especially in times when we are not upset. By familiarizing ourselves with this more comprehensive understanding of the other person, we strengthen our mindfulness and will be able to call it to mind more quickly when a difficult situation arises.

If we have difficulty seeing any good qualities in the person, then we should generate compassion for her, thinking of the karma she is creating and the kind of results she will experience due to it. Considering that she will likely have an unfortunate rebirth, or if born human, will encounter numerous obstacles and sufferings, there is no use wishing her harm. It is similar to seeing someone who is ill: the person is already suffering, so compassion, not malice, is appropriate. To overcome resentment toward someone whose behavior is vulgar and harmful, Śāriputra advises us to contemplate the following (AN 5.162):

> May this respectable individual abandon improper physical actions and cultivate proper ones. May he abandon improper verbal actions and cultivate proper ones. May he abandon improper mental actions and cultivate proper ones. Why? So that this respectable individual will not be reborn in a state of loss, in an unfortunate realm, in ruin, or in hell after the dissolution of the body and death.

Another method to dispel animosity is to reflect on the karmic result of holding on to it. Here we reflect that we are the owner of our deeds and are the heir of our actions. We ask ourselves: "Is my way of thinking going to lead to awakening? Will it create the cause for a fortunate rebirth so I can continue practicing the Dharma? Or will this anger cause me to be separated from the Dharma, from companions in the holy life, and from an excellent spiritual mentor?"

Thinking of the Buddha's responses when he faced the aggression of others in his previous lives as a bodhisattva can inspire us to forgive others their faults and relax our mind. The *Jātaka* tells many stories of the bodhisattva's previous lives as human beings or as animals, in which others harmed him, were ungrateful, or betrayed his trust. In all of these, he responded with compassion, never retaliating or holding a grudge. His ability to forgive and love those who harmed him were important factors in his attaining full awakening. The bodhisattva's behavior is an inspiring role model and emulating it will release the pain of our anger.

Another technique to free our mind from anger is to reflect that all sentient beings have been our mother, father, siblings, and children. As our mother, they carried us in their womb, gave birth to us, fed us, cleaned us, played with us, and taught us. As our mother or father, they worked hard to earn an income to feed and support us. As our siblings, they helped us and played with us. As our children, we loved them unconditionally and they brought us great joy by trusting and loving us. Earnestly reflecting in this way, we come to see that we have received outstanding benefit from all sentient beings in the past. It is unfitting that we now harbor enmity for them. In this way, our feelings of affection and gratitude overpower any resentment or grudge we may hold against others (Vism 9.36).

Bringing in analytical wisdom is also useful. Ask yourself, "What am I angry at? Is it the hair on his head? His teeth? Nails? The water element in the body? The earth element?" Or we examine, "Among the five aggregates in dependence on which this person is called so-and-so, what aggregate am I angry with? His body? His mind? A primary mind or a mental factor?" Searching for the real person who is the source of our anger becomes like painting in space (Vism 9.38).

Another idea is to give the person a gift. Others' animosity toward us and ours toward them subside when a gift is given and received earnestly (Vism 9.39).

When anger has subsided by employing one of these methods, we experience the satisfaction of having transformed our mind into either a neutral or wholesome state. We experience happiness or equanimity and increase our ability to prevent and abandon anger in the future. Both our body and mind are tranquil.

REFLECTION

1. Think of a person whom you are angry with. Think, "This person is a complex human being with good qualities and faults." Focus on their admirable qualities.
2. Contemplate the karma this person is creating by doing the action that you find objectionable: what a sad situation it is that they want to be happy but are creating the causes for suffering. Try to feel how much they want happiness, yet through their harmful actions they are preventing their own happiness. In addition, they will have to experience the suffering results of their actions. Generate compassion for the person.
3. Reflect that you're in a similar situation—wanting happiness, not suffering, yet by holding on to anger and resentment you too are creating the cause for suffering. Have compassion for both the other person and yourself and release the anger.

Continuing the Meditation on Love

Once anger and resentment have dissipated, cultivate love toward the hostile person, just as you did toward the others.

Reciting the formula "May they be happy and free from suffering; may they be free from animosity, affliction, and anxiety, and live happily" is a tool. Cultivating love is not about reciting the formula; it is about generating the state of mind that corresponds to the words that you are saying. If the recitation becomes mechanical and monotonous, change the formula by expressing it in your own words; contemplate in more detail the types of happiness and good fortune you would like someone to experience. Imagine that person in their ordinary state with confusion and suffering. Then imagine how he would feel and act if he were free from specific miseries and had specific types of opportunities, good qualities, and conducive conditions. Imagine him having these. Making the meditation detailed and personal opens your heart to the experience of love. When the feeling of love arises, it will gain momentum, and after a while the meditation will carry on by itself without your having to use the formula.

Follow this by breaking down the barriers: see the five individuals—ourselves, the respected person, the friend, the neutral person, and the hostile person—as equal and generate love equally for each of them. Buddhaghosa describes the sign of having succeeded in breaking down the barriers: Let's say five people are being held hostage and one has to give up his or her life. If you feel no difference among the five when the hostage-taker selects one, you have succeeded in breaking down the barriers. In other words, you lack any animosity that hopes the hostile person is chosen, no self-disparagement in wanting yourself to be sacrificed, no attachment in not wanting the dear one or respected person to be selected, and no apathy in not caring if the neutral person is chosen.[7]

According to Buddhaghosa, when barriers of extending love to the five individuals have been broken down and a meditator is able to radiate love equally to all five, simultaneously the counterpart sign (P. *paṭibhāga-nimitta*) appears, and access concentration (P. *upacāra samādhi*) is attained. Continuing to meditate, she attains the full concentration (P. *appanā samādhi*) of the first dhyāna by developing and repeatedly practicing the counterpart sign. In the first dhyāna, the five hindrances have been suppressed and the five factors—investigation, analysis, joy, bliss, and one-pointedness—are present. She also attains the liberation of mind with love. As meditation continues, the second and third dhyānas will be gained.

Only when a meditator has attained one of the dhyānas does she have the ability to train her mind in extending love so that she (MN 43.31)

> dwells pervading one direction with a mind (heart) imbued with love, likewise the second direction, the third direction, and the

> fourth direction. Thus above, below, across, and everywhere, and to all as to herself, she dwells pervading the entire world with a mind imbued with loving-kindness, vast, exalted, measureless, without animosity, without malice.

Meditators begin by extending love to one direction—the east—so that it pervades all sentient beings there. When doing this, it is recommended to begin small, thinking of one dwelling and extending love to everyone there. When the mind is malleable, then expand it to two dwellings, radiating love there. Gradually extend the radius of love to the town, state, and the entire eastern sector. When that meditation is firm, add on the other directions—the remaining three cardinal directions, the four intermediate directions, up, and down—sending love to each place, one by one.

Then radiate love everywhere without specifying a particular direction. Love is extended equally to all beings regardless of their realm of existence, social status, race, ethnicity, religion, and so forth. Love is shared with everyone, be they friend, enemy, or stranger, irrespective of how they feel about us or treat us. This love is measureless or boundless in that love for each being is unlimited, it extends to immeasurable sentient beings, and meditators are totally familiar with it. Without any pollution by bad feelings, grief, or suffering, this love is pure, impartial, and unconditional.

To practice love as a divine abode, meditators contemplate it at all times when they are awake and in all postures—sitting, standing, lying down, and walking. This leads to the liberation of mind with love—that is, love at the level of the full concentration of a dhyāna. It is called "liberation of mind with love" because while in that absorption, the mind is liberated from anger and animosity. Any manifest anger will disappear and anger that hasn't arisen will not arise. The suppleness of such love is available only to those whose minds have reached absorption.

Together with extending the range of their love, meditators also intensify the experience of love. This is done by seeing all sentient beings as their children. The *Mettā Sutta* says (Sn 1.8):

> As a mother would, with all her life, protect her only child, so one should develop a boundless heart toward all beings.

A mother loves her only child with all her being and does not lament relinquishing her own happiness—even her life—to protect her child. In a similar way, meditators view other sentient beings with intense affection, care, and concern. Remembering that in our beginningless infinite rebirths we have all been one another's mothers helps us eliminate feelings of separateness and self-concern and open our hearts to unconditionally love all beings just as a mother loves her only child.

To cultivate love we must contemplate many points: why our anger is unreasonable, others' kindness, the wide variety of living beings, and so forth. Given that so much thinking and visualization are involved, we may wonder, how can we attain the single-pointedness of dhyāna?

In the early stages of cultivating love, thought and imagination are necessary. But once love is aroused and becomes strong and stable, these are no longer needed. Instead, we abide in the experience of love and radiate that to others. Radiating love does not depend on verbalization or conception. When the mind is well trained and very familiar with love, mentally reciting "extend love to the east, to the west . . ." is not necessary. Rather, the mind becomes absorbed in the experience of love, and radiating love assumes a momentum of its own. Cultivating love in meditation leads to a level of samādhi that corresponds to dhyāna. Interestingly, the four brahmavihāras were not explained as states of dhyāna in the early sūtras, but Pāli commentaries say that practitioners can develop them to the level of dhyāna.

The liberation of mind with love is practiced with unspecified pervasion by thinking, "May all beings be happy and free from suffering. May they be free from anger, affliction, and anxiety, and live happily." Then "all breathing things," "all creatures," "all persons," and "all those with a personality" are substituted, one by one, for "all beings," and love radiated to them. Although these five terms are synonymous with "all beings," meditating on each of them one by one gives us different perspectives on the object of our love.

The liberation of mind with love can also be practiced in seven ways with specified pervasion by thinking in this order: "May all women be happy and free from suffering. May they be free from animosity, affliction, and anxiety, and live happily." Then "men," "āryas," "ordinary beings," "devas," "human beings," and "those born in unfortunate realms" are substituted for "women" and love spread to them.

The liberation of mind with love is cultivated to pervade the ten directions in ten ways, by thinking as above first toward all beings in the east, then the west, north, south, northeast, southeast, southwest, northwest, above, and below. Then each of the twelve types of beings[8] can be thought of in each of the directions: "May all beings in the east . . . " up to "May all those in unfortunate realms in the downward direction be free from animosity, affliction, and anxiety, and live happily." In addition, each of the phrases for well-being—"be free from animosity," "be free from affliction," "be free from anxiety," and "live happily"—is one meditative absorption, so when put together there are quite a number of absorptions. Developing any of the liberations of mind with love with any of these absorptions will bring the eleven benefits mentioned below.

REFLECTION

1. Imagine the person who you are upset with in their ordinary state afflicted with confusion and suffering.
2. Then imagine how they would feel, act, and speak if they were free from specific miseries and had specific types of opportunities, good qualities, and conducive conditions. Imagine them having these.
3. Seeing the person in a different light, let love wishing them to have happiness arise.
4. Do the above reflection for other beings until you get to the point where it is easy to extend the wish for them to be happy to all sentient beings.

Cultivating Love Benefits Self and Others

The Buddha speaks of eleven benefits accruing to those who practice the liberation of mind with love regularly (AN 11.15):[9]

1. They sleep well, free from restless sleep and apnea.
2. They awake well, without groaning, yawning, and rolling over to go back to sleep.

3. They do not experience nightmares but have auspicious dreams, such as paying respects at a stūpa or offering homage to the Three Jewels.
4. They are dear to humans, who appreciate and respect them.
5. They are dear to nonhumans, who are grateful for their serenity that brings peace among them.
6. Deities protect them.
7. Fire, poison, and weapons do not affect them. Here a story is told of a hunter who threw a spear at a cow who was nursing her calf. The spear bounced off her due to the power of her love that wished for the well-being of her calf.
8. Their minds are easily concentrated, not subject to sluggishness.
9. The expression on their face is serene.
10. They die without confusion, as if they were simply falling asleep.
11. If they do not attain a supramundane realization, after death they will be born in the Brahmā world in the form realm. Meditators who have attained any of the four immeasurables—that is, a mind of dhyāna with any of these four as its object— during their life will have the intention associated with this immeasurable arise as they die. This is an invariable karma that will ripen by the person being reborn in the corresponding level of the Brahmā world.[10]

The cultivation of love benefits our own mind as well as the society around us. At the time of the Buddha, a murderous bandit named Aṅgulimāla terrorized the land. Having killed 999 people and made a necklace of their finger bones, he was seeking his next victim when the Buddha intervened. The power of the Buddha's peace and love subdued Aṅgulimāla, who became one of his monastic disciples. Then one day when King Prasenajit went to visit the Buddha, the Buddha introduced him to Aṅgulimāla. The king reacted with terror and dread, but the Buddha assured him that there was nothing to fear. Conversing with Aṅgulimāla, the king was astounded by the change and relieved that his subjects could now live without fearing this serial murderer. Addressing the Buddha, King Prasenajit said (MN 86.13):

> It is wonderful, venerable sir, it is marvelous how the Blessed One tames the untamed, brings peace to the unpeaceful, and leads to nibbāna those who have not attained nibbāna. Venerable sir, we

> ourselves could not tame him with force and weapons, yet the Blessed One has tamed him without force or weapons.

Love is also effective at stilling disturbance by spirits, negative energy, and threats from human beings. The Buddha taught the famous *Sutta on Love* because his disciples' meditation was being disturbed by antagonistic spirits. By the monastics cultivating profound love for all beings, the spirits were subdued and their interference ceased. When Devadatta released a wild elephant with the hopes it would trample the Buddha, the Buddha's meditation on love soothed the elephant, who bowed to him instead. The laywoman Sāmāvati was protected from the actions of her jealous husband by meditating on love. The Buddha also instructed monastics to contemplate love for snakes, scorpions, centipedes, spiders, lizards, and rodents, and to speak of the excellent qualities of the Three Jewels to protect themselves from being bitten by these creatures.

Cultivating love in a dangerous situation cannot be done out of fear or anger, for such emotions are the antithesis of love. Rather, understanding the suffering of these beings and wishing them well, cultivate love and compassion for them. Love, particularly in a mind of dhyāna, protects you from external and internal disturbances. Furthermore, the liberation of mind with love energizes practitioners to reach out and directly help others whenever the possibility arises. In the process of helping others, it is important not to transgress whatever precepts we have taken.

Meditating on love reduces interferences and increases conducive circumstances so that meditation on other topics will proceed smoothly. Here a practitioner generates love for members of the Dharma community where she lives; this results in their living harmoniously together. Then she meditates on love for the deities in the area, who respond by protecting her. She continues by cultivating love for her benefactor, who, feeling her genuine concern, wishes to provide her with the requisites to continue her Dharma practice. She expands her love to include all the sentient beings in the area, which is conducive to having good relations with them such that they do not feel malice toward her and do not cause problems or interfere with her Dharma practice. In modern-day Thailand, some disciples cite the power of their spiritual mentor's love as creating peaceful and conducive circumstances to meditate in that monastery.

The cultivation of love aids in the three types of abandonment of defilements: temporary abandonment, abandonment by suppression, and abandonment that eradicates. Developing love toward others can be used as an antidote to anger, resentment, spite, and other hostile emotions, and leads to *temporary abandonment* or abandonment by substitution of the opposite. For example, when we become angry because someone criticizes us or when resentment surges when remembering a harsh event from years ago, we can cultivate a loving feeling that replaces the disturbing emotion. This temporarily removes the affliction.

By attaining the full concentration of dhyāna on love, the five hindrances are suppressed by the power of concentration and cannot manifest.[11] This is *abandonment by suppression*, and it lasts as long as the meditator remains in dhyāna or until the strength of the dhyāna has diminished to such a point that gross afflictions arise again.

By using the liberation of mind with love as the basis for developing insight, a meditator can attain arhatship, a state of *abandonment that eradicates the defilements* so that they can never return. This is done by meditating in a dhyāna, then leaving the dhyānic state and analyzing its components. Through this method, the meditator sees that even the blissful state of concentration is impermanent, unsatisfactory in nature, and selfless. This understanding of the three characteristics in turn leads to the realization of nirvāṇa, in which the fetters are forever eradicated.

Cultivating love benefits ourselves and others. The Buddha explains (SN 47.19):

> "I will protect myself." Monastics, thus should the establishments of mindfulness be practiced. "I will protect others." Monastics, thus should the establishments of mindfulness be practiced. Protecting oneself, one protects others. Protecting others, one protects oneself.
>
> And how is it that by protecting oneself one protects others? By the pursuit, development, and cultivation [of the four establishments of mindfulness] . . . And how is it that by protecting others one protects oneself? By fortitude, harmlessness, love, and empathic joy.

The commentary to this nikāya explains "protecting oneself, one protects others" as follows: Practicing the four establishments of mindfulness well by abandoning worldly pursuits, a meditator protects himself from duḥkha by attaining arhatship. Others who see his serene conduct develop the virtuous minds of confidence and inspiration. This will lead others to have a heavenly rebirth and to practice the path to liberation themselves. In this way, by protecting himself, a meditator protects others.

It further explains "protecting others, one protects oneself": By cultivating fortitude, compassion (nonharm), love, and empathic joy, a meditator develops the dhyānas by taking the four immeasurables as the object. In this way, she protects others. By then employing the dhyānas as the basis for cultivating insight into the three characteristics and realizing nirvāṇa, she becomes an arhat, and in this way protects herself.

Some readers may wish that the Buddha had used the meditation on love to stimulate his disciples to become social activists and directly benefit suffering sentient beings. Here, however, the Buddha is focusing on meditation and its relationship with liberation. In other contexts, he explains how to apply fortitude, compassion, love, and empathic joy to improve living standards and educational opportunities and to promote social equality, justice, and environmental protection. For example, in *The Kindred Sayings* the Buddha recommends that lay followers plant trees, dig wells, construct dams, and provide shelter for the homeless, and in another sūtra he advises monarchs to share their wealth with their subjects in order to create a harmonious society that is easy to govern. In *Precious Garland* (*Ratnāvalī*), Nāgārjuna spends considerable time advising the king on social policy and how to benefit the denizens of his kingdom as well as travelers and refugees staying there.

Meditation on Compassion

Similar to the meditation on love, begin the cultivation of compassion by contemplating the disadvantages of lacking compassion and the benefits of having it. Choose someone who is suffering greatly as the first person who is the object of your compassion. This person may or may not be someone you know personally; the media provides us with more than enough images of people who live in miserable conditions. Still, the compassion will be stronger if you have direct contact with the person.

If you don't encounter an appropriate person, cultivate compassion for someone who is creating horrendous destructive karma, even if that person appears to be happy at the moment. This person is like someone who is given delicious food just before he is executed. He may look happy at the moment, dining on sumptuous food, but that happiness is false. Similarly, someone who legally or illegally orders the death of many people, steals their wealth, or creates massive disharmony through lying and dissimulation may appear to enjoy good circumstances now. However, due to lack of constructive karma, horrible suffering in unfortunate rebirths awaits him.

After generating compassion for a miserable person, do so for a dear person, followed by a neutral person, and finally a hostile person. Should anger or fear arise toward a hostile person, counteract it by employing the methods described above. Even if these hostile people are not experiencing extreme suffering at the moment, they are still under the control of afflictions and polluted karma and therefore are not free from the pervasive duḥkha of conditioning in saṃsāric existence. For this reason alone, they are worthy of compassion. Even if some of them have created constructive karma yet are experiencing troubles with their health, family relations, job, and so forth, they are deserving of compassion.

Then break down the barriers between the four kinds of people—ourselves, dear ones, neutral people, and hostile people—until the counterpart sign appears and access concentration is attained. By repeatedly meditating on the counterpart sign, attain the first three dhyānas. With that concentration, develop malleability and versatility by generating compassion for all the various beings in all directions as described in the meditation on love. The eleven advantages as detailed above also accrue.

When viewing others' suffering and cultivating compassion, if your mind becomes overwhelmed by feelings of despair or helplessness, you have missed the mark. Distress about others' suffering, anger at societal forces that cause suffering, and frustration with others for carelessly getting themselves into predicaments may be natural emotions for ordinary beings, but they are far from the Buddhist understanding of compassion. Compassion is the wish for others to be free from all duḥkha, and to cultivate it we must remain focused on responding with tender concern and the wish to help.

REFLECTION

1. Think of someone undergoing great suffering and imagine what it would feel like to be in their situation. Think of that person's buddha nature and good qualities—their potential to contribute to the world and their potential for good.
2. Let the wish for them to be free from suffering arise in your mind. That is compassion.
3. Then go through the above steps thinking of friends, neutral people, hostile people, and finally generalize to all sentient beings of the six realms in saṃsāra. Let compassion arise in each case.

Meditation on Empathic Joy

Empathic joy is feeling joy at others' success, merit, good qualities, and happiness. Here the first person to cultivate empathic joy toward is a dear person who is good-natured and happy and whose happiness and success is worthy of rejoicing over. Sincerely rejoicing at others' good fortune fills our mind with delight and is an excellent antidote to dispel jealousy and envy. Empathic joy is extended not only for the person's present good fortune but also for their past successes and future virtuous actions. Having generated empathic joy toward this dear person, proceed to cultivate empathic joy for the success and happiness of a neutral person and then a hostile one. Proceed to subdue anger for the hostile person, break down the barriers, and cultivate and repeatedly practice the counterpart sign to increase the absorption up to the third dhyāna in accord with the explanation above. Similarly, cultivate versatility and then reap the benefits of generating empathic joy as explained before.

Meditation on Equanimity

To develop equanimity fully entails previous attainment of the third dhyāna on the basis of cultivating immeasurable love, compassion, and empathic joy. Having become familiar with the third dhyāna, the meditator emerges from it and contemplates the risks of the previous three divine abodes and the benefits of equanimity. The first three divine abodes are risky because attachment and anger are not far away. For example, when developing love and wishing for others to be happy, attachment may arise instead. Also, the first three immeasurables are associated with happiness, which lessens the depth of concentration. For these reasons, the meditator now seeks equanimity, which is a constancy or steadiness of mind when seeing the happiness and suffering of others. The mind is free from longing and repugnance regarding others. Seeing that their happiness and suffering are results of their own karmic actions, the mind of equanimity remains balanced when seeing sentient beings' felicity and misery.

The chief benefit of equanimity is its peacefulness, and peace comes when the mind is balanced. This equanimity is not indifference or apathy, for meditators have already gained dhyāna on love, compassion, and empathic joy. These three imbue equanimity with calm affection for sentient beings and balanced involvement with them, while equanimity remains peaceful and receptive.

Having contemplated the first three immeasurables, meditators now focus on a neutral person and cultivate equanimity. When this is stable, they then develop equanimity toward a dear one, and then toward a hostile person.

Breaking down the barriers between the neutral person, the dear one, the hostile one, and themselves is the same as in the meditation on love, compassion, and empathic joy. So too is cultivating and repeatedly practicing the counterpart sign. Through this they enter the fourth dhyāna. Meditators can gain the fourth dhyāna only on the basis of having attained the third dhyāna by means of meditation on one of the other immeasurables. In other words, only after attaining the first, second, and third dhyāna on love, compassion, and empathic joy can meditators attain the fourth dhyāna on equanimity. In addition, they cannot attain the fourth dhyāna on equanimity on the basis of having attained the third dhyāna with another meditation object, such as the earth kasiṇa, because that object differs considerably from equanimity. Developing versatility and receiving the advantages are similar to the other immeasurables. In the fourth dhyāna, the dhyānic factor of bliss has ceased and the predominant feeling is equanimity. However, as explained below, the divine abode of equanimity and the feeling of equanimity are not the same.

The sequential cultivation of the four immeasurables is compared with the evolving attitude parents have toward their children. When the baby is in the womb, the parents think with a *loving* mind, "May our child be healthy." After he is born, when the adorable baby lies on his back and cries because he is hungry or has been bitten by insects or has had a bad dream, the parents feel *compassion*. When the child grows up and the parents see him playing, being inquisitive about the world, and learning, they feel *empathic joy* and rejoice at their child's happiness. When the child is grown and becomes a successful person in his own right, the parents have *equanimity*, knowing that he can take care of himself.

This analogy shows the usefulness of each attitude in a specific situation. However, do not take this analogy too far. It does not mean that equanimity is the superior attitude to have toward all sentient beings. Nor does it mean that equanimity is to be favored more than the other immeasurables or that it is higher or more desirable. Skill in all four is helpful because depending on the situation, love, compassion, or empathic joy may be more appropriate than equanimity. As we see by the parents' response to their child at different times, love is called for at one time, compassion at another, empathic joy in one circumstance, and equanimity in another. Versatility in the dhyānas and in the range of positive emotions meditators experience expands their practice. It also affects their ability to reach out and benefit others in their daily life.

Even after his awakening, when he had nothing further to cultivate or attain, the Buddha continued to meditate on all four immeasurables. Most likely this was because of the benefit they bestow on others and to encourage his direct disciples and future generations of practitioners to cultivate them. Certainly the four immeasurables were satisfying and pleasant abodes for the Buddha himself. As we see from the example of his life, the Buddha was a loving, compassionate, and joyful individual whose evenness of mind enabled him to be effective in all situations and with all people.

Types of Equanimity

"Equanimity" has a variety of meanings, depending on the context. Buddhaghosa differentiates ten types of equanimity (Vism 4.156–66). The prominent six are as follows:

1. The *feeling of equanimity* is a neutral feeling, one that is neither pain nor pleasure. It can arise in virtuous, nonvirtuous, and neutral states of mind.
2. *Even-minded equanimity* maintains an even attitude, balances the mind and its accompanying mental factors, and makes our responses even and balanced. It is present in virtuous minds but absent in nonvirtuous minds. The next four are types of even-minded equanimity that are differentiated according to the circumstance in which they arise.
3. The *equanimity of purity* is the equanimity of the fourth dhyāna. In the first three dhyānas, even-minded equanimity maintains the balance of investigation, analysis, joy, and bliss, but in a sense it is overshadowed by them. In the fourth dhyāna, these four dhyānic factors are absent and the feeling of equanimity is present, which enables even-minded equanimity to shine forth purely.
4. The *divine abode of equanimity* is the fourth immeasurable. It is a blend of equanimity toward dear ones, strangers, and enemies with the evenness of the mind and its accompanying mental factors. Being very peaceful, divine-abode equanimity differs from the equanimity of purity only in terms of its object. Equanimity of purity arises in relation to the counterpart sign, while divine-abode equanimity arises toward sentient beings.
5. The *awakening factor of equanimity* is the balance among the various factors of the mind that realizes nirvāṇa. It is one of the thirty-seven harmonies with awakening.[12]
6. *Six-limbed equanimity* keeps the mind balanced when it contacts attractive or unattractive sense objects and when it experiences pleasure or pain. Only arhats have perfected this type of equanimity, which may be accompanied by pleasant, painful, or neutral feelings. It is the equanimity spoken of when describing an arhat: "(When) he sees form with his eye, he becomes neither mentally pleased, nor mentally displeased, but remains equanimous, mindful, and discriminating (and so on for all six senses)."[13]

Dhammapāla speaks of unknowing equanimity, which is ignorance combined with the feeling of equanimity. This is the dull apathy that is a defilement.

Of the four immeasurables, immeasurable equanimity is the most potent in helping a meditator develop the awakening factor of equanimity that is needed to realize nirvāṇa.

The Four Divine Abodes and Insight

Meditation on the four divine abodes can be done for several purposes: for protection when suffering or in danger, as a path to rebirth in the Brahmā world, and as a basis for insight. When perfected, these four immeasurables become "immeasurable liberations of mind,"[14] which are states of dhyāna that are liberated from attachment to sensual objects and free from the five hindrances. Although these immeasurable liberations of mind alone cannot bring liberation from cyclic existence, when these minds of deep concentration are used to meditate on the three characteristics and nirvāṇa, the resulting insight will lead to the ultimate goal of liberation from saṃsāra.

For example, meditators who develop the first dhyāna based on love enter into that dhyāna through love. After stabilizing their concentration in the dhyāna on love, they emerge from the dhyāna and, looking back at it, they examine it. The experience in dhyāna is so blissful that if they did not examine it, attachment for it would easily arise and they might forgo liberation in favor of the bliss of samādhi.

But when analyzing the dhyāna they see the dhyāna of love as a composite phenomena consisting of the five aggregates. There is a pleasant or equanimous feeling, some discrimination, and other miscellaneous factors such as love, attention, contact, intention, and concentration, as well as the mental primary consciousness. In short, the four mental aggregates and the physical body were present when they were in dhyāna. They see each of the dhyānic factors as a distinct mental factor, instead of their usual experience of seeing them as a seamless whole. With insight, these meditators see the dhyāna is impermanent because it is produced by causes and conditions and it ceases with the cessation of its causes and conditions. Because it is impermanent—unceasingly arising and perishing in every moment—it does not bring ultimate satisfaction; thus it is in the nature of duḥkha. Because it is impermanent and duḥkha in nature, it is not worthwhile clinging to—it is not I, mine, or my self. There is no substantially real person findable within or separate from the ever-changing combination of physical and mental aggregates.

Continuing to investigate their experience of the dhyāna more deeply by seeing it in light of the three characteristics, meditators increase their wisdom until there is a breakthrough to seeing or vision. With this insight perceiving the unconditioned, nirvāṇa, comes the abandonment of the first three fetters—view of a personal identity, doubt, and view of rules and practices. Having used the dhyāna on love to develop insight and realize nirvāṇa, these meditators have now become stream-enterers.

As they continue cultivating wisdom, stream-enterers reduce their malice and their attachment to sense pleasure sufficiently so that they become once-returners. When these two are abandoned completely, they become nonreturners, and if they don't attain arhatship in that life, they will be reborn in the pure lands where they will attain it.

Some meditators cultivate the four immeasurables after becoming āryas, but before attaining arhatship. In this case, they will be reborn in the Brahmā worlds in the form realm after death, continue to practice insight there, and become arhats. This is very different from worldlings who, rather than seeking liberation, cultivate the four immeasurables for the purpose of being born in the Brahmā world. While attainment of the four immeasurables will bring rebirth in the Brahmā world, because these practitioners lack insight and wisdom as well as the interest in developing them, they may be reborn in an unfortunate realm after the karma for rebirth in the Brahmā world has been exhausted.

REFLECTION

1. Meditate on one of the four divine abodes as taught above until you experience it.
2. Step back from the experience and see it is simply a mental state.
3. Note the feeling, discrimination, and any other mental factor such as mindfulness, intention, or concentration that are present. Note that the mental primary consciousness is present and that your body is there too.
4. Dissecting the experience of the divine abode into the five psychophysical aggregates in this way, see that it is a state composed of many changing factors.

5. Note that the mental state is impermanent because it's produced by causes and conditions. Because it is impermanent, it does not bring ultimate satisfaction and is thus in the nature of duḥkha. Because it is impermanent and duḥkha in nature, it is not worthwhile clinging to—it is not I, mine, or my self. There is no substantially real person findable within or separate from the aggregates.

Near and Far Enemies of the Four Immeasurables

Each of the four immeasurables has a "near enemy" and a "far enemy." The near enemy is an affliction that is similar in some way to that virtuous immeasurable; the far enemy is an affliction that is the opposite of the emotion we are trying to cultivate.

The near enemy of love is attachment because both love and attachment see the good qualities in the other person. However, attachment clings to others with unrealistic expectations; it wants something from others, and thus the affection we feel is polluted with possessiveness and neediness. Malice is the far enemy of love. We must ensure that our love is free of both these dangers.

Compassion's near enemy is personal distress or grief based on worldly life. This grief is the sadness and distress felt when we or those we care about cannot get what we want. It may be sorrow over past frustrations or present disappointments. The grief is similar to compassion in that both have an element of sorrow due to others' misery. Compassion's far enemies are cruelty and violence.

The near enemy of empathic joy is joy based on worldly life—that is, delight at receiving sense pleasures in the past or present. Here our mind becomes giddy with excitement; we become too involved and attached to someone else's happiness. Empathic joy's far enemies are jealousy and boredom, which interfere with our experiencing empathic joy at others' successes and happiness. Jealousy resents the other person's successes and happiness, and boredom doesn't care about them.

Equanimity's near enemy is the equanimity of unknowing based on worldly life; this is the indifference and apathy that people often experience.

Indifference and apathy are similar to equanimity in that none of them notices the faults or good qualities of others. Equanimity's far enemies are anger and attachment, which push some beings away and hold others near and dear.

THE FOUR IMMEASURABLES AND THEIR NEAR AND FAR ENEMIES

IMMEASURABLE	CHARACTERISTIC	NEAR ENEMY	FAR ENEMY
Love	Sincere wish for the welfare and happiness of beings	Personal attachment, worldly affection, clinging or possessive love	Malice, hatred
Compassion	Wanting to dispel the suffering of others	Worldly grief, personal distress	Cruelty (the wish to inflict suffering on others), violence
Empathic joy	Joy produced by seeing the success and good fortune of others	Worldly happiness, giddiness, and excitement that is too involved with others' success	Jealousy, boredom
Equanimity	Impartiality toward living beings	Indifference, cold uncaring apathy	Attachment and anger, partiality

It's good for us to keep the near and far enemies of each immeasurable in mind so that when we cultivate each of the four, our meditation will be on target. The near enemies are much harder to detect, so special vigilance regarding them is needed. How disappointing it would be to think we were cultivating love when actually we were building up attachment toward someone! And how deleterious it would be to try to generate compassion but get stuck in personal distress. By precisely understanding the qualities of each immeasurable and monitoring our mind closely, our meditation will have a transformative effect.

Meditation on love is recommended for people whose anger and malice are strong; it will help them overcome those obstacles. Meditation on compassion is advised for people who tend toward cruelty, because with compassion they will cease wanting to inflict suffering on others and instead will want sentient beings to be free of suffering and its causes. Meditation on empathic joy is especially helpful for people with strong jealousy and boredom, as it will enable them to rejoice and take delight in others' happiness instead of resent or disregard it. Meditation on equanimity is suitable for those who suffer from much attachment, anger, prejudice, and partiality, because it helps them to accept all others and have an equal and balanced attitude toward them.

Buddhaghosa says we should practice the four immeasurables like a mother with four children—a young child, a sickly child, one in the flush of youth, and one who is busy with her own life. A mother wants to nurture the young child so he will grow up and become a happy and ethical adult; she wants her sickly child to recover and regain his health. She hopes the one in the flush of youth will enjoy the benefits of good health and many opportunities for as long as possible, and she does not intrude or worry about the one who is handling her own affairs, but peacefully lets her be.

Joyous effort is crucial when beginning to practice the four divine abodes. Taming the hindrances by applying their antidotes is important in the middle as practice continues. Meditative absorption is essential at the conclusion. The object of any of the four divine abodes is a single living being or as many living beings as we think of.

As noted above, immeasurable equanimity and the feeling of equanimity differ. Immeasurable equanimity is impartiality with respect to all sentient beings; it is a mental factor in the aggregate of miscellaneous factors. The feeling of equanimity is a neutral feeling that is neither pain nor pleasure; it belongs to the feeling aggregate.

REFLECTION

1. Contemplate the near and far enemies of each of the four immeasurables.
2. Are there particular ones that you tend to fall into?
3. What ideas do you have to remedy that, so that you can experience genuine love, compassion, empathic joy, and equanimity?

The Four Immeasurables in the Mahāyāna

The four immeasurables are an important practice in the Mahāyāna as well. As in the Pāli tradition, they are objects for cultivating the dhyānas, and practicing them culminates in attaining the dhyānas. However, they also play a strong role in creating the causes to attain bodhicitta and in strengthening bodhicitta when it has been generated.

Chapter 5 of the *Bodhisattvapiṭaka Sūtra*, which is part of the *Sūtra of the Heap of Jewels*, has an extensive explanation of the four immeasurables.[15] In general, the four are contemplated at the beginning of a meditation session in order to stabilize and increase bodhicitta. The short version of the four immeasurables is as follows:

> May all sentient beings have happiness and its causes. (love)
> May all sentient beings be free of suffering and its causes. (compassion)
> May all sentient beings not be separated from sorrowless bliss. (empathic joy)
> May all sentient beings abide in equanimity, free of bias, attachment, and anger. (equanimity)

The long version:

> How wonderful it would be if all sentient beings were to abide in equanimity, free of bias, attachment, and anger. May they abide in this way. I shall cause them to abide in this way. Guru Buddha, please inspire me to be able to do so.
>
> How wonderful it would be if all sentient beings had happiness and its causes. May they have these. I shall cause them to have these. Guru Buddha, please inspire me to be able to do so.
>
> How wonderful it would be if all sentient beings were free from suffering and its causes. May they be free. I shall cause them to be free. Guru Buddha, please inspire me to be able to do so.
>
> How wonderful it would be if all sentient beings were never parted from fortunate rebirths and liberation's excellent bliss.

> May they never be parted. I shall cause them never to be parted.
> Guru Buddha, please inspire me to be able to do so.

In the long version of the four immeasurables, each verse has four parts, which gradually serve to intensify the emotion: (1) a wish (How wonderful it would be . . .), (2) an aspiration (May they . . .), (3) a resolution (I shall cause them . . .), and (4) a request for inspiration (Guru Buddha, please inspire me to be able to do so).

Using love as an example, first we have the wish that sentient beings have happiness and its causes. Focusing our attention on this wish, the wish intensifies and becomes an aspiration that they have happiness and its causes. After that aspiration takes root in our mind, it grows into a resolution to get involved, and we take responsibility to make our aspiration a reality. Because we may feel inadequate to fulfill this grand resolution, we seek inspiration from the Buddha and our spiritual mentor. In this way, we feel supported by the buddhas who have perfected their ability to fulfill this resolution. Our love becomes stronger and more stable, as does our confidence to engage in whatever is necessary so that sentient beings will have happiness and its causes.

In the short version of the four immeasurables, equanimity comes at the end, while in the long version it comes at the beginning. Placing equanimity at the end emphasizes our wish that others enjoy the peace of being free from attachment to friends, anger toward enemies, and apathy toward strangers.

By putting equanimity first, the long version becomes a synopsis of the method of generating bodhicitta called the "seven cause-and-effect instructions," which will be described in chapter 3. Cultivating equanimity at the beginning pacifies the attachment, animosity, and apathy that all too often constitute our reactions to others. Such partiality renders generating equal compassion for all beings impossible, and such compassion is a prerequisite for generating bodhicitta, the mind aspiring to attain full awakening in order to benefit all sentient beings more effectively. Equanimity—a state free from attachment and aversion toward all beings—is preliminary to the seven instructions.

With a mind of equanimity, we then generate love for all beings. Love is the fourth of the seven instructions and the result of the first three—

seeing all sentient beings as our mother, recognizing their kindness, and wishing to repay it. The third immeasurable, compassion, is the fifth instruction. This leads to the great resolve and bodhicitta, the sixth and seventh instructions. With bodhicitta, we work for the welfare of all sentient beings, which includes their temporal happiness in saṃsāra, such as taking fortunate rebirths, and their ultimate happiness—liberation and full awakening. This is the meaning of empathic joy that wishes sentient beings to never be separated from fortunate rebirths or liberation's excellent bliss. Empathic joy rejoices at their well-being and wants it to arise and continue.

REFLECTION

1. Meditate on the four immeasurables in the short way, with equanimity as the fourth point.
2. Meditate on them with equanimity as the first point.
3. What difference do you experience?
4. Meditate on the four immeasurables in the long way with all four phrases.
5. Both methods are effective; it's good to develop familiarity with both.

When meditating on the four immeasurables, we aim to generate these four thoughts or emotions in our mind. Unlike meditation on impermanence or emptiness when we try to apprehend an object not previously realized, in these meditations we want to transform our mind into that mental attitude. Using love as an example, we do not meditate on love as an object of contemplation—that is, we do not focus on love and its definition, reciting them over and over again—but we try to imbue our mind with love.

In both the Pāli and Sanskrit traditions, we are instructed to develop the four immeasurables first toward specific individuals—ourselves, a friend, a stranger, and an enemy—and then gradually extend them to include all others, including sentient beings in other realms of existence.[16] A Pāli sūtra, the *Simile of the Cloth*, says (MN 7.13):

> He abides pervading one quarter with a mind imbued with love (compassion, empathic joy, equanimity), likewise the second, likewise the third, likewise the fourth; so above, below, around, and everywhere, and to all as to himself, he abides pervading the all-encompassing world with a mind imbued with love (compassion, empathic joy, equanimity), abundant, exalted, immeasurable, without hostility and without malice.

If we immediately jumped to cultivating the four immeasurables toward all sentient beings as an amorphous group, our love, compassion, empathic joy, and equanimity will be only intellectual. It is comparatively easy to think of a vague group of beings who are far away and wish them well. But to feel love, compassion, empathic joy, and equanimity toward specific individuals with whom we come in contact daily is another matter. Therefore, while knowing our aim is to extend these emotions toward all beings, we must begin by cultivating them toward specific individuals and extend them in stages so they become immeasurable and heartfelt toward all sentient beings.

Empathic joy is expressed as wishing all beings to attain liberation—the state of undeclining peace that is free from sorrow—as well as rejoicing in their virtuous actions that create the causes of happiness. It also rejoices in others' temporal happiness and wishes them never to be separated from whatever worldly happiness they have.

The great Nyingma master Longchenpa (1308–1363) makes empathic joy more immediate by emphasizing its relationship to sentient beings' buddha nature. Because we want them to experience the joy of awakening, we rejoice that they already have the blissful, pure nature of mind that enables that awakening to be possible.

In the Mahāyāna, equanimity is expressed as a mental state in which we wish all sentient beings' minds to be free from gross attachment, anger, and apathy. In the *Compendium of Knowledge*, Asaṅga (fourth century) explains that immeasurable equanimity thinks, "May all sentient beings receive benefit." This can be interpreted in two ways, the first wishing that they all receive equal benefit, without some receiving more and others less, the second wishing that sentient beings free their own minds from bias, attachment, and anger and thus benefit by developing equanimity themselves. Tsongkhapa explains in the *Great Treatise* that equanimity may refer to the meditator feeling equanimity toward others, and to all sentient beings having equanimity whereby their minds are free from bias, attachment, and anger. Either way, equanimity is a calming attitude that helps us live harmoniously both inside our own hearts and together with others.

Similar to the explanation in the Pāli tradition, Maitreya says in the *Ornament of Clear Realizations* (*Abhisamayālaṃkāra*) that equanimity, love, compassion, and empathic joy are not immeasurables unless they are accompanied by an actual dhyāna. Here we see that the four immeasurables may be meditated upon in the Mahāyāna not only to increase our bodhicitta but also as an object of meditation for cultivating serenity.

It is also important to combine wisdom with equanimity, love, compassion, and empathic joy by viewing their agents, objects, and actions—also known as the "circle of three"—as empty of true existence. Taking love as an example, we contemplate the emptiness of inherent existence of the meditator who is generating love for sentient beings (the agent), the sentient beings who are the object of her love (the object), and the action of wishing them to have happiness and its causes (the action). These three factors exist dependent on one another. Having such "objectless" wisdom—that is, the wisdom that does not grasp an inherently existent object because it has realized its emptiness of inherent existence—combined with love, compassion, empathic joy, and equanimity, will lead to liberation. Without this wisdom, abiding in the four immeasurables will lead only to rebirth in the Brahmā realm within cyclic existence.

Some masters, such as Atiśa, say that the four immeasurables are preliminary to generating bodhicitta. Other masters, such as Maitreya and Asaṅga, emphasize their development as practices of bodhisattvas. This doesn't mean that the four are developed only after generating bodhicitta and becoming a bodhisattva. Rather, the four immeasurables act to strengthen the bodhicitta that was generated previously.

The *Vimalakīrtinirdeśa Sūtra* (chapter 7) speaks of the immeasurable love of bodhisattvas:

> Mañjuśrī then asked further, "Noble sir, if a bodhisattva considers all living beings in this way, how does he generate the great love toward them?"

Vimalakīrti replied, "Mañjuśrī, when a bodhisattva considers all living beings in this way, he thinks: 'Just as I have realized the Dharma, so should I teach it to living beings.' Thereby, he generates the love that is truly a refuge for all living beings,

the love that is peaceful because it is free of grasping,
the love that is not burning because it is free of afflictions,
the love that accords with reality because it is equanimous in all three times (past, present, and future),
the love that is without conflict because it is free of the violence of the afflictions,
the love that is nondual because it is involved neither with the external nor with the internal,
the love that is imperturbable because it carries through to the end.

"Thereby he generates the love that is firm, its high resolve unbreakable, like a diamond,

the love that is pure, purified in its nature,
the love that is even, its aspirations being equal,
the ārya's love that has eliminated its enemy [anger],
the bodhisattva's love that continuously develops living beings,
the Tathāgata's love that understands reality,
the Buddha's love that causes living beings to awaken from their sleep,
the love that is spontaneous because it is fully awakened spontaneously,
the love that is awakening because it is unity of experience,
the love that has no presumption because it has eliminated attachment and aversion,
the love that is great compassion because it infuses the Mahāyāna with radiance,
the love that is never exhausted because it knows that all [persons and phenomena] is empty and selfless,
the love that is giving because it bestows the gift of Dharma free of the tight fist of a bad teacher,

the love that is ethical because it improves unethical living beings,
the love that is fortitude because it protects both self and others,
the love that is joyous effort because it takes responsibility for all living beings,
the love that is meditative stability because it refrains from indulgence in tastes,
the love that is wisdom because it causes attainment at the proper time,
the love that is skillful means because it has manifestation suited for every occasion,
the love that hides nothing because it is pure in motivation,
the love that is without deviation because it acts from decisive motivation,
the love that is high resolve because it is without afflictions,
the love that is without deceit because it is not artificial,
the love that is happiness because it introduces living beings to the happiness of the Buddha.

"Such, Mañjuśrī, is the great love of a bodhisattva."

Mañjuśrī: "What is the great compassion of a bodhisattva?"
Vimalakīrti: "It is the giving of all accumulated roots of virtue to all living beings."

Mañjuśrī: "What is the great joy of the bodhisattva?"
Vimalakīrti: "It is to be joyful and without regret in giving."

Mañjuśrī: "What is the equanimity of the bodhisattva?"
Vimalakīrti: "It is what benefits both self and others."

The Four Immeasurables in the Vajrayāna

The four immeasurables are found in many tantric sādhanas (meditation texts) as well. One example is in the sādhana of the meditational deity Cakrasaṃvara:

> May all sentient beings come to hold the special sublime bliss.
> May all sentient beings be freed from duḥkha and its causes.
> May all sentient beings never be separated from the bliss of liberation.
> May all sentient beings be free from afflictions and their associated defilements.

The first line is love, but here the happiness we wish for all beings is the special sublime bliss that arises in tantric practice and is used to realize emptiness. Tantra specializes in the development of blissful wisdom, so it is natural here to wish that all sentient beings will be able to generate this special bliss that leads to the penetrating wisdom that eradicates all defilements and brings full awakening. The tantric meaning of empathic joy is similar to the meaning in the general Mahāyāna—that is, it is not simply rejoicing at others' worldly well-being, but wishing them to have the bliss of liberation, which here means full awakening. For that to come about, their being free from afflictions is essential—thus equanimity is wanting them to be free from afflictions and their associated defilements through the generation of bodhicitta and the realization of emptiness.

In the Yamāntaka sādhana, the four immeasurables are expressed like so:

> May all sentient beings be endowed with bliss.
> May all sentient beings be parted from duḥkha.
> May all sentient beings never be parted from bliss.
> May all sentient beings be placed in a state of equanimity unperturbed by preconceptions of apprehender and apprehended or by the eight worldly concerns.

Here, too, love wishes that all sentient beings have the great bliss that leads to realizations in tantric practice. How does the experience of great bliss do this? Through melting the subtle drops of the subtle body, great bliss is produced, and this is used to make manifest the fundamental innate mind of clear light. When this mind realizes emptiness, even subtle defilements can be eradicated quickly.

Equanimity here includes two wishes. The first, that sentient beings be unperturbed by preconceptions of apprehender and apprehended, is the wish that they realize emptiness directly. When the absence of inherent existence is known nonconceptually, there is no appearance whatsoever of an apprehending mind and an apprehended object. That is, emptiness is perceived nondually, without any feeling at all of "I am perceiving emptiness." It is said the subject (the mind realizing emptiness) and the object (the emptiness of inherent existence that is apprehended) are experienced inseparably, like water poured into water. Since Yamāntaka is the wrathful form of Mañjuśrī, the Buddha of Wisdom, immeasurable equanimity wants all sentient beings to attain that liberating wisdom.

The second wish associated with equanimity is that all sentient beings be free from the eight worldly concerns—attachment or aversion regarding material gain and loss, fame and disrepute, praise and blame, pleasure and pain.[17] While these eight worldly concerns and methods to subdue them are taught early in the stages of the path, they are difficult to counteract while our body and mind are in the desire realm. While meditative absorption suppresses them, it cannot eradicate them completely from the mind. Only the wisdom directly realizing emptiness can do this. Thus, wishing that sentient beings be free from delight regarding money and possessions, praise and approval, reputation and image, and pleasant sense objects, and free from dejection when confronting poverty, blame and disapproval, notoriety and a bad reputation, and unpleasant sense experiences, is wishing that they have this supreme wisdom.

An Intimate Feeling with All Beings

The four immeasurables are important for all of us, be we spiritual practitioners or not. A mind imbued with these four thoughts is tranquil and spreads peace to those around us. For this reason, many Theravāda masters encourage their disciples to meditate on the four immeasurables at the beginning of meditation sessions on mindfulness or insight, and Mahāyāna masters encourage their disciples to contemplate them early in every meditation session.

The use of the mother-child analogy in cultivating love and bodhicitta is found in both the Pāli and Sanskrit traditions. While imperfect, this analogy is the best one found in our world because this connection between parent and child is precious—it is the closest example we have to illustrate unconditional love and gratitude. The Pāli tradition recommends seeing sentient beings as our children and cultivating unconditional love for them, wanting to protect them from harm and misery as a parent does his or her child. The Sanskrit tradition encourages contemplating sentient beings as our mother and feeling gratitude and the wish to repay their kindness through attaining buddhahood.

Personally speaking, I (Chodron) find contemplating others' kindness very helpful to do before meditating on the four immeasurables. Doing this changes how I feel about others and myself and opens my heart, because I realize a fact that I am often blind to—that I have been, am, and will continue to be the recipient of incredible kindness from others. Dear ones, neutral people, hostile people, friends, strangers, and enemies—all have been kind to me not only because they have been my parents in previous lives but because I receive the benefits of the labors and various jobs they undertake in this life as well. With this awareness, turning my mind to being concerned about their well-being and wishing them to have happiness and be free from suffering comes much easier, almost automatically.

2 | The Altruistic Intention of Bodhicitta

The Fundamental Vehicle and Mahāyāna

IN THIS VOLUME, bodhicitta—the altruistic intention to become a buddha in order to benefit others most effectively—will be front and center. Bodhisattvas are those who have cultivated spontaneous bodhicitta that arises with respect to every sentient being. Because of being motivated by bodhicitta, bodhisattvas fulfill the two collections of merit and wisdom and attain the resultant full awakening of a buddha with the four buddha bodies. Bodhisattvas follow the Bodhisattva Vehicle, also called the Mahāyāna or Universal Vehicle.

Śrāvakas and solitary realizers, on the other hand, are motivated by the aspiration for liberation. Although they realize the same emptiness as the bodhisattvas do, they do not gather the same amount of merit; the awakenings they attain from practicing their vehicles are the awakenings of śrāvakas and solitary realizers. They attain liberation and become arhats.

There is some difference between the way arhatship is described in the Pāli and Sanskrit traditions. Although both agree that Śākyamuni Buddha was an arhat, the Sanskrit tradition distinguishes arhatship and buddhahood. Arhatship is the abandonment of all afflictive obscurations, whereas buddhahood involves the abandonment of both afflictive obscurations and cognitive obscurations.

The choice of vehicle depends on the disposition of the individual. The practitioners of all three vehicles are to be respected for their spiritual attainments. We must admit, however, that some Mahāyāna sūtras may appear to denigrate those who seek arhatship rather than buddhahood. This was done to encourage practitioners inclined toward the Bodhisattva Vehicle to see the value of bodhicitta and put energy into generating it. Unfortunately this has been misunderstood and has become the source of sectarianism. This and other misconceptions that Buddhist traditions have about one another have been passed down historically. Remedying them was one reason why we wrote *Buddhism: One Teacher, Many Traditions*, which explains the doctrines of the Pāli and Sanskrit traditions. Here we see that both traditions contain teachings on the Śrāvaka, Solitary Realizer, and Bodhisattva Vehicles, and that many teachings practiced by bodhisattvas are built on the foundation of the practices of śrāvakas and solitary realizers. For example, we can easily see that the teachings on bodhicitta are founded on the teachings of the four immeasurables, which are contained in both traditions. That is, the teachings on immeasurable love, compassion, empathic joy, and equanimity are available to all Buddhist practitioners. The teachings on bodhicitta are not separate from those on the four immeasurables; they simply take these four wonderful thoughts a step further.

In extolling the magnificent qualities of bodhicitta and bodhisattvas, there is the danger that ordinary people who aspire to enter the Mahāyāna may look down on the Fundamental Vehicle. That is wrong. The greatness of any approach must be explained contextually. In the Mahāyāna, the primary motivation that inspires practitioners is seeking the awakening of all sentient beings. From this point of view, striving for our own personal awakening is limited. However, from the viewpoint of people drowning in saṃsāra, the Fundamental Vehicle that leads to nirvāṇa is magnificent.

By examining the practice and the results of these two vehicles, we see one is more expansive, while the other is more modest. Those following the Fundamental Vehicle seek their own liberation and practice the three higher trainings as the method to attain arhatship. Those following the Mahāyāna must do all the practices taught in the Fundamental Vehicle, including generating renunciation of saṃsāra and practicing the three higher trainings. However, they renounce not only their own saṃsāra but also that of all sentient beings, and for this reason they aspire for full awakening. Practitioners of the Fundamental Vehicle and the Mahāyāna share the ethical conduct of restraining from the ten paths of nonvirtue and abiding in the prātimokṣa ethical code. Mahāyāna practitioners additionally train in the ethical conduct of restraining from actions motivated by self-interest alone and practice the ethical conducts of accumulating virtue and benefiting sentient beings.

Fundamental Vehicle practitioners aspire to attain nirvāṇa without remainder, in which they abide in the personal peace of nirvāṇa. Mahāyāna practitioners seek to attain the enjoyment body of a buddha because through it they will be able to fulfill the purpose of others: leading all sentient beings out of saṃsāra and to full awakening.

These differences do not mean that the Fundamental Vehicle teachings or its practitioners should be denigrated. The sixth root bodhisattva precept is to not abandon the holy Dharma by saying that texts that teach the three vehicles are not the Buddha's word. Mahāyāna practitioners must not denigrate the scriptures of the Fundamental Vehicle by saying they are faulty and therefore were not spoken by the Buddha. The thirteenth root bodhisattva precept is to abandon causing others to forsake their prātimokṣa precepts and embrace the Mahāyāna. Mahāyāna practitioners must not disparage maintaining prātimokṣa precepts in an attempt to bring Fundamental Vehicle practitioners into the Mahāyāna fold. The fourteenth root bodhisattva precept is to abandon causing others to hold the view that the Fundamental Vehicle does not abandon attachment and other afflictions. Such a view is untrue and could adversely affect Fundamental Vehicle practitioners by making them lose faith in the Śrāvaka and Solitary Realizer Vehicles, which do lead to liberation.

Nevertheless, the Fundamental Vehicle and the Mahāyāna bring different results. Nāgārjuna says in *Commentary on Bodhicitta* (*Bodhicittavivaraṇa*, 83–85):

> Because of their detachment,
> did not the śrāvakas attain less awakening?
> By never abandoning sentient beings
> the fully awakened buddhas attained [full] awakening.
>
> Thus when one considers the occurrence of
> the fruits of beneficial and nonbeneficial deeds,
> how can anyone remain even for an instant
> attached [only] to one's own welfare?
>
> Rooted firmly because of compassion,
> and arising from the shoot of bodhicitta,

> [full] awakening that is the sole fruit of altruism—
> this is what the bodhisattvas cultivate.

Based on the firm foundation of the practices of the Fundamental Vehicle, bodhisattvas go beyond the aspiration for their own liberation; seeing that others are trapped in cyclic existence, they seek full awakening.

REFLECTION

1. The Buddha taught three vehicles to correspond to the different dispositions and interests of sentient beings. Practitioners follow the vehicle that corresponds to their disposition and way of thinking.
2. The more we learn about the three vehicles, the more we see what a skillful teacher the Buddha was.
3. The teachings in each vehicle originate from the Buddha and thus are worthy of our respect, appreciation, and honor. Likewise, all practitioners are to be respected.

The Ultimate Purpose of Dharma Practice

From a Mahāyāna perspective, the ultimate purpose for practicing the Dharma is to attain buddhahood, a state that is completely free of all defilements and is fully endowed with all positive qualities. Buddhas have attained their own ultimate peace as well as made themselves fully able to benefit all others. They have accomplished their own purpose in that they have attained a buddha's omniscient mind, the truth body, in which they know all phenomena that exist as clearly as we can see an apple in our hand. They have accomplished the purpose of others in that they have attained a buddha's form bodies—the enjoyment body and the emanation body—with which they can work to benefit sentient beings and lead them to awakening.

All other Dharma practices are either preliminaries to bodhicitta or subsequent practices through which bodhisattvas express their bodhicitta and fulfill their altruistic intention. Preliminaries include the meditations in common with the initial- and middle-capacity practitioners, as well as all the meditations done to generate bodhicitta, such as the seven cause-and-effect instructions and equalizing and exchanging self and others. Subsequent practices include the six perfections and the four ways of assembling disciples (*saṃgrahavastu, saṅgahavatthu*). Vajrayāna's specialty lies in enhancing the perfections of meditative stability and wisdom, and possessing bodhicitta is one of the chief criteria to enter the Vajrayāna. Due to the importance of bodhicitta, the Kadampa masters of eleventh- and twelfth-century Tibet advised us to apply whatever abilities we have to only one purpose—the cultivation of bodhicitta if we have not yet generated it, and to sustain and enhance it once we have.

The principle cause of the wonderful state of buddhahood is bodhicitta. Without it, buddhahood is impossible. Why? Because bodhicitta is the mind aspiring to attain full awakening in order to benefit all sentient beings most effectively, and without this intention, someone will not engage in the practices to attain full awakening. To become a buddha we must first generate bodhicitta and then engage in the actual practice of an advanced practitioner: the six perfections—generosity, ethical conduct, fortitude, joyous effort, meditative stability, and wisdom.

Deep and continuous meditation on the defects of cyclic existence imprints on our mindstream the understanding that the happiness found in saṃsāra is transient and unsatisfactory in nature. Pursuing saṃsāra's limited happiness is not worthwhile when we can attain liberation from saṃsāra, which offers actual peace and joy. When this is clear in our mind, we have no reluctance in relinquishing saṃsāra and attaining liberation. This is compassion for ourselves.

But the question still remains: What about everyone else? We are surrounded by sentient beings, all of whom are like us in wanting happiness and not wanting suffering. In addition, any happiness we have had, are having, and will experience in cyclic existence is dependent on them. Would we feel right to seek only our own liberation? Āryaśūra questions us (LC 2:14):

> When people see that joy and unhappiness are like a dream
> and that beings degenerate due to the faults of ignorance,
> why would they strive for their own welfare,
> forsaking delight in the excellent deeds of altruism?

When we can enact so much good in this and other worlds, why not aspire for full buddhahood, a state of body and mind in which exists full wisdom, compassion, and skillful means for benefiting all beings? To do this we must first generate bodhicitta. The *Array of Stalks Sūtra* (*Gaṇḍavyūha Sūtra*) says (LC 2:17):

> O child of good lineage (bodhisattva), bodhicitta is like the seed of all buddha qualities.

Each and every awakened quality depends on bodhicitta. Regarding this precious mind, Śāntideva reflects (BCA 1.8, 1.26):

> Those who long to overcome the abundant miseries of mundane existence,
> those who wish to dispel the adversities of sentient beings,
> and those who yearn to experience a myriad of joys
> should never forsake the altruistic intention [of bodhicitta].
>
> How can one measure the merit of the jewel of the mind,
> which is the seed of the world's joy
> and is the remedy
> for the world's suffering?

What Is Bodhicitta?

The word "bodhicitta" has two syllables, *bodhi* and *citta*. *Bodhi* means awakened or enlightened, and *citta* means mind. What type of mind? There are two types of mind: primary consciousnesses and mental factors. Primary consciousnesses know the general nature of an object, be it an object of sight, sound, smell, taste, or touch, or a mental object. Auxiliary mental factors know the specifics of the object. As a primary consciousness, bodhicitta focuses on the general nature of its object, which in this case is bodhi. "Bodhi" implies both purification and realization. To show this, Tibetan translators translated "bodhi" or "awakening" as *byang chub* (pronounced *jang chup*) in Tibetan. *Byang* indicates purification; we can understand that through purification of all mental obscurations it's possible for the mind to directly know all phenomena. *Chub* indicates enhancing our good qualities so we can attain that state. In this way *byang chub* connotes that the awakening that comes about by completing the purification process is omniscience—buddhahood with the four buddha bodies.

Similarly, Tibetan translators rendered the word "buddha" as *sangs rgyas* (pronounced *sang gyey*). *Sangs* means to eliminate, and refers to the eradicating of all faults and obscurations, and *rgyas* means to expand, in the sense of knowing all phenomena and actualizing all excellent qualities. Someone who has done this is *sangs rgyas*, or buddha.

Looking at the words *byang chub* and *sangs rgyas*, we see that they have similar meanings: both *byang* and *sangs* portray the purification of all obscurations, while both *chub* and *rgyas* indicate the expansion of good qualities and the development of all realizations, especially the direct realization of emptiness. This realization of emptiness is common to āryas of all three vehicles—the Śrāvaka, Solitary Realizer, and Bodhisattva Vehicles, each of which has its own awakening. Due to how śrāvakas, solitary realizers, and bodhisattvas practice before attaining their respective awakenings, there are differences in these three types of awakening. In the present case, "bodhi" refers to Mahāyāna bodhi or great awakening, so *byang* indicates the purification of both afflictive obscurations and cognitive obscurations, and *chub* is a buddha's realization of ultimate reality in which meditative equipoise and post-meditative realization cannot be differentiated. A buddha's awakening has the ability to simultaneously remain in the union of meditative equipoise and post-meditative realization until the end of space; unlike sentient beings, buddhas are omniscient and can directly perceive all veiled truths and ultimate truths simultaneously.

Bodhicitta is a primary mental consciousness.[18] As such, it is accompanied by (is concomitant with) various mental factors, a principal one being the aspiration to attain full awakening. How does this aspiration arise? Contemplation of the kindness of sentient beings and their duḥkha in saṃsāra causes great compassion, which is a mental factor wishing sentient beings to be free from suffering. The observed object of compassion is sentient beings. Strong meditation on great compassion causes the aspiration to benefit sentient beings. This aspiration leads us to examine how best to benefit sentient beings, and we conclude that it is through attaining the qualities of a buddha. Thus the aspiration for full awakening is born. This aspiration accompanies the primary mind of bodhicitta. The observed object of bodhicitta is bodhi—our own full awakening. Bodhicitta is directed toward full awakening because we want to work for the welfare of all sentient beings by attaining full awakening. Wisdom is the force that will purify our mind and transform it into the fully awakened mind of a buddha. The observed object of this wisdom is emptiness.

To have the aspiration for full awakening, we have to understand what we are aspiring toward, and to do this we first need to be convinced of the possibility of attaining true cessations, nirvāṇa. This returns us to the topic of the mind's nature being pure and the afflictions being adventitious, which was discussed in an earlier volume.[19] This, in turn, leads us to investigate the ultimate nature of the mind, through which we come to understand and then have an inferential realization of emptiness. Sharp-faculty practitioners generate bodhicitta on the basis of an inferential realization of emptiness that confirms the possibility of attaining full awakening. Their bodhicitta is especially firm and cannot degenerate because it is based on reasoning. Modest-faculty practitioners, inspired by their teachers, past practitioners, and the scriptures, assume that awakening is possible. With this vague understanding of awakening, they generate bodhicitta. Because their bodhicitta is based on faith, it is not firm and is vulnerable to degeneration.

In the *Ornament of Clear Realizations* Maitreya describes twenty-two types of bodhicitta that will be explained in a later chapter. Practitioners on the initial level of the path of accumulation have earth-like bodhicitta, which may degenerate so that the practitioner loses his bodhicitta and relapses to the state of a non-bodhisattva. However, gold-like bodhicitta, attained on the middle level of the path of accumulation, is stable and cannot degenerate. Bodhicitta divorced from the wisdom realizing emptiness cannot develop beyond the initial level of the path of accumulation; thus it is important to further our understanding of emptiness while we also create the causes to generate bodhicitta.

This wisdom mind that focuses on bodhi is completely developed at buddhahood. To arrive at the state of mental enrichment indicated by *chub*, we must understand the observed object of bodhicitta—full awakening. The potential to attain full awakening is not something that must be newly generated; it is an innate quality of our mind present from beginningless time. The Buddha said (AN 1.51):

> This mind, O monastics, is luminous, but it is defiled by adventitious defilements.

And Maitreya said in the *Sublime Continuum* (RGV 1.50):

> The pollutants are adventitious; the good qualities exist innately.

Dharmakīrti makes a similar statement (PV 2.208ab):

> The nature of the mind is clear light;
> the defilements are adventitious.

Both of these masters emphasize two reasons why pollutants can be eliminated from the mind. First, there exist strong counterforces capable of destroying the pollutants. Second, the nature of the mind is clear light—that is, the pollutants do not abide in the nature of the mind. The ability to cognize and understand objects is the innate nature of mind. When the obscurations are overcome and this ability is perfected and focused on worthwhile objects, the mind is purified and all obscurations removed. At that time, our mind will become the omniscient mind of a buddha.

If the ability to realize something is in the nature of the mind, why doesn't our present mind realize all existents? Because it is polluted by obscurations. While *chub* indicates enriching the mind with realizations, to arrive at the state of perfect enrichment or realization, total purification is necessary. That is, purification must happen for enrichment to come about. Thus *byang* comes first, followed by *chub* in the word *byang chub*—the Tibetan word for awakening—because without purification there is no possibility of knowing all objects.

However, saying that the ability to cognize and understand that an object—even an object such as the emptiness of inherent existence—is an innate quality of the mind does not mean that we can sit back and relax and awakening will come to us without effort. Bringing to fruition the two aspirations associated with bodhicitta involves effort and diligence because serenity and insight must be cultivated and unified in order to nonconceptually realize ultimate bodhicitta—the wisdom directly realizing emptiness. Only that wisdom has the capacity to remove all obscurations from the mind in such a way that they can never reappear.

REFLECTION

Contemplate the meaning of bodhicitta in order to orient and motivate yourself to cultivate it.

1. Bodhicitta is a primary mental consciousness with two aspirations.
2. The causal aspiration is rooted in great compassion and seeks to benefit all sentient beings by freeing them from saṃsāra and leading them to full awakening.
3. The second aspiration is to attain one's own full awakening in order to be able to benefit all beings in these ways.
4. It is possible to attain full awakening because all mental defilements can be eradicated from the mindstream.
5. All defilements can be eradicated because strong counterforces that can eliminate the defilements exist and the nature of the mind is clear light.

The Causes of Bodhicitta

Like all other conditioned phenomena, bodhicitta does not arise without causes, nor does it arise from discordant causes—that is, factors that do not have the ability to produce it. Some causes of bodhicitta are internal, others are external. The internal causes lie in our own mind. We have the mental factors of love and compassion within us now. Love is the virtuous mental factor of nonhatred. It overcomes and prevents anger and hatred and is the basis for increasing patience and fortitude. Compassion is the virtuous mental factor of nonharmfulness that lacks any intention to cause harm and wishes all sentient beings to be free of duḥkha. The inability to bear the duḥkha of others is the basis of the desire to benefit sentient beings and to not disrespect them by harming them. Compassion is said to be the essence of the Buddha's teachings.

Although the mental factors of love and compassion already exist in our mindstreams, they must be nourished and expanded through habituating ourselves with these emotions. Releasing hindrances by purifying destructive karma and making our mind receptive by accumulating merit are also necessary causes of bodhicitta. In addition, we must listen to teachings and study texts that describe the method to generate bodhicitta and the conduct of bodhisattvas and then contemplate and meditate on what we learn. Remembering the qualities of the Buddha inspires us to generate bodhicitta, as do understanding the advantages of bodhicitta and wishing that the Mahāyāna teachings last forever.

External causes of bodhicitta include being guided by a Mahāyāna spiritual mentor, who compassionately teaches us the method to develop bodhicitta, and living near others who aspire for and practice bodhicitta. In addition, our generating bodhicitta depends on sentient beings. Kind sentient beings provide the requisites for living so we are free to practice bodhicitta; they also give us the opportunities for practice by being the objects of our generosity, ethical conduct, and fortitude. Their suffering and their kindness are the prime motivating forces leading us to generate bodhicitta. If we admire bodhicitta and seek the benefits of generating it but dislike sentient beings, then we've failed to understand that without caring for sentient beings it's impossible to generate bodhicitta.

Practice and training are necessary to learn any skill, be it car mechanics or compassion. As with gaining any ability, first coarse hindrances must be eliminated and then subtle ones. Therefore, at the start of your practice, removing or reducing obsession with the happiness of only this life is a must, as that is the coarsest hindrance to Dharma practice. With an attitude concerned for only our own happiness in this life, we try to procure what we think will bring us happiness and destroy what seems to bring us misery, without caring about the effects of our actions on others. Blinded by ignorance, we engage in a plentitude of destructive actions to gain or protect name and fame, material possession and wealth, approval and praise, and sense pleasures. Doing this puts us in conflict with people and creates greater problems. Thus the eight worldly concerns and the destructive actions of body, speech, and mind that result from them are the first and principle factors to subdue at the beginning of the path.

Subduing our attachment and anger regarding the eight worldly concerns does not come about from simply telling ourselves that attachment and animosity are hindrances. Rather, we must reflect deeply on their disadvantages so that we gather the inner strength to oppose them. By examining our own life, we see how worldly concerns and obsession with the happiness of only this life make us unhappy now and create the causes for unhappiness in future lives. We observe how they prevent us from practicing and realizing the path. Our efforts in virtue can be reinvigorated also by contemplating the advantages of a precious human life so that we will be energized to abandon harmful actions and engage in constructive ones in order to receive another precious human life in the future. This is the practice in common with the initial-level practitioner.

Having done this, we then reflect that although a precious human life with many excellent conditions is advantageous, our very existence is still under the control of afflictions and polluted karma, and thus we have no lasting freedom or security. This will motivate us to renounce the duḥkha of cyclic existence and its causes and generate a strong aspiration for liberation. In this way, our enchantment with the pleasures of future lives comes to an end. This is the practice in common with the middle-level practitioner. Both the initial and the middle levels constitute preparatory practices for the generation of bodhicitta. On this basis, we now turn our mind to the cultivation of bodhicitta, that most noble of all aspirations.

The cultivation of bodhicitta depends on many causes. Among these, one is to learn about the qualities of buddhas and bodhisattvas from a reliable spiritual mentor or from scriptures. By admiring the magnificent abilities of these beings, faith arises in our mind and we aspire to attain these qualities. This aspiring faith is essential for overcoming the complacency thinking that attaining nirvāṇa alone is sufficient to fulfill our own spiritual purpose.

How do we gain conviction that full awakening is necessary to fulfill our own purposes so that we turn away from seeking only our own liberation? By knowing that (1) śrāvakas have not abandoned all defilements or actualized all realizations, (2) śrāvakas are liberated from cyclic existence but not from the drawbacks of the personal peace that is an arhat's nirvāṇa, and (3) a buddha's truth body is the fulfillment of our own purpose because it's the complete abandonment of all obscurations and the full realization of all excellent qualities. A buddha's form bodies fulfill the purpose or aim of others by manifesting in diverse forms in order to teach and guide sentient beings to awareness. By knowing and admiring the qualities of the buddhas, we aspire to attain them in order to accomplish our own *and* others' purposes.[20] Fulfilling others' purpose is not sufficient, nor is fulfilling only our own purpose. Buddhahood enables us to do both. This is important to prevent us from backsliding and seeking personal liberation alone.

Another cause of bodhicitta is understanding that the existence of the bodhisattvas' teachings is not stable in our degenerate world; they will disappear. Finding this unbearable and wanting these precious teachings to remain a long time so that sentient beings' suffering can be eliminated, we aspire to gain a buddha's pristine wisdom.

Yet another cause is seeing that it is difficult enough in this age to generate a śrāvaka's aspiration for liberation; generating bodhicitta is even more difficult. Knowing the rarity of this opportunity and knowing the preservation of the bodhisattvas' teachings for future generations depends on people actualizing them now, we aspire to attain buddhahood.

While compassion and bodhicitta are cultivated separately from the wisdom realizing emptiness, the realization of emptiness in the mindstream of someone who already admires and appreciates bodhicitta and who aspires to generate it will help their compassion grow. Deep realization of emptiness by those inclined toward the Mahāyāna gives rise to understanding that ignorance is the fundamental cause of their own duḥkha. These practitioners will more thoroughly understand the relationship between ignorance, afflictions, and their karmic actions. Furthermore, the realization of emptiness will undermine their ignorant view of the world, giving them stronger conviction in the possibility of attaining liberation. When they extend this understanding to other sentient beings, it leads to feeling strong compassion for others, which, in turn, gives rise to bodhicitta.

REFLECTION

Contemplate the conditions of bodhicitta to enable yourself to cultivate it.

1. Bodhicitta is a conditioned phenomenon that arises as a result of causes and conditions.

2. External causes of bodhicitta include being guided by a Mahāyāna spiritual mentor, who compassionately teaches us the method to develop bodhicitta, and living near others who aspire for and practice bodhicitta. It also depends on sentient beings, the object of our great compassion.

3. Internal causes include the seeds of love and compassion we have right now, recognizing the defects of saṃsāra, knowing the qualities of the buddhas and bodhisattvas and wanting to attain them, recognizing the disadvantages of the self-centered attitude, and being endowed with great compassion.

4. Knowing the rarity of our present situation with its excellent conditions to practice the Dharma and wanting the precious teachings to remain in our world are also causes to generate bodhicitta.

The Benefits of Bodhicitta

Bodhicitta, the essence of the path of the advanced practitioner, brings inconceivable and inexpressible benefits to self and others in this and future lives. Having even a general awareness of these benefits will stimulate us to enthusiastically cultivate bodhicitta. In this life, personal happiness and peace come from practicing bodhicitta. Why? When we sincerely wish to benefit others, we forgo judgmental and critical attitudes toward them. Without these negative thoughts churning around in our mind, we automatically feel better. When our mind is filled with kind thoughts, our physical health improves, as do our relationships with family and friends. If we practice bodhicitta during illness or injury, our mind will be calm, and we will be able to take our physical situation and its treatment in stride. Having the altruistic intention at the time of death brings peace to our minds; we die with no regrets because our life was worthwhile.

Generally, when an ordinary person encounters difficulties she becomes frustrated, angry, and resentful. At that time she may believe that anger is her friend, supporting her and enabling her to have the courage to face the problem. Gaining inner strength through the force of anger is not simply foolish, it is dangerous. We do not think clearly or express ourselves well when we are angry, and actions done in a rage generally worsen the problem.

Some analogies illustrate the benefits of bodhicitta:

- It is like supreme nectar that prevents death and replaces our unclean body with the form body of a buddha.

- It resembles an inexhaustible treasure because it nourishes and sustains us spiritually.
- It is a supreme medicine because it cures the illness of the afflictions.
- It resembles a resting tree in that it gives us protection of the exhaustion of saṃsāra.
- It is like a boat that keeps us safe while we're still in the ocean of saṃsāra with its dangerous sea monsters of afflictions and karma.
- Bodhicitta is like soothing moonlight that calms our entire body and mind.
- It is like water from a pond that cools the fire of afflictions.
- Bodhicitta resembles bright sunlight in that it sheds light on dark corners and broadens our perspective so we can see possibilities we couldn't see before.
- It resembles perennial flowers that continue to bring the beautiful blossoms of virtue.

Compassion and bodhicitta bring genuine self-confidence and self-esteem. The courage and conviction that come from them have a strong foundation in reason. These qualities enable us to face problems and suffering without being overwhelmed by confusion, depression, or low self-esteem. We will be able to deal with what life brings with determination and confidence. Why? Because with bodhicitta we are aware that suffering arises from causes and conditions such as afflictions and karma, and we know that these causes and conditions can be overcome. In this way, bodhicitta brings optimism and hope.

Bodhicitta is the best way to deal with an enemy. If we get angry, the enemy has been successful in harming us, but if we maintain a peaceful mind, the enemy has failed to bring us trouble. Of course, sometimes we still have to run away to protect ourselves from harm—for example, if a mad dog is nearby—but in many cases, when we practice compassion and altruism, someone who was previously an enemy will become our friend. This is evident in international relations. The Allies helped to rebuild Germany and Japan after World War II, and now those countries are friendly.

People ask what enables me to remain optimistic, considering all that has happened in my homeland, Tibet, and to me personally due to the tragedy there. Bodhicitta gives me a sense of hope, for I see the basic good in human beings and know that their mistaken actions occur not because they are evil people but because their afflictions overwhelm them. For that reason, I do not harbor grudges or wish for revenge and thus can work with optimism to help improve the situation.

We may think that when we practice compassion, the primary beneficiaries are other sentient beings. But in fact we benefit even more than others do from our practice of compassion. When I practice compassion, I receive 100 percent benefit—my mind is upbeat—but the extent to which others benefit from my compassion is uncertain. Some people may even become suspicious when I act with compassion! Love and compassion make our mind joyful; bodhisattvas on the first ground are called the Very Joyful because their happiness is much greater than that of an arhat, even though they haven't abandoned all afflictions as arhats have done. The great joy of these bodhisattvas derives from their mind that cherishes others and enables them to manage problems and difficulties with ease. After hearing bad news, they swiftly regain their sense of well-being and optimism. Compassion is like nectar that immediately calms their mind. Someone who has peace of mind and inner calm as a result of practicing compassion and understanding emptiness is not easily dispirited.

Bodhicitta motivates us to act in ways that bring peace in the larger society. I often tell people half-jokingly that if they are going to be selfish, they should be wisely selfish. And the best way to do that is to help others because when the people around us are happy, we naturally are too! However, when our self-centered behavior damages others, we live surrounded by miserable people who make their pain known to us.

With bodhicitta, we care for the environment because we care about other species as well as the future generations of human beings who will inherit this planet. These benefits of a kind heart and bodhicitta are obvious. There is no controversy about them, and no special logic is needed to understand them.

Meditating on bodhicitta enriches our practices of the initial and middle levels of the path. At the initial level, the goal is to pacify our coarse destructive actions and prepare for a good rebirth. A mind wishing to benefit others abstains from harming them and thus stops engaging in destructive actions that destroy their happiness. Bodhicitta also inspires us to purify previously accumulated destructive karma and to act in beneficial ways. As a result of this, a fortunate rebirth will naturally follow.

As a middle-level practitioner, the aim of our practice is to abolish the afflictions that cause cyclic existence. Many of these afflictions are disturbing emotions, such as resentment, jealousy, or belligerence toward living beings. When we generate bodhicitta, we see others as loveable and dear, so afflictions directed toward them are dramatically curtailed.

Those who exclusively practice the initial and middle levels of the path aspire for liberation from cyclic existence but not for the full awakening of buddhahood. Following the Fundamental Vehicle, they meditate to gain the direct realization of emptiness that will cut the continuity of their afflictions forever. Although they realize the same emptiness that bodhisattvas do, their wisdom eliminates only the afflictive obscurations preventing liberation. It does not become the antidote to the cognitive obscurations preventing omniscience. Those practicing the advanced level of the path develop bodhicitta, which gives their wisdom extra force, enabling it to cut through the subtle obscurations and attain buddhahood. Dza Patrul Rinpoche cautions:

> Even if you have the generation and completion stages [of Tantra]
>   and single-pointed concentration,
> if they are not linked to authentic bodhicitta,
> they're just the seeds of rebirth in the deceptive appearances of
>   saṃsāra
> and are no help in attaining the state of omniscience.[21]

Without bodhicitta and the direct realization of emptiness, the merit created by reciting tantric sādhanas and mantras and by doing vase breathing and so forth becomes the cause of rebirth in saṃsāra, not of a buddha's omniscient mind.

Bodhicitta is a vast mind because it wants to benefit all beings and seeks to attain the highest awakening in order to do so. All actions motivated by bodhicitta accumulate merit corresponding to the vastness of this intention. This enables a practitioner to accumulate quickly the great collection of merit needed to attain full awakening. Bodhicitta also enables the wisdom realizing emptiness to become powerful enough to remove from the mindstream subtle latencies and the dualistic appearances they create. For this reason, it leads to buddhahood. Without this altruistic intention, attaining the ultimate bliss and magnificent qualities of buddhahood is not possible. In sum, everything positive and admirable in cyclic existence and nirvāṇa can be accomplished with bodhicitta. As Nāgārjuna says (BV 105–7):

> This bodhicitta is stated
> to be the highest [ideal] in the great vehicle,
> so with an absorbed [determined] effort
> generate this altruistic intention.
>
> To accomplish the welfare of yourself and others
> no other methods exist in the world;
> apart from the bodhicitta,
> to date the buddhas saw no other means.
>
> The merit that is obtained
> from mere generation of bodhicitta,
> if it were to assume form
> it would fill more than the expanse of space.

Not understanding the value of bodhicitta, some people say that generating it is too difficult and put it aside. Giving in to ignorant arrogance, others say bodhicitta is a preliminary practice that is not so important and they're engaged in more profound tantric practices. Such thoughts impede our spiritual growth. Someone who has cultivated bodhicitta will attain awakening whereas someone meditating on any profound tantric practice without this altruistic intention will not attain awakening.

REFLECTION

Contemplate the benefits of bodhicitta to energize yourself to cultivate it.

1. It increases our self-confidence, inner strength, and optimism by giving us a long-term inspiring goal to work toward.

2. Bodhicitta motivates us to act in ways that bring peace in society at large.
3. It enriches our practices of the initial and middle levels of the path.
4. The merit created by even simple actions done with bodhicitta is limitless because we're working for the benefit of limitless sentient beings.
5. Buddhas and bodhisattvas are role models that inspire us to transform our actions of body, speech, and mind into virtue. In this way, we become the kind of person we would like to be.
6. Spiritual realizations will come quicker due to the power of working for the benefit of all beings.

Bodhisattvas as Inspiring Role Models

The examples of bodhisattvas' lives and their marvelous activities inspire us to want to become like them. Personally speaking, thinking about the bodhisattvas encourages me to practice more than does thinking about the buddhas. If I thought just of the buddhas' qualities without being attentive to the qualities of bodhisattvas on the training paths, I could become disheartened, thinking that the buddhas are too high and I can never catch up to them. For example, when I view Tsongkhapa as an emanation of Mañjuśrī, I think he had all those marvelous qualities because he was the emanation of a buddha. But when I regard him as an ordinary person who sincerely took on serious spiritual practice and gained high realizations in his lifetime, I am encouraged. Since both of us began as ordinary beings, if I practice just as he did, I will become like him.

It is similar to being in a race. If someone is a kilometer in front of us, we feel we can never catch up and quit trying. But if someone is only a few steps in front of us, we do not lose courage. We try harder because we know that if we make effort, we can draw near to them. This could be called a positive kind of competition that results from comparing ourselves to others in a way that is not completely egocentric. I encourage you to read about the great deeds of bodhisattvas and the biographies of past great practitioners. Let your mind feel joyous and inspired knowing that people like this exist in the world and that you can become like them by developing bodhicitta.

In the Pāli tradition and also in the *Ornament of Clear Realizations* by Maitreya, six recollections are taught: recollections of the Buddha, Dharma, Saṅgha, generosity, ethical conduct, and deities. The recollection on deities can refer to mundane gods (*devas*) or to transcendental divine beings who are ārya bodhisattvas. In the Fundamental Vehicle, recollection of the deities focuses on being mindful of the qualities that caused beings to be born in these celestial states, thus inspiring us to emulate them in our practice of generosity, ethical conduct, and meditation. In the Mahāyāna, recollection of the deities is done so that they will serve as witness to our proper cultivation of the path. Recollection of the compassionate qualities of the bodhisattvas also gladdens and inspires our mind. This deepens our refuge in the bodhisattva saṅgha and inspires us to practice bodhicitta in order to work for the benefit of all beings, as they do.

The Perfection of Wisdom sūtras and the Mahāyāna sūtras in general contain stories of many bodhisattvas. Eight of these—Mañjuśrī, Avalokiteśvara, Vajrapāṇi, Kṣitigarbha, Ākāśagarbha, Sarvanivāraṇa-viṣkambhin, Samantabhadra, and Maitreya—are especially close spiritual heirs of Śākyamuni Buddha. Of these bodhisattvas, Avalokiteśvara is seen as the manifestation of compassion, and so meditating on and making supplications to Avalokiteśvara is extremely helpful when practicing compassion and bodhicitta.[22]

If we doubt our ability to generate bodhicitta and become bodhisattvas, it is helpful to reflect on Dharmakīrti's teachings in chapter 2 of *Commentary on the "Compendium of Reliable Cognition"* (*Pramāṇavārttika*). Using reasoning, he first establishes the existence of past and future lives to demonstrate that since it takes time to familiarize ourselves with great compassion for all sentient beings, we can cultivate it gradually over many lifetimes. He continues by comparing physical and mental development. The physical abilities of an athlete have limitations due to the limitations of the body. In addition, to improve, an athlete, such as a high jumper, must cover the area they previously jumped plus some. Mental development is different; the mental factors of love and compassion already exist in our minds. The mind is a stable basis for the cultivation of these emotions, and the love and compassion we generate today can build on what we generated yesterday, so that these qualities continually increase.

Two factors are necessary to train the mind in developing compassion: consistency and intensity. Consistency involves training our mind in compassion every day through having a stable meditation practice, and intensity involves doing our practice with sincerity and concentration without letting the mind be distracted. Together they enable us to familiarize ourselves with great compassion repeatedly so that it becomes a natural part of our mind and arises easily. Overcoming adverse conditions, such as anger, resentment, and jealousy, is also an important element. It is possible to do this because these mental factors that are contrary to love and compassion are based on ignorance and have antidotes.

If we doubt that we can develop great compassion at all, Dharmakīrti reminds us that we have all been one another's parents and children in previous lives. Parents and children have natural bonds of affection, love, and compassion for one another. Since we have the imprints from such close relationships with all others in previous lives, it is possible to cultivate great compassion for everyone now. Although effort is needed at the beginning of our practice, by increased familiarization with love and compassion, they will arise more easily in our lives.

Two Types of Mahāyāna Disciples

Some Mahāyāna disciples have sharp faculties, whereas others have more modest faculties. Here "faculties" refers in particular to wisdom, but more broadly to the five faculties of faith, effort, mindfulness, concentration, and wisdom. The disciples with sharp faculties first seek the correct view of emptiness. Through using reasoning, they understand that ignorance apprehends phenomena to exist inherently, whereas phenomena exist dependently. Seeing that the wisdom that realizes emptiness can eradicate this ignorance that is the root of saṃsāra and can thus cease saṃsāra completely, they are convinced that attaining awakening is possible through gaining insight into emptiness. They then develop compassion and generate bodhicitta. In this way, sharp-faculty disciples aspire for full awakening, enter the bodhisattva path, overcome the self-grasping ignorance, practice the six perfections, and attain awakening.

The disciples of modest faculties admire bodhicitta due to the strong faith they have in the teachers who speak about bodhicitta, and their aspiration to attain awakening derives from their faith in the Three Jewels. They cultivate heartfelt compassion for others' duḥkha and build up altruism on that basis. These disciples have not yet gained the wisdom to deeply appreciate selflessness and its essential role in attaining awakening. They generate uncontrived bodhicitta, enter the bodhisattva path, and then make effort to gain an inferential understanding of emptiness.

Bodhisattvas with sharp faculties are not content to believe that liberation and full awakening are possible because their spiritual mentors stated that or because it is written in sūtras. They want to know, What is the root of all afflictions? Can afflictions be removed? What is the realization that can eradicate them? What is the object perceived by the wisdom that eradicates afflictions? With strong compassion and altruism, these disciples examine whether sentient beings' duḥkha can be totally eliminated and whether a path to liberation exists. This leads them to understand emptiness at least on an intellectual level, because the wisdom realizing emptiness is what will destroy the afflictions and directly bring about awakening. Based on understanding emptiness, these disciples generate the conviction that a way to eradicate the origins of duḥkha exists, liberation is possible, and there is a path leading to it.

In short, modest-faculty bodhisattvas first cultivate compassion and bodhicitta and then turn their mind to understand emptiness; sharp-faculty bodhisattvas first emphasize the cultivation of wisdom and then, on the basis of understanding that liberation is possible, generate great compassion and bodhicitta.

In the Autocommentary to the *Ornament of the Middle Way* (*Madhyamakālaṃkāra-vṛtti*) Śāntarakṣita explains the sequence of meditation for the two types of Mahāyāna disciples:[23]

> First searching to know reality,
> they ascertain well the ultimate [truth]
> and then generate compassion
> for the world obscured by bad views.
>
> Emboldened to undertake migrators' welfare
> and skilled in the vast mind of awakening,

they practice the Subduer's discipline (the bodhisattva deeds)
adorned with wisdom and compassion.

Followers of pure faith (modest-faculty disciples) generate
the mind of perfect awakening (bodhicitta),
and then assume the discipline of the Subduer,
and strive for knowledge of reality.

Cultivating compassion and wisdom in tandem is very beneficial. As one's understanding of emptiness increases, so will one's compassion for sentient beings who are under the influence of ignorance. Furthermore, generating wisdom is difficult when the mind is tormented by coarse afflictions. Decreasing the intensity and frequency of the coarse afflictions through practicing compassion makes meditation easier and opens the mind to be more receptive to realize emptiness.

The compassion that is not complemented by the wisdom realizing emptiness differs from the compassion that is. While the former compassion may be so powerful that bodhisattvas continuously think of others and work for their welfare, those bodhisattvas do not yet know how to accomplish their own or others' liberation. In contrast, compassion complemented by the wisdom realizing emptiness knows that self-grasping ignorance binds sentient beings to cyclic existence and that the wisdom directly realizing emptiness can free them. Bodhisattvas who generate bodhicitta with wisdom have great enthusiasm and courage because they know a path to liberation exists. This is the way of generating bodhicitta taught by Śāntideva (eighth century)—equalizing and exchanging self and others.

To explain the path for sharp-faculty bodhisattvas in more detail: Having gained a general idea of the path to awakening, these disciples focus on gaining ultimate bodhicitta—the wisdom realizing emptiness—by cultivating the wisdom of suchness in terms of dependent arising.[24] That is, they meditate on dependent arising as the reason that proves all persons and phenomena lack inherent existence. When they have developed a conceptual understanding of the ultimate truth, they recognize that the root of our duḥkha is the ignorance that misapprehends the ultimate truth. This ignorance is the first link of the twelve links of dependent origination,[25] and sharp-faculty bodhisattvas know that it is erroneous.

Through this, these sharp-faculty bodhisattvas come to understand buddha nature—the clear light nature of the mind—and know that the pollutants that defile the mind are adventitious and can be separated from the mind, as the quotations from the Buddha, Maitreya, and Dharmakīrti earlier in this chapter state. In this way, they generate a deep, stable, genuine aspiration to seek liberation from suffering. This is truly well-grounded renunciation.

Having such genuine renunciation, these sharp-faculty bodhisattvas then direct their thoughts to other sentient beings and know that just as their own suffering is not endless, it is possible for other sentient beings' duḥkha to come to an end. They know that other sentient beings also have the buddha nature. This certainty stimulates such strong compassion to arise that whenever they perceive any sentient being whatsoever, their instinctive response is, "How terrible it is that they suffer! Their suffering can and must be ended!" This is a genuine wish that others be free from duḥkha and is called "compassion in the form of a wish." Such compassion can also arise in śrāvakas, but when this compassion is cultivated further, it culminates in a profound level of compassion called "compassion that wants to liberate sentient beings." Here the element of wanting to act to bring about others' freedom from suffering is much stronger, and these bodhisattvas are committed to help eliminate sentient beings' duḥkha. This is the great compassion that culminates in the altruistic resolve and bodhicitta.

From the perspective of this sequence of mental development, Nāgārjuna says that with regard to bodhisattvas with sharp faculties, insight into suchness in terms of dependent arising will lead to the arising of compassion (BV 73):

> In a yogi in whom the realization
> of emptiness has arisen,
> there is no doubt that
> compassion for all beings will arise.

Before these sharp-faculty disciples investigate the ultimate nature of phenomena, they already have a strong tendency toward compassion, bodhicitta, and the Mahāyāna. When they cultivate an understanding of emptiness, this aids them in generating bodhicitta. However, it is not the case that the realization of emptiness alone will enable them to generate great compassion and bodhicitta. In that case, arhats would have realized these. Rather, practitioners must also learn, contemplate, and meditate on the methods for generating great compassion and bodhicitta.

3 | How to Cultivate Bodhicitta: The Seven Cause-and-Effect Instructions

Training the mind in bodhicitta can be done by two methods. The first is the seven cause-and-effect instructions and the second is equalizing and exchanging self and others. Tsongkhapa received the lineages of both methods to generate bodhicitta and combined them.

In both of these methods, the principal cause of bodhicitta is great compassion, and seeing others as pleasing and lovable is the key to cultivating compassion. Without seeing sentient beings in a positive light, wishing them to be free from suffering is difficult. Thus the strength of our compassion depends on the degree to which we see others as lovable and feel close to them as well as the depth of our understanding of their suffering. If either one of these is missing or weak, our compassion will be either flat or fake.

The seven cause-and-effect instructions sets forth three steps to see sentient beings as pleasing and lovable: recognizing that all sentient beings have been our parents (especially our mother) in previous lives, contemplating the kindness of our parents, and wishing to repay their kindness. Since all sentient beings have been our parents and have been kind to us at that time, a natural feeling of wanting to reciprocate that kindness arises in our hearts. These three steps produce in us feelings of affection and heart-warming love for all beings, which leads to having love and compassion for them.

Equalizing and exchanging self and others depends more on reasoning to generate compassion for others. Here, we see that all beings—not only friends and relatives but also strangers and enemies—have been kind because we have been, are, and will continue to be dependent on the kindness of others to stay alive. In addition, each and every sentient being wants happiness and freedom from suffering as intensely as we do; there is no difference among us on that account. In fact, differentiating ourselves from others is only a matter of perspective. We say "I" in reference to our body and mind, but others say "I" in reference to their bodies and minds. Furthermore, limitless benefits come from cherishing others, while self-centeredness leads only to misery. Seeing this, a wise person generates love and compassion for all beings.

The Seven Cause-and-Effect Instructions

The seven cause-and-effect instructions is a popular method for generating bodhicitta practiced in the Sanskrit tradition. Its origins are traced to Maitreya's *Ornament of Clear Realizations*—especially the chapter on mind generation (bodhicitta)—and the teaching of his disciple Asaṅga. Candragomin, Śāntarakṣita, and Kamalaśīla generated bodhicitta through this method, which was also popular among the early Kadampa masters. Kamalaśīla writes about this method of developing bodhicitta in his middle *Stages of Meditation* (*Bhāvanākrama*), and Candrakīrti speaks of it in his commentary on Āryadeva's *Four Hundred*.

To practice the seven cause-and-effect instructions we begin by understanding the order of the stages, how compassion is the root of the Mahāyāna, and that six of the instructions are either the causes or the effects of compassion. We then begin training the mind to be intent on others' well-being, which is followed by developing the attitude that is intent on others' welfare.

The seven points that are meditated on in sequence are (1) seeing all sentient beings as having been our mother, (2) recalling their kindness to us when they were our parent or caregiver, (3) wanting to repay that kindness, (4) love, (5) compassion, (6) the great resolve, and (7) bodhicitta.

Of these seven, compassion is the root of the Mahāyāna. At the beginning of our practice compassion motivates us to cultivate bodhicitta and to engage in the bodhisattva deeds. In the middle, compassion enables us to look beyond our own happiness and suffering and to take others' joy and misery to heart. In this way, it keeps us involved and encourages us to continue accumulating the collection of merit and the collection of wisdom, two essential requisites to attain supreme awakening. At the completion of the path, compassion enables bodhisattvas to attain nonabiding nirvāṇa in which they dwell neither in the extreme of saṃsāra nor the extreme of personal liberation. Compassion motivates buddhas to manifest in innumerable forms until saṃsāra ends in order to guide sentient beings to full awakening.

The seven points center around compassion, with the first four being the causes of compassion, and the last two being the effects of compassion. For this reason, some masters consider the cause-and-effect instructions to refer to the causes and effects of compassion. Other masters say that the first six points are the causes for the seventh point, bodhicitta.

To cultivate compassion two elements are needed: we need to be aware of the three types of duḥkha of sentient beings and to see them as endearing so that the compassion—the wish that they be free from duḥkha—arises easily in our mind. The awareness of their duḥkha comes from first contemplating our own duḥkha in saṃsāra and cultivating the wish to be free from it and then seeing that all other sentient beings are in the same position. To see sentient beings as endearing we must first free ourselves from attachment to friends and dear ones and animosity for enemies—enemies here being anyone who disturbs our well-being. We do this in the equanimity meditation, which is a forerunner to the seven points.

To cultivate affection and a sense of endearment toward others, we contemplate that they have all been our parents in previous lives and will be our parents in the future as well. As our parents—especially as our mother who carried us in her womb and in general was the chief caregiver when we were little—they were extremely kind to us. In response to their kindness, we develop a wish to repay their kindness. In this way, the first three points result in heart-warming love that cares for sentient beings as a mother cares for her only child. Heartwarming love is the fourth point and is the cause of the compassion that is the fifth point.

There is another kind of love too—the love that wishes others to have happiness and its causes. This love does not have a cause and effect relationship with compassion. Whether we then develop love and compassion depends on whether we first consider sentient beings as bereft of happiness and want them to have happiness and its causes (love), or whether we consider sentient beings' duḥkha and want them to be free of it and its causes (compassion). The first four points are the cause for both of these.

The great resolve and bodhicitta are the effects of compassion. Fundamental Vehicle practitioners may have developed immeasurable love and compassion, but they do not have the resolve to act on these and bring about others' happiness and the alleviation of their duḥkha. With great resolve, Mahāyāna practitioners make a commitment and assume the responsibility to do so.

Once we have made this commitment, we must consider how to fulfill it. In our ordinary condition, we are incapable of doing this. As an arhat, we will be able to lead some sentient beings to liberation but not to the omniscient state of a buddha. Because only a fully awakened buddha has the compassion, wisdom, and capacity to do this most effectively, we generate bodhicitta, resolving to attain buddhahood.

Training the Mind to Be Intent on Others' Well-Being

To train our mind to be intent on others' well-being, as noted above, we must develop a sense of impartiality that is free of attachment and animosity toward others and then cultivate a sense of affection and endearment toward them. The first is done by cultivating equanimity, the second by meditation on the first four of the seven points.

Genuine compassion for all sentient beings is based on having evened out any tendency toward bias that we may have, bias meaning seeing some beings as close and worthwhile and seeing others with animosity as distant. As long as our mind has strong attachment or animosity toward others, our compassion will extend only to those to whom we are attracted and attached. Such compassion isn't stable; if those people later harm us, our compassion for them vanishes.

Equanimity

In general, the Sanskrit tradition speaks of three types of equanimity:

(1) The *feeling of equanimity* is a feeling toward all phenomena that is free from pleasure or pain and is part of the feeling aggregate. It is also the feeling that is dominant in the fourth dhyāna.

(2) The *virtuous mental factor of equanimity* prevents restlessness and laxity when cultivating serenity and does not let the mind be affected by them. It does not unnecessarily apply antidotes when the mind is concentrated and

the faults impeding serenity are not present. This mental factor is developed during the nine sustained attentions leading to serenity.

(3) *Immeasurable equanimity* is one of the four immeasurables. It is an evenness of mind that enables us to be impartial without being indifferent toward sentient beings. It has two types: one wishes all sentient beings to be free from bias, attachment, and antipathy toward others; the second is cultivating equanimity ourselves so that we are free from attachment and animosity. The second type of immeasurable equanimity is the precursor to love, compassion, and bodhicitta. It ensures that we spread these good qualities to all beings.

In cultivating equanimity, we do not seek to abandon the notions of friend and enemy but to abandon the biased emotions of attachment and antipathy that we feel toward them. In his second *Stages of Meditation*, Kamalaśila suggests two ways to do this.

The first is to contemplate that from the perspective of others, each and every living being is equal in wanting happiness and freedom from suffering. Therefore it isn't reasonable for us to favor some with a mind of attachment and to dismiss others with an attitude of animosity. Being even-minded toward all is more suitable.

Think about this deeply. This contemplation is good to do when you are in a public place such as a store or a traffic jam. Look around and reflect that each person there is just trying to be happy and avoid suffering. That thought motivates every one of their actions. For us to hold either attachment or antipathy toward these beings who have the same fundamental human wish is not at all appropriate.

The second way to generate equanimity is to reflect that from our own perspective, in our beginningless previous lives, we have been in every kind of relationship possible with every sentient being. None of these relationships are fixed, and a slight change of circumstance can turn attachment to antipathy and vice versa. For example, someone gives us a gift today; we consider her a friend and become partial toward her. But if tomorrow she criticizes us, our fondness evaporates and we are angry. Meanwhile, another person talks about us behind our back today, triggering our animosity, but tomorrow he praises us and we think he's great. We see similar changes in the shifting alliances of international politics. The *Tantra Requested by Subāhu* (*Subāhuparipṛcchātantra*) advises (LC 1:282):

> Within a short space of time an enemy can become a friend,
> and a friend can become an enemy.
> Likewise, either one may become indifferent,
> while those who were indifferent may become enemies or intimate friends.
> Knowing this, the wise never form attachments.
> They give up the thought of delighting in friends
> and are content to focus on virtue.

When we take the vacillations of rebirth into consideration, the instability of relationships becomes even more pronounced. These roles change from one life to the next, depending on the vagaries of karma. During our beginningless lives in cyclic existence, we have been friends, enemies, and strangers to one another countless times. Considering the changeable nature of our relationships, feeling close and attached to friends and relatives and distant and angry toward enemies is not suitable. A sense of equanimity and impartiality toward all is more realistic.

REFLECTION

1. Because it is easier to generate equanimity toward people for whom we have neutral feelings, begin by focusing on strangers. Release any attachment or aversion you may have toward them.

2. Focus on a friend or relative and recall that, given the instability of relationships, it is unsuitable to be attached to him. Release the attachment and cultivate equanimity.

3. Consider someone for whom you have hostile feelings and similarly see that she has not always been and will not continually be your enemy. People change and relationships change. It doesn't make any sense to develop a rigid image of someone and think that is the whole of that person's life when it is merely fabricated conceptualization on your part.

4. Maintain mindfulness on the understanding that no one is a friend, enemy, or stranger forever. If you meet them in a different situation or if their

behavior changes, your feeling close to or distant from them will change too. Therefore feeling attachment or animosity toward them doesn't make sense. Be aware of the calm that equanimity brings to your mind and the way in which it makes your behavior more thoughtful and considerate.

Although equanimity ceases bias and partiality in our mind, we do not necessarily treat or trust everyone equally. Conventional roles and relationships still exist. We don't treat colleagues whom we don't know well like family members whom we do. We don't confide in the cashier at the grocery store; we discuss private matters with people who are interested and who will understand. We give people the trust they deserve in different areas. For example, we may love a child, but we don't trust him with matches, whereas we trust an adult who is a stranger to fly the plane we're on because that person is a trained pilot. We trust our dog to warn us of danger, but we don't expect our aged grandparents with health problems to do this.

It requires skill to reflect on what areas to trust what people in, and if we slow down and do this wisely, many difficulties are prevented. However, despite interacting with living beings in different ways, we respect them equally and care about their well-being equally. From our side, the attachment and antipathy that foster prejudice, emotional swings, and rash actions are gone. We trust old friends more than we do strangers, even though we want both equally to be happy and free from suffering. We deal with difficulties that arise through the words and actions of those who are hostile toward us but without anger or resentment. Although I want all beings to be happy, in my position as the Dalai Lama I must still point out that Tibetans suffer under the policies of the Communist Chinese government and advocate for their rights.

Here is another way to meditate on equanimity that includes strangers and freeing ourselves from feeling apathy toward them. This method includes the mind-training teaching in which we practice seeing that individuals can vacillate from one category to another depending on whatever distorted judgments and emotions we may have at that moment. The categories of friends, enemies, and strangers are fabricated by our mind, and when we practice mind training, we come to see all sentient beings as teachers.

REFLECTION

1. Imagine three people in front of you: a dear one to whom you are very attached and from whom you don't want to be separated; an enemy toward whom you feel anger, resentment, and fear; and a stranger toward whom you are apathetic. Think of specific individuals.
2. Focus on the dear one and ask yourself, "Why am I so attached to this person?" There are no right or wrong answers, and the answer isn't an intellectual one. Just listen to what your mind replies.
3. Now focus on the enemy and inquire, "Why do I have so much anger, resentment, or even belligerence toward this person? Again, without judging your thoughts, observe the reasons you give for holding animosity toward this enemy.
4. Focus on the stranger and ask yourself, "Why do I feel apathetic and indifferent toward this person?" Once more, listen to what your mind replies.
5. In observing your responses to the above three points, what word did you hear repeatedly?

That word was "I," wasn't it? We classify people as friends worthy of attachment, enemies deserving of our anger, and strangers whom we usually ignore based on how they relate to *Me*. We believe our opinions about people are true—that people are inherently good, bad, or indifferent—but when we stop and question why we think that, we see that it depends on how they relate to *Me*. If someone is kind to us, they are a friend, but if someone is kind to our enemy, we are upset. Their trait of kindness is the same, but who they show the kindness toward makes the difference between whether I like them or hate them. If someone ruins my reputation, they are evil, but if they ruin the reputation of a person I don't like, then they are good and I applaud their action. Our views of people are very subjective, very biased; they invariably depend on how they treat *Me*, as if we were the most important person alive.

When we're able to see this clearly, we relax our opinionatedness and self-righteousness. We release the rigid categories of friend, enemy, and stranger, together with our fixed beliefs and emotions toward them. This brings space in our mind for another perspective, one that cares equally about the welfare of all beings.

Reflecting on the faults of attachment, animosity, and apathy helps us to release those unrealistic and unbeneficial emotions and cultivate a state of equanimity that is open and receptive toward all beings. Although anger is difficult to release, understanding its harm opens our mind to forgiveness. Releasing resentment and grudges, no matter how "right" our anger may seem, is essential not only to cultivate equanimity but also to be happy in this life. An angry, bitter person who cannot forgive events that happened years ago is miserable.

Śāntideva wrote a marvelous chapter on fortitude, the antidote to anger, in his book *Engaging in the Bodhisattvas' Deeds.* Some of his methods for working with our anger will be discussed in the next volume, where the six perfections are explained. If we understand fortitude as Śāntideva explained it, our mind and heart will be deeply affected. Of course it takes time and effort to transform habitual negative reactions and to release judgments about people, but the more we generate equanimity, the more peaceful we will be.

Meditation on equanimity complements sociological, psychological, and neuropsychological research on prejudicial attitudes people bear toward others. Most people have spontaneous compassion for a hungry, impoverished child in another part of the world, but if that child lived down the street from us, how would we feel? If that child were of a different race or nationality, would our empathy be the same? What if a group of those hungry children roamed our neighborhood searching for food, emptying the garage bins and scattering the rubbish around? Researchers have found that context plays an important role in how we feel about others.

We are easily influenced by the attitudes of those around us and of those in authority. Stanley Milgram's famous research in 1963 showed that average people would administer what they believed to be strong electric shocks to others when a person they saw as an authority figure ordered them to do so. Similarly, in 1971 the Stanford University professor Philip Zimbardo wanted to observe the effects of perceived power and studied the interactions of college students who volunteered to be "prisoners" and "guards" in a simulated prison. Both of these research projects were halted before completion because of the violence inflicted by normal people when given power. In our meditation, we should examine how power and authority affect our prejudices, empathy, and equanimity.

Emile Bruneau, a cognitive neuroscientist at MIT, has found that the strength of our identity with a group affects our empathy and thus our equanimity. The more we identify with a particular group—be it racial, ethnic, religious, political, and so on—the less we can empathize with the situation and feelings of those from another group, even if our group is not in conflict with that group.[26]

When we have strong prejudice against a particular group of people, it is difficult to accept new information about that group. Should we befriend a person from that group, we view them as not a real member of that group, whereas when we met someone who fits our stereotype, we use that to justify and strengthen our prejudice. Similarly, when we are biased toward a particular group, if a person from that group abrogates social norms, we see them as an exception—perhaps someone who has mental problems—instead of allowing that our favored group also contains individuals with antisocial behavior.

In short, to develop true equanimity entails deep exploration of our own prejudices and fears. Without identifying and addressing these aspects of ourselves, our equanimity will be superficial and unstable.

Seeing All Sentient Beings as Having Been Your Mother

Having leveled the field by dampening attachment and animosity toward others, we now turn to cultivating a sense of affection and endearment toward sentient beings. This is done by means of the first four points, beginning with seeing all sentient beings as having been our mother, remembering their kindness, wishing to repay it, and generating heartwarming love. When our heart is opened by heartwarming love, compassion for them will easily arise.

In ancient India at the time of the Buddha and in many present-day cultures too, people assume the existence of past and future lives; it was not necessary to prove it to them. However, in Western cultures, this idea is foreign and people do not automatically assume there are past and future lives. If accepting the idea of multiple lives is difficult for you, try provisionally accepting it and see if considering that all beings could have been your mother helps you to cultivate a feeling of closeness with them. You may also want to review explanations of rebirth in previous volumes. See chapter 2 of *Approaching the Buddhist Path* and chapter 7 of *The Foundation of Buddhist Practice.* There are also reliable accounts of people who remember their previous lives.[27]

If you accept the idea of past and future lives, then it seems reasonable that in your beginningless previous lives each and every sentient being has been your mother at one time or another. Contemplating that all sentient beings have been our parents helps us to overcome feelings of alienation and isolation. We see that in previous times we and others have been very close, and that others have cared for us with the unconditional love parents have toward their infants. This feeling of closeness helps us to trust others more readily and to give them the benefit of the doubt instead of instantly believing habitual suspicious thoughts that may arise.

The Indian sage Dharmakīrti uses reasoning to prove the existence of rebirth in *Commentary on the "Compendium of Reliable Cognition"* (*Pramāṇavārttika*). There are also many sūtra passages that affirm past and future lives (LC 2:38):

> I have difficulty seeing a place wherein you have not been born, gone to, or died in the distant past. I have difficulty seeing any person in the distant past who has not been your father, mother, uncle, aunt, sister, master, abbot, guru, or someone like a guru.

In short, in infinite previous lifetimes we have been born in all realms in saṃsāra, done everything (except practice the Dharma leading to direct realization of emptiness), and been in intimate relationships with all sentient beings. No one is a stranger; no one has not helped us in the past. The *Mother Sutta* in the Pāli canon says (SN 15.14):

> This saṃsāra is without discoverable beginning . . . It is not easy to find a being who in this long course has not previously been your mother . . . your father . . . your brother . . . your sister . . . your

son . . . your daughter. For what reason? Because, monastics, this saṃsāra is without discoverable beginning.

Reflect on this repeatedly. Remember that we haven't always been who we are now, and neither have others. Even in this life, as infants we are very different from the adults we became and the senior citizens we will become. Similarly others are not the same from one rebirth to the next and our relationships with them can vary a lot. When we have a sense of multiple lives, then recalling the kindness of others during them is surely reasonable.

Recalling the Kindness of Sentient Beings When They Were Your Mothers

To cultivate a feeling of closeness and endearment toward sentient beings, we choose someone who has been very kind to us as an example and then generalize that to all other sentient beings. Generally speaking, most human beings and animals regard their mother as someone extremely dear and close. Of course, exceptions exist, so if you have a closer feeling toward your father, grandparent, sibling, another relative, or a friend, focus on seeing the kindness of that person. Every one of us has had caregivers when we were infants, toddlers, and children. The proof is that we are alive today. We lacked the ability to do simple tasks to care for ourselves and needed the care of others. Although I refer to the mother, please apply it to whomever took care of you when you were little.

Our mother carried us in her womb for over nine months and gave birth to us. She then took care of us or, if she was unable to do so, she made sure that someone else did. She fed us, changed our diapers, protected us from danger, comforted us when we cried, covered us when we were cold. She held us gently, looking upon us with love. We may not remember this nurturing from infancy, but we can get an idea by observing how mothers around us care for their young children. We can see this loving devotion in the animal world too. At a monastery where I (Chodron) lived in Nepal, there was an old, crippled dog named Sasha, who dragged herself around on her front paws because her back legs had been injured. Even though it was so difficult for her to take care of herself, after she gave birth to a litter of puppies, she nursed and protected her pups with amazing love. Watching her painfully drag herself here and there to find food so she could nurse her pups would bring tears to my eyes.

Similarly, when we were toddlers, our parents and caregivers protected us from harm, rescuing us when we were about to tumble down a flight of stairs or stick a paper clip into an electric outlet. They taught us to speak, to tie our shoelaces, and to walk. In their efforts to teach us the disadvantages of self-centeredness and to make us more considerate of others so that we could get along with people, they taught us manners and disciplined us when we misbehaved. They also had to endure our childish bad behavior, teenage rebelliousness, and the way in which we took them for granted. So many abilities that we take for granted as adults we learned from our parents when we were young. Without their kindness to us then, where would we be now?

My mother was my first teacher of compassion. There was no school in our village and she was illiterate, but she was naturally kind and I experienced her compassion from the day I was born. My father had a temper, so I avoided him when possible. One time I yanked his moustache and was hit hard in return, but my mother was kind to everyone. She gave birth to sixteen children; seven survived. When I was a young boy, I had no toys to play with, but instead rode on her shoulders, hanging on to her long, braided hair as she went about her work in the fields or with our animals. We, her children, never saw an angry expression on her face. She was kind to us, kind to our neighbors, and when victims of famine came to the door, she always found something for them to eat. It's because of her that I am the happy, smiling person I am today. The way she lived showed me the value of kindness and compassion. All of her children, children-in-law, and grandchildren loved her in return. Tibetans called her Gyalmo Chenmo, the Great Mother.

In general, there are some differences between how people who grow up in traditional Asian cultures and in contemporary Western cultures view their families and parents. Over the last hundred years or so in Western society some people have begun to speak publicly about the ill treatment they experienced from their parents when they were children. As mentioned above, if emotions resulting from childhood abuse make contemplating the kindness of your parents difficult, contemplate the kindness of whomever cared for you as an infant and young child, and in this way, develop awareness of others having cared for you with kindness. Later, after the turbulent emotions from childhood abuse have lessened or been resolved completely, turn your mind to consider the kindness of your parents.

Your parents did the best they could given their emotional, social, and financial situation. As a result of karma, they experienced physical and mental problems, but they still cared for you in the best way they knew how and to the best of their abilities given the constraints they faced from their own upbringing. Developing an attitude of acceptance, appreciation, and forgiveness of others' foibles will prevent you from being encumbered by bitterness and hatred. Instead of dwelling on what was lacking in your upbringing, focusing on the care and compassion you received as a young child is psychologically and spiritually therapeutic.

Opening your heart to experience gratitude in response to whatever kindness you have received is an important element in being a healthy adult and good parent to your own children. By contemplating the kindness of your parents or other caregivers, recognize that you have been the recipient of tremendous kindness during your life. Instead of holding on to feelings of resentment, relax the mind and allow gratitude to arise—gratitude is a natural human response to kindness. There is no sense in denying yourself the opportunity to experience that wonderful emotion.

Having seen the kindness of your mother or caregiver, consider that your friends and relatives have all been your mother in previous lives and have been as kind to you as your present mother. Let yourself feel grateful and close to them. Then recognize that strangers have also been kind to you in that same way when they were your mother in previous lives, and allow the same positive emotions to arise. Continue by seeing that your present enemies were kind to you in the past when they were your parents. Finally, extend that awareness of kindness to all sentient beings, all of whom have been your mother in beginningless saṃsāra, all of whom will continue to be your kind mother in future lives until you are free from saṃsāra. Just as you feel great gratitude and love toward your present mother, open your heart and feel that toward all sentient beings.

Wishing to Repay Their Kindness

Seeing the kindness we have experienced from all sentient beings when they were our parents throughout our beginningless previous rebirths, how can we turn our backs on them and seek our own liberation? Thinking that because we don't recognize them as our parents in this life there is no connection between us and that therefore there is no reason to repay their kindness is a poor excuse. Let's say you were separated from your kind mother when you were a young child. Fifty years later you meet an elderly impoverished woman sitting on the corner begging for food. You begin to talk with her; one thing leads to another and you discover that she is your long-lost mother. An intense feeling of love for her arises. Would you just give her a dollar and leave her there, or would you do everything in your power to help her?

Recognizing all beings as having been your mother and as having been kind to you in countless previous lives, consider that most of your mothers are completely ignorant about their existence in saṃsāra. Thinking that the self-centered attitude is their friend, they follow its demands, thereby creating so many causes for suffering. They don't even know "ignorance is the root of cyclic existence" and, unaware, they don't try to overcome it. Attachment, animosity, and confusion arise easily in their minds, implanting them deeper in the wheel of life held in the hands of the lord of death. Isn't this reason enough to benefit them, especially considering the kindness they have shown you as your mother in infinite previous lives? Even people who are foolish or deceitful, or who have poor ethical conduct, have affection for people who were kind to them and want them to be safe.

For many years I (Chodron) have worked with incarcerated people—some who have inflicted horrible suffering on others—and have witnessed the deep love and affection they and their mothers have for each other. Many inmates tell me that they were extremely inconsiderate of their mother's feelings and well-being when they were young. Seeking only their own pleasure, they were blind not only to the effects of their actions on others but also to the affection and support their mother continually offered and the hardships she endured for their sake. Once imprisoned, they reflected on their lives and, much to their own surprise, realized this about their mothers. This realization led many of them to connect with their mother and appreciate her in ways they never would have imagined before. They say how much it pains them that their mother is old now and they are not able to take care of her. It is truly moving to see big burly men who put on a tough face in prison to protect themselves soften and get teary-eyed when speaking of their mother and their wish to repay her kindness.

This wish to repay the kindness of sentient beings—all of whom have been our parents countless times—is not simply the wish for them to live comfortably and enjoy the pleasures of saṃsāra. Having contemplated the disadvantages of saṃsāra, we see that such comfort is without essence. Our mothers, blinded by ignorance and wounded by karma, wander near the precipice of unfortunate rebirths, aimlessly searching for happiness in a land of deceptive illusions. As their child who has been the recipient of their tremendous kindness since beginningless time, we cannot turn our backs on them. When we were young and immature, we may have mistreated them or left them to their own devices, but now our gratitude for them is too strong to do this. We must help them to be free from saṃsāra. In *Heart of the Middle Way* (*Madhyamakahṛdaya*) Bhāvaviveka says (LC 2:40):

> Furthermore, like applying salt
> to the wounds of those who have been possessed
> by the madness of their afflictions,
> I created suffering for those sick with suffering.
>
> Now, what else is there other than nirvāṇa
> to repay the help of those
> who in other lives
> helped me with love and service?

REFLECTION

1. Reflect that the mind is a continuum. The clarity and awareness that constitute the mind do not cease at death and the mindstream continues to another rebirth.
2. In most rebirths we have had parents. Since there is no beginning to our previous lives, every sentient being at one time or another has been our parent.
3. Think of the kindness of your mother or of whoever took care of you when you were little. Remember how she fed and cleaned you and protected you from danger when you were an infant. She loved and encouraged you;

she rejoiced in your successes, and taught you skills to deal with difficulties. She taught you to speak and how to cooperate and get along with others. She made sure you received an education and helped you to grow into a responsible adult. And much more.

4. All other sentient beings, who have been your mother in previous lives, were similarly kind and loving toward you.
5. Seeing sentient beings as endearing, let the wish to repay their kindness arise in your heart and feel heartwarming love toward all beings.

The above meditations—equanimity, recognizing all sentient beings as having been our mother, remembering the kindness of our mother or other caregiver and wishing to repay it—are the basis for developing the attitude intent on others' welfare. Through these meditations we come to cherish sentient beings and feel a sense of affection and endearment toward them. Such feelings of closeness and endearment are likened to the love a parent has for their child. This affectionate love is the fourth point, heartwarming love. It arises naturally as a result of the first three points; a separate meditation is not necessary to cultivate it.

Developing the Attitude That Is Intent on Others' Welfare

There are different types of love. Heartwarming love that sees all sentient beings as endearing is the fourth point, which is the sum of the first three points—seeing that all sentient beings have been your mother, remembering their kindness, and wishing to repay it. This love is a necessary cause for the fifth point, compassion. One is not the cause or effect of the other. Love that wishes sentient beings to have happiness and its causes and compassion do not have a fixed order. Generating love or compassion depends on whether we first think of sentient beings as lacking happiness or as being overwhelmed by duḥkha. In the former case, we generate love; in the latter, compassion.

The next meditations—love, compassion, and the great resolve—bring about the attitude intent on others' welfare. Bodhicitta, the firm aspiration to work for others' welfare and the aspiration to attain buddhahood in order to do so, is the result of the previous six meditations.

Love

The seed of love is in the mind of each of us. The seed doesn't need to be newly generated, but we do need to learn the method to enhance it; both love and compassion need to be consciously cultivated. The observed object (*ālambana*, *ārammaṇa*) of love is sentient beings who are bereft of happiness and its subjective aspect is the wish for them to have happiness and its causes.

Love wishes others to have happiness and its causes as in "How wonderful it would be if they had happiness and its causes. May they have these." Because love is preceded by equanimity toward friends, strangers, and enemies, we seek to cultivate love toward all beings, excluding none. This kind of love is immense. Its field is vast: it extends to each and every sentient being, no matter how they treat us. Its goal is vast: it wishes them to have every happiness, from the smallest pleasure up to the happiness of having eliminated all obscurations and being able to easily work for the benefit of all sentient beings. Its time is vast: to work to benefit sentient beings for as long as space exists. We also relinquish a vast amount: we willingly give up our own enjoyments and even our own life for the benefit of sentient beings.

We use words to describe this kind of love, but actually it is difficult to understand and experience. To cultivate it from the depth of our heart, understanding its benefits is a necessary first step. By understanding the advantages of cultivating great love and the disadvantages of not doing so, our interest and enthusiasm to cultivate great love and compassion will increase, giving us the inner strength to actualize these qualities no matter what comes our way in the process of doing so.

Here and now we can experience for ourselves the benefits of an unbiased, kind, and loving heart. In my own case, I meet many different people and regard all of them as my friends. This loving attitude brings me much inner peace, regardless of how others respond to my friendliness. Nevertheless, people usually respond with a friendly and kind demeanor. Meditators who cultivate serenity and the dhyānas on love are well-loved in this life. Their presence influences the people and environment around them in a positive way, making them more peaceful. In future lives, these practitioners are reborn in the peaceful celestial realm of Brahmā if that is their wish. Bodhisattvas' love goes beyond that and leads to bodhicitta and full awakening. Nāgārjuna speaks of eight benefits of love (RA 283–84):[28]

> Even offering three hundred cooking pots of food three times
> a day
> does not match a portion of the merit in one instant of love.
>
> Although [through love] you are not liberated,
> you will attain the eight good qualities of love—
> (1) gods and (2) humans will be friendly, and
> (3) even [nonhumans] will protect you.
> (4) You will have mental pleasures and
> (5) many [physical] pleasures.
> (6) Poison and weapons will not harm you,
> (7) effortlessly you will attain your aims and
> (8) be reborn in the world of Brahmā.

In short, having love and compassion for others is the source of all temporal happiness in saṃsāra and the ultimate happiness of liberation and full awakening. Having a precious human life and not cultivating love and compassion is a great loss and waste of our potential.

REFLECTION

Contemplate these benefits of love and compassion one by one and make examples of them in your life.

1. You will have less anger, jealousy, arrogance, and resentment, so your mind will be more peaceful.
2. You will refrain from nonvirtuous actions, so your relationships with others will improve.
3. People and animals will feel comfortable around you, and you will be able to influence them to take a positive direction in life.

4. You will abstain from the ten nonvirtues and practice the ten virtues, creating a wealth of causes for fortunate rebirths.

5. You will die peacefully without regret or guilt and feel satisfied that you had a life well-lived.

6. You will easily develop bodhicitta, enter the Mahāyāna path, and attain full awakening.

7. From now until full awakening you will be able to benefit countless sentient beings and lead them on the path.

8. You will become an ārya bodhisattva and be able to create a pure land where you will attain full awakening and teach ārya bodhisattvas. You can also establish a pure land where ordinary sentient beings can be born and thrive in the Dharma.

9. By having single-pointed concentration on love and compassion, you will be able to travel to many pure lands and receive teachings from many buddhas. You will also attain the six super-knowledges.

Feel joyful at your opportunity to cultivate love and compassion and be enthusiastic to use this opportunity.

In *Tale of a Wish-Fulfilling Dream* (*Svapna-cintāmaṇi-parikathā*), Nāgārjuna spoke of five reasons why it is necessary to generate love for all sentient beings. The first reason is that we and all sentient beings are equal in wanting happiness and not suffering (SCP 2):

> I and all sentient beings are equal [with regard to] happiness and suffering.
> Being equal [with regard to] happiness and suffering, we are family.
> It is not right to completely abandon these [beings],
> yet enter nirvāṇa.

Our equality in seeking peace and avoiding pain was discussed in the meditation on equanimity above. Reflect that in the same way you have problems, so do all sentient beings. In the same way you don't want pain, neither do they. Just as you want freedom from suffering, so do others; just as you want happiness, they do too. Just as family members go through good and bad together, you and all sentient beings are like family in these ways. In addition, you and all others are equal in having the same enemy, the afflictions.

Think about others' difficulties and what it would be like to have them: to be a refugee, to be poverty stricken or terminally ill, to have a disability or chronic pain, to face the death of your child, to be oppressed or to constantly face racism or gender discrimination, and so on. Imagine being left on your own to face these problems and contemplate how strong your wish to receive help, or at least understanding and empathy, would be. Remember times when you have faced trying experiences and how relieved you were when someone stepped up to help you. Think that that's how others would feel if you reached out to them.

Just as you are joyful when you're able to accomplish your goals, so are others. Just as you feel supported when others show appreciation for your talents and contributions, so do others. Since beginningless time in saṃsāra, we've been desperately searching for lasting happiness and for meaning in our lives, but haven't been successful. We already know this, but we forget it. As we repeatedly familiarize ourselves with these points, they will arise more frequently in our mind. Then when we encounter situations that require our help, we won't hesitate to give it.

Seeing that there are no significant differences between ourselves and others in our deepest longings, and considering that we are close like family, it is not suitable to abandon others. Especially if someone has understood the four truths and knows the disadvantages of saṃsāra and the possibility of attaining nirvāṇa, it would be completely unacceptable to seek one's own liberation and abandon others. For example, someone has great wealth and lives in a mansion that overlooks a slum, yet he doesn't think at all about the suffering of his neighbors and at times even ridicules them. We would consider that person to be cold-hearted and his actions despicable. This is similar to attaining our own nirvāṇa and leaving others—especially our kind parents— drowning in saṃsāra.

We have heard of people who have jumped onto the train tracks to protect a complete stranger who has fallen there from an oncoming train. When asked afterward why they did that, the rescuer inevitably says that it was only the right thing to do; they couldn't have done otherwise. Similarly, if we understand the horror of saṃsāra, how can we not help others escape from it?

The second reason: It is important and possible to love other sentient beings because we have gone through the same experiences in saṃsāra repeatedly. This common experience brings us close to each other. Nāgārjuna says (SCP 3):

> Together with these beings I experienced
> the sufferings of the unfortunate realms and
> all sorts of happiness of the higher realms.
> Since we dwelt as one, I am fond of them.

We've had countless rebirths in saṃsāra—experiencing intense pain in unfortunate realms and incredible bliss in celestial realms. In all these rebirths we've been with other sentient beings, experiencing joy and misery together; for a long time we have dwelt as one, confronting problems and enjoying pleasures together. The feeling of familiarity opens the door to feeling fondness for them. They helped me when I needed caring companions or even strangers to reach out and give me a hand. Now that my situation is better, I have the responsibility to help them. It wouldn't be right for me to abandon them and enter nirvāṇa myself.

The third reason is that in limitless previous lives we've been one another's parents and children. Nāgārjuna observes (SCP 4):

> Not just once did I reside in every womb,
> nor is there a single sentient being
> who did not reside in my womb.
> Therefore, we are all family.

This and the previous verse rely on the notion of rebirth. If you have accepted the notion of rebirth or are at least open to it, it is not difficult to think that we have all been one another's relatives in previous lives and will be family in future lives as well. If rebirth is still difficult to imagine, it's fine to set it aside for the time being and come back to it later. You may also want to review the explanation of the nature of mind and its continuum from one life to the next, as discussed above, and look into the resources mentioned in note 27.

For those who accept rebirth, think that all sentient beings have been your parents and children numerous times. Since you change bodies in each birth, you don't recognize each other, but the connection is still there. If you were to remember your previous relatives—and in the future when you develop the superknowledges, you will—the feeling of closeness and affection you had for them will arise again. Given our long and deep connections, it is only fitting that I wish all these beings to have happiness and its causes.

The self-grasping ignorance spawns the feeling of being an isolated, independent individual when in fact we are dependent on and interrelated with everyone else. If there is a person you find despicable now, remember that they haven't always been that person. They are conditioned beings, and as the external and internal conditioning changes, so do their personalities, beliefs, and actions. Remember that we are in the nature of impermanence, so you have loved people you may not be fond of now, but you will be close to and fond of them again in the future.

Someone could say: If all sentient beings have been my parents, then I've also been their parents, so shouldn't they appreciate me for my kindness? Someone may also say: If others have been kind to me in countless previous lives, they've also harmed me countless times too, so why should I try to benefit them now? Although there may be some truth to these statements, thinking like this benefits neither ourselves nor others. It only stimulates thoughts of revenge and resentment that create more turbulence and unhappiness in our mind and motivate destructive actions. On the other hand, reflecting on our close and endearing relationships with others stimulates thoughts of kindness and love and leads to harmony and virtuous actions. When we adopt a positive perspective on others, we have many opportunities to be happy; when we hold a critical, judgmental view, unhappiness follows us wherever we go.

The fourth reason supporting the importance and possibility of loving others takes a different approach. Here we reflect on the Buddha's relations with all these living beings: The Buddha purified his mind and accumulated merit for a long time because he cherished all sentient beings, and he sought full awakening so he could benefit them most effectively. Since I have respect and devotion for the Buddha and he sees sentient beings as being so precious, I should too (SCP 5):

> Further, I am fond of the Buddha.
> As he worked hard for the sake
> of these [sentient beings] for a very long time,
> that too makes me fond of sentient beings.

Parents love their children dearly, so if we help their children, the parents are delighted. In fact, they're happier than if we helped them! Because of anger and partiality, we don't see sentient beings accurately and undervalue the kindness and help we receive from them. Ārya bodhisattvas and buddhas know their past relationships with sentient beings and cherish sentient beings more than themselves. Because we admire and respect these highly realized holy beings, it makes sense for us to cherish sentient beings who are so dear to their hearts. It would seem rather strange if we said to the Buddha, "You've got it all wrong. Sentient beings are not trustworthy; they're conniving and two-faced. I don't cherish them, and neither should you!" Are we wiser than the Buddha?

The fifth reason is that just as benefiting and harming our spiritual mentors brings happiness or suffering, respectively, so does helping and harming sentient beings (SCP 6):

> In this way, since benefiting and harming
> are the [respective] causes of immeasurable
> happiness and suffering,
> sentient beings are also my gurus.

We create virtuous and nonvirtuous karma in dependence on the recipients of our actions. Our spiritual mentors are powerful fields of merit for us because of their spiritual qualities and because of their kindness in leading us on the path. For that reason, we create enormous merit by offering material possessions and service to them. Similarly, if we get angry with our spiritual mentors, if we criticize, insult, or beat them, we create great nonvirtuous karma. The situation is similar with respect to ordinary sentient beings. Sentient beings have been our parents, friends, and dear companions in previous lives, and even as strangers doing their jobs in society, they have benefited us greatly. When we benefit them they are happy, and in addition we reap the result of temporal and ultimate happiness. When we harm sentient beings physically, verbally, or mentally, they are pained and we create great destructive karma that will ripen in our own misery. In this way sentient beings are like our spiritual mentors.

When we contemplate the kindness we have received from sentient beings in this life and from beginningless lives, it is clear that our ability to stay alive depends on them, and a feeling for the endearing qualities of sentient beings arises in our heart. In this way, they are precious and endearing.

Sentient beings are also precious and endearing in that our creation of virtue depends on them. Our being able to practice the six perfections and progress through the ten bodhisattva grounds to attain buddhahood depends on sentient beings (SCP 14–18):

> If those sentient beings did not exist,
> with whom could one be generous?
> If living beings did not exist, on what basis
> could one achieve the ethical discipline of the Vinaya?

We don't practice generosity by making offering to a chair, nor do we practice ethical conduct by abandoning harming a rock. We need impoverished beings in order to practice generosity; and we need sentient beings in order to practice the ethical conduct of abandoning harm.

> For whose sake does a hero meditate
> on patience with those who commit a fault?
> For the sake of whom does he diligently work
> to achieve his deeply desired object of attainment?

We can't practice fortitude with holy beings because they don't harm us. Fortitude can only be cultivated with harmful and quarrelsome sentient beings. Our practice of joyous effort likewise depends on sentient beings. To accomplish our own purpose and the purpose of others—which is to attain the truth body and form body of a buddha—we need sentient beings. Otherwise there would be no use in generating joyous effort to accomplish the path.

> If living beings did not exist,
> how would one—by correctly depending on
> love, compassion, joy, and equanimity—
> attain the bliss of meditative absorption?

Among the meditation objects for cultivating the dhyānas are the four immeasurables. We can't cultivate love, compassion, empathic joy, and equanimity for empty space. Sentient beings are the necessary objects of these meditations.

> Knowing the functioning and nonfunctioning bliss of liberation,
> presenting dispositions, attitudes, and tendencies,
> the thoroughly afflicted or completely pure,
> if [sentient beings] did not exist how could those be known?

"Functioning and nonfunctioning" refers to the two truths. "The thoroughly afflicted or completely pure" are factors pertaining to saṃsāra and nirvāṇa, respectively. Saṃsāra and nirvāṇa exist because of sentient beings; we cannot develop the wisdoms realizing the two truths without sentient beings.

> Since all these sentient beings are
> the cause of the factors of awakening,
> therefore, all who wish for complete awakening
> should regard sentient beings as gurus.

All of the above practices would be impossible without the existence of sentient beings. They are indeed precious and are as essential for our spiritual progress and buddhahood as our spiritual mentors are. For this reason, how can we not value, respect, and have love and compassion for sentient beings? Śāntideva exclaims (BCA 8.129):

Whatever joy there is in this world
all comes from desiring others to be happy;
and whatever suffering there is in this world
all comes from desiring myself to be happy.

All these points that show the value and necessity of benefiting sentient beings are based on the reasoning of dependent arising. Sentient beings have benefited us and will continue to do so. In addition, both we and sentient beings benefit when we cherish them, extend love and compassion to them, and work for their benefit. The more we ponder these points, the clearer it becomes that benefiting sentient beings is the wellspring of all joy—now and in the future—and harming them is the source of all misery. As your heart and mind evolve on this point, you'll find yourself being less angry and upset and more content and peaceful. The pain and problems brought on by the critical, judgmental, self-centered mind fade away.

REFLECTION

1. Think of all the practices the Buddha did and the hardships he endured to become a fully awakened one. He did all this because he cherished sentient beings even more than himself. Feel respect, gratitude, and devotion for the Buddha.
2. Reflecting that the Buddha's magnificent qualities—the superknowledges, the fulfillment of the ten perfections, the ten powers[29] and four fearlessnesses[30] of a buddha, and so on—are all dependent on his cherishing sentient beings, open your heart to cherish those whom the Buddha cherishes.
3. Contemplate that sentient beings, just like your spiritual mentors, are precious because it is in dependence on them that you create virtue.
4. Seeing them as precious and endearing, generate love, wishing them to have happiness and its causes, and compassion, wishing them to be free from suffering and its causes.

To generate love, contemplate that sentient beings want only happiness and its causes but lack these. Focusing first on friends, then strangers, and finally on enemies, wish them to have happiness and its causes and imagine them happy as well as happily creating the causes for well-being. Meditating earnestly in this way will heal many of your own unresolved disturbing emotions left over from previous experiences.

From a Buddhist perspective, several types of happiness exist, and it is good to wish that sentient beings have all of them. The first is the happiness derived from having the basic requisites for life—food, shelter, clothing, and medicine—as well as other factors that bring happiness in this life—good health, harmonious relations with relatives and friends, safety, money, possessions, social standing (even animals seek that!), and worldly success. This is what most people think of as happiness, even though it is unstable, transient, and difficult to control. While having good external conditions brings a certain type of happiness, it does not guarantee well-being. Worldly pleasures bring an assortment of difficulties—the fear of losing what we have, the anxiety of not getting what we desire, and jealousy of those who have more and better.

Another type of happiness is emotional peace—acceptance of who we are, the lessening of anger, releasing grudges. The causes of this type of happiness are internal reflection and the deliberate cultivation of wholesome mental states. Psychotherapy can help with this, as can nonviolent communication,[31] secular mindfulness practices, and other skills.

In general, working hard is the social ethic and norm across cultures, and society identifies one's chosen work as the cause of happiness and well-being. Some people recognize that a society's social, economic, and political systems can either bring about or interfere with the type of happiness that is dependent on work. But looking deeper, we see that the cause of temporal happiness depends on merit—virtuous actions (good karma) created through generosity and benefiting others, ethical conduct, and fortitude.

Still greater than the happiness of emotional well-being is the joy, bliss, and equanimity derived from states of meditative absorption. This peace is experienced by those who have suppressed manifest afflictions by attaining the deep states of concentration of the four dhyānas and the four formless absorptions. While this bliss is more stable than the happiness that depends on external circumstances, such as the people and environments we live in, it does not last forever. The causes of well-being derived from meditative states involve practicing the steps to gain serenity—eliminating the five hindrances, overcoming the five faults by the eight antidotes, traversing the nine stages of sustained attention, accomplishing the seven mental contemplations, and so forth.[32]

An even higher level of happiness is the fulfillment of our ultimate spiritual aims—nirvāṇa and full awakening. This necessitates subduing and then completely overcoming afflictions such as craving, ignorance, animosity, jealousy, and arrogance. Imagine the kind of peace, fulfillment, and bliss we and others would feel if our minds were free of these! The bliss and joy experienced in these states does not decline or disappear. In nirvāṇa, the mind is totally free from the vagaries of afflictions and polluted karma and dwells peacefully in the realization of emptiness. With full awakening, the mind is free from afflictive and cognitive obscurations and all beneficial internal qualities have been limitlessly developed. This is ultimate security, satisfaction, and fulfillment that enables us to benefit and bring meaning not only to ourselves but also to others.

Our wish for sentient beings to have spiritual happiness entails wishing that they have all the conducive circumstances needed to meet, learn, and practice the Dharma, beginning with having a fortunate rebirth, meeting qualified spiritual mentors, and having supportive Dharma friends and environments. We also wish them to be imbued with interest in spiritual matters and to question how persons and phenomena exist—that is, to seek the truth. The causes for this are observing karma and its effects as well as studying, reflecting, and meditating on the Buddha's teachings to the best of our ability in the present life.

The cause of nirvāṇa is the mind of renunciation and the practice of the three higher trainings, especially wisdom. The causes of full awakening are—in addition to those for nirvāṇa—bodhicitta, the six perfections, and the generation and completion stages of Tantra. We wish that all sentient beings create these causes that come about from a qualified disciple meeting a qualified spiritual mentor and then practicing diligently with joyous effort.

When meditating on love, wish that sentient beings have all these levels of happiness and peace as well as their causes. When done in depth, this meditation is quite extensive and expansive. Please continue to contemplate in this way, looking ever deeper.

Like self-respect, loving ourselves in a realistic and practical way is important. Self-love must be distinguished from self-indulgence. Self-indulgence is fraught with selfish attachment and leads to anxiety and guilt, whereas loving ourselves involves caring for ourselves with an acceptance and kindness that are free from unrealistic expectations. Like all sentient beings, we seek happiness. Self-indulgence involves thinking we must fulfill all our worldly wishes; self-centeredness is believing that our happiness is more important than anyone else's. Genuine self-love enables us to love others, while self-centeredness uses others for our own pleasure. Self-love cares for self and others in an expansive way and enables us to live harmoniously with others. At its most exalted levels, genuine love and compassion for ourselves wish us to be free from cyclic existence and to attain full awakening. Working toward these spiritual goals is true kindness to ourselves, and it brings about the joy of others as well.

REFLECTION

What is happiness? Reflect on the various types of happiness there are and then wish sentient beings to have it and its causes.

1. The happiness of having the basic requisites for life—food, shelter, clothing, and medicine—as well as good health, harmonious relations, safety, money, and possessions.
2. The happiness of emotional peace—acceptance of who we are, the lessening of anger, releasing grudges.
3. The calm of elevated states of consciousness that is the joy, bliss, and equanimity derived from states of meditative absorption.
4. The happiness of the fulfillment of our ultimate spiritual aims—nirvāṇa and full awakening.
5. Contemplate the causes of each type of happiness and wish sentient beings to have these too.

Compassion

As we said, love and compassion do not occur in a fixed order. Which one is generated depends whether we first see sentient beings as lacking happiness and want them to have happiness and its causes, or if we first see them as being burdened by duḥkha and want them to be free from it.

Our first experiences after birth were of kindness and compassion. Love and compassion are not unfamiliar to us. Not only have we received love and compassion from others, but also each of us has the seed of love and compassion in our mindstream. By learning and practicing the methods to generate great love and great compassion, we can nurture those seeds that are already in our mindstream, enabling them to grow into the beautiful, life-sustaining love and compassion of a bodhisattva.

Although based on ordinary love and compassion, the great love and great compassion cultivated in the Mahāyāna differ from them in several important ways. First, great love and great compassion are impartial and unbiased. Usually affection arises easily toward close friends and relatives; concern about their welfare arises naturally. However, those feelings are mixed with attachment. They depend on the other person's attitude and actions toward us. When the other person's speech and behavior are pleasing, we feel affection for them. But when their attitude or behavior do not meet our expectations, wants, or needs, our love and compassion evaporate; we may even become enraged with this person. Genuine love and compassion, on the other hand, arise irrespective of others' attitudes and actions toward us. Rather, our perspective is "Others are just like me; they want happiness and don't want duḥkha as much as I do. They also have the right to overcome suffering." We feel such unbiased love and compassion even toward enemies and those whom we dislike because they, too, are sentient beings who have the wish and the right to overcome suffering.

Furthermore, unlike ordinary love and compassion, which are felt only toward a limited number of beings, great love and great compassion are extended toward all sentient beings—including ourselves, people we like, those we dislike, and those we don't know.

Ordinary love and compassion are usually dependent on our personal preferences and prejudices and arise automatically in us ordinary beings whose minds are under the influence of afflictions. Great love and great compassion, on the other hand, are consciously cultivated with a clear purpose.

Reasoning is used to overcome the bias and favoritism that color our self-centered emotions toward others. Wisdom helps our love and compassion become more stable and less influenced by the vagaries of others' behavior. This enables ordinary love and compassion to expand to include all sentient beings and to wish them to be free from all types of duḥkha and have all types of happiness, transforming them into great love and great compassion.

The focal object of compassion is sentient beings who are suffering. Its subjective aspect is the wish for them to be free from suffering. Compassion depends on two principal attitudes: a sense of closeness with others and concern for their suffering. Seeing sentient beings as endearing through remembering their kindness creates a sense of intimacy and affection toward others in our heart. Meditating on the fact that sentient beings undergo all the diverse kinds of duḥkha just as we do brings concern for their suffering. Bringing these two together arouses genuine compassion for living beings.

As with cultivating love, we begin cultivating compassion with ourselves, our dear ones, then toward those for whom we have neutral feelings, followed by enemies, and finally all sentient beings. To develop compassion for others, we must be in touch with how we ourselves are oppressed by duḥkha and wish to be free of it. For this reason, meditating on the four truths—especially true duḥkha and true origins—and the twelve links of dependent origination is essential. Without the support of these meditations, our compassion for others will lack energy and risks becoming pity instead.

It is important to cultivate compassion beginning with specific individuals because this brings a personal quality to our compassion. This is very different from feeling sorry for a large amorphous group of beings we don't know. We are generating the wish for individuals whom we feel close to and care about to be free from duḥkha and its causes. Meditating on individuals also brings to light the resentment, prejudice, and fear that interferes with having compassion. When we have successfully dealt with these hindrances, then it is suitable to extend the range of our compassion to more and more sentient beings.

Just as when generating love there are many kinds of happiness to wish sentient beings to have, when cultivating compassion there are diverse forms of duḥkha that we wish them to be free from. Here it is helpful to contemplate the three kinds of duḥkha, the six disadvantages of cyclic existence, and the eight unsatisfactory conditions one by one.[33] The more we have contemplated these faults of saṃsāra in terms of our own lives and generated the aspiration to attain liberation, the easier it will be to consider that others suffer from them as well and to generate compassion for them. The same is true when we contemplate afflictions and karma as the causes of saṃsāric suffering and wish sentient beings to be free from them.[34]

You can also begin your meditation on compassion by thinking of someone whose suffering is such that you cannot bear it. Recall that he is similar to you in wanting happiness and not wanting suffering, and by reflecting on this, in time you will feel very strong concern for him and compassion will arise. Then extend your meditation to close friends and relatives; think of them one by one and cultivate compassion for each person. Then focus on strangers—road workers, secretaries, citizens of other countries, refugees—and recall their suffering. Recall that they are just like you in wanting and deserving to be free from duḥkha and to have happiness. Finally bring to mind people for whom you have negative emotions: people who have harmed you, whom you fear, and who hold views and opinions that you find totally unacceptable. Think of them one by one, remembering that they are just like you in wanting happiness and not suffering and in having the right to be free from duḥkha. Do this until you feel that their suffering is intolerable. In this way, develop the same strength of concern toward them that you have toward those who are dear to you. Finally, extend compassion to all sentient beings in all the realms of saṃsāra. Remember that planet Earth is not the only place with living beings; there are countless sentient beings, each having their own experience of duḥkha at this moment. Enlarge your heart to include them all.

Another way to meditate on compassion is to visualize an animal—it could be a pet, an animal raised for its meat or fur, or any other animal. Contemplate the difficulties it faces in an animal rebirth—being under others' control, its vulnerability to being killed, and so forth. Unable to understand the Dharma, animals face huge obstacles to creating virtuous karma and to gaining a better rebirth. When compassion arises for this being who has the buddha nature but is trapped in a body that brings physical suffering and limits its ability to learn, change your focus to hungry ghosts and think of the suffering they experience—the strong desires that are never met; the hunger and thirst that cannot be satisfied. From there, contemplate the suffering of hell beings—their fear and terror and physical suffering. Think also of human beings: although they have less physical suffering than beings in the unfortunate realms, their mental suffering can be formidable. In addition, they are often distracted from creating virtue, as are desire-realm gods. The form- and formless-realm gods experience great pleasure, but when the karma for these rebirths is consumed, they helplessly fall to rebirths with more duḥkha. In this way, cultivate a strong wish that all of these beings be free from their duḥkha.

One especially poignant thought to contemplate when cultivating compassion is that although sentient beings long only for happiness and freedom from suffering, because they are overwhelmed by ignorance and other afflictions, they continuously create more karma that will ripen in their suffering. Śāntideva said (BCA 1.28):

> Although wishing to be rid of misery,
> they run toward misery itself.
> Although wishing to have happiness,
> like an enemy, they ignorantly destroy it.

Think about this in terms of the people you care for. They want only happiness but due to their mental afflictions they constantly self-sabotage, abandoning the causes of happiness as if they were a horrible disease. Because they are confused regarding the causes of misery, they embrace them as if they were the path to happiness. Not only are our friends in this sorrowful state but so too are all other sentient beings, including ourselves. What a sorrowful state sentient beings are in! Feeling that their experience of even the subtle pervasive duḥkha of conditioning is intolerable, allow compassion to arise in your mind.

When meditating on compassion, do not fall prey to personal distress. Keep your focus on others' experiences, not on the pain you feel from observing their duḥkha. Have deep concern for the plight of yourself and all sentient beings, but remember that the causes for all duḥkha can be eliminated, so maintain an optimistic yet grounded attitude. Love, compassion, and bodhicitta are not uncontrolled emotions that render us incapable of action. To the contrary, they make us strong and courageous. But we must work hard to generate them. Tsongkhapa cautions (LC 2:45):

> Therefore, if you are satisfied with just a little personal instruction and neglect to familiarize yourself with the explanations of the classical texts, your compassion and love will be very weak... You must then analyze these explanations with discerning wisdom and elicit the experience produced after sustaining them in meditation. You will not achieve anything with the unclear experiences that come when you make a short, concentrated effort without precisely clarifying the topic with your understanding. Know that this is true for other kinds of practice as well.

There are many types of compassion that are possessed by different people. Ordinary people who may or may not follow a particular religion or spiritual tradition have compassion when they see the evident suffering of the people and animals they care about. They may extend this compassion to more living beings, but because they usually aren't aware of the duḥkha of change and the pervasive duḥkha of conditioning, their compassion is generally confined to wishing beings to have health, wealth, job fulfillment, and happy families in this life.

Some śrāvakas and solitary realizers have immeasurable compassion (synonymous with limitless compassion). This compassion is at the level of a dhyāna, and although it is spread to immeasurable sentient beings, it is not strong enough to inspire them to shoulder the responsibility to liberate all sentient beings. Nevertheless, the immeasurable love and compassion of śrāvakas and solitary realizers are to be lauded and these practitioners are to be respected for their attainments. There is no reason for us bodhisattva-aspirants to be proud, for our present love and compassion are weak, biased, and of short duration. In all cases, it is fitting to respect those who are more spiritually accomplished than we are and to endeavor to generate the excellent qualities they possess.

In his first *Stages of Meditation*, Kamalaśīla delineates the measure for having generated great compassion (LC 2:45):

> When you spontaneously feel compassion that has the subjective wish to completely eliminate the duḥkha of all living beings—just like a mother's desire to remove her dear child's

> unhappiness—then your compassion is complete and is therefore called great compassion.

Here Kamalaśīla uses an example that is familiar to us—the compassion of a mother for her child—to give us a sense of something extraordinary that we have not yet experienced—the spontaneous, heartfelt desire to completely eliminate the duḥkha of all sentient beings. As with all analogies, however, not all aspects of the example apply to the object to understand. In this case, a mother's compassion for her child is tinged with attachment and partiality, whereas a bodhisattva's compassion is free from these. The measure of having generated great love can be inferred from the above passage.

Great compassion observes all sentient beings and its healing effect extends to all of them. Great compassion wants not only to liberate all sentient beings from the duḥkha of pain and the duḥkha of change but also to free them from the pervasive duḥkha of conditioning that afflicts all beings wandering in saṃsāra.[35] This great compassion is a prerequisite for bodhicitta and therefore must be present in order to enter the first bodhisattva path, the path of accumulation.

Knowing the characteristics of the realizations of love, compassion, and bodhicitta enables us to assess our spiritual progress. This prevents false conceit, thinking we have actualized something that we have not. For example, it is not too challenging to think, "I will attain awakening for the benefit of all sentient beings." But feeling this sincerely and spontaneously as our immediate response when seeing any sentient being is quite difficult.

Bodhisattvas' great compassion is strong, stable, and resilient. They do not succumb to despondency and feelings of hopelessness even though they may feel unsettled when observing sentient beings suffer. Deep inside their minds courage, inner strength, and optimism abound. Bodhisattvas express their compassion in creative and appropriate ways. They neither succumb to personal distress upon seeing others' suffering nor take it upon themselves to "fix" those sentient beings' predicaments by interfering in unwanted ways.

Śāntideva uttered a phrase that leads us to imagine a world where great compassion abounds: "May people think of benefiting one another." May each of us become one of those people.

The Great Resolve

By practicing the steps of mental trainings over time, our love and compassion will increase to the point where they become the great resolve, which assumes the responsibility to bring sentient beings happiness and to eliminate their suffering. This is much stronger than the wish to repay the kindness of sentient beings. It is also stronger than the love and compassion that think how wonderful it would be if sentient beings had happiness and its causes and were free of duḥkha and its causes. The great resolve has energy behind it: it is the heartfelt commitment to act in order to give happiness to each and every sentient being and to protect them from all three types of duḥkha. It thinks, "I will give happiness to all sentient beings and free them from duḥkha." It is very helpful to think like this frequently during the day so that this intention supports our physical and verbal actions. Try thinking like this during your workday and see how it transforms your attitude and relationships and increases the sense of meaning in your life.

Śrāvakas and solitary realizers may have immeasurable love and immeasurable compassion that wish sentient beings to have happiness and be free of duḥkha. This love and compassion, however, are not strong enough to induce their commitment to act to bring this about. Great compassion is so called because it goes beyond the compassion of śrāvakas and solitary realizers. When our compassion can no longer endure sentient beings' suffering, it induces the great resolve, a type of great compassion that is willing to bear the responsibility of liberating sentient beings from all duḥkha whatsoever. With the great resolve that is induced by compassion and love, practitioners have the confidence and determination to work for the benefit of all sentient beings, are willing to do it without any regret, and act to fulfill their aim.

The great resolve has overcome gross self-centeredness and is ready to act on the aspiration to benefit and protect sentient beings. The *Questions of Sāgaramati Sūtra* gives the example of a family that has only one child, who was charming and loved by his parents. One day the child was playing and fell into a pit filled with sewage and filth. His aunts and uncles screamed and lamented as they stood by the side of the pit. When his parents came along and saw the situation, their only thought was to save the child, and without hesitation or revulsion they jumped into the sewage pit and pulled the child out.

The sewage and filth are the three realms of saṃsāra; the treasured child is all sentient beings; the other relatives are the śrāvakas and solitary realizers; the parents are bodhisattvas. While the compassion of śrāvakas and solitary realizers is like that of the aunts and uncles for their beloved nephew caught in a pit of filth, it isn't moved to action. For this reason bodhisattva aspirants must generate the great resolve that is firmly committed to liberating all sentient beings oneself.

The deeper our understanding of duḥkha, the stronger our compassion will be. When our compassion reaches the point where we feel that sentient beings' duḥkha in saṃsāra is unbearable and we want them to be free from it as well as from the afflicted obscurations and cognitive obscurations, the great resolve to work for their welfare arises. We commit to work for the temporal well-being of sentient beings as well as to lead them to the highest good—liberation and full awakening.

Bodhicitta

It's important to understand precisely what bodhicitta is so that our efforts to generate it will bear fruit. In *Illumination of the Thought*, Tsongkhapa defines bodhicitta as "the wish to attain highest awakening—the object of attainment—for the sake of all sentient beings—the objects of intent."[36] This is the noble mind that we should do everything in our power to generate in our own mental continuum. Considering this definition, we see that this precious altruistic intention isn't only wishing others to be free of suffering, wishing them to become buddhas, or wanting to become a buddha ourselves. Bodhicitta isn't just being kind and cooperative, nor is it only praying to take on others' suffering. Kamalaśīla says the measure of having generated genuine bodhicitta is (LC 2:45) as follows:

> When you have committed yourself to being a guide for all living beings by conditioning yourself to great compassion, you effortlessly generate the bodhicitta that has the nature of aspiring to unexcelled perfect awakening.

Generating actual bodhicitta requires first cultivating several other attitudes. In addition to having stable experience in the paths in common with the initial- and middle-level practitioners, Śāntideva leads us through several other steps in *Engaging in the Bodhisattvas' Deeds*: contemplating the benefits of bodhicitta; practicing the seven limbs, which includes confessing innumerable nonvirtues by means of the four opponent powers;[37] taking refuge in the Three Jewels; and understanding the bodhisattva trainings.

Through contemplating the previous six steps, we generate the primary mind held by two aspirations, one seeking to benefit all sentient beings, the other aspiring to attain full awakening in order to do so. This mind is the bodhicitta. It is the seventh point, which is the effect of the six preceding causes.

A naïve assumption that awakening is easy to attain and half-hearted effort is sufficient does not bring the strong resolve necessary to generate bodhicitta. How, then, does the great resolve induce bodhicitta? It comes from reflecting, "At present, I can't even save myself from the duḥkha of saṃsāra, let alone lead others to freedom. Who is most capable of doing that?" Investigating, we see that no saṃsāric being is fully equipped to guide sentient beings to awakening. Arhats, although they have compassion for others, lack the great compassion and great resolve to do this. Although they are free from the afflictive obscurations, their minds are still affected by cognitive obscurations, so they are able to lead a few beings to liberation but not to buddhahood. Ārya bodhisattvas have bodhicitta, but their minds aren't free from the cognitive obscurations. The only ones fully equipped to benefit sentient beings most effectively are the buddhas, who have eradicated all obscurations and perfected all excellent qualities. Therefore, we must become a fully awakened buddha with stainless wisdom, unwavering compassion, and full capacity.

Buddhas cannot liberate sentient beings by themselves; if they could, they would have already done so. Sentient beings must learn and practice the Dharma themselves. To teach and guide sentient beings on the path, buddhas must have personal experience of all the practices and the paths to awakening. They must know others' individual spiritual dispositions, interests, and tendencies as well as the effective ways to practice that would help them actualize their spiritual goals. For the sake of helping others, we must fully prepare ourselves.

When we understand that the wisdom realizing the ultimate nature can remove afflictions and their seeds and lead to liberation, we can also see that eliminating the cognitive obscurations—the latencies that produce the appearance of inherent existence and cause us to see the two truths as different natures—is also possible. For this reason, we seek to eliminate all obscurations from our mindstreams and realize all excellent qualities. In short, we need to attain full awakening—the nonabiding nirvāṇa of a buddha—in which we abide neither in cyclic existence nor in the complacency and personal peace of our own liberation.

The Perfection Vehicle presents the path to full awakening, and the explanation in highest yoga tantra sharpens this understanding by revealing the extremely subtle wind-mind, the fundamental innate mind of clear light, as well as the tantric path. In this context, the possibility of attaining the four buddha bodies becomes much clearer. Once we have an accurate and stable understanding of what awakening is and how attaining it is possible, we will be able to develop genuine bodhicitta aspiring for buddhahood.

The method for developing bodhicitta is not difficult to understand. However, to gain firm love, compassion, and altruism involves training our mind and eliminating the extremely strong tendency toward considering our own happiness as more important than others. If self-centeredness were not so deeply rooted, the śrāvakas and solitary realizers—who are great and wise practitioners with high attainments—would have abandoned it. Eliminating it takes great courage and strength of mind because making the commitment to work for others' welfare for eternity and to attain buddhahood in order to do so is a radical reversal of our usual way of thinking and relating to the world.

Sometimes during meditation sessions we may feel an intense great resolve to better sentient beings' condition. But after our meditation session, our resolve falters, our love and compassion recede into the background, and self-centeredness reemerges. To remedy this requires continued vigilance and application in all aspects and activities of our life. We can't take a holiday from love and compassion in order to "enjoy the pleasures" of self-centeredness. For this reason, in the first *Stages of Meditation,* Kamalaśīla encourages us (LC 2:47):

> Cultivate this compassion toward all beings at all times, whether you are in meditative concentration or in the course of any other activity.

Tsongkhapa advises (LC 2:48):

> The mindstream which has been infused since beginningless time with the bitter afflictions will not change at all from just a short cultivation of the good qualities of love, compassion, and so forth. Therefore you must sustain your meditation continuously.

Cultivating spontaneous bodhicitta once is a wonderful start. Then you must make it stable through repeated meditation. To do this, continue meditating on the duḥkha of saṃsāra, the kindness of sentient beings, love, compassion, and the great resolve. In addition, contemplate the physical, verbal, and mental qualities of the buddhas and their awakening activities to keep your spiritual goal in mind. Meditate on the emptiness of inherent existence to abandon the obscurations on your mindstream, and continue to support all these practices by purifying and accumulating merit. In short, make your bodhicitta strong so that you won't give it up when difficulties arise.

May we follow their excellent advice and complete the entire path in good time.

REFLECTION

1. Cultivate compassion first toward one person and then gradually expand it to all sentient beings according to the instructions here and in chapter 1.
2. Generate the great resolve to actively engage in increasing others' happiness and diminishing their suffering.

Who can do this? As ordinary beings we lack the wisdom and skill. As śrāvakas we lack the compassion. Only buddhas have the ability to benefit others most effectively. Therefore, we must follow the path to buddhahood and attain full awakening.

4 Equalizing and Exchanging Self and Others

I AM OVER EIGHTY years old now. For almost seventy years, I have contemplated bodhicitta and emptiness daily. I'm not saying I have attained the bodhisattva paths and grounds, but I am getting closer. If we create the cause, the result will come. This daily contemplation has brought peace in my mind as well as the confidence that my life has been meaningful. I encourage all of you to dedicate your lives to contemplating and approaching these two bodhicittas: the conventional bodhicitta (the altruistic intention) and the ultimate bodhicitta (the wisdom realizing emptiness).

In the preceding chapter we discussed the seven cause-and-effect instructions for generating bodhicitta. The second method to cultivate bodhicitta is equalizing and exchanging self and others. This method is traced to Nāgārjuna's *Commentary on Bodhicitta* (*Bodhicittavivaraṇa*) and his *Precious Garland of Advice for the King* (*Rājaparikathāratnāvalī*). Later Śāntideva explained this method in detail in *Engaging in the Bodhisattvas' Deeds*, and it was passed down privately among the early Kadampa masters in Tibet.

The method of equalizing and exchanging self and others as well as the practice of taking and giving included in it were practiced secretly, not because practitioners wanted to deprive others of knowledge about it but because thinking according to this approach shakes us up. Although we know intellectually that we aren't the most important person in the world, in our heart the self-grasping ignorance and self-centered attitude refuse to accept this. This method hits right at the heart of our self-centered attitude and makes us question the view of self-grasping ignorance as well. The self-honesty and directness of this approach are what make it so profound.

Let's start at the beginning and gradually transform the mind that anxiously clings to I and mine into a relaxed, joyful mind that cherishes others more than self. The method to do this consists of the following steps: (1) equalizing self and others, (2) becoming convinced of the disadvantages of self-centeredness, (3) understanding the great benefits of cherishing others, (4) exchanging self and others, (5) taking others' duḥkha with compassion and giving them our happiness with love, and (6) bodhicitta.

Equalizing Self and Others

The first step is to equalize ourselves and others by recognizing that all sentient beings—ourselves and others—are equally important and worthy of being happy and peaceful and free from pain and misery. This counteracts the ingrained notion that we deserve to have every happiness and to be free of all sufferings, but others deserve these less. The hazards of this self-centered view are clear: we seek the means to eliminate only our problems and procure our happiness, while ignoring the well-being of others.

The meditation to equalize self and others differs from the equanimity meditation explained in the previous chapter. The equanimity meditation overcomes the emotional reactions of attachment and animosity with respect to friends and enemies. It steers us toward unbiased openness for these two groups of people. The meditation on equalizing self and others overcomes something deeper: our tendency to consider ourselves more valuable and important than other sentient beings. This meditation brings a deep conviction that we and others are fundamentally equal in wanting happiness and freedom from suffering. Whereas equanimity levels the playing ground of friends, enemies, and strangers, equalizing self and others levels it between us and others.

When we question our innate assumption of self-importance, we find that it is false, that we and others are equal in wanting happiness and wishing to be free from suffering. We and others have the same right to be happy and free of suffering because all of us equally have buddha nature. Try as we may, we cannot come up with a valid reason why our happiness is more important than others and why our suffering hurts more than theirs.

If our happiness and misery were unrelated to those of others, it would be reasonable to say that we do not need to bother about their joy and pain. But this is not the case. Our happiness and suffering do not arise in isolation. They are interwoven with those of others. Because we are interconnected in this way, caring more about others' happiness, helping them attain it, and eliminating their suffering are crucial, even for our own well-being. The problem with caring only about the safety and well-being of ourselves and our dear ones is that we will live in a society where the vast majority of people are miserable. They will make their suffering and unfair treatment known to us, so that all of us will live in a tumultuous society. Caring for others as we care for ourselves will easily remedy this.

To equalize self and others, on your left imagine your usual self, and on your right visualize all other sentient beings. Both have the reasonable wishes to be safe and free from suffering. Then be the judge and determine whose well-being is more important. On one side is one sentient being, on the other side are all sentient beings minus one. Better yet, hold a vote on whose welfare is more important. Wouldn't the side of all sentient beings minus one win by a landslide? Surely it is more important to bring about the happiness and remove the suffering of other sentient beings than of just ourselves.

If our self-centeredness refuses to admit defeat, we must protest against it because it is a tyrannical despot that refuses to turn over power to the rightful victor of the vote. We should plan protest marches and write editorials in the newspaper against this unjust ruler, the self-centered attitude. When an autocrat ignores the welfare of the citizens, the world condemns him as greedy, arrogant, and power hungry. Similarly, isn't our self-centered attitude a ruthless dictator that ignores the welfare of other living beings and arrogantly uses them for his own enjoyment? In the past, oppressive monarchs were overthrown by the populace, and as a result government policies and cultural customs changed. Likewise, our customs and actions will change as we overthrow the tyranny of self-preoccupation and institute the reign of cherishing others.

My junior tutor Trijang Rinpoche taught a nine-point meditation on equalizing self and others when he gave teachings on the "Guru Pūjā." This meditation has three major points, each of which has three subpoints. Two of those major points are based on conventional truths, one on ultimate truth.

1. Self and others are equal from the perspective of conventional truths. These reasons do not delve into the mode of existence of self and others, but work on the level of appearances.

A. The three reasons from the viewpoint of others primarily examine others and consider whether there is any difference between them and ourselves.

1. Everyone equally wants happiness and freedom from suffering. Not only do all six classes of sentient beings equally want this but also ourselves and others are equal in having this desire. Seeing that deep within everyone's heart, each and every being has the same wish, discriminating among them is unsuitable.
2. Favoring some beggars over others is not suitable because each of them has needs, although their specific needs may differ. Similarly, we and others equally have needs and desires, although their specifics may differ. Therefore it is not right to be partial to our friends over enemies or to favor ourselves over others. Instead, we should aim to benefit everyone equally.
3. Curing the suffering of some patients and not others is not proper. Although each one suffers from a different illness or injury, they all equally want to be free from pain. Therefore we should try to remove suffering from everyone equally without helping ourselves and neglecting others.

B. The three reasons from the viewpoint of self focus on our attitudes toward others.

1. All sentient beings have been kind to us in the past, are kind to us in the present, and will be kind to us in the future. Everything that is used to sustain our lives—food, clothing, shelter, and medicine—and all our enjoyments were produced and given to us by others. Everything we use in our life was made by others. Even our body came from others. All our knowledge and skills came because others taught and encouraged us. Seeing the immeasurable

kindness we have received from all sentient beings since beginningless time, we should help them equally in return, without abandoning any of them.

2. "But sentient beings have also harmed us," harps the self-centered attitude. If we were to weigh the help and the harm we have received, the help we have received from others greatly outweighs the harm. In fact, the harm is miniscule. In addition, when we were harmed, many sentient beings came to our aid. Our self-centered mind keeps tabs on and seldom forgets even the slightest harm we have received, while it takes for granted every benefit we have received and expects more. If we take stock of our lives, we'll see how true this is.
3. If we still cling to old hurts and indulge our resentment, let's recall that we and others are impermanent beings who are subject to death. In that light, there is no sense in discriminating against anyone, holding grudges, or seeking revenge. Such attitudes only make us miserable and create the cause for suffering in future lives. Furthermore, the beings we seek to harm in return are caught in cyclic existence; given that they are going to die in any case, what use is harming them?

2. Self and others are equal from the viewpoint of ultimate truth. These reasons examine if there is an inherently existent self and others. If not, there is no sense in being attached to these labels and distinguishing self as more worthy of happiness than others.

A. If friends, enemies, and strangers existed from their own side inherently, rather than being mere imputations, the Buddha would see this. But the Buddha makes no distinction between a person massaging him on one side and someone cutting him on the other. They are equally objects of his love and compassion.
B. If friends, enemies, and strangers were truly existent, each sentient being would always remain in whatever category he or she is presently found. However, our experience is that relationships change. The friend of one year is the enemy of the next, and vice versa. Both

can become strangers, and someone who is currently a stranger can easily become a friend or enemy. Making these differentiations is a function of our mind; they are not inherent in those sentient beings.

C. Self and others are dependent designations. They depend on each other just as this side of the valley and that side are posited in mutual dependence on the other. Depending where we stand, one side is labeled "this" or "that"; these labels change depending on our viewpoint. Similarly, calling one set of aggregates "I' or "other" is dependent. The aggregates I currently call "I" other people call "other." If they were inherently mine, then everyone would see them as mine; but most people see them as other, and therefore not so important.

The above nine points are powerful tools to cut away at our ingrained feeling of entitlement. Meditating on them produces a definite change in the mind. Self-centered attitude sees myself and others as unrelated and deems others' suffering and happiness as less important than my own. But there is no logical reason to support this belief. We all equally want happiness and not suffering. In addition, others have been kind to me and everything I have or know comes from them. Seeing this, holding myself as more worthy is unconscionable. Furthermore, myself and others are not inherently existent entities. Why is "I" to be labeled only in dependence on this set of aggregates and not on others? From the viewpoint of others, "I" is designated in dependence on other aggregates and "other" is imputed in dependence on mine. Śāntideva asks himself very pointed questions about why we care for ourselves and neglect others (BCA 9:92–96):

Although my suffering does not
cause pain in other bodies,
nevertheless that suffering is mine and is difficult to bear
because of my attachment to myself.

Likewise, although I myself do not feel
the suffering of another person,
that suffering belongs to that person and is difficult [for her] to bear
because of her attachment to herself.

I should eliminate the suffering of others
because it is suffering, just like my own suffering.
I should take care of others because they are sentient beings,
just as I am a sentient being.

When happiness is equally dear
to others and myself,
what is so special about me
that I strive after happiness for myself alone?

When fear and suffering are equally abhorrent
to others and myself,
what is so special about me
that I protect myself but not others?

Śāntideva's questions deserve some thought. He also asks us to be humble when helping others and to care for them in the same way we do for ourselves, without expecting anything in return (BCA 8.116–17):

When I work in this way for the sake of others,
I should not let conceit or the feeling that I am wonderful arise.
It is just like feeding myself—
I hope for nothing in return.

Therefore, just as I protect myself
from unpleasant things, however slight,
in the same way, I should habituate myself
to have a compassionate and caring mind toward others.

REFLECTION

This reflection is on equalizing self and others. Since nine points to contemplate are easily seen in the explanation above, please refer to them there.

1. Consider each of the points establishing why you and others are equal from the perspective of conventional truths.

2. Consider each of the points regarding why you and others are equal from the perspective of ultimate truth.
3. How will this reflection influence how you think of yourself? How will it influence how you think about and act toward others?

The Disadvantages of Self-Centeredness

Self-centeredness has several different aspects. *Coarse self-centeredness* considers ourselves more important than others and seeks primarily our own happiness in this life. This self-centeredness leads us not only to be apathetic toward others' welfare but to also create a great deal of destructive karma. A less coarse form of self-centeredness seeks our own fortunate rebirth in saṃsāra. It is a virtuous attitude, even though it cares more for ourselves than others. *Subtle self-centeredness* is the mind that seeks liberation for ourselves alone. In general, subtle self-centeredness seeking our own nirvāṇa—also called "attending to our own goal"—is not an object of abandonment; it is a valid mind that enables śrāvakas and solitary realizers to abandon harming others and to attain liberation. People inclined toward the śrāvaka path hear about or see arhats and think, "I want to attain liberation like they have," and by attending to that goal they practice well, eradicate the afflictive obscurations, and attain nirvāṇa. These arhats are worthy of our respect. However, from the perspective of bodhisattvas who seek to become fully awakened buddhas, subtle self-centeredness is to be abandoned because it leads one to forfeit the opportunity to attain buddhahood with its ability to vastly benefit sentient beings, in favor of gaining the personal peace of arhatship.

In the following sections, we will predominantly speak about the disadvantages of the coarse self-centeredness. In contemplating its faults, it is important to distinguish it from seeking the well-being of the conventional self—the self that exists. The conventional self has the capacity to practice the path and will one day attain the bliss of awakening; seeking the ultimate happiness of the mere I is a productive endeavor. The self-centered attitude, on the other hand, is an adventitious, ingrained thought on our mindstream. A limited attitude that pretends to look out for our welfare but in fact constricts our open-heartedness and potential, it can be overcome. Pointing out the disadvantages of self-centeredness is not a criticism of the legitimate wish for the conventional I to be happy and free of pain, so do not get confused and blame yourself for being selfish. Rather, recognize the self-centered attitude as the troublemaker that makes you create destructive karma and causes you misery in this and future lives. Aspire to free yourself from it so that you and all other sentient beings will not be adversely affected by it in the future.

Recalling that others and ourselves are equal in wanting to be happy and avoid suffering, consider the faults of being self-centered. All the problems we experience in cyclic existence are tied to our self-preoccupation. These problems and turmoil are the results of our own destructive actions, which are supported by self-centeredness. For example, wrongdoings such as the ten nonvirtues are supported by a self-centered motivation. Lying is done to protect ourselves and get what we want; talking behind others' backs to create disharmony is done with the thought to benefit ourselves, and so forth.

All of our emotional and physical pain is a result of the self-centeredness that motivated the karmic actions that resulted in this pain. In addition, self-centeredness adds to that pain by feeling sorry for ourselves, blaming others for our problems, and complaining about the unfairness of life.

Self-centeredness is the root of guilt, anxiety, and fear. These painful emotions swirl around a twisted sense of importance: I am hopeless, I am unworthy, I am unloved, I am mistreated. By ruminating on our own difficulties, our perspective becomes very narrow and turned in on itself. Brooding over thoughts of shame, low self-esteem, and self-hatred, our pain and distress increase.

Moreover, doing one's spiritual practice with principally one's own welfare in mind is responsible for resting complacently in nirvāṇa and relinquishing the commitment to lead others to full awakening.

In the path of the middle practitioner, we identified the faults of the afflictions and became convinced that they were the source of suffering and lack any good qualities whatsoever. Similarly, here meditate in the same way with regard to the self-centered attitude. See that it has absolutely no benefit and only harms yourself and others. Just as you previously made a firm determination to be free from afflictions and aspired to develop the wisdom realizing emptiness to overcome them, now develop the same strong determination to rid yourself of self-preoccupation and to practice cherishing others from your heart. Only through this can the joy and benefit of buddhahood be attained. When instructing us how to meditate on this topic, Tsongkhapa summarizes the defects of the self-centered attitude (LC 2:55):

> Out of attachment to self, my self-centered attitude has produced all sorts of undesirable things throughout the beginningless time of cyclic existence up to now. Although I wanted to make things perfect for myself, I emphasized my own welfare and engaged in improper methods. I have spent countless eons at this, but have not at all accomplished my own or others' aims. Not only have I not achieved these, I have been tormented only by suffering. If I had replaced concern for my own welfare with concern for others' welfare, I would certainly have already become a buddha long ago and would have completely and perfectly accomplished my own aims as well as those of others. As I did not do this, I have spent my time uselessly and laboriously.

Śāntideva warns (BCA 8.134):

> Since all the injury,
> fear, and pain in this world
> arise from the self-centered attitude,
> what use is that great demon to me?

The self-centered attitude interferes with our spiritual practice and our attainment of awakening; it creates havoc in our world. Once when I was speaking with a Muslim friend, Dr. A. P. J. Abdul Kalam, a scientist and the eleventh president of India, he mentioned that many problems of this world are due to our having overly strong clinging to concepts of "I" and "me." This is true, isn't it? If we thought more in terms of "we" than of "me versus them," we would be able to work together in a way that would benefit all of us.

A teenager once asked me (Chodron), "Do Buddhists believe in the devil?" I replied that there is not an external devil and there is no one who is thoroughly evil because each sentient being has buddha nature. Rather, the most fearsome devil is the self-centered attitude because it causes us to neglect others and seek only our own happiness.

Cherishing others from the heart is not easy, for self-centeredness sneaks in to cause many problems. For example, we might do what someone wants so that she will like us, not because we genuinely care about her. We may be kind so that others will approve of us, praise us, or speak well of us so that we have an excellent reputation. In these instances, our care for others is not genuine, for self-centeredness has polluted it by seeking some worldly gain for itself. Constant introspective awareness is necessary to flush out the many and varied deceptive intrigues of the self-centered thought and to transform the energy that was restricted in self-absorption into an open heart that cares impartially for all others.

In developing antipathy toward our self-preoccupation, do not mistakenly think that if you experience any happiness you are self-centered and that the only way to sincerely care for others is to suffer yourself. This is not correct at all. Practicing the path should be joyful, although it requires effort and there are bumps on the road. Even in terms of our relationship to sense objects, happiness and pleasure themselves are not the problem—don't feel guilty for experiencing them. They are just feelings arising as a result of karma. Self-centered attachment to them is the culprit. Thus let's strive to diminish and eventually banish self-preoccupation so we and others will be genuinely happy.

Some people may think they have to neglect themselves in order to cherish others. This too is a mistaken notion. Although we want to cease letting self-preoccupation run our lives and make our decisions, this doesn't mean that we should neglect our own situation entirely. The kind of selfishness that leads us to exploit others must be reduced, but disparaging ourselves is not helpful on the path and it is to be abandoned. Our aim is to cherish all sentient beings, including ourselves. If we neglect ourselves, then instead of being able to work for others, they will have to take care of us! Rather, we need to respect ourselves and our buddha potential and, on that basis, discern the appropriate way of caring for ourselves that will support our practice of bodhicitta.

REFLECTION

Contemplate the disadvantages of following the self-centered attitude and think of more disadvantages that haven't been listed below. Remember you are not your self-centeredness, so don't criticize yourself for being self-centered. Remember the self-centered attitude is your enemy.

1. It motivates the destructive karmic actions that bring unfortunate rebirths and many problems in future lives.
2. It is the source of all our interpersonal problems and disputes.
3. It prevents us from understanding the Dharma and especially from realizing bodhicitta.
4. It makes us extremely sensitive to anything concerning ourselves and interprets whatever others do in terms of how it affects us.
5. It causes us to think others wish to harm us when they have no such thought.
6. It is the root of guilt, anxiety, low self-esteem, self-hatred, fear, and so forth. All those disturbing emotions arise due to focusing on ourselves in an unhealthy and unrealistic way.
7. Make examples of each of the above from your own experience.
8. Make a strong determination to catch the self-centered attitude when it arises and to abandon it.

Benefits of Cherishing Others

All good comes from benefiting others. That's why I tell people: even if you want to selfishly care about yourself, the best way to achieve your own happiness is to take care of others. This applies even to people who are not interested in liberation or awakening. Cherishing others will bring them happiness and peace in this life.

We live in a society where we are completely interdependent. This is especially true now that people's careers and knowledge are narrowed to specialized fields and we must depend on one another to complete our own projects. If we look out only for our own welfare, how will we be happy in an interdependent world? If we don't care about the environment we share, we will create many difficulties and problems that future generations will experience. We see that countries that care only for their own citizens exploit other nations, thereby evoking their ire. Similarly, groups that work only for their own benefit soon find themselves abandoned by others. If one member of a family is self-centered, the other members lose their wish to help him.

If we take whatever is good for ourselves and ignore others' plight, we soon find ourselves living amidst a group of unhappy people. Their unhappiness will surely affect us; they will complain, they will resent our success, they might even try to steal our things. On the other hand, if we work for the benefit of society as a whole, there is a better chance that those around us will be content and kind, and this will certainly make our life more pleasant!

On a personal level, if we are self-centered, we will lack genuine friends and will be lonely. When we have problems, others will not extend a helping hand. However, when we are kind and fair, others reciprocate and, as a result, we feel cared for and respected.

Thinking beyond this life, cherishing others brings great benefits. We create so much constructive karma, will die without fear or regret, and will secure a good rebirth. Realizations of the path will come easily because our mind has been made fertile with merit. Bodhicitta will arise in our mind and with that we will progress through the bodhisattva's paths and grounds, attaining full awakening.

In short, our accumulation of virtue depends on cherishing sentient beings. Practicing the perfections of generosity, ethical conduct, and fortitude are dependent on sentient beings. Seeing that sentient beings are necessary for our accumulating merit and generating realizations, feel grateful to them and cherish them. In fact, our happiness and awakening depend on each and every sentient being. If one sentient being is omitted from our love and compassion, we cannot generate bodhicitta, and thus awakening will be beyond our reach. Only by depending on each insect and animal, each hungry ghost, each hell being, each human being, and each deva can we generate bodhicitta. By creating the causes to attain a buddha's truth body, cherishing others fulfills our own purpose. By creating causes for a buddha's form bodies, we are enabled to fulfill others' purpose. In short, in the long term only benefit and never harm results from cherishing other sentient beings.

From beginningless time until now, our sworn enemy—the self-centered attitude that is responsible for all our problems—has been residing comfortably inside us as if it were our best friend. It keeps whispering in our ear, "If I don't take care of you, no one will," and in our confusion we believe it. On the other hand, our true friend—the mind cherishing others, which is the source of all happiness—has been kept at a distance with suspicion. Now that we clearly see the disadvantages of self-preoccupation and the benefits of caring for others, let's rectify this injustice and cherish others as much as possible in our daily life.

Maintaining and enhancing bodhicitta depends on continuously cherishing sentient beings, and that depends on understanding with valid reasons the importance of doing so. If we cherish others because they praise us, give us gifts, agree with our ideas, and act in other ways that gratify our self-centered attitude, we will not be able to sustain that affection for a long time, and our bodhicitta will suffer as a result. As soon as others blame us, lie to us, disagree with our opinions, or act in ways that we don't like, our affection will dry up and be replaced by anger. However, if our reasons for cherishing others are sound, we will withstand the vacillations in sentient beings' moods, behavior, and feelings toward us. For this reason, we must frequently remember the kindness of sentient beings and the benefit we receive from cherishing them. In addition, it's good to recall that the buddhas cherish sentient beings more than themselves. Since we take refuge in the buddhas, we should cherish whom they cherish—sentient beings. If we give up cherishing sentient beings, we neglect what is most valuable to the buddhas. After all, each buddha practiced the Dharma for eons in order to attain awakening so they could be of the greatest benefit to sentient beings. How can we neglect, or worse yet, harm those the buddhas cherish more than themselves? Therefore, remembering the sound reasons why sentient beings are worthy of our love, compassion, and care, let's continuously maintain a positive attitude toward them.

REFLECTION

Contemplating the benefits of cherishing others will inspire you to do so. Then, when you actively cherish others, you'll experience the benefits yourself.

1. It is the source of all happiness in this and future lives.
2. Others are happy and your life becomes meaningful.
3. By being kind to others, they will be drawn to you and you will have harmonious relationships.
4. Others will respect you and will take your words to heart.
5. You will create great virtuous karma that will bring a fortunate rebirth and happiness in future lives.
6. This virtue will also fertilize your mind so that the teachings will enter at a deeper level.
7. You will die free of regrets.
8. Generating love, compassion, and bodhicitta will come easily.
9. Whenever you look at any sentient being you'll have a feeling of warmth.
10. Make more examples from your experience.

Exchanging Self and Others

Seeing that self-preoccupation is the path to suffering and cherishing others is the path to bliss, we now exchange the object of our cherishing, replacing self with all sentient beings. Exchanging self and others does not mean that I become you and you become me. Nor does it mean your possessions are mine and mine are yours. Rather, we exchange the attitude with which we hold each one important. We consider others as we would ourselves—we cherish them, want them to be happy and free from pain, seek their success in temporal and spiritual endeavors. Whereas previously we held ourselves as most important, now we hold others as supreme. Whereas previously we thought others' misery was of secondary importance, now we consider our own problems as minor.

We may have some doubts: Is it possible to exchange ourselves with others? Is there benefit in doing so? If it were useful but not possible, or possible but not useful, then meditating to exchange ourselves with others would just be a waste of time. However, on examination, we find that it's both possible and useful.

But aren't living beings biologically programmed to look out for their own benefit first? Could exchanging ourselves and others bring about the demise of the human species because we would be totally defenseless in the face of others' aggression?

In fact, holding ourselves as foremost is a matter of habit. For example, we may dislike someone and even fear him at one point in our life, but later we meet him in different circumstances and discover that he is very amicable. Developing a close friendship, we miss him when he is absent. This change in feeling is due to our adopting a different attitude about the person and becoming familiar with it.

"But," we may retort, "I don't feel the pain and pleasure that another person's body does, so how could I have the same attitude toward it as I do toward my own body?" Here, too, the answer is that our considering this mass of organic matter "my body" is a matter of familiarity. When we look closer, what about this body is ours? The sperm and egg and genetic material belong to our parents and ancestors. The rest is the result of the food we have eaten, which came from the earth and was given to us by others. It is simply by habit that we consider this body mine. By closely examining the parts of the body and the feelings of pain and pleasure in the body when practicing mindfulness of the body and of feelings, we will see that there is no I or mine in them. There are simply elements and feelings; the notions that there is an inherently existent person and that the body is inherently mine are our mental fabrications. Śāntideva tells us (BCA 8.101–2):

> Such things as a continuum and a collection
> are false in the same way as a rosary and an army.
> There is no real owner of duḥkha;
> therefore who has control over it?
>
> There being no inherent owner of duḥkha,
> there can be no distinction at all between the duḥkha
>   of myself and others.
> Thus I shall dispel duḥkha because it hurts.

The basis for designating the I is the collection of the body and mind; the I is a continuum made up of many moments. There is no inherently existent I to be found in the continuum of I or in the collection of the body and mind. The I exists by being merely conceived and designated. Therefore we cannot make a hard and fast line between my duḥkha and others' duḥkha, saying that one hurts more than the other. Because suffering hurts no matter whose it is, we should work to eliminate it.

As for the concern that the human species would be obliterated if we were more concerned with others' well-being than with our own, I believe that in our case survival of the most cooperative overrides survival of the fittest. Unbounded self-concern and competition lead to destruction, whereas caring and cooperating with one another lead to the benefit of all. Ants and bees survive because they cooperate and care for one another; we human beings do as well. If each ant refused to trust and care for others, all of them would soon die. It is the same with us human beings sharing life on planet Earth. We flourish when we work for the common good; we destroy each other when we think only of our own benefit.

Two principal obstacles block our exchanging self and others. The first is thinking self and others are inherently separate; the second is believing that since others' happiness and suffering doesn't affect us, we don't need to care about it. Regarding the first obstacle, self and others depend on each other. "Self" is posited only when "others" is also posited, similar to one side of the valley being this side only when the other side is that side. Of course, which is this side and which is that side depend on our perspective—where we happen to be standing. They are not inherently this and that; when we go to the other side of the valley, it becomes this side.

The second obstacle is thinking that it's not necessary to dispel others' suffering because it doesn't harm us and it's not necessary to care for others because that doesn't benefit us. This, too, is based on seeing self and others as unrelated and entirely separate, when in fact we living beings depend on one another. It would be similar to thinking, "There's no need to save money for my old age because that old person is a different person and her suffering doesn't harm me." It would also be similar to the hand refusing to pull a thorn out of the foot because they are unrelated and the foot's pain doesn't hurt the hand.

We might think that ourselves and the old person we will become are in the same continuum and that the hand and the foot are parts of the same body, so it is suitable for them to care for each other. But what we call "continuum" is simply a label imputed in dependence on a collection of moments and what we call "body" is similarly a name designated in dependence on a collection of parts. There is nothing inherently existent in either of these. The various moments of mind and the various parts of the body have no inherent relationship that binds them together. It is simply a matter of conception and designation. Śāntideva says (BCA 9.115–16):

> Just as in this form, devoid of I,
> the thought of self arose through long habituation,
> why, in dependence on the aggregates of living beings,
> should not the thought I, through habit, be imputed?
>
> Thus when I work for others' sake,
> there is no reason for boasting or amazement,
> for it is just as when I feed myself—
> I don't expect to be rewarded.

Contemplating this for some time will open our mind to seeing the possibility and benefit of exchanging self and others.

Wishing to exchange ourselves and others is a heartfelt desire that stems from having clearly seen the disadvantages of self-centeredness and the benefits of cherishing others through repeated meditation. Śāntideva recounts his own internal dialogue about this (BCA 8.125, 8.130–31):

> "If I give this, what will be left for me?"
> Concern for my own welfare is the attitude of demons.
> "If I keep this, what will be left to give?"
> Concern for others' welfare is the approach of the divine beings.
>
> All the joy the world contains
> has come through wishing happiness for others.
> All the misery the world contains
> has come through wanting pleasure for myself.

Is there need for lengthy explanations?
Childish beings look out for themselves,
while buddhas work for the good of others:
see the difference that separates them!

When the mind is unripe, the thought of exchanging self and others by placing others foremost and ourselves last is frightening. Should fear arise, remember that it is the self-centered attitude that is anxious because it is losing its ascendency and control. Develop a courageous attitude to weather that fear; it will not destroy you. Still, it is important to go at a pace that is suitable for us and be content to create the causes so that our meditation on this topic will be successful. Pushing ourselves is counterproductive. Thus if you don't feel capable of exchanging self with others yet, focus on cultivating love and compassion and engage in practices of purification and collection of merit to strengthen your mind. It is also helpful to request your spiritual mentors and the buddhas for inspiration. When you feel more confident, return to the meditation of exchanging self and others.

Although we practice the meditation of exchanging self and others, on a practical level we still must take care of our body and mind. We're the only one who can do that, and we need to preserve our precious human life for the sake of others. Looking out for our own well-being at the expense of others is selfish, yet caring for our health and safety as one person among many is a valid concern. Everyone has a natural sense of wanting happiness and freedom from suffering. In and of itself, this wish is not negative. When supported by wisdom, it induces us to discern the causes of happiness and the causes of suffering and to practice the former and abandon the latter. As our compassion and wisdom grow, so will our ability to exchange self and others.

Deep understanding is necessary to effect such a dramatic change in attitude. Exchanging ourselves with others is not something we can intellectually force on ourselves, and simply telling ourselves we should feel it will not change our attitude. Firm conviction that self-centeredness is our enemy and that cherishing others is beneficial is needed. This conviction comes only through familiarization over time. There is no shortcut. While exchanging self and others may initially seem frightening, with familiarity and practice it will become joyful and easy.

Using Jealousy, Competition, and Arrogance in the Exchange

To demolish our self-centered attitude and hit it at its vulnerable points, Śāntideva describes a meditation in which we exchange ourselves with others and then cultivate jealousy, rivalry, and arrogance toward our old self. This mimics and then inverts the emotions our self-centered attitude usually holds toward people we consider better, equal, or inferior to us. In the following verses, "I" refers to other sentient beings, those who are to be cherished, and "he" refers to our self-centered attitude that is the source of our misery. In other words, we adopt the perspective of others—now called "I"—and criticize our self-centered attitude—now called "he" or "others" (BCA 8.146):

> Indifferent to the plight of living beings,
> who tread the brink of unfortunate rebirths,
> he makes an outward show of virtues,
> even sets himself among the perfect!

This verse shows contemptuous jealousy toward the self-centered attitude, looking at it the same way as other beings do. He (our self-centered attitude) does not care about others' plight but sees himself as the most wonderful being, making a show of being virtuous when he is anything but that. Furthermore, he has high status; we are no one and are jealous of and resent him. Thinking in this way helps us to see how misplaced our self-preoccupation is, generating within us the determination not to bow to its antics.

The following verses are the means to compete with our self-centered self (BCA, 8.148–49):

> By every means I'll advertise
> my gifts to all the world,
> ensuring that his qualities
> remain unknown, ignored by everyone.
>
> My faults I will conceal, dissimulate,
> for I, not he, will be the object of devotion;
> I, not he, will gain possessions and renown;
> I will be the center of attention.

Usually we compete with others, bragging of our own good qualities and ignoring theirs; we make ourselves the center of attention, the one who is famous and respected, and we either put others down or treat them as if they were nonentities. In the above verses, we identify with others and turn that same attitude toward our self-centered attitude, the source of all pain and misery. Truly, our self-centered attitude should be disparaged and neglected.

The following verse illustrates arrogance toward our self-centered attitude. The voice of others (now I) is being arrogant toward our self-centeredness (he) (BCA 8.153):

> Granted, even if he does have something,
> I'm the one he is working for!
> He can keep enough just to survive,
> but with my strength I'll steal away the rest.

If the self-centered self possesses wealth, reputation, and so forth, since it is now the servant of others, it should work for their benefit. We (others, whose welfare is more important) will allow him (our self-centered attitude) to keep enough to stay alive, but even then that is just so that he has the energy to serve us.

This verse reminds us of a useful attitude to cultivate toward our possessions, good reputation, and so forth. With love we offer ourselves to all sentient beings as their servants to lead them to temporal and ultimate joy. Mentally we give them all our possessions. Having done so, we must now use these items only for their benefit, never with self-centered concern. Similarly, any good reputation we have is offered to others and used solely for their benefit; we are not arrogant with respect to our own accomplishments, bragging or showing off to others in a way that humiliates them. Gradually training ourselves to think in this way will free us from the tyranny of self-centeredness.

Initially we may encounter difficulties with the meditation cultivating jealousy, rivalry, and arrogance toward our self-centered attitude and our old self. One obstacle is that we are so habituated with self-identification, referencing everything to ourselves, that it's hard to understand the use of "I" and "he" in these verses. With repeated practice, this can be overcome.

Another obstacle is that emotions of resentment, competition, and conceit are so despicable that we wonder what the use of cultivating them is;

in fact, it seems rather unbecoming or perhaps even damaging as Dharma practitioners to dredge up these feelings. This meditation does indeed play on the repulsiveness of these emotions, but this time their object is our self-centered attitude, not other sentient beings. In this way, they are used as tools to show us just how contemptible our self-centeredness is so that we will stop following its dictates.

How to View the Body

After exchanging self with others and caring for others the way we care for ourselves, we need to adopt a suitable view toward our present body. In the four establishments of mindfulness, we contemplate the foul nature of this body produced by afflictions and polluted karma. That meditation spurs us to seek liberation from cyclic existence to free ourselves from taking problematic bodies that age, fall ill, and die. Śāntideva now builds on that meditation, encouraging us to cease pampering our bodies and instead use them to work for others' welfare and create the causes for buddhahood. Similar to the meditation on selflessness in mindfulness of the body, Śāntideva encourages us to counteract the grasping that holds this body as I and mine and to release the obsessive, self-preoccupied worry and attachment we have toward the body. Doing that lessens the suffering caused by clinging to this body and enables us to dedicate our body to practice the path to awakening and to engage in activities that bring happiness to all sentient beings. In his usual forthright style, Śāntideva says (8.178–80, 8.184):

> In the end my body will turn to dust;
> unable to move by itself, it will be propelled by other forces.
> Why do I grasp this unbearable
> and unclean form as I, my self?
>
> Whether it lives or whether it dies,
> what use is this machine to me?
> How is it different from a clod of earth?
> O why do I not dispel this conceit of self?
>
> Through lavishing attention on this body,
> such sorrow have I brought myself, so senselessly.

What use is all my wanting, all my hating—
for what indeed is like a log of wood?

Therefore, in order to benefit all beings
I shall give up this body without any attachment.
Although it may have many faults,
I should look after it while experiencing the results of my
previous karma.

Our body is simply a compilation of material elements. Why, then, do we think of it as I and mine? Since it is like an inanimate machine or a clod of dirt, it doesn't make sense for me to generate the conceit of "I am" toward it. Since beginningless time I've treasured and pampered whatever body I had as if it were a pleasure palace. I've craved sensory pleasures, hated others who prevented me from getting them, and created great destructive karma by doing so. My past behavior was senseless because this body itself is like an inanimate log. Seeing my folly, I will now devote my physical energy to benefiting others. Even though this body has faults—it ages and dies—I will care for it properly and use it for a good purpose.

The *Akṣayamati Sūtra* instructs bodhisattvas how to think about the body:[38]

> "I should throw this body into the needs of all sentient beings" . . . Regarding the body as dedicated to this goal, [a bodhisattva] looks at physical pain and is not distressed, but takes care of sentient beings.

Bodhisattvas who cherish others from the depth of their hearts and have practiced exchanging self and others can practice this sincerely, without fear for what will become of themselves. Thinking in this way gives them great joy—joy that is greater than any self-centered happiness we may ever experience.

Such bodhisattvas imbue habitual daily actions with love and compassion and transform what ordinary beings consider unpleasant into an opportunity to benefit others. For example, the *Heap of Jewels Sūtra* (*Ratnakūṭa Sūtra*) counsels bodhisattva monastics who enter a village on alms round but do not receive any food to think:[39]

> "These Brahmins, leading merchants, and religious wanderers are so busy, they certainly [have no time] to give to me. It is a wonder that they notice me at all! How much more unusual it would be if they gave me alms." Not discouraged in this way, he should go for alms.
>
> And as for those sentient beings who come into his field of vision, women, men, boys, and girls, even including animals, he should arouse thoughts of lovingkindness and compassion towards them all . . .
>
> Whether the alms-food he receives is of good quality or of poor quality, he should look around to all four directions, thinking, "In this village, town, or city, who is a poor person with whom I can share this alms-food?" If he sees a poor person, he shares his alms-food with that person. If he does not see any poor people, he should think, "There are unseen sentient beings who do not come into my field of vision. I give them the best share of this alms-food. May they accept it and eat it!"

For people who have equalized and exchanged self and others, such thoughts and practices as these arise spontaneously in their minds. Those of us in training should try to remember to think like this. Although initially such thoughts are fabricated and our self-centered attitude may rebel, with repeated meditation on exchanging self and others and continuous practice in daily life situations, our minds will come to cherish others as much as, if not more than, we currently cherish ourselves.

Taking and Giving

The taking-and-giving meditation has its source in the *Precious Garland*, where Nāgārjuna says (RA 484cd):[40]

> May their ill deeds ripen on me
> and all my virtues ripen on them.

This meditation is also championed by Śāntideva. Because it is so powerful, in the past it was practiced privately and taught only to advanced disciples who were spiritually prepared. Even the thought of experiencing our own suffering, let alone taking on others' suffering, is anathema to most people. Similarly, to consider offering our body, hard-earned wealth, and merit to others is antithetical to our ingrained self-centeredness.

It wasn't until the twelfth century that the spiritual mentor Kadampa Geshe Chekawa (1102–76) dared to publicly teach this meditation. He taught the practice to a group of lepers, who cured themselves of leprosy by doing it. Wanting these teachings to be available to others, he composed the now-classic text *The Seven-Point Mind Training*. In our time the practice is taught more openly and people find it very helpful.[41]

The taking-and-giving practice helps to further increase our love and compassion and our capacity to exchange self and others. *Taking* entails generating the compassionate wish "I will take all problems, sufferings, and confusion of other sentient beings on myself so that others may be free from them." *Giving* is motivated by love: "I will give my body, possessions, and virtuous qualities and their causes to others so that they may be peaceful and happy." Through this we generate a very courageous and resolute mind that will make our bodhicitta effective.

Taking

To practice taking, imagine a specific person or group of people in front of you and contemplate the duḥkha they experience. As compassion arises, think, "I will take on their duḥkha so that they will be free of it." Imagine their duḥkha leaving them in the form of dark clouds, smoke, or pollution and entering you as you inhale. Think how wonderful these beings feel now that their duḥkha has left them.

Now use what sentient beings don't want—their suffering and afflictions—and use it to destroy what you don't want—your self-centered attitude and self-grasping ignorance. At your heart is a dark lump, the embodiment of your own self-centered attitude and self-grasping ignorance. As the clouds, smoke, or pollution enters you, it transforms into lightning that strikes this lump, shattering it so that it no longer exists. Feel the freedom and great spaciousness at your heart now that these two have been forever destroyed.

If it is initially difficult to think of taking on others' suffering, begin by taking on the suffering you will experience later on in this life as you age, fall ill, or have interpersonal problems. Take on this suffering of your future self voluntarily, and imagine that doing so eliminates your present self-centeredness. Then imagine transforming your present body, possessions, and merit into everything you will need in the future, and give it to your future self, who receives it happily. After you become familiar with this practice, contemplate taking on others' suffering and its causes and giving them your happiness in the form of whatever will bring them temporal and ultimate bliss.

When you are ready to develop this meditation further, imagine taking the duḥkha of the sentient beings of the three realms. Then take the obstacles to the long life and successful deeds of the spiritual masters, buddhas, and bodhisattvas, as well as the hindrances to the existence and flourishing of the Buddha's teachings in the world.

After taking these, think that all beings are liberated from their suffering and its causes because you have taken them and think that your self-centeredness and grasping an inherently existent I are destroyed. In other words, you have taken what others don't want—their duḥkha—and used it to destroy what you don't want—your self-centered attitude. Meditate on emptiness for a while, feel the spaciousness, the absence of self-grasping and self-centeredness. Then, thinking that everything is dependently arising and is like an illusion, train in generosity.

Giving

In that clear, open space at your heart (the heart cakra at the center of your chest) appears a beautiful light, the embodiment of your love. With that sentiment, give to others all they need to find temporal happiness while they are in saṃsāra and, more important, all the conditions to attain the ultimate bliss of buddhahood. Here, visualize giving first your body, which transforms into a wish-fulfilling body that gives others everything they desire, principally a precious human life so they can practice the Dharma. Your wish-fulfilling body purifies sentient beings' environments so they have the necessities of life, including a good education, understanding friends, and community members who think of benefiting one another. Imagine they have all the necessary circumstances for practice, especially interest from their own side as well as spiritual mentors, teachings, and Dharma friends nearby. Think that they practice and then realize the entire path to awakening. Second, visualize giving your possessions, which transform into what others need. These give others perfect conditions so they have temporal happiness and conducive circumstances to learn and practice the Dharma. Third, visualize giving your merit, which gives others the good karma you have accumulated so they can progress on the path.

When you give to āryas and arhats, think that their last remaining obstacles to liberation and omniscience are purified and that they become buddhas. When giving to buddhas, imagine that your body, possessions, and merit transform into magnificent offering objects that please them, giving rise to great bliss in them.

Do the visualization of giving as you exhale; imagine offering to sentient beings whatever they need on light rays radiating from your heart. Feel great contentment and joy that you are able to benefit sentient beings in this way.

How to Progress in This Practice

At the beginning, it may be helpful to imagine taking on your own future suffering of tonight, tomorrow, and the rest of this life and giving happiness to your future self. Then expand to take the suffering of dear ones and to give them happiness. Expand it further to take and give to strangers, then enemies, then all beings.

Having taken on sentient beings' duḥkha, don't neglect to transform it into lightning (or whatever cleansing agent appeals to you) and destroy your self-centered attitude and self-grasping ignorance. Stop and feel the effect of that within yourself. Imagine what it would be like to be free from the constant attachment, fear, and worry about the self. Imagine feeling the openness of genuine love and compassion that can welcome anyone into its space.

Take your time doing these visualizations and allow yourself to feel love and compassion as well as relief and delight at being instrumental in dispelling others' burden of duḥkha and bringing them both ordinary and long-term satisfaction and bliss. Taking and giving can be done elaborately, taking on each suffering, cause, and obstacle of each realm individually and giving each object to beings in each realm separately. The practice can also be done in a condensed way, according to the time available.

This practice is very effective when you're sick or depressed, when you have obstacles in your practice, or when someone you are close to is sick. Do it to remove hindrances in the world around you, such as political turmoil, climate change, corruption, and so forth. Instead of rejecting this duḥkha, take it on yourself so that others are free from it and you are liberated from the self-centered attitude and self-grasping.

After the riots in Tibet in the spring of 2008 during which many people—Tibetans and Chinese alike—were killed or injured, I did the taking-and-giving meditation with respect to the Chinese leaders and policymakers. Cultivating compassion toward them, I imagined taking on their suffering, anger, and negativities and giving them my happiness and virtues. Although my meditation did not remove their animosity or change their policies toward Tibet, it did give me a greater sense of stability and calm as well as courage and compassion in the face of the tragic situation in my country.

When you are familiar with this practice, it can be incorporated with your breathing, taking on others' sufferings and their causes during each inhalation and giving them your body, possessions, and merit during each exhalation. If you wish, when taking imagine that others' duḥkha leaves them from their right nostril and enters into your left nostril. When giving, imagine that your gifts leave through your right nostril in the form of white light and enter others through their left nostril.

Practicing taking and giving for someone who is ill or experiencing difficulties and then dedicating the merit from that practice to them can benefit them by nourishing the conditions for their own good karma to ripen. Although we cannot in fact take the sufferings of others and give them our happiness, imagining that it is possible strengthens our courage, love, and compassion. It also eliminates any hesitation or reluctance to help others when we have the opportunity and propels us toward full awakening where we will have all the faculties necessary to be of the greatest service.

When doing the meditation seriously, anxiety may arise, fearing that perhaps this is not just a visualization but we may actually experience the suffering of others. At this time, use the fear to identify the object of negation in the meditation on emptiness, because at that time the ignorance grasping an inherently existent I is clearly manifest. Then using Madhyamaka analysis, refute the existence of such an I.

REFLECTION

1. With compassion take on the problems and confusion of others by inhaling it in the form of black smoke.

2. This turns into a thunderbolt of lightning that completely obliterates the black lump of selfishness and ignorance at your heart.

3. Feel the open space, the lack of wrong conception about self and others, the absence of self-preoccupation.

4. In this space, imagine a white light that radiates to all beings and think that you are increasing and transforming your body, possessions, and merit into whatever others need and giving it to them.

5. Imagine them being satisfied and happy and rejoice that you've been able to bring this about.

True Practitioners

One of my students told me about research he had done into the invasion of Nalanda Monastery in the thirteenth century. At that time, large numbers of monks were slaughtered. It seems that many monks were not afraid when they were being stabbed. We can't say that they didn't feel pain, because without pain they could not have practiced fortitude. They felt pain but, as a result of their great compassion, did not respond with anger or fear.

I heard a moving story of a monk who was the tutor of Jamyang Shepa's tulku.[42] I met him in 1955. He was a good monk and great learned adept who practiced the taking-and-giving meditation. In 1958 there was an uprising against the Communist Chinese in Amdo, the eastern area of Tibet. About two hundred monks from Labrang Tashikhyil Monastery were arrested, and about fifteen or twenty monks were executed. Among the latter was this monk. When he was brought to the execution place, he asked if he could pray before they shot him and recited the taking-and-giving verse from the "Guru Pūjā" (95):

> Thus, venerable compassionate gurus, inspire me so all negativities, obscurations, and sufferings of mother beings ripen on me right now and I give my happiness and virtue to others, securing all wanderers in bliss.

This shows that he was a true practitioner. Ordinary beings would have had far too much fear and anger to even think of exchanging their happiness and virtue for the pain of others. Before beginning the taking-and-giving meditation, you may find it helpful to recite this verse.

Comparing and Combining the Two Methods

The equalizing and exchanging self and others method for generating bodhicitta is more suitable for sharp-faculty disciples because it employs reasoning to establish others' equality. In the seven cause-and-effect instructions our fondness and compassion for sentient beings arises based on our family relationships and how family members have acted toward us personally—the kindness they have shown to us as our relatives. Equalizing and exchanging self and others does not require seeing ourselves as having been the recipient of kindness in a privileged relationship with sentient beings in the past. Rather we connect with them on a more fundamental level—each of us wants happiness and not suffering. Thus this method enables us to see the kindness of enemies without first transforming their appearance into someone pleasing, such as a relative.

The reasoning used by equalizing and exchanging self and others also brings in an understanding of the ultimate truth, emptiness. What we designate "I" and cherish and what we call "other" and neglect is not based on some inherent nature that I and others have. I and others are dependent on each other; they are also seen as mere designations, which loosens our grasping at self. For these reasons, equalizing and exchanging self and others is seen as a more profound method that is directed toward disciples with sharp faculties.

The two methods of cultivating bodhicitta may also be combined. This method is more effective for some people. Here the order for contemplating the topics is (1) equanimity regarding friends, enemies, and strangers, (2) recognize all sentient beings have been your mother, (3) remember the love and kindness of others both when they have been your mother and when they have not, (4) wish to repay that kindness, (5) equalize self and others, (6) examine the disadvantages of self-centeredness and (7) the benefits of cherishing others, (8) exchange self and others, (9) take others' suffering with special emphasis on compassion, (10) give away your own happiness with special emphasis on love, (11) make the great resolve, and (12) generate bodhicitta.

To close this chapter, I'd like to quote a passage by Tsongkhapa that encapsulates the essential instructions. I found it very moving because bodhicitta is dear to my heart (LC 2.59):

> Whether you plant the roots of the Mahāyāna or not, or whether you have genuinely entered the Mahāyāna or not, is all founded upon this [bodhicitta]. Therefore always consider what you should do to develop this. It is excellent if you do develop this; if you have not, do not let it remain that way. Always rely on a teacher who gives this kind of teaching. Always associate with friends who are training their minds in this way. Constantly look at the scriptures and commentaries that describe this. Amass the [two] collections [of merit and wisdom] as causes for this. Clear away the obstructions that prevent this. Moreover, if you train your mind in this way, you will definitely acquire all the seeds for developing this, so this work is not insignificant; take joy in it.

What better way is there to live than to generate bodhicitta? We live in challenging times where some ideologies of hate and prejudice are prevalent. Do not let yourself fall under their sway, but nourish the seeds of love, compassion, and altruism in yourself and then share the fruit of doing so with all living beings.

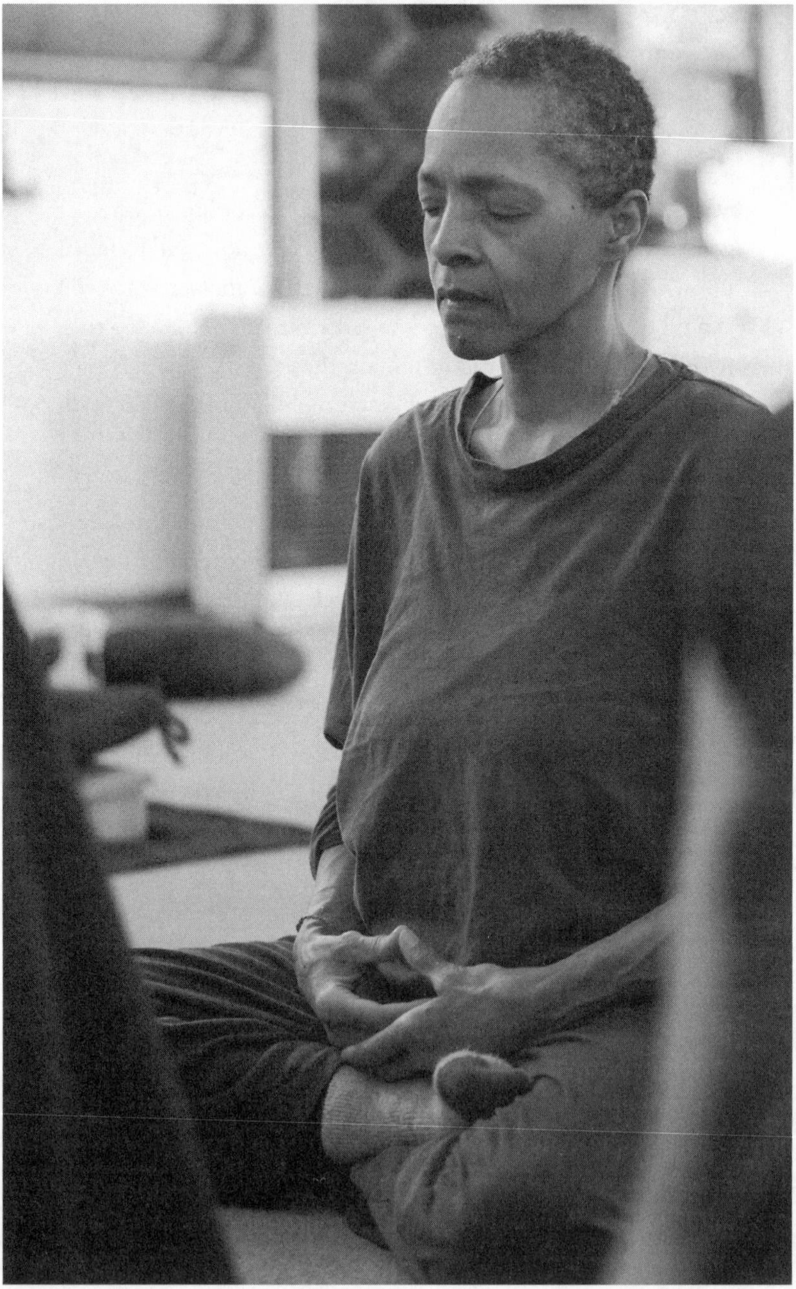

5 | Becoming a Bodhisattva

The Self-Centered Attitude and Self-Grasping Ignorance

SELF-CENTEREDNESS (T. *rang gces 'dzin*) and self-grasping (*ahaṃkāra*, T. *bdag 'dzin*) are not the same, although both hinder our progress on the bodhisattva path and are obstacles to buddhahood. Self-centeredness holds our own happiness as more important than that of others; self-grasping apprehends the self as inherently existent.

The self-centered attitude is neither an afflictive nor a cognitive obscuration. It is not a pollutant (*āsrava*, *āsava*) or a defilement (*mala*), nor is it the root of cyclic existence. It is often called an "inferior obscuration" that those following the bodhisattva path must prevent because it impedes their attainment of the nonabiding nirvāṇa of a buddha—the nirvāṇa that abides neither in the extreme of cyclic existence nor in the extreme of personal liberation. Although the self-centered attitude is called an "obscuration," it is not an actual obscuration because it is not the object of abandonment of a path, as are the afflictive and cognitive obscurations. However, it is a hindrance for bodhisattvas to abandon.

Self-grasping ignorance is the root of saṃsāra; it grasps persons and other phenomena to exist inherently. It is an afflictive obscuration that has been eliminated by arhats and eighth-ground bodhisattvas.

Self-centeredness and self-grasping do not have a causal relationship—one does not cause the other. They are also not the same nature: if one exists in a person's mindstream, the other is not necessarily present. Arhats have abandoned self-grasping but have subtle self-centeredness. Bodhisattvas below the eighth ground who freshly enter the Mahāyāna path (that is, they are not arhats who later enter the bodhisattva path) have self-grasping but do not have coarse self-centeredness. Coarse self-centeredness is abandoned upon generating spontaneous bodhicitta and entering the bodhisattva path; subtle self-centeredness and its latencies are overcome upon attaining the eighth bodhisattva ground, although some sharp-faculty bodhisattvas eliminate them before that. Subtle self-centeredness does not manifest once sharp-faculty bodhisattvas reach the path of preparation and when middle-faculty bodhisattvas attain the path of seeing.

The self-centered attitude and self-grasping ignorance also have different counterforces. Bodhicitta is the opposite of subtle self-centeredness; the wisdom realizing emptiness is the antidote eradicating self-grasping ignorance. Bodhicitta is easier to understand than emptiness, but it is more difficult to realize and fully integrate in our mind. While emptiness is harder to understand, once understood properly it is easier to realize than bodhicitta. Śrāvakas lack the fortitude, effort, and courage to cultivate bodhicitta, although they understand and admire it.

Arhats have abandoned self-grasping; when they eat or put on clothes, they do so without any self-grasping or craving. But their motivation for doing these everyday actions is not concerned with benefiting all sentient beings; it is neutral, neither virtuous nor nonvirtuous. Bodhisattvas—even those who have not realized emptiness directly—do all activities, including everyday ones such as eating, dressing, breathing, or walking, with the virtuous motivation of bodhicitta. Although they are attending to their own needs, their motivation is to dedicate their lives to benefiting sentient beings. With great love and great compassion, they constantly direct their minds to what is most beneficial in the long term for all sentient beings. Here we see that it's not so much what we do, but the motivation with which we do it that determines whether or not an action is altruistic.

In Mahāyāna teachings, the disadvantages of self-centeredness are discussed at great length because it is an obstacle to generating bodhicitta and an impediment to attaining full awakening and to benefiting all sentient beings. A verse in the "Guru Pūjā" says, "This chronic disease of self-centeredness is the cause giving rise to unwanted suffering." This does not mean that self-centeredness is the root of saṃsāric duḥkha. It is not; self-grasping ignorance is. Self-centeredness is the major impediment for entering the Bodhisattva Vehicle, and in this context it is considered worse than ignorance.

All people recognize coarse self-centeredness as harmful. It believes that our happiness and suffering are more important than that of others, that what we want to happen should happen, and that our opinions are right and our ideas are the best. This is the self-preoccupation that we see in children and that as adults we learn to hide under the pretense of gentility, although it is still present. Coarse self-centered attitude lies behind the creation of all destructive karma. It is involved with low self-esteem, guilt, rage, jealousy, greed, anxiety, and unhealthy fear. Self-centeredness chases others away and then we feel sorry for ourselves because we lack friends. Coarse self-centeredness supports afflictive minds and actions, and it harms living beings, whether or not they are spiritual practitioners. For that reason, the practice of loving-kindness and compassion in daily life is essential for combating it.

REFLECTION

1. The self-centered attitude is neither an afflictive nor a cognitive obscuration. It is called an "inferior obscuration" that those following the bodhisattva path must prevent because it impedes attaining buddhahood.
2. Coarse self-centeredness considers ourselves more important than others. It is abandoned on generating spontaneous bodhicitta and entering the bodhisattva path.
3. Subtle self-centeredness is the mind that seeks liberation for ourselves alone. It and its latencies are abandoned upon attaining the eighth ground, although some bodhisattvas abandon it earlier. Bodhicitta is its antidote.
4. Self-grasping ignorance grasps persons and other phenomena to exist inherently. It is an afflictive obscuration that has been eliminated by arhats and eighth-ground bodhisattvas. The wisdom realizing emptiness is its antidote.
5. As you practice more, you'll be able to identify these in your mind and overcome them.

Self-Interest and Self-Confidence

When we hear about bodhisattvas and their ability to cherish others more than themselves, doubts may arise: If we abandon all self-interest and only cherish others, does that mean we neglect ourselves? If so, won't our own suffering increase?

Cherishing others does not mean that we ignore our own needs and care only for others. If we did that, we would fall into a deplorable state in which we could neither benefit others nor practice the Dharma. In that case, instead of our helping others, they would need to take care of us!

Not all self-interest is negative. While one type of self-interest is selfish and looks out only for ourselves, another is wise self-interest that understands that benefiting ourselves and helping others are not necessarily contradictory. The Buddha had both self-interest and care for others. As mentioned in the teachings on refuge, the Buddha's truth body is the fulfillment of his own interest or purpose in that he has purified his mind completely and possesses direct knowledge of all existents. His form bodies are the fulfillment of others' interest or purpose in that they enable him to manifest in various forms in order to be of benefit to all the sentient beings who are receptive. A practitioner attains the truth body and form bodies simultaneously, achieving her own purpose at the same time as achieving the purpose of others.

Similarly, while one sense of self (T. *nga'o snyam pa'i blo*, literally "the mind experiencing I am"), is a troublemaker, the sense of a conventional self is useful. The former is the self-grasping that is the root of saṃsāra. The latter is the sense of the conventional self that exists; it allows for us to have stable and realistic self-confidence. This self-confident sense of self must be stronger in bodhisattvas than in ordinary people because bodhisattvas are ready to forgo their own happiness in order to benefit others. Although many Westerners believe that healthy self-esteem is demonstrated by being a unique individual, for bodhisattvas self-esteem is connected with extraordinary generosity and joyful relinquishment of self-centeredness.

Śrāvakas also have firm self-confidence and a strong, positive sense of self. They think, "I will restrain from destructive actions and cultivate the three higher trainings. I will attain liberation no matter what it takes." Such self-confidence is not egotistical or arrogant; it aspires for what is virtuous without clinging to it. Wisdom is required to differentiate self-confidence and arrogance.

Self-confidence is essential to begin, continue, and complete the path to awakening. Without self-confidence at the beginning, we won't even think to start on the path; without self-confidence in the middle, we'll get discouraged and quit before attaining any enduring qualities; and without self-confidence at the end, we won't share the results of awakening with others or work for their welfare.

Buddha nature is a valid basis on which to generate such self-confidence. Our buddha nature is stable and cannot be destroyed. Reflecting on emptiness helps us to recognize this buddha potential, for we see that the defilements are adventitious and can be removed. Compassion for others also builds self-confidence, as does remembering our precious human life, its meaning and purpose, and its rarity. It's important that, as aspiring bodhisattvas, we cultivate such strong and resilient self-confidence.

REFLECTION

1. There are two types of self-interest. One is selfish and looks out only for ourselves; another is wise self-interest that understands that benefiting ourselves and helping others can go together.
2. There are two senses of self. One is the self-grasping that is the root of saṃsāra, which is the source of our duḥkha. The other is the sense of the conventional self that exists, which allows for stable and realistic self-confidence. Bodhisattvas must have strong self-confidence to complete the path and attain buddhahood.

Integrating the View with Bodhicitta

Integrating the view of emptiness according to the Yogācāra or Prāsaṅgika Madhyamaka perspective aids our cultivation of bodhicitta by loosening rigid clinging to friend, enemy, and stranger, and to self and others. It also deepens our compassion for sentient beings under the control of afflictions and karma.

According to the Yogācāras, the seemingly external objects that appear to our sense consciousnesses have in fact arisen as a result of seeds on our foundation consciousness. These objects do not exist as separate entities from our mind, although they appear that way because the mind is obscured by ignorance. Regarding phenomena, they are like illusions in that they arise due to the same seed as the consciousness perceiving them. Some of the seeds on our foundational consciousness are karmic seeds that color our perspective according to the realm we are born in. For example, the appearance of fluid being pure nectar in the deva realm, water in the human realm, and pus and blood in the hungry ghost realm is a result of karmic seeds placed on our foundational consciousness by previous actions.

Seeing whatever appears to us as a karmic appearance loosens the solidity with which we ordinarily view sentient beings and the environment. From this perspective, friends, enemies, and strangers are simply karmic appearances, and thus having attachment, anger, and apathy toward them is misplaced. Similarly, attractive and unattractive objects, praise and blame, reputation and notoriety, and wealth and poverty are simply appearances to the mind due to the activation of karmic seeds. They lack any real external existence that is separate from the mind to which they appear.

Everything we encounter or experience that seems to be external and "out there" is created by the seeds on our foundational consciousness. Becoming angry when others criticize us or steal our possessions is inappropriate because these events occur due to the ripening of the seeds of our own previous actions that were nourished by self-centeredness. If we seek happiness, we need to subdue the self-centered attitude so that it does not provoke the creation of destructive karma. Ignoring others' welfare only plants seeds of destructive karma on our mindstream, and these lead to our own suffering. On the other hand, if we habituate ourselves with cherishing others and work to benefit them, our actions will be constructive. As a result, these seeds of constructive karma will ripen so that we will encounter pleasant situations and have all conducive circumstances for continuing Dharma practice. According to the Yogācāras, in addition to increasing our compassion and bodhicitta, meditating on the nonduality of subject and object is crucial. This meditation brings the understanding that the subject and object of our perceptions are produced from the same substantial cause—the seed in our foundational consciousness—in order to eradicate the ignorance that propels cyclic existence.

According to the Prāsaṅgika view, to integrate the view with bodhicitta we train ourselves to see that sentient beings as well as their suffering and happiness do not exist inherently. They are not solid things existing independent of all other factors, and their appearance to us as self-enclosed objects that exist from their own side is false. In this view, the chief culprit is self-grasping ignorance. The last three of the nine points of the meditation on Equalizing Self and Others show the falsity of seeing self and others as existing from their own side. In other words, what we call "self" does not exist in its own right; it exists by being merely designated in dependence on many factors, one of them being our perspective. From the perspective of all sentient beings except one (ourselves), what we call "self" is labeled "other." As that is the case, what is so special about me? From the viewpoint of the vast majority of sentient beings our suffering and happiness are considered the experiences of another person, which makes them much less significant. When we understand that exchanging self and others is possible, then others' happiness and suffering become our own, so how can we possibly dismiss them? Contemplating these questions enables us to greatly reduce our self-centered attitude and to increase our care for and engagement with the welfare of others.

Sometimes when we consider engaging the deeds of the great bodhisattvas, our mind is overcome with trepidation. What will happen to *me* if I help others selflessly? At these times, meditating on the lack of an inherently existent self is helpful to dispel this fear and clinging attachment to the self. In addition, contemplating that pain and pleasure, suffering and happiness, all exist as mutually dependent and thus are empty of having their own inherent essence lessens our fear of suffering. In this way, our mind will be more courageous in extending ourselves to others.

Cultivating the compassion observing phenomena and the compassion observing the unapprehendable, which will be explained in chapter 6, changes our perspective. Briefly explained, with compassion observing phenomena we view sentient beings as impermanent and lacking a self-sufficient substantially existent self. Seeking happiness, ordinary beings turn to impermanent phenomena such as their aggregates, as well as people and things in the external environment, in the hopes of finding it. Because these phenomena lack the ability to give them lasting happiness, they remain continually disappointed, disillusioned, and frustrated. Seeing them suffer in this way due to the erroneous self-grasping in their minds increases our compassion for them.

Compassion observing the unapprehendable views sentient beings as empty of true existence. Because they grasp their own self, the selves of others, and all other things as truly existent, ordinary beings believe that such things can give them genuine happiness and are again left disappointed and befuddled. Configuring the world around a truly existent I, they divide others into friends, enemies, and strangers and think that they truly exist in that way. Grasping true existence, sentient beings continuously generate afflictions, which create karma, which in turn leads to duḥkha. Seeing sentient beings in this predicament increases our compassion for them.

Who Can Generate Bodhicitta?

The precious bodhicitta can be newly generated by sentient beings with the physical support (body) of any of the six classes of migrating beings who have faith and regard for the Mahāyāna teachings and for awakening. There is some discussion about hell beings who newly generate bodhicitta, however. There is a story about Śākyamuni Buddha, who, before he became a buddha, was born in a hell realm in a previous life. Some say he generated bodhicitta then, although others assert that he generated the cause of bodhicitta—compassion—at that time, and generated bodhicitta in a later rebirth. Clearly, doing the meditations to cultivate bodhicitta and actually generating it are easier when we have a precious human life.

Regarding the mental support for newly generating bodhicitta, some say it must be either a preparation of the first dhyāna or an actual dhyāna. Others say that serenity is not necessary, although certainly a good degree of concentration is necessary to familiarize the mind with the steps to develop bodhicitta and to change the ingrained habit of self-centeredness to the mind that cherishes others more than self.

In Asaṅga's *Bodhisattva Grounds* and Atiśa's *Lamp of the Path,* it is said that the support of engaging bodhicitta must be one of the Pratimokṣa ethical codes. However, this is considered a special support that is more advantageous but not necessary.

Do buddhas have bodhicitta? In the *Ornament of Clear Realizations*, Maitreya described twenty-two kinds of bodhicitta by way of similes. There he said that the last two are possessed only by buddhas. Seeking the awakening of others, their bodhicitta enables their two form bodies to lead sentient beings to full awakening. Some learned adepts say that buddhas possess bodhicitta by way of fulfillment. That is, although they have attained full awakening, their aspiration for bodhi has not been relinquished; it has been fulfilled. Nevertheless, there are some learned adepts who say buddhas don't have bodhicitta because they have already attained full awakening.

Definite and Indefinite Lineage

There are three lineages or types of beings: those of śrāvaka, solitary realizer, and bodhisattva (Mahāyāna) lineages.[43] Some people are definite in one of the lineages—that is, they will definitely enter a particular vehicle. Other people are indefinite; various conditions will influence which vehicle they enter. An ordinary being who is definite in the Mahāyāna lineage will directly enter the Mahāyāna regardless of the teacher they meet, while an ordinary person who is indefinite in the Mahāyāna lineage may first enter the Śrāvaka Vehicle if they meet a teacher following the Śrāvaka Vehicle, or they may directly enter the Mahāyāna if they meet a Mahāyāna teacher. In other words, there is no certainty which path the person who is indefinite in lineage will initially follow. It depends a great deal on the teacher they decide to follow. However, someone may be definite in the śrāvaka lineage, progress through the five śrāvaka paths to become an arhat, and later enter the Mahāyāna, progress through the bodhisattva paths and grounds, and become a buddha.

Why are some people definite in lineage while others are not? The main factor is what they have come to value and appreciate over many lifetimes. For example, some people may hold compassion and altruism as primary virtues and seek a path that details a step-by-step method to develop them. They may have a very courageous and strong mind that can endure assuming the responsibility to lead all sentient beings to awakening. Such people will probably be attracted to the Mahāyāna. Other people may be more cautious, thinking that there are too many sentient beings to lead them all to awakening, that the Mahāyāna path takes too long or is too difficult, or that the result of the Mahāyāna, full awakening, is too high or is impossible to attain. The mind of such people is not strong at the present moment, and as a result they will think that attaining their own liberation is best.

However, a person's karmic latencies from previous lives and the dedication prayers they made in previous lives may also play a powerful role regarding which vehicle they enter in this life. For example, someone may have followed the Mahāyāna in previous lives and have made strong dedication prayers at that time to meet, learn, and practice the Mahāyāna in all future lives. They may have made strong aspirations to meet fully qualified Mahāyāna teachers and to follow their instructions in future lives. Due to these strong latencies from previous lives, these people will meet Mahāyāna teachers and will naturally want to follow that path. Other people may have followed the Śrāvaka Vehicle in previous lives and, having felt comfortable practicing the Dharma in the way it teaches, dedicated to meet Śrāvaka Vehicle spiritual mentors and practice that vehicle in future lives. They will naturally be attracted to the Śrāvaka Vehicle and enter that.

Can Bodhicitta Degenerate?

Once generated, bodhicitta may degenerate. Although bodhisattvas who are definite in the Mahāyāna lineage will not lose their bodhicitta and fall from the Mahāyāna path, bodhisattvas who are indefinite in the Mahāyāna lineage can. This occurs on the initial level of the path of accumulation before they reach the middle level of that path. It is especially important to guard against anger and frustration, as these are the main causes of abandoning bodhicitta. For example, someone we help may return our kindness by betraying our trust, criticizing us, or blaming us when things go wrong. It is very easy in such situations to get fed up and exasperated, thinking that sentient beings—or even just this one person—are too corrupt, selfish, or unappreciative for our goodwill to affect them in a positive way. Under the sway of anger, we either strike this person from our compassion or abandon the wish to benefit all sentient beings and relinquish the aspiration to attain buddhahood for their sake. Because bodhicitta aspires to benefit *all* sentient beings, omitting even one sentient being from the scope of our bodhicitta constitutes abandoning bodhicitta.

Signs of Irreversibility

On the path to buddhahood, there are forty-four signs of irreversibility that illustrate that bodhisattvas will not turn back from seeking full awakening but will proceed directly to it. A bodhisattva who has attained any of these forty-four signs, such as having turned away from manifest grasping to forms and so forth as truly existent, is a bodhisattva with signs of irreversibility. According to the *Ornament of Clear Realizations*, such bodhisattvas range from the heat level (the first of four levels) of the path of preparation through to the end of the continuum of a sentient being (the moment just before attaining buddhahood). Bodhisattvas on the path of accumulation have stopped interest in their own liberation from manifesting, but they haven't eliminated all propensities to seek only their own liberation and they haven't received a sign of irreversibility.

Attaining irreversibility is supported by attaining fortitude of the non-arising of phenomena (*anutpattika-dharma-kṣānti*), which is a realization of emptiness. This conviction in emptiness buoys bodhisattvas as they continue to work for the welfare of sentient beings; all fear of the path being difficult is banished, for they are fully confident in emptiness. Knowing that there are no inherently existent sentient beings to be liberated from saṃsāra and no inherently existent holy beings to lead them to awakening, bodhisattvas are irreversibly headed to full awakening.

We can often, but not always, tell if a person has excellent qualities by observing how they speak and act. However, some people who have ill intentions act nicely and some people who have kind intentions don't express themselves well. Because we are limited beings who see other people through the veil of our ignorance and afflictions, we cannot clearly distinguish people's qualities and cannot see the signs of irreversibility in others. As our minds become clearer, we'll be able to discern others' excellent qualities.

Bodhisattvas may attain signs of irreversibility at three points of the path. Sharp-faculty bodhisattvas attain them at the earliest on the heat level of the path of preparation, middling-faculty bodhisattvas on the path of seeing, and modest-faculty bodhisattvas on the eighth ground.[44] The irreversible bodhisattvas of the eighth ground and above are a refuge for all beings because their pristine wisdom is close to the tathāgatas' pristine wisdom that knows things just as they are and the tathāgatas' pristine wisdom that knows the varieties of phenomena.

The stains of the self-centered attitude may exist up to the eighth ground, but not after that. By the eighth ground, bodhisattvas have completely overcome any propensity for the individual liberation of an arhat and have also eradicated the seeds of this propensity.

Classifications of Bodhicitta

The *Ornament of Clear Realizations* speaks of several ways to classify bodhicitta: according to its name, its nature, its aim, and similes and accompanying features. The *Ornament of Mahāyāna Sūtras* explains bodhicitta according to its levels. Thinking of bodhicitta from these different viewpoints gives us a broader perspective on this precious mind and how it functions to propel us on the path to awakening and to bring about the happiness of sentient beings.

According to Its Name

Here bodhicitta may be classified as conventional and ultimate:

Conventional bodhicitta is the altruistic intention that is a primary mind held by two aspirations: the aspiration to benefit sentient beings and the aspiration to attain full awakening in order to do so most effectively. This is what is commonly called "bodhicitta" or the "altruistic intention," and most of the following classifications are ways to speak about conventional bodhicitta.

Ultimate bodhicitta is the pristine wisdom in the continuum of an ārya bodhisattva or a buddha that directly perceives the emptiness of inherent existence. In other words, ultimate bodhicitta is the direct perception of the nature of complete awakening that is informed by conventional bodhicitta. While śrāvakas have realized emptiness directly, their realization is not informed or supported by conventional bodhicitta, and so they do not possess ultimate bodhicitta. The ten bodhisattva grounds (*bhūmi*) are divisions of the ultimate bodhicitta.

Ultimate bodhicitta can be understood in two ways. The first is in common with Sūtra as explained above. The second is unique to Tantra: in highest yoga tantra, the fundamental innate clear-light mind that is focused on emptiness is ultimate bodhicitta. The object is the subtlest object—the emptiness of inherent existence—and the mind realizing it is the subtlest subject—the fundamental innate clear-light mind.

Categorizing bodhicitta according to the name given indicates that the division into conventional and ultimate bodhicitta is a terminological division. That is, although given the name "bodhicitta," not all of the subdivisions are actual bodhicitta. In this case, conventional bodhicitta is actual bodhicitta, but ultimate bodhicitta is not, even though it is given the name "bodhicitta." Conventional bodhicitta is so called because it is involved with conventional truths, such as sentient beings, whereas the object of ultimate bodhicitta is ultimate truths.

Conventional bodhicitta exists from the Mahāyāna path of accumulation through the buddha ground (i.e., in the mental continuum of a buddha). Ultimate bodhicitta is a Mahāyāna ārya's primary consciousness that directly realizes the emptiness of inherent existence of full awakening. It exists from the first bodhisattva ground through the buddha ground. Together conventional and ultimate bodhicitta represent the method and wisdom sides of the path.

These two bodhicittas are the essence of the Mahāyāna path and are very precious and amazing. Nāgārjuna praises bodhisattvas (BV 87–88):

> This is indeed amazing, praiseworthy it is;
> this is the excellent way of the sublime;
> that they give away their own flesh
> and wealth is not surprising at all.
>
> Those who understand this emptiness of phenomena
> Yet [also] conform to the law of karma and its effects,
> that is more amazing than amazing!
> that is more wondrous than wondrous!

The first verse speaks of the magnificent qualities of conventional bodhicitta in terms of equalizing and exchanging self and others. That bodhisattvas cherish others to such an extent that they can give away their body—not to mention their possessions—is an amazing quality to be honored. In terms of the method aspect of the path, there is nothing more magnificent than bodhicitta.

The second verse praises ultimate bodhicitta. A bodhisattva with the correct view avoids the two extremes of absolutism and nihilism and is able to live according to the law of karma and its effects while at the same time understand that all phenomena are empty of true existence. In terms of the wisdom aspect of the path, there is nothing more marvelous than ultimate bodhicitta.

According to Its Nature

According to its nature, bodhicitta may be classified as aspiring or engaging:

Aspiring bodhicitta is the wish to attain full awakening for the benefit of all sentient beings.

Engaging bodhicitta is that wish when it is strong enough to motivate us to engage in the bodhisattva deeds and assume the bodhisattva ethical code. Both aspiring and engaging bodhicitta are actual bodhicitta. They will be explained in more depth in chapter 7.

According to the Aim

People may generate bodhicitta in different ways according to how they see themselves leading sentient beings to awakening. Each of these ways requires great self-confidence.

With *monarch-like bodhicitta*, bodhisattvas aspire to become fully awakened buddhas and, like leaders with great capabilities and power, to then work for the welfare of the general population. They think, "Just as a monarch leads others, I will attain awakening first and lead others there."

With *boatman-like bodhicitta*, bodhisattvas progress to awakening together with other sentient beings, just as a boatman rows others across a river and arrives at the other shore at the same time as the passengers. These bodhisattvas think, "Sentient beings and I are in the same boat in the ocean of cyclic existence. I will row them across, and we will reach the other shore of nirvāṇa together."

With *shepherd-like bodhicitta*, bodhisattvas intend to attain awakening after leading others to awakening, similar to a shepherd driving the flock in front of him to the destination. These bodhisattvas think, "I will guide sentient beings to awakening, like a shepherd guides his flock. After they have attained awakening and are safe, I will attain awakening."

Bodhisattvas may meditate on each of these three types of bodhicitta because each one brings out a particular quality in their bodhicitta. Nevertheless, they know that in order to benefit others most effectively, they must attain awakening first and then lead others. Guiding all sentient beings to awakening and later attain awakening or attaining awakening at the same time as all others is not the most effective way to serve sentient beings.

According to Similes and Accompanying Features

By comparing the bodhicitta found on the successive levels of the path to various pure or lovely things around us, we can see how bodhicitta spreads joy to sentient beings and acts as the source of all of a buddha's realizations. Contemplating these poetic similes of twenty-two types of bodhicitta from the *Ornament of Clear Realizations* gives us a vision of the qualities we can develop and realizations we can gain by generating bodhicitta in our hearts and minds and living our lives according to it. Each type of bodhicitta is correlated with a level of the bodhisattva path and has an accompanying feature that enhances it. All twenty-two types of bodhicitta have the same object—sentient beings—and aspect—the wish to protect them from all saṃsāric duḥkha.

1. Found on the small path of accumulation, *earth-like bodhicitta* is accompanied by aspiration. Just as the earth is the basis for planting and growing crops, the aspiration of this bodhicitta makes it the basis for all the virtuous causes of buddhahood and is the source from which all attainments of the bodhisattva paths and grounds arise.
2. Found on the middle path of accumulation, *gold-like bodhicitta* is accompanied by intention. Just as gold is pure and never loses its nature of being pure gold no matter how it is examined, the bodhicitta accompanied by an intention is stable and never loses its character of benefiting others until we attain awakening.
3. Found on the great path of accumulation, *bodhicitta like the waxing moon* is accompanied by a special resolve. Just as the moon gradually becomes brighter and eliminates darkness, the special resolve of

this bodhicitta grows in strength and helps to continuously increase the collections of merit and wisdom as well as virtuous qualities and knowledge, such as the thirty-seven harmonies with awakening.

4. Found on the path of preparation, *fire-like bodhicitta* is accompanied by application to meditate on the similitudes of the three exalted knowers. Just as fire consumes its fuel, with application to meditate on the similitudes of the three exalted knowers this bodhicitta enables bodhisattvas to meditate on emptiness with the union of serenity and insight and to burn all manifest obstructions to the direct realization of emptiness. It eliminates obstructions to knowing the three unborn natures (emptinesses) that are the objects of the three exalted knowers, as follows: (1) The exalted knower of the basis, which is the wisdom of śrāvakas āryas. It realizes the unborn nature (emptiness) of the four truths. (2) The exalted knower of the path, which is the wisdom of ārya bodhisattvas. It realizes the unborn nature of the five paths. (3) The exalted knower of all, which is the omniscient wisdom of buddhas. It realizes the unborn nature of the aspects of all phenomena.

Each of the following ten bodhicittas, from the fifth through the fourteenth, are associated with one of the ten perfections and one of the ten bodhisattva grounds.

5. Found on the first ground, the Very Joyful, *treasure-like bodhicitta* is accompanied by generosity. Someone with a great treasure never suffers from need and is able to fulfill her own and others' wishes. Similarly, this bodhicitta imbued with generosity is able to satisfy the needs of countless sentient beings. In even a single moment of generosity, bodhisattvas' virtue of generosity excels that of śrāvakas. As a result, the Very Joyful bodhisattvas never suffer from a lack of material possessions and bountifully share them with others. With this bodhicitta, bodhisattvas can convince the miserly to be generous.
6. Found on the second ground, the Stainless, *bodhicitta like a jewel mine* is accompanied by ethical conduct. A mine of jewels is filled with pure gems of various colors and sizes. Similarly, bodhisattvas with this bodhicitta engage in the surpassing practice of ethical con-

duct, which is the support of all jewel-like qualities, such as the powers of the Buddha.

7. Found on the third ground, the Luminous, *ocean-like bodhicitta* is accompanied by fortitude. Like a perfectly still, great ocean, this bodhisattva, who has a surpassing practice of fortitude, is never disturbed and remains calm no matter how much he suffers or is harmed by fire, weapons, and so forth.
8. Found on the fourth ground, the Radiant, *vajra-like bodhicitta* is accompanied by joyous effort. Just as a vajra is immoveable and unshakable, this bodhisattva, who has a surpassing practice of joyous effort, is never discouraged or shaken from her goal due to her firm conviction in unsurpassable awakening.
9. Found on the fifth ground, the Extremely Difficult to Overcome, *mountain-like bodhicitta* is accompanied by meditative stability. Just as a mountain is stable and does not move no matter what external forces are present, owing to her surpassing practice of meditative stability this bodhisattva can easily remain in firm concentration undistracted by the appearance of true existence.
10. Found on the sixth ground, the Approaching, *medicine-like bodhicitta* is accompanied by wisdom. Just as medicine cures all diseases, this bodhicitta, which is imbued with a surpassing practice of wisdom, cures all afflictive obscurations, such as attachment, and all cognitive obscurations as well.
11. Found on the seventh ground, the Gone Afar, *bodhicitta like a virtuous guide* is accompanied by skillful means. A virtuous guide or spiritual master is skilled in working for the benefit of disciples and subduing their afflictions. Similarly, a bodhisattva with this bodhicitta has the surpassing practice of skillful means, such that she never relinquishes the welfare of sentient beings and skillfully dedicates even a single moment of virtue so that it becomes infinitely great.
12. Found on the eighth ground, the Immovable, *bodhicitta like a wish-fulfilling gem* is accompanied by unshakable resolve. Someone who possesses this gem is able to fulfill all wishes by praying to it. Similarly, a bodhisattva with the surpassing practice of unshakable resolve can fulfill all his own and others' aims.
13. Found on the ninth ground, Excellent Intelligence, *sun-like bodhicitta*

is accompanied by power. Just as the sun ripens plants, this bodhisattva, who has a surpassing practice of power, ripens the virtues of sentient beings by the four ways of maturing disciples.

14. Found on the tenth ground, the Cloud of Dharma, *bodhicitta like a melodious voice* is accompanied by pristine wisdom. Just as someone with a melodious voice draws others to himself and pleases them with his voice, a bodhisattva with this bodhicitta has the surpassing practice of pristine wisdom that she uses to attract and please sentient beings with her interesting and pleasing teachings on ultimate and conventional reality.
15. Found on the three pure grounds, *monarch-like bodhicitta* is accompanied by the first five superknowledges. Just as a monarch who fulfills his or her duties properly has power and is able to benefit the populations of the land, this bodhisattva is skilled in the first five superknowledges and thus is strong, unshakable, and can manifest in many forms or display supernormal powers in order to benefit sentient beings according to their various dispositions and needs. Just as a monarch's decisions are clear and definitive, bodhisattvas with this bodhicitta clearly and correctly know what to abandon and what to practice and do not let realizations already attained go to waste.
16. Found on the three pure grounds, *treasury-like bodhicitta* is accompanied by the collections of merit and wisdom. Just as the royals' valuables are found in their treasury, one with this bodhicitta acquires the valuable collections of merit and wisdom that lead to the form body and truth body of a buddha in order to fulfill the needs of sentient beings. In the same way that the royal treasure is not easily exhausted, this bodhisattva's virtue—which is sustained by the accumulations of merit and wisdom—cannot be devastated by wrong views and so forth.
17. Found on the three pure grounds, *bodhicitta like a great path* is accompanied by the thirty-seven harmonies with awakening. Just as all travelers of the past, present, and future who are going to a magnificent land follow a great path, all ārya bodhisattvas of the three times go to buddhahood by means of practicing the thirty-seven harmonies with awakening.

18. Found on the three pure grounds, *bodhicitta like a conveyance* is accompanied by compassion and insight. Just as someone driving an excellent carriage is able to reach her destination easily and without danger, a bodhisattva with this bodhicitta excels in great compassion and insight into emptiness. He will reach the destination of awakening easily and without the danger of falling to the two extremes of saṃsāra and the personal peace of an arhat's nirvāṇa.
19. Found on the three pure grounds, *fountain-like bodhicitta* is accompanied by retention and confidence. Coming from a constant source, fountain water is inexhaustible. Similarly, those with this bodhicitta have concentration that has the capacity to retain whatever they have learned, are learning, and will learn about what the Buddha has taught, is teaching, and will teach in the ten directions. Confidence causes them never to be exhausted.
20. Found on the tenth ground, *bodhicitta like a lovely voice* is accompanied by the celebration of the four seals. Just as one with a lovely voice pleases all who hear, a buddha pleases all those seeking liberation by giving inspiring teachings on the four seals.
21. Possessed only by a buddha and found in the continuum of the enjoyment body, *stream-like bodhicitta* is accompanied by the universal path. A stream flows naturally and without interruption; it does not discriminate who drinks from it, and it tastes the same to and refreshes all who drink its water. Similarly, by the power of compassion and wisdom, one with this bodhicitta realizes the nonduality of subject and object and spontaneously engages in diverse activities to benefit sentient beings. Buddhas dedicate their body, speech, and mind equally to all sentient beings without partiality. Their aid is available to all who wish to receive it.
22. Possessed only by buddhas and found in the continuum of the emanation body, *cloud-like bodhicitta* is accompanied by the truth body. Just as in space a cloud appears and showers rain that makes plants grow, in the space-like mind of a buddha, the cloud of bodhicitta forms and, by performing the twelve deeds of a buddha and giving teachings, realizations grow in the minds of sentient beings.

According to Its Levels

Maitreya's *Ornament of Mahāyāna Sūtras* (5.2) speaks of the bodhicitta present on various levels of the path:

> Bodhicitta on the various levels is held
> To be accompanied by aspiration,
> pure special resolve, full maturity
> and the elimination of all obscurations.

The *bodhicitta of aspiration* or *belief* is found on the paths of accumulation and preparation. Of the twenty-two types of bodhicitta mentioned above, the first four are considered the bodhicitta of belief or faith. Of these, the first three are from the path of accumulation and the fourth is from the path of preparation. Generated by having faith and receiving teachings, this bodhicitta is called the "bodhicitta of belief" because bodhisattvas on the first two paths believe and think that all phenomena are empty of true existence, but they do not yet have direct realization of emptiness.

The *bodhicitta of pure special resolve* is found in the bodhisattvas from the first through the seventh grounds and includes seven of the twenty-two types of bodhicitta—the fifth through the eleventh. This bodhicitta is so-called because the bodhisattvas who possess it have direct realization of emptiness.

The *fully ripening bodhicitta*, which includes nine of the twenty-two types of bodhicitta (the twelfth through the twentieth) is found in bodhisattvas of the three pure grounds (eighth, ninth, and tenth). These three grounds are called "pure" because these bodhisattvas have purified all afflictive obscurations. The fully ripening bodhicitta is so-called because all aspirational prayers and dedication are ripening, and these bodhisattvas are about to attain the fully ripened result of full awakening.

The *bodhicitta free from obscurations* is found only in buddhas who are free from both the afflictive and the cognitive obscurations. These are the twenty-first and twenty-second types of bodhicitta. Nevertheless, the last three bodhicittas are subsumed under the category "the Buddha's bodhicitta," as the preparation, actual, and final bodhicitta of a buddha. *Bodhicitta like a lovely voice* is the preparation because the tenth ground is a preparation for full awakening. *Stream-like bodhicitta* and *cloud-like bodhicitta* are the actual and final bodhicittas of a buddha.

REFLECTION

Reflecting on bodhicitta according to the twenty-two analogies and according to its four levels will give us a good sense of how bodhicitta grows and deepens as bodhisattvas progress through the paths and grounds.

1. What type of bodhicitta is present with each path and ground and what is the activity of each bodhicitta?
2. How does each successive type of bodhicitta differ from the previous one? What does each type of bodhicitta do for the bodhisattva or buddha who possesses it?
3. How does each type of bodhicitta, which is the method aspect of the path, relate to the wisdom realizing emptiness, which is the wisdom aspect of the path?
4. Sit quietly and let your mind be inspired by knowing that there are beings who have generated such bodhicitta and that you can also generate it in the future.

6 | Homage to Great Compassion

WHETHER WE FOLLOW a religion or not, everyone appreciates compassion. Compassion is one of our first experiences as newborn infants, when our parents, doctors, and nurses welcomed us into this world with compassion. Others compassionately protected and cared for us and kept us alive when we were children. Compassion is a basic emotion, found even in animals. It arises naturally in us when beings we see as dear are suffering.

While this commonly shared compassion exists in all of us, it differs from the great compassion that Mahāyāna practitioners cultivate. Ordinary people extend compassion toward friends, family, and others who care about and help them. This compassion is usually biased and conditioned. It depends on how others treat us and is reserved for those we have cordoned off from the mass of sentient life and consider "dear ones."

At present our compassion is limited in several ways: We feel compassion only when we see someone whom we care for suffer. We have a lesser degree of compassion when we hear of strangers suffering, and for people we don't like, we may even rejoice, thinking that they are now getting a taste of their own medicine.

Our compassion is also limited in that it arises for those experiencing the duḥkha of pain—what all sentient beings consider as undesirable—but not for those who are young, healthy, rich, successful, talented, powerful, artistic, athletic, or attractive. Thinking that they are not suffering, we don't feel compassion for them. We forget that they are imprisoned in saṃsāra owing to afflictions and polluted karma, and we neglect to consider that they're experiencing the duḥkha of change and the pervasive duḥkha of conditioning.

Bodhisattvas, however, have compassion for these people, for they know that all sentient beings are submerged in the three kinds of duḥkha. Although people who are considered successful in worldly terms may not be experiencing gross suffering—the duḥkha of pain—at this moment, due to their ignorance and afflictions they are creating the causes to have such suffering in the future. Recognizing this, we cease to glorify or envy the wealthy, the powerful, and the famous. Not only do they often have great mental suffering, but through attachment, anger, and confusion, they create the causes for future duḥkha. Bodhisattvas see beyond the superficial appearances of this life and see sentient beings' actual situation in saṃsāra, which is truly terrifying. Their compassion arises naturally and impartially for all these people.

While we ordinary beings may have compassion for the poor and sick who live in other places, when we are in the same room with them, our disgust with their physical appearance or our fear of their illness or poverty squelches any compassion that may arise. We must remember that all these sentient beings, no matter their appearance during this life, want to be happy and free from pain, just like us. Furthermore, all of them have been kind to us in this or previous lives and will be kind to us in future lives.

The great compassion of bodhisattvas does not depend on whether others act kindly toward them or behave in ways that they approve of and appreciate. Great compassion extends to all beings equally and unconditionally. Spiritual practitioners who aspire to be bodhisattvas must consciously cultivate this compassion. It doesn't arise by praying to the Buddha or by sitting in a machine that alters our brain waves.

Compassion Is the Root of All Goodness

In his homage at the beginning of the *Supplement*, Candrakīrti says (MMA 1–4c):

> Śrāvakas and solitary realizers arise from the excellent sages (buddhas);
> the excellent sages are born from bodhisattvas;
> the mind of compassion, nondual awareness,
> and bodhicitta—these are the causes of bodhisattvas.

Compassion alone is seen as the seed
of a Conqueror's rich harvest, as water that nourishes it,
and as the ripened fruit that is the source of long enjoyment;
therefore, at the start I praise this compassion.

Like a bucket in a well, migrators have no autonomy;
first, with the thought "I," they cling to a self;
then, with the thought "mine," they become attached to things;
I bow to this compassion that cares for migrators.

[Homage to that compassion for] migrators
seen as evanescent (fluctuating) and empty of inherent existence
like the reflection of the moon in rippling water.

In this homage, Candrakīrti does not praise the buddhas and bodhisattvas, as we might expect, but instead praises great compassion, the attitude that wants to completely protect all the sentient beings wandering in saṃsāra under the control of afflictions and karma, and to lead them to liberation and buddhahood. There is great meaning to unpack in these inspiring verses. The first two verses praise great compassion without differentiating different types of compassion; the last two verses praise compassion by means of pointing out three types of great compassion.

The first lines of the homage say:

Śrāvakas and solitary realizers are born from the excellent sages
(buddhas);
the excellent sages are born from bodhisattvas . . .

Śrāvakas and solitary realizers are born from buddhas in that they hear teachings on the four truths and the twelve links of dependent origination from the buddhas. By contemplating and meditating on these teachings, they fulfill their spiritual aims and attain arhatship. "Śrāvaka" is translated as "listen and hear," and these practitioners are so called because they listen to correct teachings from others and later cause others to hear that they attained arhatship by saying (MN 27:26), "Birth is destroyed, the holy life has been lived, what had to be done has been done, there is no more coming to any state of being." "Śrāvaka" can also mean "hearer and proclaimer" because they hear about supreme awakening and the path leading to it from the buddhas and then proclaim these teachings to those seeking the Mahāyāna path. We might think that bodhisattvas could then also be considered śrāvakas because they hear and proclaim the Mahāyāna path. However, there is a great difference between them: śrāvakas only hear and proclaim these teachings, whereas bodhisattvas practice and actualize them.

Unlike śrāvakas who can practice the path and become arhats in three lifetimes, solitary realizers amass merit and wisdom for a hundred eons before attaining arhatship. However, unlike bodhisattvas, they lack great compassion, and because of that their collections of merit and wisdom are considered secondary collections and not the fully qualified collections of bodhisattvas that lead to full awakening. Nevertheless, their secondary collections of merit and wisdom that are beyond those of śrāvakas allow solitary realizers to attain arhatship in their last saṃsāric life in the desire realm without depending on the teaching of another master. For this reason, they are called "solitary" realizers. Śrāvakas, solitary realizers, and bodhisattvas all realize the emptiness of inherent existence and meditate with that wisdom to attain the fruits of their respective paths. Śrāvakas and solitary realizers may have immeasurable compassion, but they lack the great compassion that shoulders the responsibility to liberate all sentient beings from saṃsāra.

Buddhas are born from bodhisattvas in the sense that through practicing the path of method and wisdom of the Mahāyāna, an individual bodhisattva will abandon all obscurations, perfect all realizations and excellent qualities, and become a fully awakened buddha. That buddha is in the same substantial continuum of that bodhisattva and thus is born from him or her.

The meaning of "born" in these two cases is different. In the case of śrāvakas and solitary realizers being born from buddhas, the buddhas are the cooperative condition supporting the śrāvakas and solitary realizers so they can achieve their respective awakenings. Although the buddhas themselves do not become śrāvakas and solitary realizers, they enable others to do so by giving them Dharma instructions. In the case of buddhas being born from bodhisattvas, an individual bodhisattva is the substantial cause of the buddha he or she will become upon completing the Mahāyāna. That bodhisattva and that buddha belong to the same continuum.

Another way that a buddha can be born from a bodhisattva is the case of one bodhisattva being a cooperative condition for another bodhisattva to stabilize his bodhicitta. For instance, a senior bodhisattva encourages and instructs a beginning bodhisattva on how to secure and enhance his bodhicitta. When the younger bodhisattva later becomes a buddha, it can be said that the senior bodhisattva was a cause of that buddha because she helped his bodhicitta to expand and flourish.

Of course bodhisattvas are born from buddhas in the same way as śrāvakas and solitary realizers are—by hearing teachings given by buddhas. Candrakīrti specifically mentioned the buddhas teaching the śrāvaka and solitary realizer learners to demonstrate the crucial, indirect role that bodhicitta plays in their attaining arhatship. Even though the śrāvakas and solitary realizers don't generate bodhicitta themselves, their attainments ultimately derive from compassion because the buddhas who taught them the path attained supreme awakening in dependence on bodhicitta, which in turn is derived from great compassion.

REFLECTION

1. In dependence on a buddha's great compassion, those inclined to the Śrāvaka and Solitary Realizer Vehicles receive the teachings that will lead them to liberation from cyclic existence.
2. Because of generating great compassion, those with Mahāyāna inclination will become bodhisattvas.
3. Through practicing the path of great compassion, those bodhisattvas will become buddhas who work for the welfare of all beings.
4. Let your mind rest in reverence for great compassion as the source for all goodness. Generate the aspiration to cultivate such compassion yourself.

The Three Principal Causes of Bodhisattvas

Candrakīrti continues:

> The mind of compassion, nondual awareness,
> and bodhicitta—these are the causes of bodhisattvas.

His understanding is based on a passage by Nāgārjuna in *Precious Garland* (RA 174cd–175):

> If you and the world wish to attain
> unparalleled awakening,
> its roots are the altruistic aspiration to awakening
> firm like the monarch of mountains,
> compassion reaching to all quarters,
> and wisdom not relying on duality.

Here three main causes of bodhisattvas are set out: compassion for each and every sentient being throughout space, nondual understanding that is free from the two extremes of absolutism and nihilism, and conventional bodhicitta, the primary mind that seeks to work for the benefit of all sentient beings and aspires to attain full awakening in order to do so most effectively. These three are said to be causes for a new bodhisattva, one who is now generating bodhicitta and entering the Mahāyāna path of accumulation.

The Mind of Compassion

Many Mahāyāna authors say "compassion" when they mean "great compassion." This may be done to keep the meter of verses they are writing, or just for convenience. When Candrakīrti cites compassion as the cause of bodhisattvas in the above verse, he is referring to the great compassion that finds sentient beings' suffering unbearable and wants to alleviate it and lead them to nirvāṇa. This great compassion, which is possessed only by bodhisattvas, is a cause of bodhicitta.[45] Kamalaśīla tells us (LC 2.45):

> When you have committed yourself to being a guide for all living beings by conditioning yourself to great compassion, you effort-

lessly generate bodhicitta, which has the nature of aspiring to unexcelled perfect awakening.

We will come back to the role of compassion in giving rise to bodhisattvas later.

Nondual Understanding

A question arises: First someone generates bodhicitta and becomes a bodhisattva. Then she trains in the six perfections. Only when she practices the perfection of wisdom does she gain the wisdom free from the two extremes. So how can nondual understanding be a cause for a bodhisattva when it is developed after one has already become a bodhisattva?

The nondual understanding that Candrakīrti refers to here is not an ārya's wisdom directly realizing suchness, where the appearance of subject and object and the appearance of true existence have totally vanished. Rather, it is a conceptual realization of emptiness, an understanding of nonduality cultivated by a practitioner with sharp faculties prior to becoming a bodhisattva. This wisdom is nondual in the sense of being free from the two extremes of absolutism and nihilism. It is an inferential realization of emptiness that has the appearance of subject and object and is not nondual in that sense.

Previously we discussed Mahāyāna practitioners with sharp faculties and those with modest faculties. To review, sharp-faculty bodhisattva-aspirants first establish the correct view of emptiness and then generate bodhicitta. Establishing the correct view of emptiness removes doubt and convinces them that attaining buddhahood is possible. How does this happen? By understanding that all persons and phenomena lack inherent existence, they understand that ignorance is an erroneous consciousness. It can be eradicated by the wisdom realizing emptiness that perceives the opposite of what ignorance perceives. When ignorance is overcome, the afflictions that depend on it cease, as does the creation of polluted karma by the afflictions. In this way saṃsāra comes to an end and nirvāṇa is attained.

With the confidence that arises from knowing that liberation is possible, sharp-faculty bodhisattvas now generate bodhicitta, become a bodhisattva, and commit to follow the bodhisattva path to buddhahood. Before being certain that full awakening is possible, they do not want to make this promise.[46] Candrakīrti spoke of nondual awareness as the second of the three causes of bodhisattva and bodhicitta as the third because he was speaking primarily of sharp-faculty disciples.

A further question comes: Śrāvakas and solitary realizers also generate nondual wisdom, so why is it explicitly mentioned as a cause of bodhisattvas?

Although śrāvakas and solitary realizers cultivate the same wisdom as bodhisattvas, their spiritual aspiration is different: they seek the personal peace of nirvāṇa and, with strong renunciation of saṃsāra and aspiration to attain liberation, enter the Śrāvaka or Solitary Realizer Vehicles. By progressing through their vehicle's five paths, they attain arhatship. Some arhats have compassion and the mind wishing to benefit others, and some also have immeasurable compassion. However, they have strong yearning for their own nirvāṇa, which inhibits their wish to benefit others from being robust and resilient.

In the case of bodhisattvas, their realizations of emptiness and great compassion complement and assist each other. By realizing emptiness, they gain the direct antidote to the afflictions that cause saṃsāra. When they see sentient beings under the sway of afflictions that create the causes of suffering, bodhisattvas' compassion increases dramatically. That stimulates them to meditate on emptiness because the wisdom realizing emptiness is the only antidote that shatters cyclic existence completely. Understanding emptiness not only overcomes afflictions, it also reinforces the positive aspects of the mind, which, in turn, motivate bodhisattvas to deepen their realization of emptiness.

Bodhicitta

Another question arises concerning bodhicitta being a cause of a bodhisattva: Someone becomes a bodhisattva the moment he or she generates stable, uncontrived bodhicitta. How, then, can bodhicitta be a cause of a bodhisattva when it is simultaneous with becoming one? A cause must occur before its result.

Here, the bodhicitta that is said to be the cause of a bodhisattva is not full-fledged bodhicitta; it is the contrived bodhicitta we initially cultivate after meditating on the seven cause-and-effect instructions or equalizing and exchanging self and others. Both contrived bodhicitta and actual, uncontrived bodhicitta have the same observed object—full awakening—

and both have the same aspect—they aspire to attain it. The difference between them is compared to the difference between tasting sugarcane bark and actual sugarcane. Sugarcane bark has a sweet flavor, but it's not the full taste of sugarcane. In the same way, contrived bodhicitta wishes to attain awakening to benefit all sentient beings but lacks the actual experience; it is a rudimentary bodhicitta. Bodhicitta like sugarcane bark is going in the right direction and is a necessary step that leads to the full experience of uncontrived bodhicitta, whereas uncontrived bodhicitta is firmly committed to attaining awakening for the sake of sentient beings.

Compassion is the chief cause of bodhicitta like sugarcane bark, which itself is a cause of actual bodhicitta and of bodhisattvas, so Candrakīrti could have mentioned just two causes of a bodhisattva: bodhicitta like sugarcane bark and nondual wisdom. However, he designated compassion as a cause of bodhisattvas to emphasize its importance at the beginning, middle, and end of our practice.

Compassion as the Root Cause

The buddhas teach the Dharma to sentient beings of all three vehicles, and by practicing these teachings, sentient beings are freed from duḥkha and attain their spiritual aims. Seeing great compassion as the root of this goodness and excellence, Candrakīrti praises it.

> Compassion alone is seen as the seed
> of a conqueror's rich harvest, as water that nourishes it,
> and as the ripened fruit that is the source of long enjoyment.
> Therefore, at the start I praise compassion.

Here, Candrakīrti points to great compassion as the root of the other two causes of bodhisattvas and explains why compassion is important at the beginning, middle, and end of the path to full awakening. To reap an abundant harvest there must be the seed at the beginning, water in the middle, and the ripening of the crop at the end. Similarly, great compassion is likened in importance to a seed, water, and the ripened fruit that together produce the harvest of a buddha's magnificent qualities.

At the beginning, before we have entered the bodhisattva path of accumulation, compassion is like a seed that will grow into all the magnificent qualities of a buddha. Without compassion, bodhicitta cannot arise, but when we view the duḥkha of ourselves and others with compassion, the strong aspiration to protect all sentient beings from the misery of saṃsāra and lead them to full awakening will arise. Based on this, we make the strong, vibrant determination to attain the highest awakening—to become a buddha—in order to lead others to that state. This is bodhicitta. Seeing that to actualize this aspiration we need to amass the two collections and engage in the six perfections—the chief of which is wisdom—we immerse ourselves in these practices and cultivate nondual wisdom. In this way, compassion is the root of the other two causes of a bodhisattva and is the seed that bears the fruit of buddhahood. As Nāgārjuna reminds (RA 378):

> The universal vehicle says
> that all activities should be motivated by compassion,
> and that wisdom will make them pure—
> what sensible person would deride this?

As mentioned above, this order of cultivation—compassion leading to bodhicitta and then to nondual wisdom—is followed by those of modest faculties. Those with sharp faculties first generate compassion, then nondual understanding, followed by bodhicitta. In either case, compassion is the chief motivating force for the development of the other two realizations.

In the middle of our practice, great compassion is likened to water, for once a seed sprouts, it must be carefully nurtured in order to survive and grow. If our bodhicitta is not nourished by compassion, it will degenerate, which would be a great loss for all sentient beings as well as for ourselves. Thinking of the numberless sentient beings who are drowning in saṃsāra and the great length of time that is required to amass the collections of merit and wisdom, we may become discouraged and even relinquish bodhicitta. However, repeatedly generating great compassion nourishes our heart, giving us courage and strength to engage in the bodhisattva deeds and to meditate on emptiness. In this way, great compassion ensures that we will fulfill the two collections of merit and wisdom and complete the path to buddhahood. Compassion keeps our heart connected to the practice so we will not waver in developing all of the vast causes needed to attain full awakening.

At the conclusion of the path, after bodhisattvas have overcome the last vestiges of defilement, great compassion resembles ripe fruit. It spurs the buddhas to continually benefit sentient beings through their awakening activities for as long as saṃsāra remains. With great compassion, buddhas do not remain in their own peaceful nirvāṇa, but turn the Dharma wheel according to the disposition of each and every sentient being so as to enact their welfare. In that way, buddhas become a source of enjoyment and benefit for all beings.

To illustrate the importance and value of great compassion, the *Compendium of the Teachings Sūtra* (*Dharmasaṃgīti Sūtra*) says (LC 3.30):

> Bhagavan, bodhisattvas should not learn many teachings. Bhagavan, if bodhisattvas grasp and know one teaching, they will have all of the Buddha's teachings in the palm of their hand. What is this one teaching? It is great compassion . . . once great compassion exists, all the other bodhisattvas' qualities will appear.

Spend some time contemplating these verses and become convinced of the importance of familiarizing your mind with compassion, bodhicitta, and the nondual understanding of emptiness. Tsongkhapa recommends that we train our mind so the thought automatically arises, "If I wish to become a bodhisattva, my mind must first come under the influence of great compassion. Then in dependence on this, I must generate from the depths of my heart fully qualified bodhicitta. Once I have done this, I must engage in the general practices of bodhisattvas and in particular the profound view, and I will continue these until reaching full awakening." With such intention and determination, our efforts will go in the right direction and will bear the fruit of being able to benefit all beings.

REFLECTION

1. What is the role of compassion in generating bodhicitta?
2. Why does bodhicitta energize us to contemplate emptiness?
3. How can understanding emptiness increase our compassion and bodhicitta?

Compassion Observing Sentient Beings

In the next two verses, Candrakīrti again pays homage to great compassion. I find this section especially powerful for generating great compassion and often meditate on it (MMA 3–4ab).

> Like a bucket in a well, migrators have no autonomy;
> first, with the thought "I," they cling to a self;
> then, with the thought "mine," they become attached to things;
> I bow to this compassion that cares for migrators.
>
> [Homage to that compassion for] migrators
> seen as evanescent and empty of inherent existence
> like the reflection of the moon in rippling water.

In these two verses, Candrakīrti honors and pays respect to three types of compassion: the compassion observing sentient beings, the compassion observing phenomena, and the compassion observing the unapprehendable. All three minds of compassion have both an observed object (*ālambana*) and a subjective aspect (*ākāra*). The observed object is the basic object that the mind focuses on, whereas the subjective aspect is the way the mind relates to that object. All three types of compassion observe sentient beings, and all three have the subjective aspect of wanting to protect them from saṃsāric duḥkha. That is, while observing sentient beings (who are the observed object), the mind of great compassion has a wholehearted determination to protect them from saṃsāric suffering (this is the aspect).

The first compassion observes just sentient beings who are afflicted by one form of duḥkha after another; it does not observe them as qualified by either impermanence or by emptiness. The last two types of compassion focus on sentient beings qualified by specific attributes. Here the wisdom side of the path that involves the realizations of impermanence, selflessness, and emptiness accompanies the method side of the path, adding depth to our compassion.

The observed object of the compassion observing phenomena is sentient beings qualified by momentary impermanence or qualified by lacking a self-sufficient substantially existent I. The observed object of the compassion observing the unapprehendable is sentient beings qualified by being empty of true existence.

"Qualified by" means that a quality appears to that mind through the force of previously having brought that attribute to mind. Before the second compassion can arise in the mind, we must first ascertain that sentient beings are momentarily impermanent; for the third compassion to arise, we must first ascertain that sentient beings lack inherent existence. It is not necessary that these two compassions themselves apprehend sentient beings as impermanent or as lacking inherent existence; the appearance of these attributes to the compassionate mind due to these attributes being previously ascertained is sufficient. This is because one mind cannot have two discordant aspects—one being the wish for sentient beings to be free from duḥkha and the other being either subtle impermanence or emptiness.

Compassion observing sentient beings is a contraction for "compassion observing just sentient beings." Contractions are made for ease of speaking, and "just" in the original term indicates that this compassion observes only sentient beings, not sentient beings qualified by being either impermanent or empty like the other two types of compassion. Compassion observing sentient beings focuses on sentient beings who migrate from one saṃsāric realm to another under the control of ignorance, afflictions, and karma. The process of how we migrate again and again is extensively described in *Saṃsāra, Nirvāṇa, and Buddha Nature*, which explains the four truths and the twelve links of dependent origination. Afflictions are delineated and described in the same book, and karma is explained in depth in *The Foundation of Buddhist Practice*. We ordinary beings live in this unsatisfactory situation; saṃsāra is our daily life although we seldom recognize it for what it is. Understanding it well is the basis for generating compassion.

How does saṃsāra come about? With the thought "I," we cling to the self as an inherently existent person. Whereas the mere I or person exists by being merely designated in dependence on the aggregates, a mental factor called the "view of a personal identity" (*satkāyadṛṣṭi, sakkāya-diṭṭhi*) grasps it to exist inherently, with its own essence that is independent of all other factors.

Viewing the aggregates as under the control of an inherently existent person who regards things as "mine," the view of a personal identity then grasps mine as inherently existent. From this, attachment to what makes *me* happy and anger at what disrupts *my* happiness or causes *me* pain, as well as all other afflictions, arise. We discriminate every person and object we encounter in terms of its ability to bring us happiness or pain; this makes our view very narrow and our actions self-centered. When conjoined with the mental factor of intention, which is karma, afflictions such as craving, hatred, jealousy, pride, deluded doubt, and heedlessness create the paths of action that leave karmic seeds on our mindstream. When these seeds ripen, they influence our future rebirths, what we experience in those lives, our habitual actions, and the type of places where we are born.[47] Seeing how sentient beings are trapped in this cycle of constantly recurring problems inspires us to generate the compassion that cares for migrators.

Six analogies that compare the experience of migrators—sentient beings born in one life after another in different situations in saṃsāra—to a bucket in a well explain how sentient beings suffer in saṃsāra and help to generate great compassion in our minds.[48]

(1) Just as a bucket in a well is tied by a strong rope, sentient beings are tightly bound to cyclic existence by afflictions and karma. While we seek happiness, we are unable to move freely and lack the autonomy to choose what we encounter in life. Although we wish for happiness and freedom from suffering, afflictions such as greed, anger, and confusion overwhelm our minds and we act counter to our own best interests. In addition, governed by our previously created actions, we find ourselves facing many problems and difficulties—personal, social, political, economic, and so forth.

(2) Just as the operator of a pulley moves the bucket in the well, the afflictive mind propels sentient beings into various rebirths where again and again we find ourselves in situations of conflict and pain. Although we see ourselves and others as independent beings who are in control of our lives, in fact afflictions and karma are our overlords and determine our experiences.

(3) Just as the bucket continuously goes up and down in the deep well, sentient beings wander without end in cyclic existence, from the highest formless realm to the lowest hellish realm. We have been born and will continue to be reborn as every type of life form in saṃsāra countless times until we develop the compassion and wisdom that will liberate us.

(4) The bucket descends easily, but great exertion is needed to pull it up again. Similarly, sentient beings easily fall to lower, unfortunate rebirths, but must exert great energy to create the causes and conditions for a for-

tunate rebirth. We can see this in our lives: harsh words, harmful actions, and disturbing thoughts that embroil us in conflicts and cause unfortunate rebirth come easily. Greed and attachment readily involve us in sticky situations that we cannot free ourselves from no matter how much we dislike them. Fortitude and great effort are needed to restrain ourselves from acting out of anger or greed and to consciously change our unproductive emotional responses into ones that lead to good communication. The difficulty in reversing the ease with which sentient beings fall to unfortunate rebirths is reflected in the *Bases of Discipline* (*Vinayavastu*), which says that unfortunate rebirths are as numerous as atoms of the Earth and upper rebirths are as few as the particles of dust under a fingernail.

(5) Just as the bucket goes round and round without a discernable beginning or end, sentient beings cycle through the three sets of thoroughly afflictive links where the end of one and the beginning of another are difficult to distinguish. These three sets refer to the twelve links of dependent origination. They are the paths of afflictions—ignorance, craving, and grasping; the paths of karma—formative actions and renewed existence; and the paths of duḥkha—consciousness, name and form, six sources, contact, feeling, birth, and aging and death. By the power of neutral obscurations, such as ignorance, and meritorious karma, we temporarily wander in fortunate realms. By the power of demeritorious karma, we wander in unfortunate realms for a long time. One set of twelve links is so intertwined with many other sets that it is difficult to distinguish them. This is our experience.

(6) The bucket is constantly battered as it forcefully knocks into the side of the well. It is dented, punctured, and worn down. Likewise, sentient beings are battered by the three kinds of duḥkha—the duḥkha of pain, the duḥkha of change, and the pervasive duḥkha of conditioning. This unbearable duḥkha is our close companion and accompanies all sentient beings—our dear ones, refugees, pets, politicians, movie stars, insects, and so on—wherever we go. The duḥkha of pain is painful physical and mental feelings; the duḥkha of change is the fleeting nature of our pleasure and the ease with which a happy situation transforms into an uncomfortable one. The pervasive duḥkha of conditioning is having a body and mind under the control of afflictions and karma, such that pain can come suddenly without any warning.

Buddhas and bodhisattvas teach us the Dharma, showing us the way to free not only ourselves but all others as well. Being the recipients of their extraordinary kindness and compassion, it's only suitable that we extend compassion and benevolence to others, especially since buddhas cherish sentient beings more than themselves.

To get a deep experience of this meditation, it is necessary to think first that we ourselves are like a bucket, endlessly going up and down, getting knocked around in all the realms of saṃsāric life. If we cannot see the duḥkha in our own lives in saṃsāra, we will not be able to see that of others. Without facing this unsatisfactory experience, it will be difficult to generate stable compassion that is courageous in practicing the path and benefiting sentient beings.

The arising of great compassion depends not only on contemplating that all sentient beings are tormented in saṃsāra but also on seeing all sentient beings as endearing. To do that, freeing ourselves from attachment to friends and animosity to enemies is essential. In addition, we must contemplate sentient beings' kindness to us in this and previous lives. Without training our mind in these perspectives, we risk succumbing to our habitual tendency to be indifferent to the misery of other beings. Bodhicitta will not arise in our minds, and without bodhicitta awakening is not possible. If we lack compassion, both our own and others' well-being face obstacles.

For this reason, repeatedly training ourselves in the seven cause-and-effect instructions and equalizing self and others is essential. Neglecting to meditate on these, yet receiving many tantric empowerments and boasting of meditating on deity yoga, inner heat, and the channels, winds, and drops, fulfills neither our own spiritual aspirations nor the well-being of others.

After meditating on how sentient beings are tormented by duḥkha, and on their kindness so that we can see them as endearing, we then generate the three subjective aspects of compassion that are found in the long meditation on the four immeasurables:

(1) *How wonderful it would be if all sentient beings were free from duḥkha and its causes.* Thinking like this from our heart—not just from our mouth—opens us to imagine all beings—friends, enemies, and strangers—as free from the three types of duḥkha: the duḥkha of pain, duḥkha of change, and the pervasive duḥkha of conditioning. Spend some time imagining all beings as free from all fear, pain, and anxiety. They abide with satisfaction, fulfillment, peace, and prosperity.

(2) *May they be free from duḥkha and its causes.* With this thought, our compassion increases in intensity. We're not simply thinking it would be wonderful if sentient beings were free of duḥkha and its causes; now we are wishing and aspiring that this will come about. Nevertheless, in terms of our engagement, we are still on the sidelines. Although mentally we want sentient beings to be free of duḥkha and its causes, we're not actively participating in bringing that about.

(3) *I shall cause them to be free from duḥkha and its causes.* With this thought, our compassion becomes fearless and unmarred by self-preoccupation. We are determined to become involved, and now our actions will correspond to our aspirations.

With each of the three types of compassion—the compassion observing suffering sentient beings, the compassion observing phenomena, and the compassion observing the unapprehendable—we progressively generate the above three thoughts or subjective aspects. The third thought is the great compassion that Candrakīrti refers to in his homage. From there, generating bodhicitta flows naturally, for in order to free sentient beings from all duḥkha and all of its causes, we must first free ourselves, and that entails realizing emptiness and using that realization to cleanse our mind from all defilements so that we can attain supreme awakening.

REFLECTION

1. Visualize a bucket in a deep well—the rope that binds it, the pulley that moves it, its quick descent, and the enormous effort needed to lift it up again. Imagine it going round and round without any discernable end, being battered as it strikes rocks and debris.

2. Think of sentient beings—yourself and others—as being similar to this bucket. We are bound to saṃsāra by afflictions and karma, afflictions being the root cause of our dire situation. In cyclic existence we go up and down from the highest pleasure to the deepest pain. We easily create the causes to fall to unfortunate rebirths, but it requires great effort to reverse our habits and create the causes for happiness. We go up and down in saṃsāra without discernable beginning or end, and are battered by the

circumstance we meet in each rebirth. Contemplate the confining and confusing situation in cyclic existence.

3. Let compassion for yourself and other sentient beings arise in your mind, and stay one-pointedly on that.

4. Gradually generate the three subjective aspects of compassion: How wonderful it would be if all sentient beings were free of duḥkha and its causes. May they be free . . . I shall cause them to be free . . . Feel each one in your heart.

5. Contemplate that an escape from saṃsāra exists: by cutting through the ignorance that lies at the root of our afflictions and karma, we can stop this cycle and attain peace. Generate bodhicitta—the aspiration to attain the highest awakening in order to help all sentient beings overcome their saṃsāra.

This meditation can be very powerful for developing renunciation and compassion. When we think of ourselves in this situation, the determination to be free arises. This is the meaning of compassion for ourselves. When we think of others experiencing the same thing, compassion for them comes to the fore. This meditation also inspires us to take deep refuge in the Three Jewels: the Dharma is the cessation of duḥkha and the true paths leading to it; how kind the Buddha is to teach us the way to liberation and how kind the Saṅgha is in supporting us on the path.

Compassion Observing Phenomena

The lines "[Homage to that compassion for] migrators seen as evanescent (fluctuating) and empty of inherent existence like the reflection of the moon in rippling water" speak of the second and third forms of compassion: compassion observing phenomena and compassion observing the unapprehendable. Reading those lines as "I pay homage to the compassion that views beings as subject to moment-by-moment disintegration, as fluctuating as the reflection of the moon in water that is being stirred by wind" is paying homage to the compassion observing phenomena. Reading the lines as "Homage to the compassion that views beings who, although appearing to exist inherently, are like the reflection of the moon in water, devoid of inherent existence" is paying homage to compassion of the unapprehendable.

In a clear pool of water shimmering with ripples caused by a breeze, the reflection of the moon appears. The excellent ones who understand its nature understand the impermanence of the reflection and also know that it is empty of being a real moon. Similarly, bodhisattvas under the sway of compassion observe sentient beings suffering in the ocean of the view of a personal identity, which is continuously filled by the vast river of ignorance. The water is stirred by the wind of distorted conceptions, and the reflections of sentient beings' virtuous and nonvirtuous karma are like the moon in the sky that is reflected in front of them. In this way, wise bodhisattvas, observing sentient beings as disintegrating in each moment and as empty of inherent existence, generate compassion for them.

Although the view of a personal identity is a form of ignorance, here Candrakīrti speaks of ignorance as nourishing this view to point out that the ignorance that induces the view of a personal identity is the self-grasping ignorance of phenomena. In other words, based on grasping our aggregates of body and mind as having their own, independent, inherent nature, we then grasp the person, the I, as being a self-enclosed entity with its own inherent nature.

Compassion observing phenomena is a contraction for "compassion observing sentient beings who are designated on just phenomena, such as the aggregates and the like."[49] The collection of aggregates is the referent of the term "phenomena" in "compassion observing phenomena." But the observed object of this compassion is not sentient beings' aggregates; it is sentient beings qualified by impermanence, sentient beings qualified by lacking a permanent, unitary, and independent self, or sentient beings who lack a self-sufficient substantially existent self, depending on whether compassion is affected by an understanding of impermanence; the lack of a permanent, unitary, and independent self; or the absence of a self-sufficient substantially existent self.

What does it mean to say that great compassion observes sentient beings as qualified by subtle impermanence? Sentient beings have had the quality of subtle impermanence since beginningless time, so this quality is not being made up or projected on them. Sentient beings appear impermanent and the mind apprehends them as impermanent. That is, a wisdom that has previously apprehended the momentary impermanence of sentient beings accompanies great compassion. Here "accompanying" means that the wisdom apprehending the impermanence of sentient beings influences the present consciousness of great compassion that has the intense wish to protect sentient beings from all saṃsāric duḥkha. Some learned adepts say that the wisdom knowing impermanence and the mind of great compassion are explicitly conjoined—that is, both of these minds are manifest simultaneously in a bodhisattva's continuum. A bodhisattva now apprehends sentient beings with a compassion that intensely wishes to deliver them from all saṃsāric duḥkha and a wisdom that knows them to be impermanent. Other learned adepts have a different view: they say that the mind of great compassion is manifest, but the wisdom understanding impermanence is a subliminal mind (T. *lkog gyur gyi blo*). Still, these two mental consciousnesses are simultaneous.

Bodhisattvas observe sentient beings as momentarily impermanent, "evanescent . . . like the reflection of the moon in rippling water." The rippling of the water indicates both the gross impermanence of death that all of us are subject to and the subtle impermanence of disintegrating in each moment. The water's nature is to change; it can never remain static. Similarly, sentient beings' bodies, minds, environments, companions, and enjoyments arise and cease in each moment. To get a strong sense of sentient beings' impermanence, imagine a reflection of the moon shimmering in rippling water as the breeze constantly blows. Then think that constant, rippling change is like the unstoppable momentary change of our body and mind in saṃsāra.

Blind to this transitory nature, we cling to the notion that we and everything around us is reliable and unchanging. When a loved one is injured or we receive a terminal diagnosis, when we lose our job or our country is torn apart by war, or when things don't turn out as we wish, we sentient beings suffer. Holding what is impermanent to be permanent makes the mind inflexible; we refuse to accept the reality of a situation that doesn't agree with our expectations. Observing that sentient beings suffer by holding what is impermanent as permanent, bodhisattvas experience compassion for sentient beings.

When we realize that sentient beings change moment by moment, we implicitly know that they do not have a permanent, unitary, and independent self or soul, as asserted by non-Buddhists. If sentient beings are not independent, they must be dependent. In this case, they depend on their aggregates—the body and mind. This dependent self is not a different entity from the aggregates that compose it. Sentient beings are designated just on the collection of their impermanent aggregates. In this context being designated just on the collection of aggregates eliminates sentient beings being separate entities from their aggregates. Sentient beings do not exist apart from their body and mind; they are not self-sufficient substantially existent selves. This is the common selflessness of persons; it is called "common" because it is shared by all Buddhist tenet systems. For Prāsaṅgikas, this is not the final or deepest selflessness.

Saying that the person is designated on just the collection of aggregates means that in order to cognize the person, we have to cognize one of their aggregates. To know that Joe is here, we must either see his body or hear his voice. The meaning of being designated here is not the same as Prāsaṅgikas saying that the person is merely designated in dependence on the aggregates, where "merely designated" indicates that aside from only being imputed by name and concept, the person has no objective existence.

Considering the fact that sentient beings change moment by moment, like the reflection of a moon in water rippling in a breeze, wakes us up to a reality about our lives: there is no lasting or fixed security in saṃsāra. Our bodies and minds—and therefore our identities and our selves—are like the reflection of the moon in rippling water, changing in each moment. Observing that sentient beings grasp impermanent things as permanent and knowing that they suffer intensely because of this will stimulate compassion in our hearts.

When sentient beings appear to our mind as momentarily impermanent or as lacking self-sufficient substantial existence, the quality of our compassion for them deepens. On the one hand, we understand more clearly how and why they suffer by grasping themselves as permanent or as self-sufficient substantially existent persons. On the other hand, we know that they can change and develop their good qualities because they are not fixed, static beings with a substantial self. Seeing their potential increases our compassion for them.

REFLECTION

1. Contemplate that phenomena—the body and mind as well as the sentient beings that depend on them—are in a constant state of flux, arising and ceasing in each moment without respite.

2. Consider how much sentient beings suffer by grasping themselves and everything in saṃsāra as static, secure, and predictable. Make examples from your life and the lives of beings around you.

3. Focus on sentient beings as qualified by momentary impermanence. Generate great compassion aspiring to release these sentient beings, who arise and cease in each moment, from all duḥkha and its causes.

Compassion Observing the Unapprehendable

The phrase *compassion observing the unapprehendable* is a contraction for "compassion observing sentient beings qualified by lacking true existence, which is unapprehendable although it is the conceived object of grasping true existence." In other words, true existence is unapprehendable because it doesn't exist; nevertheless it is the conceived object of the erroneous mind grasping true existence.

Compassion observing the unapprehendable arises after a practitioner meditates on emptiness, when that mind understanding the emptiness of sentient beings informs the compassion wishing to protect all sentient beings from all saṃsāric duḥkha. At that time, the observed object of the mind of compassion is sentient beings qualified by the lack of true existence. Here too compassion does not apprehend emptiness, although emptiness appears to it because the person has previously ascertained sentient beings as empty of true existence.

As with the compassion observing phenomena, some learned adepts say that both the mind of compassion and the mind knowing emptiness are manifest simultaneously, while other learned adepts assert that the mind of great compassion is manifest and the wisdom understanding emptiness is subliminal. Both agree that these two mental consciousnesses are simultaneous and that the aspect of emptiness appears in dependence on the practitioner who possesses compassion having first ascertained sentient beings as empty of true existence.

In this way, preceded and supported by an inferential realization of the emptiness of true existence of sentient beings, compassion observing the unapprehendable views sentient beings qualified by their emptiness of true existence, like the reflection of the moon in water. Previously, to illustrate the compassion observing phenomena, the analogy of the moon's reflection in water emphasized the transient nature of sentient beings: just as the reflection of the moon in rippling water is constantly changing, so too are sentient beings. Now, in the context of the compassion observing the unapprehendable, the analogy emphasizes the illusory nature of sentient beings: just as the moon reflected in water falsely appears to be a real moon, although it isn't, sentient beings falsely appear to be truly existent, although they are not. If we reach over and try to touch the moon in the pond, we will be disappointed because a real moon is not there. If a space mission sends an astronaut to walk on the moon in the pond, the mission will fail because there is only the false appearance of the moon. Similarly, although all persons appear to be "real," having their own essential nature that makes them who they are, they are actually reflections of their previously created karma. We are continually baffled, depressed, and upset when illusion-like people and things do not fulfill our expectations that they should be predictable and reliable.

Recall the analogy: the water corresponds to the ocean of the view of a personal identity that grasps I and mine as truly existent. This ocean is fed by the powerful river of ignorance grasping the five aggregates to exist truly. While sentient beings struggle to stay afloat, the powerful winds of distorted conceptions agitate the water where sentient beings appear as reflections of their virtuous and nonvirtuous karma. They lack true existence, yet unaware of this fact, they continue to grasp themselves and all other phenomena as truly existent and generate afflictions that bind them in saṃsāra. Seeing sentient beings as qualified by being empty of true existence, and knowing that they suffer due to grasping themselves and everyone and everything around them as truly existent entities, bodhisattvas generate strong compassion wanting sentient beings to be free from ignorance, afflictions, and polluted karma, and all the duḥkha that these cause.

Although there is no moon in the water of a still pond, the reflection exists as a dependent arising, the product of the water, moon, and light coming together in a certain arrangement. Just as there is no truly existent person in either the body or mind or in the collection of the two, a person still exists. The I is a dependently arising product of conceiving and designating the person in dependence on the collection of physical and mental aggregates.

Compassion observing the unapprehendable is not content to wish sentient beings to be free from duḥkha; it actively engages in ways to reduce and eventually eradicate their duḥkha and its causes. Taking the meaning of compassion to heart increases our respect and admiration for great compassion and for the bodhisattvas who possess it. It also stimulates us to see sentient beings as bodhisattvas do and to respond with the same love and compassion. Because the buddhas cultivated such great compassion as well as the wisdom realizing emptiness, they attained buddhahood and continue to turn the wheel of Dharma to benefit us sentient beings. As such, Buddhapālita admires them:[50]

> Though seeing transmigrators as empty,
> because you wish to remove their suffering
> you have toiled for a long time.
> This is most amazing!

The great bodhisattvas and the magnificent buddhas do not see us transmigrating sentient beings as truly existent, "concrete" personalities, yet they are concerned with our welfare and work for our benefit. Let's emulate these great beings!

Compassion observing the unapprehendable enables bodhisattvas to know that realizing emptiness is not antithetical to having compassion for sentient beings. That is, emptiness does not mean that sentient beings are nonexistent; it means they lack inherent existence, a false type of existence. That the wisdom realizing emptiness and great compassion are not only compatible but necessary for bodhisattvas is apparent in Nāgārjuna's *Praise to the Supramundane* (*Lokātītastava*, LS 2):

> That apart from the mere aggregates
> no sentient being exists, you uphold.

Yet, great sage, you continue to remain
perfectly immersed in the welfare of beings.

The first two lines affirm that sentient beings do not exist separate from their physical and mental aggregates. Rather, the person is understood on the basis of and in dependence on the collection of the physical and mental aggregates. Similarly, all phenomena are understood only on the basis of the coming together of the parts that constitute them.

Buddhapālita expresses the same meaning in another way. In his commentary on chapter 22 of Nāgārjuna's *Treatise on the Middle Way*, he makes this challenge: If phenomena exist inherently, in their own right, what need is there to characterize them as being dependent on other factors? If they possess an inherent reality, when we ask, "What is the true referent of a term?" we should be able to point to one thing and say, "This is it." However, this is not the case. We are able to understand things only in the context of their dependence on other things.

Does that mean there are no suffering sentient beings who are worthy of compassion because no sentient being can be found when searched for among the aggregates or separate from them? In the third and fourth lines, Nāgārjuna praises the Buddha for being completely immersed in working for the well-being of sentient beings despite the fact that sentient beings are not findable under ultimate analysis. Sentient beings exist dependently. Similarly, duḥkha is empty of inherent existence yet exists dependently. Thus sentient beings exist and are worthy of our compassion, and we must strive to relieve their duḥkha. The Buddha instructs Śāriputra in a Perfection of Wisdom sūtra:

> When bodhisattvas mahāsattvas cultivate the perfection of wisdom, there are no sentient beings. However, a continuum of empty [mind] is designated "sentient being." O Śāriputra! Bodhisattvas mahāsattvas rely on the two truths—conventional truth and ultimate truth—in order to teach sentient beings. O Śāriputra! Although sentient beings are intangible in either truth, bodhisattvas mahāsattvas practice the perfection of wisdom and use the power of skillful means to teach sentient beings.

Although sentient beings lack inherent existence, they exist by being merely designated in dependence on their aggregates, especially the continuum of their mental consciousness. Their emptiness is an ultimate truth; their nominal, dependent existence is a veiled or conventional truth. They are empty yet exist dependently. These two attributes are compatible, not contradictory. The two truths are perceived by different types of minds—ultimate truth is known by the probing awareness realizing emptiness, veiled truths are known by a conventional reliable cognizer. When ārya bodhisattvas abide in meditative equipoise on emptiness, they do not perceive any conventional objects, including sentient beings; they perceive only emptiness. However, that does not negate the conventional existence of sentient beings, whom ārya bodhisattvas perceive as illusion-like in the postmeditation time. They have great compassion and work for the benefit of these illusion-like sentient beings; the realization of emptiness nourishes the bodhisattvas' compassion. Nāgārjuna says in *Commentary on Bodhicitta* (BV 63, 73):

> In brief, the Buddha taught that agents,
> actions, and consequences
> are, in conventional terms,
> empty things generated from empty things . . .
>
> In this way, when yogis practice
> meditating on that emptiness,
> without a doubt, they grow attached
> to the well-being of others.

Here "attached to the well-being of others" means bodhisattvas care deeply for the welfare of sentient beings.

Sentient beings are burdened by saṃsāric suffering because they grasp themselves and all phenomena as truly existent. This grasping can be eliminated and their duḥkha ceased. Thus the duḥkha they currently experience is unnecessary. It is not predetermined or unavoidable; it exists only because its root cause—self-grasping ignorance—exists, but this cause can be eradicated so that it never returns. Viewing sentient beings this way arouses intense compassion that seeks to liberate them from unnecessary misery and its causes. This strengthens the resolve to attain buddhahood to be fully capable of guiding them to awakening.

Seeing sentient beings as empty of existing from their own side protects compassion and altruism by preventing afflictions from arising when we seek to benefit them. If we see sentient beings as truly existent, our relationships with them could easily become complicated. We may expect them to follow our advice and to appreciate our guidance, or we may be attached to the outcome of our efforts. By remembering that no inherently existent person is there, our mind is freer to meet situations freshly, as the Buddha prescribed in the *Diamond Sūtra* (*Vajracchedikā Prajñāpāramitā Sūtra*):

> Subhūti, what do you think? You should not maintain that the Tathāgata has this thought, "I shall take living beings across." Subhūti, do not have that thought. And why? There are actually no living beings taken across by the Tathāgata. If there were living beings taken across by the Tathāgata, then the Tathāgata would hold the existence of a self, of others, of living beings, and of a life. Subhūti, the existence of a self spoken of by the Tathāgata is no existence of a self, but common people take it as the existence of a self.

Inherently existent living beings do not exist, even conventionally, even though common people believe they do. However, living beings who arise dependently do exist; it is these living beings that the Tathāgata takes across to freedom.

Compassion in the continuum of someone who has not realized impermanence or emptiness does not necessarily focus on permanent, unitary, and independent sentient beings. It often focuses just on sentient beings—that is, sentient beings who are not qualified by either momentariness or emptiness. Even in the mindstreams of those who have realized impermanence and emptiness, their compassion frequently focuses on mere sentient beings, not on sentient beings qualified by either of those characteristics. For example, someone who has realized emptiness may have compassion for the unapprehendable when her mind of compassion is explicitly conjoined with wisdom apprehending emptiness, but at another time her compassion may observe mere sentient beings.

All three types of compassion have the aspect of wanting to protect all sentient beings from all duḥkha, and the great bodhisattvas possess all three. Such great compassion differs from the compassion of śrāvakas and solitary realizers. Bodhisattvas' compassion does not just wish sentient beings to be free from duḥkha and its causes, it also wants to be actively involved in making this happen, and thus it leads to the generation of bodhicitta.

While the third compassion depends on a deep understanding of emptiness, in general compassion and emptiness are cultivated separately. The former involves transforming the mind into the entity of compassion; the latter entails realizing an object not previously known: emptiness, the nature of reality. These require different types of meditation. Compassion will not automatically arise in our minds from realizing there is no inherently existent self to be attached to. We must also contemplate sentient beings' duḥkha as well as their kindness and see them as endearing by following one of the methods to generate bodhicitta.

Nevertheless, an understanding of emptiness deepens our compassion and vice versa. For example, when I sit down to teach I notice that everyone in the audience appears to me to exist from their own side, not through the power of thought. They appear to be "out there," each person on their own seat. I remind myself that this is a false appearance, that none of them are either inherently one with or separate from their body-mind. Looking out at everyone, I see that each person is thinking, "I, I, I," as if they had their own inherent essence and that is who they really are. This mistaken view brings forth their afflictions, which create polluted karma that leads them to experience difficulties in this life and in future rebirths in saṃsāra. Seeing that, I cultivate compassion.

Candrakīrti's homage to great compassion is most precious and profound. I hope you feel joyful in learning about it and will keep it in your heart as an invaluable treasure.

REFLECTION

1. Investigate how sentient beings exist: Are they one and the same as their aggregates? Are they completely different from their aggregates? Con-

clude that they cannot be found in either way when searched for with ultimate analysis.

2. Contemplate how much these sentient beings suffer because they grasp inherent existence and generate afflictions based on this ignorance. All this suffering is unnecessary because phenomena do not exist with an inherent nature, from their own side.

3. Focus on sentient beings who do not exist inherently. These sentient beings are like illusions—appearing to exist inherently but actually existing dependently. Let the great compassion arise that wants to release them from all duḥkha and its causes.

Combining Wisdom and Compassion

Compassion observing the unapprehendable is a powerful example of one way that bodhisattvas combine wisdom and compassion in their practice. Sharp-faculty Mahāyāna disciples first gain an inferential cognizer of the emptiness of inherent existence. This gives them the confidence that defilements can be removed from the mind and awakening attained. On this basis, they meditate on one of the two methods to generate great compassion and bodhicitta. Mahāyāna practitioners with modest faculties first develop faith in the Buddha, Dharma, and Saṅgha through reading the scriptures and accepting the teachings because the Buddha explained them. On that basis, they generate compassion and bodhicitta. For them, the realization of emptiness comes later, and compassion observing the unapprehendable only thereafter.

Try to become a sharp-faculty disciple whose faith is based on reasoning, not just thinking that the teachings are true and awakening is possible because the Buddha said so. Apply reasoning to understand emptiness and then gain deeper understanding of the ultimate nature without remaining content to simply understand it intellectually. Some old and infirm people may have little choice but to follow the path on the basis of faith because physical liabilities now prevent them from engaging in deeper studies. But when you are healthy and have the ability to do so, study well and follow the path without hesitation, just as sharp-faculty practitioners do. Disparaging yourself by thinking you lack intelligence or potential is ignorant and self-sabotaging. So is thinking that you cannot cultivate sharp faculties in this life but must be born with them. Without falling prey to fallacious or discouraging thoughts, make yourself into a sharp-faculty disciple and cultivate your potential to become a buddha.

When we examine our situation, it is clear that all our destructive emotions arise based on false appearances. Things appear to exist objectively, and we assent to that appearance and grasp them to exist in that way. Even scientists are changing their ideas about external objects. Quantum physicists now believe that external objects don't exist objectively but depend on the observer. It seems that they are approaching the Yogācāra view, which asserts that although blue and the mind perceiving blue appear to be substantially different and unrelated, they do not exist in that way. The appearance of duality between the subject and object of a perception is false. In fact, the blue does not exist as an external object but is a reflection of the latency to perceive blue. This latency exists on the foundation consciousness and gives rise to both the subject—the visual consciousness perceiving blue—and the blue color that is the object of this perception.

Prāsaṅgikas explain the ignorance that underlies these false appearances differently but agree that things appear to exist objectively, "out there," independent of the mind. We ignorantly grasp them to exist in this way. This leads to distorted conceptions and inappropriate ruminations that exaggerate the desirable or undesirable qualities of objects or project qualities that aren't there. This, in turn, gives rise to attachment, anger, and other afflictions. Nāgārjuna explained this process clearly.

The American scientist Aaron Beck, who was instrumental in the development of cognitive therapy, has worked for decades with clients whose minds are very disturbed by anger. He once told me that the object we get angry at—usually another person—appears to us to be completely negative. But 90 percent of this negativity is actually mental projection. This accords with what Nāgārjuna stated in chapters 18, 22, and 24 of the *Treatise on the Middle Way*. That some scientists are coming to some of the same conclusions as Buddhist sages is intriguing.

Although Yogācārins assert that external things do not exist objectively, they say that our internal feelings and consciousnesses are truly existent. Madhyamaka philosophy disagrees; Nāgārjuna and Candrakīrti both say that the apprehending subject and the apprehended object of a cognition do not exist independently.

Within the Madhyamaka system, there is debate whether the object of negation, what we seek to prove does not exist—in this case, true or objective existence—appears to our sense consciousnesses or not. Those who assert that the object of negation does not appear to sense perception—the Svātantrika Mādhyamikas—accept that on the conventional level things exist by their own characteristics—that is, conventionally, things inherently exist. According to them, phenomena lack inherent existence ultimately but not conventionally. For Svātantrikas, the object of negation is true existence, which they say exists neither ultimately nor conventionally. They define true existence as existence without being posited by the force of appearing to a nondefective awareness. A nondefective awareness is a mind free from superficial causes of error, such as having bad eyesight or being under the influence of hallucinogens. They say that two criteria are necessary for things to exist: they must appear to a nondefective consciousness and be designated by mind. Grasping true existence is apprehending things as existing by appearing to a nondefective awareness without their also being designated by mind.

Prāsaṅgika Mādhyamikas, on the other hand, assert that even conventionally there's no objective existence—neither external objects nor our internal experiences of pain and pleasure have their own, independent essence. It's clear from our experience that things appear to have some objective existence, but Prāsaṅgikas say that appearance is false. Candrakīrti makes the point in his *Supplement* that if you assert that phenomena exist by their own characteristics, then ultimate analysis should establish veiled (conventional) truths. In other words, when you analyze the entity of phenomena with reasoning, you should find some essential nature. However, when we search with reasoning for such an inherent essence in phenomena, nothing can be found.

Through our own experience, we know that external objects as well as internal feelings and mental states affect us; they benefit or harm us. But if we actually search within their parts or their bases of designation, we discover that the way they exist is not the way they appear to exist. They don't exist from their own side, objectively, independent of all other factors. External objects and internal experiences exist, but if we search for their identity, we cannot find anything that we can point to as being them. The more we search for the objects in our environment or for our subjective, internal experiences, the clearer it becomes that they do not have any objective existence from their own side, even though they appear to.

How, then, do they exist? Only by convention. They exist nominally, merely in name. When we don't search for them they appear, but when we analyze to seek their essence, there is nothing to be found except the emptiness of any inherent essence.

Although the quantum physicists agree that nothing exists objectively, when it comes to the observer, they don't know what to say. If Yogācāras say that external things don't exist objectively, they should also say that internal experiences don't exist objectively. How can there be a difference in the mode of existence between the two? Prāsaṅgikas, on the other hand, negate the true existence of both the perceiving subject and perceived object. They say there's no other way that external and internal phenomena can exist except nominally, by convention, by being merely designated. That alone is the way phenomena exist. Seeing that things exist by being merely designated is very powerful. The more you think about it, the more you'll understand its significance.

The understanding that things exist by being merely designated tallies with reality. It is an awareness of reality. Afflictions, on the other hand, arise due to distorted conceptions, which, in turn, are rooted in grasping true existence. Nāgārjuna says (MMK 18.5):

> Through ceasing karma and afflictions there is nirvāṇa.
> Karma and afflictions come from conceptualizations.
> These come from elaborations.
> Elaborations cease by (or in) emptiness.

Karma comes from afflictions, which depend on distorted conceptions. Distorted conception is the aspect of our mind that exaggerates the positive or negative qualities of an object or person, or projects good or bad qualities that the object or person lack. These conceptualizations are rooted in the ignorance that grasps true existence, a mental factor that grasps phenomena to exist objectively, inherently, from their own side.

Grasping at true or inherent existence apprehends inherently existent objects that don't exist, whereas the wisdom realizing emptiness apprehends the opposite: the emptiness of inherent existence. This is the way that phenomena actually exist. That is, grasping inherent existence is a mental state that is discordant with reality, whereas the realization of emptiness accords with how phenomena exist.

In short, phenomena appear to us to exist objectively. Even though that appearance is false, self-grasping ignorance holds phenomena as having some objective existence. But when we search for the inherently existent object that ignorance grasps, we can't point to anything that is it. Instead we find their emptiness. Since phenomena do exist, there is only one way they can exist—as mere name, mere designation, nominally. There is nothing existing from the side of the object; things exist in dependence on the mind conceiving and designating them.

When we understand that grasping true existence is not in accord with reality, whereas the awareness that phenomena exist nominally is in accord with reality, we see the possibility to overcome afflictions and attain true cessation. That is done by applying the antidotes that can eradicate the self-grasping ignorance that is the root of the afflictions. The principal antidote is the wisdom realizing emptiness. This wisdom will overcome not only ignorance and afflictions but also cognitive obscurations, which are the latencies of ignorance and the mistaken appearances it produces.

In his commentary on the *Ornament of Clear Realizations*, Haribhadra spoke of two powerful characteristics of bodhisattvas: With wisdom they focus on awakening, and with compassion they focus on sentient beings. But even before we become bodhisattvas, if we are sharp-faculty disciples our wisdom can understand emptiness and know that it is possible to eliminate the afflictions as well as all other obscurations.

When we understand this, we can also clearly see that the ignorance grasping true existence and its latencies bind sentient beings in saṃsāra and impede their becoming buddhas. Although sentient beings have the possibility of overcoming these defilements, they are ignorant of their potential and thus continue to create polluted karma under the influence of afflictions. In this way their saṃsāra, with all its attendant duḥkha, continues without any end in sight. Although sentient beings do not want suffering, they are unaware that afflictions dominate their minds and that on a daily basis afflictions instigate them to create the causes for duḥkha. As a result, sentient beings sink deeper into saṃsāra. Seeing this desperate situation, how can compassion for sentient beings not arise?

If their duḥkha were innate and unavoidable, we could not do anything about it. But that is not the case. Śāntarakṣita says (MA 96):

> Therefore, the intelligent who follow the system of [the Tathāgata]
> will generate intense compassion
> for those believing in tenets
> that are based on mistaken [views].

Unless we have full conviction in the possibility that all afflictions and obscurations can be eradicated and that the counterforce to do this is the wisdom realizing emptiness, our bodhicitta will be weak: we won't feel completely confident that it's possible to attain full awakening, let alone to lead other sentient beings to that state. If we don't gain certainty in this through the path of reasoning, we're left with saying, "This is so because the Buddha said so," or "This is so because my spiritual mentor said so," and there's not much weight in this. If you follow like those with modest faculties, your conviction and understanding will not be stable. You may sometimes find contradictions in the scriptures or the teachings of your spiritual mentor and, not having developed astute wisdom through reasoning, you won't know how to make sense of these and will become confused and doubtful.

But if you are able to follow the Buddha's teachings as the sharp-faculty disciples who follow reasoning do, awakening will be yours and the Buddhadharma will remain for centuries. Even if someone criticizes the Dharma, as a sharp-faculty disciple, you will be able to respond by using reason, just as Nāgārjuna and his followers did. Try to develop the wisdom knowing reality, beginning with a correct assumption, progressing to an inferential reliable cognizer, and finally gaining a wisdom consciousness that knows emptiness directly. As Śāntarakṣita says in *Ornament of the Middle Way* (*Madhyamakālaṃkāra*, MA 75):

> [Those who realize emptiness are] those who know it inferentially
> with reasonings that make [the lack of a real nature] known
> and that cut superimpositions,
> as well as those powerful yogis who know it clearly by direct
> perception.

Śāntarakṣita was one of the seventeen Nalanda masters whose writings are the life force of the Buddhadharma in Tibet. If we follow and practice the teachings by using reasoning as they did, we will sustain the Dharma for a long time, as the great Indian and Tibetan masters have done. They studied all the texts of the Nalanda masters and wrote commentaries on them, using reasoning to explain the points. In *Destiny Fulfilled* (vol. 2), Tsongkhapa advised us not to be partial or superficial when studying the texts of the great masters:

> Therefore, not content with a partial or superficial understanding
> of the treatises of the Invincible Lord of Dharma
> and those of [the great sages] widely renowned in India
> as the six ornaments and two supreme ones,
> I studied them all in great detail.

The invincible Lord of Dharma is Maitreya, also known as Ajita. The Vinaya masters Guṇaprabha and Śākyaprabha are the two supreme ones. Nāgārjuna and Āryadeva are ornaments of the Madhyamaka; Asaṅga and Vasubandhu are ornaments of the Abhidharma; and Dignāga and Dharmakīrti are ornaments of epistemology. Tsongkhapa recommends we study their texts thoroughly and put what we learn into practice, just as he did. What excellent advice!

7 | Aspiring and Engaging Bodhicitta

THE PRECIOUS MIND of bodhicitta is spoken of in many different ways. In the *Ornament of Clear Realizations*, Maitreya calls bodhicitta "mind-generation" and defines it as "the desire to [attain] perfect, complete awakening for others' welfare." It is a mental consciousness that is associated with two aspirations: the first is the causal aspiration that seeks the welfare of others; the second is the assisting aspiration that seeks full awakening. The general understanding is that the causal aspiration occurs first, followed by the aspiration for wakening, at which time the actual bodhicitta is born.

Identifying Aspiring and Engaging Bodhicitta

One way of speaking about bodhicitta is in terms of aspiring and engaging bodhicitta. *Aspiring bodhicitta* is the initial wish to become a buddha in order to benefit all sentient beings. This bodhicitta is generated before making the formal commitment to engage in the bodhisattva deeds by taking the bodhicitta vow. *Engaging bodhicitta* arises when someone follows up on the initial wish of aspiring bodhicitta by taking the bodhisattva vow and making the commitment to create the causes for buddhahood. Aspiring bodhicitta is analogous to wishing to go to Dharamsala; engaging bodhicitta is acting on that wish by buying the air ticket, packing the bags, getting on the plane, and so on.

These two types of bodhicitta are generated sequentially as part of a single substantial continuum of bodhicitta. That is, someone meditates on either the seven cause-and-effect instructions, equalizing and exchanging self and others, or their combined instruction, and when they generate bodhicitta, the continuum of that mind becomes aspiring bodhicitta. When bodhisattvas, upon taking the bodhisattva vow, engage in acts of generosity, ethical conduct, or fortitude, and so forth, the continuity of their bodhicitta becomes engaging bodhicitta. Both bodhicitta and the active practice of the bodhisattva deeds must be manifest to be engaged bodhicitta.

There is some debate on whether bodhicitta is present when an ārya bodhisattva enters meditative equipoise directly perceiving emptiness. Some learned adepts say that during this profound meditation on the path of seeing or path of meditation, aspiring bodhicitta exists in an unmanifest state in the mindstream of the meditator and only emptiness appears to that mind. In short, the substantial continuum of bodhicitta is always present in that individual, and it becomes aspiring or engaging bodhicitta depending on what the bodhisattva is doing.

Other learned adepts say that to be present, a mind has to be manifest. In this case, it is impossible for bodhicitta to accompany a mind of meditative equipoise directly perceiving emptiness because it would be manifest and during meditative equipoise directly perceiving emptiness no conventional phenomenon appears to the mind; only emptiness appears. Therefore they say conventional bodhicitta is not present and does not exist in the bodhisattva's continuum at that time. However, the bodhisattva still possesses bodhicitta because their bodhicitta hasn't degenerated and will manifest in post-meditation time.

It is worthwhile to spend time developing a good understanding of the importance and meaning of bodhicitta with its objects and aspects. When we feel that the time has come to seriously undertake the cultivation of bodhicitta, we may generate contrived bodhicitta in the presence of our teacher. This is called *cultivating aspiring bodhicitta in a ceremony*. This helps stabilize our determination to cultivate bodhicitta.

Later, when we feel capable to train in the four causes for keeping our bodhicitta from deteriorating in this and future lives, we can do the ceremony again in the presence of our teacher and generate bodhicitta with the thought never to give it up. This is called *receiving aspiring bodhicitta with commitment in a ceremony*.

After training the mind in aspiring bodhicitta with commitment, we can take the bodhisattva vow. Our bodhicitta at this time is engaging bodhicitta. Even if we engage in the six perfections with a mind aspiring "May

I become a buddha," or "I will become a buddha," as long as we have not taken the bodhisattva vow, engaging bodhicitta is not yet present in our mindstream. Kamalaśīla says (LC 2:49):

> The initial aspiration thinking "May I become a buddha in order to benefit all sentient beings" is aspiring bodhicitta. Once you have taken the vow and you engage in the collection [of merit and wisdom], the initial aspiration becomes engaging bodhicitta.

Both aspiring and engaging bodhicitta are the thought seeking to attain awakening for the benefit of all sentient beings. Their difference lies in that engaging bodhicitta is present when, conjoined with the bodhisattva vow, a practitioner is engaged in physical, verbal, or mental activities leading to awakening; aspiring bodhicitta is not conjoined with the bodhisattva vow.

Who can generate aspiring and engaging bodhicitta? All those attracted to the bodhisattva practice and of sound mind can generate aspiring and engaging bodhicitta. Optimally, they should have antipathy for cyclic existence, be mindful of impermanence and death, and have trained in wisdom and compassion. In short, they should have studied and practiced the earlier stages of the path in common with the initial- and middle-level practitioners and have some experience of compassion that deeply inspired them.

REFLECTION

1. *Aspiring bodhicitta* is the wish to become a buddha in order to benefit all sentient beings. It is generated before making the formal commitment to engage in the bodhisattva conduct.

2. *Engaging bodhicitta* is the thought to become a buddha to benefit sentient beings that has formally committed to engage in the bodhisattva deeds and create the causes for buddhahood.

3. Reflect on the benefits of bodhicitta, the duḥkha of sentient beings, and their wish to be happy and not suffer. Aspire to become a buddha in order to benefit them.

4. Sentient beings are overpowered by afflictions and karma and as a result

they cycle in saṃsāra. They have been, are, and will be kind to us and are endearing. Reflecting deeply on these two points, generate the aspiration to become a buddha. Make a firm commitment to engage in the bodhisattva conduct in order to benefit sentient beings most effectively.

The Ceremony for Generating Aspiring Bodhicitta

We may have an intellectual understanding of bodhicitta, but to become a buddha the experiential feeling is essential. Once we have even an inkling of that feeling, we can develop it further and transform it into uncontrived bodhicitta. One way to generate the experience of bodhicitta is to undergo the ceremony of cultivating aspiring bodhicitta. The ceremony for receiving aspiring bodhicitta with commitment is the same; the difference is whether your intention is simply to generate aspiring bodhicitta or to make a commitment to not let it decline in this or future lives.

The spiritual mentor in whose presence you generate bodhicitta in a ceremony should have the bodhisattva vow and practice bodhicitta. He or she will guide you in the ceremony. Visualize in the space in front of you the Buddha, his body made of golden light. Think of him as a living being, not a statue or painting. He is surrounded by all the buddhas and bodhisattvas who look at you with delight because you're joining them in generating bodhicitta and dedicating yourself to awakening and to benefiting living beings. Also visualize the great Indian masters: Nāgārjuna, Āryadeva, Asaṅga, Vasubandhu, and others. Think they are holding their precious texts that you can still read and learn. If you follow another Buddhist tradition, imagine the lineage masters from that tradition too. If your own spiritual mentor is not living, imagine him or her as well.

If a spiritual mentor who can perform the aspiring bodhicitta ceremony is not available, you can generate and perform the ceremony alone by visualizing the Buddha and all the buddhas and bodhisattvas in front of you as explained above. Then proceed as follows.

Mentally offer your body, speech, and mind to your spiritual mentors and the Three Jewels. In the presence of all these esteemed beings, recite and contemplate the meaning of the seven-limb prayer. The following are the opening verses of "The King of Prayers: The Extraordinary Aspiration of the Practice of Samantabhadra" from the *Flower Ornament Sūtra* (*Avataṃsaka Sūtra*) (POW 2:64–74). If you prefer, recite verses from *Engaging in the Bodhisattvas' Deeds* (chapter 2 and the beginning of chapter 3).

I bow down to the youthful Ārya Mañjuśrī.
You lions among humans,
gone to freedom in the present, past, and future
in the worlds of ten directions,
to all of you, with body, speech, and sincere mind I bow down.

With the energy of aspiration for the bodhisattva way,
with a sense of deep respect,
and with as many bodies as atoms of the world,
to all you Buddhas visualized before me, I bow down.

On every atom are Buddhas numberless as atoms,
each amidst a host of bodhisattvas,
and I am confident the sphere of all phenomena
is entirely filled with Buddhas in this way.

With infinite oceans of praise for you,
and oceans of sound from the aspects of my voice,
I sing the breathtaking excellence of Buddhas,
and celebrate all of you Gone to Bliss.

Beautiful flowers and regal garlands,
sweet music, scented oils, and parasols,
sparkling lights and sublime incense,
I offer to you Victorious Ones.

Fine dress and fragrant perfumes,
sandalwood powder heaped high as Mount Meru,
all wondrous offerings in spectacular array,
I offer to you Victorious Ones.

With transcendent offerings peerless and vast,
with profound admiration for all the Buddhas,
with strength of conviction in the bodhisattva way,
I offer and bow down to all Victorious Ones.

Every harmful action I have done
with my body, speech, and mind
overwhelmed by attachment, anger, and confusion,
all these I openly lay bare before you.

I lift up my heart and rejoice in all merit
of the Buddhas and bodhisattvas in ten directions,
of solitary realizers, śrāvakas still training, and those beyond,
and of all ordinary beings.

You who are the bright lights of worlds in ten directions,
who have attained a Buddha's omniscience through the stages of awakening,
all you who are my guides,
please turn the supreme wheel of Dharma.

With palms together I earnestly request:
You who may actualize parinirvāṇa,
please stay with us for eons numberless as atoms of the world,
for the happiness and well-being of all wanderers in saṃsāra.

Whatever slight merit I may have created,
by paying homage, offering, and acknowledging my faults,
rejoicing, and requesting that the Buddhas stay and teach,
I now dedicate all this for full awakening.

Now review the steps for generating bodhicitta according to either the seven cause-and-effect instructions, equalizing and exchanging self and others, or the combined instructions. Arouse the bodhicitta in your heart just as the great masters visualized before you have done.

I often offer the aspiring bodhicitta rite using three of my favorite verses.

The first verse is taking refuge, the second is generating aspiring bodhicitta, and the third is dedicating the merit. I will include these here for you to contemplate if you have not yet generated aspiring bodhicitta, and to use as part of your daily practice to renew your bodhicitta if you have (POW 2.73).

> With the wish to free all sentient beings,
> I take refuge at all times
> in the Buddha, the Dharma, and the Saṅgha
> until the attainment of full awakening.
>
> Today in the presence of the awakened ones,
> inspired by compassion, wisdom, and joyous effort,
> I generate the mind aspiring for full buddhahood
> for the well-being of all sentient beings.
>
> For as long as space endures,
> and for as long as sentient beings remain,
> until then may I too abide
> to dispel the misery of the world.

Guidelines of Aspiring Bodhicitta

Because the mind of bodhicitta cherishes others more than self, it runs counter to the well-entrenched self-centered attitude. As we ordinary beings cultivate bodhicitta, and even after we generate spontaneous bodhicitta and enter the bodhisattva path of accumulation, our bodhicitta is fragile and vulnerable to the power of self-preoccupation. Until we reach the middle level of the path of accumulation, our bodhicitta may degenerate and even be lost. To prevent this, after having received aspiring bodhicitta with commitment in a ceremony, follow the four guidelines that prevent bodhicitta from deteriorating in this lifetime. If you follow these, there is no doubt that your bodhicitta will grow.

1. To increase enthusiasm for generating bodhicitta, *repeatedly recollect the benefits of bodhicitta.* Reflect on the great merit you create by generating bodhicitta, the increased ability you will have to be a positive

influence in the lives of people around you and in the world, and the delight of placing yourself firmly on the path to awakening.

2. To increase the intention to become awakened, *generate bodhicitta three times during the day and three times at night.* Dividing the day and the night into three periods each and generating bodhicitta during each of these periods is excellent. It's like regularly eating nourishing food. If this is not possible, at least once in the morning and once at night generate bodhicitta three times. Even if you don't recite the verse, reflecting on the object of intent—awakening—and the motivation for attaining it—to benefit all sentient beings—strengthens your bodhicitta.
3. *Do not give up or neglect the welfare of even one sentient being.* If you develop a negative attitude toward someone—for example, an insect that frightens you or a person who criticizes you—and exclude this person from the scope of your bodhicitta, you are no longer working for *all* sentient beings and your bodhicitta has degenerated.
4. As much as possible, try to *fulfill the two collections of merit and wisdom.* Fulfilling the collection of merit involves engaging in virtuous activities. Fulfilling the collection of wisdom necessitates generating the understanding of the uncommon Madhyamaka view. Because this is difficult, at least maintain the wish and put effort into understanding the Yogācāra system.

To prevent your bodhicitta from deteriorating in future lives, train in four wholesome actions and avoid four unwholesome ones. The unwholesome actions to abandon are the following:

1. *Lying to your abbot or spiritual mentor* makes it impossible for them to trust you or to guide you. Being open and honest with your abbot or abbess and your spiritual mentors enables you to receive and be receptive to their wise advice. Trying to make yourself appear to be someone you're not only muddles the relationship and plants the seeds of destructive karma on your mindstream.
2. *Causing others to regret their virtuous actions* runs counter to a bodhisattva's wish to lead sentient beings to full awakening. Regretting virtuous actions destroys the merit created from doing them.

3. *Criticizing or blaming a bodhisattva* creates impediments in your practice and interferes with that bodhisattva's virtuous actions to be of benefit to others. Bodhisattvas are your role models and criticizing them turns your mind away from their excellent example. Disparaging those who have compassion for all beings is a warning of how twisted your views have become.
4. *Acting with pretension or deceit* in order to receive offerings and service leads you down the malignant path of manipulation and fraud. Pretension is pretending to have good qualities you lack; deceit is covering up your bad qualities.

To prevent and counteract the above unwholesome actions and to preserve your bodhicitta in future lives, practice these virtuous actions:

1. *Abandon deliberately lying to any living being.* Being truthful creates trust, which is an essential quality for harmonious relationships. This remedies the first unwholesome action.
2. *Be honest, straightforward, and sincere with all living beings.* If you do so, they will act similarly toward you. This counteracts the fourth unwholesome action.
3. *Consider bodhisattvas as great teachers and treat them respectfully.* Since knowing who is a bodhisattva is difficult, it is best to treat everyone with respect. Does this mean that we don't point out anyone's harmful actions because they might be a bodhisattva? By differentiating the person and the action, we can say the action is harmful without denigrating the person who did it. This guideline remedies the third unwholesome action.
4. *Directly or indirectly encourage the people who rely on you to seek full awakening.* This is a wonderful way to aid sentient beings and counteracts the second unwholesome action.

We diligently protect our valuables by putting them in a safe at home, a safe-deposit box at a bank, or in other safe places. Bodhicitta is a treasure beyond any worldly money or jewels, so we must protect it assiduously. If we preserve our bodhicitta well in this life, just a small condition will trigger us to remember bodhicitta in future lives. Admiring bodhicitta and manifesting compassion from childhood will definitely be an advantage for our Dharma practice in future lives.

REFLECTION

1. Contemplate each guideline of aspiring bodhicitta. In what way does each one keep your bodhicitta from degenerating in this life? In future lives?
2. Would it help you in your Dharma practice to follow these guidelines? You can try to do so without formally taking them.

Engaging Bodhicitta

During a ceremony in the presence of our spiritual mentors and the Three Jewels visualized in front of us, we may cultivate contrived bodhicitta. Although we may experience a special feeling when generating the aspiring bodhicitta at that time, for most of us this is not genuine bodhicitta, and we have not yet become actual bodhisattvas. The difference between contrived and actual bodhicitta is that the former arises with effort and will later fade, whereas the latter is deep, stable, and continuous. It arises spontaneously whenever a sentient being is brought to mind. The cultivation of uncontrived, genuine bodhicitta requires effort and persistence and may take many months, years, or lifetimes.

Do not become discouraged thinking that you're not making progress or that despite your effort, your bodhicitta is still contrived. Rather, remember the noble and extraordinary qualities of bodhicitta and be willing to familiarize yourselves with it over the course of many years because you know in your heart that this is of real value and meaning in your life.

As your bodhicitta becomes even stronger, you will naturally want to engage in the bodhisattva's deeds—generosity and the other perfections—that lead to awakening. When that wish arises and you start to engage in the bodhisattva deeds conjoined with the bodhisattva vow, engaging bodhicitta is present.

During the ceremony of taking the bodhisattva vow, you promise to observe the bodhisattva precepts from now until awakening. Unlike the various prātimokṣa ethical codes, the bodhisattva and tantric vows are not lost at the time of death but continue with our mental continuum into future lives. Does this mean that we might commit transgressions in a future life even if we are not aware at that time of having received the bodhisattva or tantric vow in a previous life? No, it does not, because we lack conscious awareness of having assumed that vow. However, having received and kept the bodhisattva or tantric vow in a previous life is very advantageous in that it plants the latencies for being able to meet these practices in a future life and receive the precepts again, thus reinforcing the ethical conduct practiced in the previous life.

Most people who take the bodhisattva vow in a ceremony are not yet full-fledged bodhisattvas with uncontrived bodhicitta. As long as you have the aspiration to become a bodhisattva and a buddha and the intention to keep the bodhisattva vow as best you can, taking it is beneficial. The bodhisattva vow in your mindstream is a similitude, not the actual bodhisattva vow, but doing your best to live in accord with the bodhisattva precepts will help you to develop bodhicitta and to conduct yourself like a bodhisattva. When transgressions occur, reciting the *Sūtra of the Three Heaps: The Bodhisattva's Confession of Ethical Downfalls*, together with prostrations to the thirty-five buddhas, is an excellent way to purify.[51] In time you will generate spontaneous bodhicitta and become an actual bodhisattva.

If you admire bodhicitta and want to practice it but are hesitant to take the bodhisattva vow, you can practice living according to the precepts of aspiring and/or engaging bodhicitta without taking them. Mindfulness of your motivations and actions will increase and you will create merit by doing this. Later, when you feel confident and more prepared, you can join an aspiring or engaging bodhisattva vow ceremony.

Becoming a bodhisattva is highly admirable. All the buddhas praise bodhisattvas. Candrakīrti comments that they do so for four reasons. First, being a bodhisattva is a cause of becoming a buddha and thus is precious and profound. In addition, by praising bodhisattvas as the causes of buddhas, we implicitly praise the buddhas as well. Furthermore, new bodhisattvas are like the sprout of a medicinal plant that will bear great fruit as it grows. Finally, others will be inspired to enter the Mahāyāna path to buddhahood by hearing the bodhisattvas being praised. If buddhas praise bodhisattvas, needless to say, we should too!

Taking the Bodhisattva Vow

Regarding those who can generate engaging bodhicitta, Atiśa says in the *Lamp of the Path* (LP 21):

> Those who maintain any of the seven kinds
> of the prātimokṣa ethical codes
> have the ideal (prerequisite) for
> the bodhisattva vow, not others.

The seven kinds of prātimokṣa ethical codes taken for life are those of male and female lay followers, male and female novice monastics, nuns in training, and male and female fully ordained monastics. Maintaining one of these seven ethical codes is a "special support" for human beings who generate engaging bodhicitta. However, desire-realm gods, form-realm gods, and formless-realm gods also can generate engaging bodhicitta, even though they cannot take the prātimokṣa precepts because they are not human beings.

During large Dharma gatherings attended by people who are at various stages of spiritual practice, I often allow all those who see the value of aspiring bodhicitta to generate it during a ceremony. However, those taking the bodhisattva vow must have at least taken refuge in the Three Jewels. Although living in one of the seven types of prātimokṣa ethical codes is the ideal basis on which to receive the bodhisattva vow, it is not required. However, you should have a very strong determination to abandon the naturally negative actions such as killing, stealing, unwise sexual conduct, and lying. Without living in an ethically disciplined way that refrains from gross negativities, it will be difficult for your actions to accord with the bodhisattva vow or to benefit others. The precepts included in the bodhisattva vow are more difficult to keep than the prātimokṣa precepts because they regulate mental activities, not just physical and verbal behavior. For that reason, many people find training in one of the prātimokṣa ethical codes a good preparation before receiving the bodhisattva vow.

There are several ceremonies for taking the bodhisattva vow and a variety of verses that may be recited to do so. The spiritual mentor in whose presence you take the bodhisattva vow should be someone who herself has the bodhisattva vow and practices engaging bodhicitta. Atiśa recommends that this spiritual mentor have specific qualities (LP 23):

> Understand that a good spiritual mentor
> is one skilled in the ordination ceremony,
> who lives by the precepts, and
> has the confidence and compassion to bestow them.

In cases when it is not possible to receive the precepts the first time in the presence of a spiritual mentor, the ceremony may be done by visualizing the buddhas and bodhisattvas in front of you and reciting the verse of taking the bodhisattva vow. This procedure is unique to taking the bodhisattva vow; both the prātimokṣa ethical restraints and the tantric vow must be taken from a spiritual mentor, although a tantric practitioner, after doing the approximation retreat and concluding fire pūjā, can renew the tantric vow by doing the self-empowerment.

The place in which the bodhisattva vow will be given should be decorated in a joyous way befitting a celebration. Participants should bathe and put on fresh clothing and sit respectfully while the spiritual mentor delivers an encouraging talk. Purify and collect merit by reciting the verses of one of the seven-limb prayers mentioned above, and then crouch or kneel and recite after the spiritual mentor a verse to take the bodhisattva vow, such as this one from Śāntideva's *Engaging in the Bodhisattvas' Deeds* (BCA 3.23–24):

> Spiritual masters, buddhas, and bodhisattvas, please listen to what I now say from the depths of my heart. Just as the sugatas of the past have developed bodhicitta and dwelt in the sequential trainings of the bodhisattva, so I too, to benefit migrating beings, will develop bodhicitta and practice the sequential trainings of the bodhisattvas.

As you recite each phrase after the spiritual mentors, think about what you are saying. Make this a living experience in which you generate your deepest aspiration in the presence of your spiritual mentor, the buddhas, and bodhisattvas.

The verse of taking the bodhisattva vow from the *Guhyasamāja Root Tantra*, quoted by Nāgārjuna at the beginning of his *Commentary on Bodhicitta*, is quite powerful:

> All buddhas and bodhisattvas, please give me your attention.[52] Just as the blessed buddhas and the great bodhisattvas have generated bodhicitta, I, too, shall from now until I arrive at the heart of awakening generate bodhicitta in order that I may liberate those who are not liberated, free those who are not free, relieve those who are not relieved, and help to thoroughly transcend sorrow those who have not thoroughly transcended sorrow.

There are three ways of interpreting the phrases "liberate those who are not liberated, free those who are not free, relieve those who are not relieved, and help to thoroughly transcend sorrow those who have not thoroughly transcended sorrow." Examining them reveals many ways of understanding this brief passage that can enrich our meditation on bodhicitta.

Version 1

"Liberate those who are not liberated" refers to liberating sentient beings who have cognitive obscurations; these are śrāvaka arhats and ārya bodhisattvas. "Free those who are not free" indicates freeing sentient beings who have afflictive obscurations. "Relieve those who are not relieved" means to lead to higher rebirth those sentient beings who are inflicted with evident pain and misery, especially those in unfortunate realms. "Help to thoroughly transcend sorrow those who have not thoroughly transcended sorrow" summarizes benefiting the above three groups of sentient beings.

Version 2

This version is in relation to the four truths. "Liberate those who are not liberated" refers to liberating sentient beings who are subject to true duḥkha. "Free those who are not free" means to free sentient beings who are not free from the bondage of the true origins of duḥkha. "Relieve those who are not relieved" is to relieve sentient beings who are not yet relieved from the grasping at true existence by teaching them how to generate true paths. "Help to thoroughly transcend sorrow those who have not thoroughly transcended sorrow" is to enable those who are not endowed with true cessations to have them.

Version 3

This version is explained in relation to four vehicles as set forth in *Laṅkāvatāra Sūtra*. Because sentient beings have diverse inclinations and ways of thinking, different vehicles or paths exist in order to meet their needs.

(1) The vehicle of humans and devas (celestial beings) contains instruction on how to abandon harming others and to help them. Seeking the elimination of pain, it encourages us to have contentment, love, compassion, fortitude, generosity, and other qualities acknowledged as virtuous in the world. This vehicle seeks to eliminate the duḥkha of pain and enables people to attain a good rebirth and have good facilities in this life. Theistic religions fall into this category, as they generally emphasize attaining a pleasurable heavenly state after death by means of living an ethical life and being kind to others.

(2) The vehicle of Brahmā is followed by non-Buddhists who seek rebirth in the form and formless realms. It encompasses the teachings of many ancient Indian schools that emphasize the cultivation of samādhi, serenity, and worldly insight. Worldly insight is insight cultivated on the basis of seeing the coarseness of lower states of mind and the peacefulness of higher states. By seeing the faults of attachment to sense objects—for example, so many problems ensue from trying to procure and protect them—practitioners become disinterested and repulsed by sense objects. They are drawn to focus inwardly and gain mental peace through attaining various levels of samādhi. This vehicle leads practitioners to attain the meditative absorptions of the form and formless realms, which are delineated according to the depth of meditative concentration. For example, those who attain the fourth dhyāna as human beings are free from the duḥkha of pain and the duḥkha of change. They are born as devas in the fourth dhyāna, where they experience only neutral feelings. However, they are not yet free from the pervasive duḥkha of conditioning and continue to cycle in saṃsāra.

(3) The Śrāvaka and Solitary Realizer Vehicles have the goal of being free from all three types of duḥkha and attaining liberation. They seek to eliminate the self-grasping that acts as the basis for all other afflictions. Practitioners accomplish this by cultivating the wisdom realizing emptiness,

which counteracts the self-grasping ignorance. While there are some slight differences between the vehicles of śrāvakas and solitary realizers, broadly speaking they can be classified together because they both seek liberation from all three types of duḥkha, which is gained by eliminating the afflictive obscurations.

(4) The Bodhisattva Vehicle seeks to eliminate not only afflictive obscurations but also cognitive obscurations so that its practitioners attain nonabiding nirvāṇa—the nirvāṇa of a buddha that is free from the extreme of saṃsāra and the extreme of the personal peace of śrāvakas' and solitary realizers' nirvāṇa. These practitioners have the aim of freeing all sentient beings—themselves and others—from all obscurations both afflictive and cognitive.

With this as background, "liberate those who are not liberated" means to liberate those who are not free from the duḥkha of pain—human beings, desire-realm devas, and especially those born in unfortunate realms. This is done by guiding them so that they will abandon the ten nonvirtues and practice the ten virtues, and as a result will take rebirth in fortunate rebirths. This is how a bodhisattva liberates followers of the vehicle of humans and celestial beings.

"Free those who are not free" means to free the followers of the vehicle of Brahmā from the duḥkha of pain and the duḥkha of change. Although followers of the vehicle of Brahmā have renounced sensual pleasures, they are ensnared by craving for the calm of samādhi and for rebirth in the form and formless realms. To be free from this craving and the rebirths it brings, they need to learn and practice the Śrāvaka and Solitary Realizer Vehicles that eliminate all duḥkha completely by overcoming afflictive obscurations.

"Relieve those who are not relieved" refers to liberating those following the Śrāvaka and Solitary Realizer Vehicles from afflictive obscurations by giving them teachings on the four truths and twelve links of dependent origination. When these sentient beings engage in those practices, they will attain nirvāṇa.

"Help to thoroughly transcend sorrow those who have not thoroughly transcended sorrow" indicates leading bodhisattvas—especially those who have attained the ten grounds of the Perfection Vehicle—to the practice of highest yoga tantra. While the fundamental innate clear-light mind is naturally free from coarser levels of mind, sentient beings must learn how to access it and then free it from both afflictive and cognitive obscurations by the practices of highest yoga tantra. In this way, they will attain the full awakening of buddhahood. Here we wish to lead sentient beings to make manifest through the power of meditation the fundamental innate clear-light mind that is freed from the coarser levels of mind, which are called "sorrow" here. By transcending these coarser levels of mind, they will access the innate clear-light mind and use it to realize emptiness directly. In this way, they will quickly become fully enlightened buddhas.

While reciting and contemplating this verse from the *Guhyasamāja Tantra*, recollect all sentient beings and pledge to attain awakening for their benefit. Dedicating all your lives for this purpose is truly worthwhile and rewarding.

The Bodhisattva Ethical Code in the Tibetan Tradition

After receiving the bodhisattva vow, take it yourself each morning and evening by visualizing the buddhas and bodhisattvas in the space in front of you and reciting three times one of the verses for taking the bodhisattva vow, such those cited above.

The bodhisattva vow entails avoiding eighteen root downfalls and forty-six misdeeds. As explained in the Tibetan tradition, the Buddha taught the bodhisattva precepts at different times and they are dispersed among several Mahāyāna sūtras. Asaṅga collected many of these percepts and explained the four root downfalls and forty-six misdeeds in the "Chapter on Ethical Conduct" in his *Bodhisattva Grounds* (*Bodhisattvabhūmi*). The lay practitioner Candragomin (seventh century) condensed this longer explanation and wrote *Twenty Verses on the Bodhisattva Ethical Code* (*Bodhisattva-saṃvara-viṃśaka*). Śāntideva also searched the Mahāyāna sūtras and, drawing principally from the *Ākāśagarbha Sūtra*, he compiled a list of fourteen root precepts, which is found in his *Compendium of Training* (*Śikṣāsamuccaya*). One of the fourteen is almost the same as the first one in Asaṅga's list, so the duplication was removed and Śāntideva added the eighteenth root precept from the *Sūtra on Skillful Means* (*Upāyakauśalya Sūtra*). In short, of the root precepts, numbers 1–4 were gathered by Asaṅga and Candragomin, and numbers 5–18 by Śāntideva. All forty-six auxiliary precepts are from Asaṅga's and Candragomin's texts.

The ethical conduct of bodhisattvas consists of three aspects: refraining from destructive actions, gathering virtue, and benefiting sentient beings. The eighteen root downfalls pertain to the ethical conduct of refraining from destructive actions; the first thirty-four of the auxiliary precepts are included in the ethical conduct of gathering virtue, and the last twelve auxiliary precepts pertain to the ethical conduct of benefiting sentient beings. In this way, keeping all the bodhisattva precepts, both root and auxiliary, fulfills the three types of ethical conduct for bodhisattvas.

The precepts are described briefly below. I recommend studying them in depth; in that way, you will know all the factors involved in a complete downfall or misdeed so that you can avoid them. Asaṅga's *Bodhisattva Grounds* and Candragomin's *Twenty Verses* are good places to start.[53]

While only people who have taken the bodhisattva vow are capable of transgressing these precepts, you will benefit from training yourself to avoid these activities even if you haven't taken the vow. These precepts point out specific activities as well as states of mind to be aware of with mindfulness and introspective awareness. Reciting and studying the precepts helps us to identify which actions to practice and which to abandon. Contemplating the precepts informs us about how to direct our body, speech, and mind so that they are compassionate, wise, and peaceful, like those of a bodhisattva.

The Eighteen Root Bodhisattva Precepts

When a precept has more than one aspect, engaging just one aspect constitutes a transgression of the precept. Abandon these actions:

1. (a) Praising yourself or (b) belittling others out of jealousy for others' possessions, status, or good qualities or with attachment to receiving material offerings, praise, and respect.
2. (a) Not giving material aid or (b) not teaching the Dharma to those who are suffering and have no one else to turn to for help, because of miserliness. When we have the opportunity to help someone who is in deep suffering and is without friends or support by giving material aid or explaining the Dharma to them, we should do it. This does not mean we have to give to every charity or every beggar.
3. (a) Not accepting someone's sincere apology, continuing to be angry at the person and verbally abusing them, or (b) angrily striking or

injuring them. When someone genuinely wants to make amends, we should accept their apology and not continue to hold a grudge.

4. (a) Abandoning the Mahāyāna by saying that Mahāyāna texts are not the words of the Buddha or (b) teaching false doctrines that appear to be Mahāyāna teachings but are not. This involves thinking or saying that bodhicitta is impractical and bodhisattva practices are too vast and difficult to actually practice, and that therefore they could not have been taught by the Buddha, or propagating views that contradict the Dharma and encouraging others to practice false teachings. Doing either of these not only harms us but also has a deleterious effect on others' spiritual practice.
5. Taking things belonging to the (a) Buddha, (b) Dharma, or (c) Saṅgha. This entails taking back, robbing, or embezzling offerings given to any of the Three Jewels, using material given to either an ārya or the monastic community for your own purposes without permission, or borrowing and not returning things belonging to the Saṅgha.
6. Abandoning the holy Dharma by saying that texts that teach any of the three vehicles (the Śrāvaka, Solitary Realizer, or Bodhisattva Vehicles) are not the Buddha's word—for example, criticizing or declaring that any of the Fundamental Vehicle or Mahāyāna teachings are not the Buddha's word or despising the three baskets (Vinaya, Sūtra, and Abhidharma) of any of the three vehicles.
7. With anger, (a) taking the robes of a monastic, beating and imprisoning them, or (b) causing them to lose their ordination and return to lay life even if they have impure ethical conduct—for example, by saying that being ordained is useless.
8. Committing any of the five heinous actions: (a) killing your mother, (b) killing your father, (c) killing an arhat, (d) intentionally drawing blood from a buddha, or (e) causing a schism in the Saṅgha community by supporting and spreading sectarian views.
9. Holding wrong views that are contrary to the teachings of the Buddha, such as denying the existence of the Three Jewels, rebirth, or the law of cause and effect, and so forth. Holding such views makes having confidence in and practicing the Buddhadharma very difficult.
10. Destroying a (a) town, (b) village, (c) city, or (d) large area by means such as fire, bombs or other explosives, pollution, or black magic, with

the intention to harm others. Today, this would be considered a hate crime.

11. Teaching emptiness to those whose minds are unprepared. If we teach emptiness to a person who is not well-trained in the fundamental teachings, especially in the law of karma and its effects, there is the danger that this person will misunderstand the meaning of emptiness and conclude that nothing exists. Teachers must check the mental capacity of students before instructing them.
12. Causing those who have entered the Mahāyāna to turn away from working for the full awakening of buddhahood and encouraging them to work merely for their own liberation from duḥkha. For example, discouraging someone who has interest in the Bodhisattva Vehicle by telling them that practicing the bodhisattva deeds for three countless great eons is too difficult or that there are too many sentient beings to lead them all to awakening. We recommend that they instead seek an arhat's liberation, and as a result of our words, they relinquish bodhicitta.
13. Causing others to abandon completely their prātimokṣa (monastic) precepts and embrace the Mahāyāna. Here we tell a monastic that there is not much benefit in keeping their monastic precepts and it would better if they disrobed and practiced the Mahāyāna. A transgression occurs if they follow this bad advice.
14. Holding and causing others to hold the view that the Fundamental Vehicle does not abandon attachment and other afflictions. For example, telling someone who follows the Fundamental Vehicle that they won't be able to eradicate all afflictions and attain liberation. This could cause the person to hold that erroneous view and give up their efforts to attain liberation.
15. Falsely saying that you have realized profound emptiness and that if others meditate as you have, they will realize emptiness and become as great and as highly realized as you. This hypocritical action involves lying and claiming to possess a realization of emptiness that we do not have.
16. (a) Not giving offerings to the Three Jewels that others have given you to give to them, (b) fining a monastic and thereby obliging him or her to steal from the Three Jewels to pay the fine, or (c) accepting property

stolen from the Three Jewels. These actions involve an abuse of power related to the Three Jewels.

17. (a) Depriving those engaged in serenity meditation of their belongings or of offerings intended for them by giving them to those who are merely reciting texts, or (b) making harmful rules that interfere with monastics' Dharma practice.
18. Abandoning aspiring bodhicitta by resolving to exclude even one sentient being from your bodhicitta. It is important to guard against deep anger and grudges toward any sentient being.

The eighteen root downfalls are closely related to our mental state. For sixteen of them, all four binding factors must be present to commit a defeat. For the other two root downfalls, numbers 9 and 18, only the action itself is required for a defeat to be committed. When a defeat is committed, the bodhisattva vow is lost. Unlike the prātimokṣa vow of a monastic, which cannot be retaken in this lifetime if a defeat has been committed, the bodhisattva vow may be restored in this lifetime by taking it again in the presence of a spiritual master or in the presence of the objects of refuge—the buddhas and bodhisattvas—visualized before you. However, just as it's better not to break our leg than to break it and have it reset, it is better not to commit any of the root downfalls or misdeeds than to engage in them and then purify.

The four binding factors are the following:

1. Not regarding our action as negative, or not caring that it is even though we recognize that the action is transgressing a precept.
2. Not wanting to abstain from the action in the future and wanting to do it again.
3. Being happy and rejoicing in the action.
4. Not having a sense of integrity or consideration during or after doing the action. Integrity is abandoning destructive actions because of respecting our principles and precepts. Consideration for others is abandoning harmful behavior because we don't want to adversely influence others or cause them to lose faith.

If the first binding factor is present—that is, the person doesn't regard the action as negative or even if they do, they don't care—and the other three factors are missing, a medium fault is committed. If the first factor is absent—that is, the person is aware that what they are doing is negative—and the other three factors are present, they commit a lesser misdeed.[54] If all four binding factors are not present, the bodhisattva vow is not lost. Nevertheless, the transgression inhibits the possibility of generating a great store of merit for awakening.

To prevent experiencing the results of transgressing a precept, it is important to purify by employing the four opponent powers—regret, making a determination to restrain from such actions in the future, taking refuge and generating bodhicitta, and engaging in remedial actions.[55] Prostrations to the thirty-five buddhas and the Vajrasattva meditation and recitation are excellent methods to purify the destructive karma created by transgressing precepts.

Only three conditions can make someone lose their bodhisattva vow: holding wrong views that are contrary to the teachings of the Buddha, abandoning aspiring bodhicitta, or committing a root downfall with all four binding factors complete. If none of these is present, the bodhisattva vow is not lost at death and is still present in our mindstream regardless of where we are reborn. Although we may forget the vow in our future life, we can retake it from a spiritual mentor to refresh our memory and our commitment to attaining full awakening in order to benefit all sentient beings.

The Forty-Six Auxiliary Bodhisattva Precepts

The first thirty-four auxiliary precepts that constitute the ethical conduct of gathering virtue are classified according to the six perfections. The seventh group is included in the ethical conduct of helping others.

The bodhisattva auxiliary precepts may be transgressed in three ways: (1) by being under the influence of manifest afflictions, in which case an afflictive fault will be incurred; (2) by being subject to conditions such as laziness or forgetfulness, in which case a nonafflictive fault is incurred; or (3) as a result of legitimate reasons such as sickness or attending to more important activities, in which case no fault is incurred.

Attachment and miserliness are the chief obstacles to practicing generosity. To eliminate obstacles to the perfection of generosity and obstacles to the ethical conduct of gathering virtuous actions, abandon these actions:

1. Not making offerings to the Three Jewels every day with your body, speech, and mind. These could be physical offerings (bowing, circumambulating), verbal offerings (reciting texts or prayers), or mental offerings (contemplating the teachings, having faith in the Three Jewels, remembering their good qualities). The transgression is heavier if it is done with a lack of respect or faith in the Three Jewels or delight in worldly activities.
2. Following thoughts of desire, dissatisfaction, attachment to material possessions, and attachment to signs of respect without trying to oppose them. This mental action is a transgression; if we don't oppose it, we'll soon find ourselves acting out these thoughts.
3. Disrespecting your elders (those who have taken the bodhisattva vow before you). Paying respect to those who have received the bodhisattva vow prior to you helps you to better abide in the vow.
4. Not answering sincerely asked questions that you are capable of answering. When people ask sincere questions—Dharma questions or ordinary questions—you should sincerely answer them. If you don't know the answer, don't humiliate the other person; simply tell them you don't know and refer them to someone who does.
5. Not accepting invitations from others out of anger, pride, or other negative thoughts. Not accepting their invitations denies them the opportunity to practice generosity. If you're busy or the invitation is to a place you'd better not go, it's fine to decline. Abandon declining invitations because you think you're too good to associate with those people or you're angry or spiteful.
6. Not accepting gifts of money, gold, or other precious substances that others offer to you. With anger or ill will, refusing a gift. If you're concerned that accepting an object will create hardship for the giver, that you may become attached to it, or that it was stolen from others, it's fine to decline. Normally, it's good to accept the gift so that the other person can create merit; you can then give it away to someone else.
7. Not giving the Dharma to those who desire it. Refusing to share the Dharma out of miserliness, anger, ill will, or jealousy is counter to cherishing others. Exceptions are if we don't know the teachings or if the person who requests is not a suitable vessel, has a bad motivation, or is disrespectful.

To eliminate obstacles to the perfection of ethical conduct, abandon these actions:

1. Forsaking or scorning a person who has engaged in many destructive actions or who has broken their precepts. If such a person sincerely apologizes or requests help to improve, you should accept. Refusing out of anger, vengefulness, or malice is a lack of compassion on your part.
2. Not acting according to your trainings as it would generate or sustain faith in others. We should keep well whatever prātimokṣa ethical restraints we have taken as well as all the bodhisattva precepts. Our behavior influences others and misbehavior or flagrant neglect of our prātimokṣa precepts could ruin someone's faith in the Dharma.
3. Doing only limited actions to benefit sentient beings, such as strictly keeping the Vinaya rules in situations when not doing so would be of greater benefit to others. For example, not helping someone of the opposite sex who is injured if you're the only person there because it would involve touching them.
4. Not doing the seven nonvirtuous actions of body and speech with loving-compassion when circumstances deem it necessary to benefit others. This is for the spiritually advanced, people whose compassion is so great that they are willing to accept the karmic result of their action. However, spiritually advanced monastics should not transgress their root prātimokṣa precepts; if they truly feel it is necessary to do so, they should disrobe first. Do not misconstrue this bodhisattva precept to rationalize or justify doing negative actions.[56]
5. Acquiring requisites—food, shelter, clothing, or medicine—and other goods by any of the wrong livelihoods of hypocrisy, hinting, flattery, coercion, or bribery. Be honest and appreciative without selfishly exploiting others' generosity.
6. With attachment and excitement, engaging in amusement, entertainment, parties, talking and laughing loudly, and so forth without any beneficial purpose, or leading others to join in these distracting activities. If there is a useful purpose that benefits others without harming your practice, this is not a transgression.

7. Believing and saying that followers of the Mahāyāna should remain in cyclic existence and not try to attain liberation from afflictions. When it is said that bodhisattvas remain in saṃsāra to benefit sentient beings, it does not mean that they do not strive with effort to eradicate all obscurations and attain awakening. Bodhisattvas know that their attaining full awakening is more useful to sentient beings so they work diligently to do that. Ārya bodhisattvas may make emanations that work for the benefit of others in saṃsāric realms.
8. Not trying to overcome disrepute by either admitting our mistake or clarifying the situation if we did not err, or not avoiding actions that would cause us to have a bad reputation. If we have bad habits that provoke others' scorn or aversion, we must work to change them. The motivation for having a good reputation is so that others will trust us and we can help them; it is not attachment to our reputation.
9. Not helping others to correct their destructive behavior when doing so would be helpful. If we can influence someone positively, we should try to. If we don't get involved and let others create negativity because we don't want to lose face or because it is inconvenient for us or we simply don't care, it is a transgression.

To eliminate obstacles to the perfection of fortitude, abandon these actions:

1. Returning insults, anger, beating, or criticism with insults and the like. Practicing fortitude by overcoming anger is crucial at these times. Learn the antidotes to anger;[57] practice them in meditation so that you are familiar with these new perspectives and can apply them when you encounter difficulties.
2. Neglecting those who are angry with us by not trying to pacify their anger. If we have acted in a way that provoked others' anger, even unintentionally, we should do what we can to assuage their anger and upset.
3. Not accepting someone's apology and remaining angry at them. The difference between this and the third root transgression presence is that the four binding factors are present for the root transgression.

4. Following thoughts of anger and not counteracting them by applying antidotes. If you are angry but don't try to calm yourself and instead let the anger increase or harbor resentment, it constitutes a transgression.

To eliminate obstacles to the perfection of joyous effort, abandon these actions:

1. Gathering a circle of friends or disciples because you desire respect or profit. We should not attempt to attract people if our motivation is bad—for example, wanting to impress them in order to receive offerings, become famous, or be respected. Rather, we should give teachings, build monasteries, or work in Dharma centers with a sincere motivation to share the Dharma.
2. Not dispelling the three types of laziness: (1) sleeping excessively and lounging around, (2) being very busy doing worldly activities or harmful actions, and (3) indulging in self-pity or self-criticism that results in discouragement.
3. With attachment, indulging in idle talk and joking. Exceptions are chatting or joking for a good purpose—for example, to connect with someone who feels left out or depressed. Otherwise we should not waste time gossiping or engaging in meaningless conversations just to amuse ourselves.

To eliminate obstacles to the perfection of meditative stability, abandon these actions:

1. Not seeking proper instructions on how to develop concentration. Avoid doing so with pride, thinking you know everything about this subject.
2. Not abandoning the five hindrances: sensual desire, malice, lethargy and sleepiness, restlessness and regret, and doubt. Not learning how to overcome these or not trying to overcome them are transgressions.[58]
3. Becoming attached to the good qualities of meditative absorption after experiencing them. Attachment to the bliss or equanimity of meditative absorption can impede our cultivation of wisdom and attainment of awakening.

To eliminate obstacles to the perfection of wisdom, abandon these activities:

1. Abandoning the scriptures or paths of the Fundamental Vehicle as unnecessary for one following the Mahāyāna. Thinking or saying these teachings are not important or necessary for someone following the Bodhisattva Vehicle is a transgression. In fact, Mahāyāna practice is based on the practice of the Fundamental Vehicle. In addition, bodhisattvas must know and practice these teachings in order to teach Fundamental Vehicle practitioners.
2. Exerting effort principally in the Fundamental Vehicle while neglecting your own tradition, the Mahāyāna. Although we should study and practice the Fundamental Vehicle, beginning to favor it over the Mahāyāna is unwise; this slows our practice in the Mahāyāna and could eventually lead to abandoning bodhicitta.
3. Exerting effort to learn or practice the treatises of non-Buddhists that are not proper objects of your endeavor, or studying them without good reason. Becoming so interested in non-Buddhist practices that we neglect studying, thinking, and meditating on the Mahāyāna is a transgression. However, we can study non-Buddhist philosophies to understand and help practitioners of these religions.
4. Beginning to favor and take delight in the treatises of non-Buddhists while studying them for a good reason. We can study non-Buddhist treatises in order to refute wrong views, but we should not begin to favor these views or become attracted to them because doing so will impede our development of wisdom.
5. Abandoning any part of the Mahāyāna because you don't understand it or think it is uninteresting. This includes criticizing or rejecting essential Mahāyāna teachings—such as the teachings on emptiness and bodhicitta—or thinking it's not possible to develop the wisdom realizing selflessness as taught by the Mahāyāna. This differs from the fourth root transgression, which entails saying a particular Mahāyāna teaching was not taught by the Buddha.
6. Praising oneself or belittling others because of arrogance, anger, and so on. This differs from the first root transgression, which is done with the desire to receive gifts or respect.

7. Not going to Dharma gatherings or teachings due to arrogance or anger. Exceptions are being sick, not knowing the teaching is occurring, suspecting the person teaching doesn't know the topic well, knowing our teacher would not want us to attend, being very learned on that topic already, or if it would interrupt our meditation.
8. Scorning, disrespecting, or being rude to our spiritual mentor, or not paying attention to the meaning of the teachings but picking at faults in the presentation. We need guidance from a living spiritual mentor. If we prefer books and neglect listening to or thinking about our spiritual mentors' teachings, we lose much benefit.

To eliminate obstacles to the ethical conduct of benefiting others, abandon these actions:

1. Motivated by anger or spite, not helping those who are in need—for example, those needing help in making a decision, settling a question, traveling, doing a task, protecting possessions, reconciling with a friend, planning events, and organizing celebrations. Exceptions are if we are ill, have another appointment, are busy doing something more important, lack the knowledge or ability to help or if the activity contradicts the Dharma, the person can complete the task themselves, others are already helping, it is better for the person's spiritual development not to receive help, our help would upset many other people, or the task is counter to our prātimokṣa precepts.
2. Avoiding taking care of the sick due to anger, arrogance, or other afflictions. Exceptions include if we are ill, are already helping another sick person, need to focus on our studies and practice or if the sick person is already receiving help or can do things themselves, we have helped for a long time and the person is getting better, or helping would create negative karma.
3. Not alleviating the sufferings of others out of anger, spite, pride, and so forth. This includes not helping travelers, the distressed, the blind, the deaf, the abused, those who are being trafficked, or those who have lost their job or social position. As people committed to compassion, when we are able to help others or alleviate their suffering, we should.

4. Not explaining what is proper conduct to those who are reckless. People who are careless and not conscientious can't discriminate the wholesome from the harmful. They make bad decisions or engage in actions that are harmful to themselves or others. We should advise them skillfully and make them aware of the possible painful results of their actions. Exceptions are when helping would lead to difficulties, we lack the knowledge to help, a qualified person is already helping, or the person doesn't like us or isn't receptive to help.
5. Not repaying the kindness others have shown to us because of ill will or lack of conscientiousness. When people have helped us in some way or contributed to our welfare, we should have a kind attitude toward them and reciprocate when possible. Exceptions are when we lack the capacity to help, they don't want help, we try to help but aren't successful, and so forth.
6. Not relieving the sorrow of others, not consoling the distressed who are separated from loved ones or have lost their wealth or property as a result of theft or natural disasters. Exceptions are similar to those in previous precepts in this category.
7. Not giving material possessions to those in need—such as food, clothing, and other necessities to the poor and needy who ask for help—out of miserliness, anger, or other afflictions. Exceptions: we don't have what they need, they may misuse the gift, the substances they want are dangerous to them, or others would be harmed.
8. Not working for the welfare of your circle of friends, disciples, relatives, or employees by teaching them the Dharma and helping them materially if needed.
9. Not acting in accordance with the wishes of others if doing so does not bring harm to you or others. We should try to be pleasant, polite, and considerate of others' wishes and feelings and have genuine care for them.
10. Not praising those with good qualities. When others have good qualities, knowledge, or Dharma realizations, we should rejoice and praise them. Similarly, let's rejoice and praise them if they have specific practical skills or artistic or athletic talents and so forth.
11. Not taking corrective action when the situation demands it—for example, when someone is acting harmfully or behaving in a way

detrimental to the Dharma or a Dharma community. When peaceful means do not help, this may entail using strong measures, such as criticizing the person in public or even having him arrested. If we allow them to continue their harmful actions when it is within our ability to stop them, we commit a transgression.

12. Not using psychic powers if you possess them, in order to stop others from doing destructive actions.

REFLECTION

1. Contemplate each precept of engaging bodhicitta. In what way does each one help guide your life as well as your thoughts, words, and actions in a good direction?
2. Would it help you in your Dharma practice to follow these bodhisattva precepts? You can try to do so without formally taking them. For example, pay special attention to live according to the first nine of the root precepts for a week, then do the same for the second nine.
3. Following that, focus on the precepts to eliminate obstacles to the perfection of generosity for a week. Do the same for each subsequent group of auxiliary bodhisattva precepts.

A Kind Heart

In short, developing a kind heart is most important for sustaining life on our planet and improving the quality of life. Needless to say, a kind heart is crucial for our individual spiritual progress. Without affection we will not be fulfilled personally, and without cooperation born from respecting others our communities will not be happy. Affection and compassion are part of our human nature; they go beyond religious precepts. When we are born, our parents' or caregiver's compassion nurtures us. When we die, we feel comforted if a trusted, compassionate person is nearby. Any person, no matter what their religious or political beliefs, responds to kindness and compassion and shares their own affection and compassion with others.

We must increase this feeling in society, and doing that begins with ourselves. Then as individuals we come together to work for the welfare of all. Just as isolated fingers are not very powerful without the central palm, we human beings cannot function well without affection and compassion binding us together. People in every country and walk of life must generate and increase their feelings of kindness and interconnectedness with all others.

Compassion must be deliberately cultivated. It will not arise simply by stilling the mind and developing concentration. Nor will it arise by realizing emptiness, although understanding emptiness will deepen our compassion. We know that sentient beings suffer by the power of their ignorance, and this ignorance can be removed through realizing emptiness. However, we must still practice the causes of compassion as explained in this book, in order to generate it fully and maintain its strength within ourselves.

Some people understand emptiness first and then generate great compassion; others develop great compassion first and then realize emptiness. This is due to differences in their aptitudes. Although understanding compassion is easier than understanding emptiness, actually generating compassion in our mindstream is more difficult than realizing emptiness. These virtuous emotions and attitudes won't appear in us magically by praying to the Buddha. How worthwhile it is to put in effort to cultivate them!

8 | Love, Compassion, and Bodhicitta in Chinese Buddhism

BUDDHISTS OF MANY countries—China, Tibet, Vietnam, Korea, Japan, and so forth—share the Mahāyāna scriptures, teachings, and practices from India. Each tradition has its distinct teachings and interpretations as well. In this chapter, we'll look at some of the ways that love, compassion, and bodhicitta are cultivated in Chinese Buddhism.

Love and Compassion—Prerequisites to Bodhicitta

Chan (Zen) Buddhism says that all sentient beings possess buddha nature, which is by nature pure—"pure" meaning it transcends the duality of purity and impurity. When the buddha nature is fully manifested, that is buddha. However, being obscured by afflictions and defilements, the buddha nature is not presently manifest in sentient beings. Similarly, all sentient beings possess compassion, but our compassion is weak because it is obscured by grasping at self.

Love and compassion are prerequisites for actualizing bodhicitta, the "pure nature." Without having love and compassion for all beings, the aspiration for buddhahood cannot arise, and generating this aspiration is necessary to enter the first of the five bodhisattva paths. Overcoming grudges and forgiving others is very difficult for ordinary people. Someone mired in resentment, spite, and anger has no wish to help the enemy who destroys their happiness. Love and compassion are the antidotes we must cultivate to dispel this hatred.

In Chinese Buddhism, several methods are used to cultivate love and compassion. One is meditation on the four immeasurables. Another is the seven-round compassion meditation, which has its source in Vasubandhu's autocommentary on the *Treasury of Knowledge* (*Abhidharmakośa-bhāṣyam*) in the Chinese canon.[59] This meditation is so called because there are seven rounds and each round consists of seven steps. The seven steps involve contemplating our relationship with seven groups of people:

1. Our elders—parents, grandparents, aunts and uncles, teachers, bosses, people of higher rank, and those who were our elders in previous lives.
2. Our peers—siblings, classmates, friends, associates, coworkers, helpers, and those who were our peers in previous lives.
3. Our juniors—employees, students, children, and people whom we take care of.
4. Enemies of our elders in this and previous lives.
5. Our own enemies in this and previous lives.
6. Enemies of our juniors in this and previous lives.
7. Neutral people with whom we do not have a close relationship in this life.

First step: Recollect with fondness all the elders that you have known during this life. Recall each person who has taken care of you, raised you, taught you, guided you, protected you, and was a good role model. Take your time in doing this. Contemplate the many ways they influenced your life in a positive way. Then think: My elders have done so much for me. They have raised and taught me. They have risked their life for me. They have selflessly helped me, so it would seem natural that I would try to repay their kindness. However, I don't do that. Instead, I often argue with them, make them angry, and cause them to worry. I don't listen to them and I treat them rudely, without appreciating all they have done to help me during my life. I confess and regret this.

Feel this in your heart. Now think of all the merit you have accumulated and dedicate it to all of your elders: I dedicate my merit to these elders. I share with them all the merit I have created in my Dharma practice and all the merit from all virtuous deeds I have done. May my elders' suffering cease and may they attain full awakening.

Then think about all the elders you had in past lives: Just as I have parents and teachers in this life, I had parents and teachers in previous lives. I don't know who they are now because all of us have been reborn. Still, they were kind to me, so I dedicate my merit to return kindness to them whenever and however I meet them in this and all future lives.

Second step: Think in the same way regarding your peers—all the friends and companions you have had during your life. Remember your siblings and childhood friends as well as colleagues, team members, and associates. Reflect: My friends, siblings, and helpers have kept me company. They have befriended me and assisted me when I needed help. My colleagues have worked with me on projects; I worked and played together with fellow team members. It would only be natural for me to help them when they need help, to care about them and comfort them; but instead I have argued with them, competed with them, fought with them, called them names, been inconsiderate, and sometimes even jealous of their successes. On projects we did together, I claimed the success and ignored their contributions. I confess and regret this. Now I dedicate my merit to them. May their suffering be eliminated and may they attain full awakening.

Then contemplate the friends and peers you had in previous lives and think in the same way.

Third step: Recall your juniors. These people look to me for help, education, and guidance. They trust and respect me. I should help them and be patient with them, but instead I lose my temper or get frustrated. Neglecting to treat them fairly, I shout at them and use my authority to humiliate them or to force them to do things. I don't encourage and help them in the best way possible but make sure they are always subordinate to me. I confess and regret this. I dedicate all my merit to them. May they be free from all suffering and attain awakening.

After that, think in the same way with regard to your juniors or subordinates in previous lives.

Fourth step: Think about all the enemies of your elders—all the people who have created nonvirtuous karma with your elders and interrupted their happiness. Reflect: I should be compassionate toward these people, but instead I hold rancor toward them because they harmed the people I care about. I must release my negative feelings and wish them to be happy. May they purify their harmful karma and act constructively. No matter who they are, whether they hurt or cheated my parents, may they be free from suffering and have happiness.

Similarly, if your elders mistreated people, think: May these people toward whom my elders felt malice be free from suffering and have happiness. I dedicate my merit to the enemies of my elders. May they be happy and attain awakening.

Then think in the same way toward those who were enemies of your elders in previous lives.

Fifth step: Consider your own enemies—people who have hurt you, interfered with your happiness, cheated you, lied to you, betrayed your trust, or taken advantage of you. This is the hardest group to generate love and compassion for because it concerns sentient beings who have hurt us directly. Recall all of these beings. Reflect on the suffering they experienced that made them think that hurting you would relieve their misery. Recall that they are saṃsāric beings who are controlled by ignorance, craving, and hatred.

In addition, think of all the people whom you have hurt. Reflect that your bad relationships with others are not just because they have hurt you but also because you have harmed them. Think: I forgive all those who have hurt me. I let go of all hostility toward them. I will not retaliate or do anything to further antagonize them. I regret any harmful words and actions I have inflicted on them. Feel this in your heart. Then think: I dedicate my merit to them, with the wish that they will practice the path and become buddhas. May I help them on the path. Sincerely dedicate your merit to them.

Then think of those who were your enemies in previous lives—whether they harmed you or you harmed them—regret the harm and dedicate your merit for their welfare.

Sixth step: Think similarly toward those who are the enemies of your children, employees, students, and so forth—people who have hurt your juniors or whom your juniors have hurt by bullying them, taking advantage of them, ridiculing them, and so forth. Think: I regret and relinquish any hard feelings I hold toward them. I dedicate my merit to them. May they be free of misery and have happiness.

Then do the same for the people who were enemies of your juniors in previous lives.

Seventh step: Contemplate neutral people—those who have neither helped nor harmed you, those you don't know, whom you pass in the street, or clerks in the store—all those with whom you don't have strong karmic relationships at this moment. Think: I dedicate my merit to them too. May they be happy and free from suffering. May they take refuge in the Three Jewels and become awakened. Think this as well for all those who were neutral in previous lives. In this step there is no confession or regret, because you have not interacted with them. Of course those who are strangers and neutral now could have been friends or enemies in previous lives, and vice versa.

Contemplating the seven steps in this way constitutes one round. The second round is thinking in the same way toward these seven groups, this time in reverse order beginning with neutral people and ending with your elders. The third round is done by going through the seven steps again, this time from your elders to neutral people. The meditation is done, back and forth, in this way seven times, making it the seven-round compassion meditation.

At the conclusion, meditate on emptiness. During the seven-round compassion meditation you think a lot, so at the end make sure to turn the mind to emptiness. Empty your mind of all thoughts, ideas, and grasping at true existence, and keep pure awareness.

Take your time contemplating each step. Really feel others' kindness toward you and your responsibility toward them. Regret the mistakes, misunderstandings, and bad decisions made in these relationships. Cultivate love and compassion for these people and dedicate your merit for their well-being in this and all future lives as well as for their awakening. As you become more familiar with the steps, you will sometimes be able to do them more quickly but with the same depth of feeling. Anyone who practices this compassion contemplation for some months will definitely see a change in their life and relationships with sentient beings.

The four immeasurables and the seven-round compassion meditation are the two standard meditations used to develop love and compassion for sentient beings. The seven-round compassion meditation principally deals with human beings, whereas the four immeasurables concern all sentient beings from all six realms. The four immeasurables covers not only this world system but also all world systems in all directions throughout infinite space. For this reason, the seven-round compassion meditation is usually taught first, followed by the four immeasurables.

REFLECTION

1. Do the seven-round compassion meditation as explained above by contemplating with affection your relationships with your elders, peers, and juniors. Think of their kindness and love for you.
2. Regret when you have treated them poorly.
3. Express the loving and compassionate wishes and aspirations you have for them.
4. Reflect on your relationships with the enemies of your elders, your own enemies, and the enemies of your juniors. Release any anger you may have toward them and wish them well.
5. Reflect on your relationship with neutral people and wish them well.
6. You may want to do purification practice to clear any destructive karma you created with these seven groups of people. This removes obstacles to having sincere positive aspirations for their well-being.
7. Rest your mind in feelings of love and compassion for sentient beings.

Causes and Conditions to Generate Bodhicitta

In "On Generating the Resolve to Become a Buddha," the sixth chapter in Nāgārjuna's *Treatise on the Ten Grounds* (*Daśabhūmikavibhāṣā*), he speaks of seven causes and conditions that facilitate generating bodhicitta: the influence of a tathāgata, observing that the Dharma is on the verge of destruction in our world and wanting to protect it, feeling compassion for sentient beings, receiving instructions from a bodhisattva on how to generate bodhicitta, observing the conduct of a bodhisattva and wanting to emulate it, being inspired after being generous, and being delighted by seeing the signs and marks of a buddha.[60] These are different ways through which a person may generate bodhicitta, depending on his or her disposition and tendencies.

1. The Influence of a Tathāgata

Through his supernormal powers, a buddha is able to see that a person's roots of virtue are sufficiently mature that they are capable of taking on the commitment to become a fully awakened buddha. That buddha then instructs them, "Child of a good family, come forth. You are now capable of bringing forth the resolve to liberate beings from duḥkha and afflictions." In this way the person generates bodhicitta.

2. Observing that the Dharma Is on the Verge of Destruction in Our World and Wanting to Protect It

Thinking about the vast and profound qualities that the Buddha practiced and the hardships he endured as a bodhisattva in order to attain awakening for our benefit, feel grateful and indebted to the Buddha. Be aware that as a result of the degeneration of sentient beings' minds, these precious teachings are on the verge of vanishing in the world. Resolve to plant firm roots of virtue and to generate bodhicitta in order to cause the Dharma to be preserved for countless eons in the future.

3. Feeling Compassion for the Duḥkha of Sentient Beings

Observe sentient beings beset by afflictions, drowning in cyclic existence, experiencing terror and adversity as they cycle in the six realms, separating from their loved ones, encountering happiness infrequently, taking one rebirth after another without any foreseeable end, and having no protector. Find this unbearable and, spurred by compassion, proclaim, "I shall become a protector for those who have no protector. I shall become a refuge for those who have no refuge. I will become one on whom those with no one to rely on may depend. Once I have succeeded in making my way across saṃsāra, I shall endeavor to bring beings across as well. Once I have gained liberation, I shall liberate these beings as well. Once I have succeeded in gaining peace, I shall see that all beings are established in peace as well."

4. A Bodhisattva Instructs Us in Generating Bodhicitta

There are those who, simply by hearing others talk about bodhicitta and full awakening, generate bodhicitta. Sometimes it could happen that they later lack instructions on bodhicitta and the perfections and adopt the path to arhatship instead. But before they attain the stage of the fortitude of the nonarising of phenomena (*anutpattika-dharma-kṣānti*) of the śrāvaka path, they meet an ārya bodhisattva on the seventh to tenth grounds, who knows their faculties and disposition. The Buddha or bodhisattva will then instruct these people again on bodhicitta and the bodhisattva path and, due to the ripening of their roots of virtue, they will again abide in the bodhisattva path upon realizing the stage of the fortitude of the nonarising of phenomena, which is attained with the eighth bhūmi.

5. Observing the Conduct of a Bodhisattva and Wanting to Emulate It

Some people observe how bodhisattvas practice and want to emulate it. They see that bodhisattvas proceed on the path with the protection of compassion, engage in countless beneficial deeds without self-centeredness toward their own body and life, have vast and profound learning and meditation experience, are sources of protection for those afflicted with the misery of cyclic existence, and possess pure minds. Being inspired by the example of these great bodhisattvas, these people think: I, too, want to generate bodhicitta and attain unsurpassed awakening for the welfare of all sentient beings.

6. Inspiration after Being Generous

Some people, when making offerings to the Buddha or the Saṅgha, call to mind the great bodhisattvas of the past who excelled in the perfection of generosity. Being inspired by their example, they immediately generate bodhicitta and then dedicate the merit from their generous action to full awakening.

7. Delight upon Seeing the Signs and Marks of a Buddha

Some people hear about those who have directly seen the thirty-two signs or eighty marks of a buddha. These are physical signs, such as the imprint of the Dharma wheel on a buddha's palms and the soles of his feet, the crown protrusion on his head, and the golden color of his body. They become delighted and inspired by seeing these, and think: I, too, wish to possess these exquisite physical signs and marks so I will practice what these buddhas have practiced and generate the same realizations as they have. In this way, they generate bodhicitta.

People may generate bodhicitta as a result of any of these seven causes and conditions. However, only those who have generated bodhicitta by means of the first three ways—(1) instruction by a buddha who understands their faculties, (2) respecting the Dharma and wishing to protect it in the world, or (3) having strong compassion for sentient beings experiencing duḥkha—will certainly be successful in attaining full awakening. This is because the roots of virtue created by generating bodhicitta in these three ways are very deep.

Those who generate bodhicitta in any one of the other four ways—(1) instruction by a bodhisattva who influences them to generate bodhicitta, (2) having observed the practice of bodhisattvas and been inspired by them, (3) having performed an action of generosity that made them recall bodhisattvas' virtues, or (4) having seen or heard about the physical signs on a buddha's body—are not certain to be successful because their roots of virtue are not firmly established. However, those who practice well will be successful.

Ten Factors to Spur the Generation of Bodhicitta

Sheng'an Shixian (1686–1734), a meditation master and pure-land patriarch, wrote *Exhortation to Resolve on Buddhahood*, in which he expressed the importance of generating bodhicitta, urged the reader to generate it, and gave ten points for reflection to spur the generation of bodhicitta. But first, to encourage us to cultivate bodhicitta purely and perfectly, he discussed eight distinctions in the characteristics of practitioners' aspirations: deviant or correct, genuine or false, great or small, and one-sided or perfect.

Some practitioners do not examine their mind and are very concerned with external matters. Seeking wealth, fame, or sense pleasures, their aspiration is *deviant*. On the other hand, some practitioners are not attached to personal profit, reputation, and pleasure either in this life or the next. Their generation of bodhicitta is *correct*.

We should constantly direct our mind to the Buddha's path and try to benefit sentient beings in every thought by teaching and guiding them. Hearing of all the perfections that need to be practiced for countless eons, we should not become intimidated and retreat but should go forward with courage and confidence. Observing the depth of sentient beings' defilements and the difficulty in teaching and guiding them, we must abandon discouragement and not give in to exhaustion. Like someone climbing a high mountain or building a huge stūpa, we must complete the path to its end. Such bodhicitta is *genuine*.

On the other hand, not purifying our destructive karma or the downfalls from transgressing precepts, being internally confused while acting as if we were clear, undertaking projects with excitement but not completing them, having virtuous thoughts that are mixed with attachment to wealth and reputation, following the virtuous path but remaining defiled with destructive karma—generating bodhicitta on such a basis is called *false*.

When we resolve to maintain our bodhicitta motivation, to keep the bodhisattva vow until all sentient beings are awakened, and to practice until we attain awakening, this is a *great* resolve. On the other hand, if we see cyclic existence like a prison and aspire only for our own liberation without caring for the situation of others, this resolve is *small*.

Thinking that the Buddha's path is separate from and outside of our own mind, we may aspire to become awakened and lead others to awakening but remain attached to our own merit, knowledge, and views. Such resolve is *one-sided*. On the other hand, when we realize that others want happiness and not suffering, just as we do, and that all of us are empty of inherent existence; when we realize that our nature is in line with the Buddha's path and thus aspire to actualize it; and when we see that no phenomenon exists independent of and unrelated to the mind, we are going in the correct direction. When we then generate bodhicitta and take the bodhisattva vow with a mind supported by the wisdom realizing emptiness, when we engage in the perfections with a mind grounded in the understanding of emptiness and do not view emptiness itself as existing by its own characteristics, then our generation of bodhicitta is *perfect*.

By understanding these eight distinctions, we know what constitutes bodhisattva practice and what does not. We must then continuously examine our mind to see if our bodhicitta is deviant or correct, genuine or false, great or small, one-sided or perfect. With mindfulness of this we should then proceed to rid ourselves of the deviant, false, small, and one-sided and cultivate the correct, genuine, great, and perfect. A bodhisattva practice done in this way will certainly be successful.

The ten points for reflection follow. The first five concern mindfulness of the kindness that we have received from the Buddha, our parents, teachers, benefactors, and all sentient beings. Recognizing that we have been the recipient of tremendous kindness inspires in us the wish to repay that kindness, and the most effective way to do that is to generate bodhicitta and practice the bodhisattva path. The remaining five points support and direct our bodhicitta.

1. Mindfulness of the Extreme Kindness of the Buddha

Many eons ago, the person who was to become Śākyamuni Buddha with great compassion generated bodhicitta and practiced the path until he attained buddhahood. Where would we be had he not done this for our sake? How would we learn the Dharma and practice the path in this degenerate age, had the Buddha not vowed to lead us on the sacred path?

When we created destructive karma, the Buddha experienced agony because we were creating the cause for our own suffering. He tried to lead us to virtue with his skillful means, but we were often too obtuse, skeptical, and cynical to accept the teachings or to have confidence in them. When we floundered in unfortunate rebirths, the Buddha was overwhelmed with compassion and wanted to take on our destructive karma and suffering so that we would not have to experience them. However, our karma was so heavy that he could not free us from this torment. When we finally gained a human rebirth, he tried to lead us in the virtuous path and his loving attention never strayed from its focus on us.

When the Buddha was alive, we were sunken in unfortunate rebirths. Now that we have a precious human life, he is in parinirvāṇa. Due to our previously created destructive actions, we have been born in this degenerate time. Yet, due to constructive karma, we have become the Buddha's followers and have the opportunity to practice the Dharma. Due to mental obscurations, we cannot see Śākyamuni Buddha now, but due to virtuous karma and open-mindedness, we can hear the teachings. Understanding the Buddha's kindness and the rare opportunity we have at present, let's generate bodhicitta, accomplish the bodhisattva path, attain buddhahood, and liberate sentient beings from cyclic existence. If we don't do this to repay the kindness of the Buddha, then how else can we repay it?

2. Mindfulness of the Kindness of Our Parents

Our parents gave us this body, which is the support for us to practice the Dharma. They spent years caring for us when we were unable to take care of ourselves. They taught us basic living skills: how to speak, eat, and clean ourselves. They taught us social skills: how to get along with others, deal with the frustration of not getting what we want, and work as a member of a team. If our parents were not in a position to do these things for us because of poverty, illness, or their own confusion and limitations, they made sure that others cared for and guided us. They had great hopes and wishes for us to be happy and successful. Yet we often repaid their kindness with self-centeredness, not caring how our actions affected them, not appreciating what they had done for us but just expecting more.

If we do not put energy into generating bodhicitta, all their sacrifice and efforts for our sake would be wasted. But if we study and practice the Mahāyāna, we will be able to liberate our present parents, all those who have been our parents in previous lives, and everyone's parents. To guide them over the abyss of cyclic existence to the security and peace of awakening—what a wonderful thing to be able to do!

3. Mindfulness of the Kindness of Our Teachers and Senior Practitioners

Those who teach us skills useful in the secular world and especially those who teach us the Dharma have been and continue to be immeasurably kind to us. Everything we know has come from the kindness of our teachers. Without them we would not know how to read and write, nor would we have basic ethical values. Our behavior would be like that of an animal.

Our opportunity to learn the Buddha's teachings is due to the effort of our spiritual mentors and senior practitioners. They guide us on the path, encouraging us when we feel tired, steering us in the right direction when wrong views or bad behavior threaten our practice, and practicing patience when we are stubborn, rebellious, or ungrateful. The fact that we have been able to take refuge and the five lay precepts, to become monastics, to take the bodhisattva precepts—all this is due to the kindness of our Dharma teachers. Whatever transformation in our thoughts and behavior has occurred since we started to practice the Dharma can be traced to their instructions and guidance. What better way to repay their kindness than to tame our mind and train in bodhicitta so that we will be able to humbly share the Dharma with others just as they have shared it with us?

4. Mindfulness of the Kindness of Benefactors

Those who support us so that we can learn and practice the Dharma are very generous indeed. Monastics do not earn wages. We are completely dependent on kind benefactors who provide us with the four requisites of life: food, clothing, shelter, and medicine. We should live simply as part of our practice of developing contentment and counteracting attachment in order not to inconvenience those who so kindly support us.

Our benefactors work hard all day, often laboring overtime and becoming stressed as a result of their job. Yet, out of the kindness of their hearts, they share what they have earned with us. We do not live in poverty as many people in the world do. We are in a position to choose to moderate our consumption and care for the planet. Taking benefactors' support for granted is certainly not appropriate. Having a nicer living situation with better food and clothes than our supporters would be repugnant to the wise; it is the path to an unfortunate rebirth for us and deprives the kind benefactors of benefiting from our Dharma practice. The only appropriate way to repay their kindness is to keep our precepts well, generate bodhicitta, and fulfill the collections of merit and wisdom for their sake.

5. Mindfulness of the Kindness of Sentient Beings

All sentient beings have been our loved ones in so many previous lives. How do we know that the crawling and flying insects we see were not once our parents? Or that the meat we eat or leather we wear is not the flesh and skin of our friends? Our dear ones have changed form since we knew them as friends and relatives in previous lives, so we may not instantly recognize them. If a child was separated from her parents, she may not recognize them when she encounters them as an adult. But once someone has pointed out to her, "Those people are your parents who cared for you with so much love many years ago," her feeling of familiarity will return and she will be overjoyed to be reunited with them. Similarly, when the Buddha points out to us that all sentient beings have been our loved ones many times in previous lives, we lose our sense of distance and hesitation and come to cherish them again.

Some of our dear ones may now be screaming in torment in the hell realms, starving as hungry ghosts, or befuddled and used as beasts of burden in the animal realm. Surely they would appreciate our help. Were it not for the Buddha informing us about this, we would be oblivious to their situation. Thus, we must remain ever-mindful that the sentient beings around us—enemies included—have been our dear ones and have the potential to become buddhas in the future. We must continuously contemplate how to benefit them and be aware of our responsibility to do so. Thinking of all the past benefits we have received from sentient beings stimulates us to care for them in return by giving rise to the bodhi mind.

6. Mindfulness of the Suffering of Repeated Birth and Death in Cyclic Existence

Under the influence of afflictions and karma, we go up and down in saṃsāra—sometimes born amidst the delights of the celestial realms, other times trapped in the pain and agony of the hell realms. Once a seed of destructive karma has ripened, we cannot purify it; we are left with experiencing its result. At this time, we may realize that our misery is brought about from our own harmful actions and regret them, but there is no possibility to go back and undo them. Later, when our immediate suffering has ceased, we forget about the law of karma and its effects, going back to our old ways of seeking pleasure in the present moment, lacking conscientiousness regarding the effects of our actions on others or on our own future experiences. With this mindset, we will undoubtedly create more nonvirtuous karma, leading to more misery. Seeking happiness, we slaughter animals to fulfill our desire for meat, yet these beings have been our kind mothers and friends in previous lives. Although we seek security and safety, there is none to be found as long as ignorance, afflictions, and karma rule our lives.

If we truly understood our relationships with others and the law of karma, we would feel horrified by our many destructive actions. If we actually understood what being in saṃsāra meant, we would laugh at the tiny problems our afflictive mind makes into catastrophes on a daily basis. Our ignorance causes us to believe we are happy, or if we are not, to believe that simply improving our situation in saṃsāra will bring the relief we long for. How wrong we are! People who don't know the Buddha's teachings have difficulty grasping this, as do people who are obsessed with the happiness of only this life; they live and die in confusion. Their wealth and reputation cannot protect them at the time of death, when their agony can be immense. For a tortoise to have its shell ripped off is less anguish than for those whose minds are immersed in ignorance and craving to separate from their bodies at death.

Having a precious human life at this moment, we are unbelievably fortunate. Yet this life goes by so quickly. As youngsters, we just want to play; any talk of karma or future lives seems irrelevant to us. As young adults, desire takes over the body and mind, and we work hard to procure and protect the pleasures of this life. But in the blink of an eye, we are old, our skin dried out, our muscles withering, our mind forgetful. While we think we can control things, we actually have little control over our own body and mind, let alone the people and environment around us. If the tears we have shed in previous lives were amassed, they would be greater than the ocean. If the bodies we have taken in saṃsāra were piled up, they would fill the universe.

Thinking about this, we see that cyclic existence is a desperate situation. Without the Buddha's teachings, where would we be? We would have no knowledge of how to liberate ourselves, let alone liberate others, from this wretched situation. It is in this life—and with our precious human life—that we have the opportunity to attain buddhahood. If we do not make use of this rare and precious chance, when will it come again? Using this special situation wisely is of utmost, long-lasting importance. We must aspire to liberate ourselves and all sentient beings from the broad and deep ocean of cyclic existence through practicing bodhicitta.

7. Respect Your Own Buddha Nature

The nature of our mind is no different from the nature of the Buddha's mind. Yet we are still struggling for pleasure amidst confusion while Śākyamuni Buddha enjoys unending bliss. Why is it that the Buddha has compassion, wisdom, and superknowledges, and is adorned with the ten perfections, while we are confused by wrong views and have a storehouse of afflictions and destructive karma? This occurred because even though the person who is now the Buddha was once drowning in saṃsāra, he took hold of the life raft of the Dharma, practiced it, and attained full awakening. Meanwhile we neglected the precious jewel of our beautiful buddha nature, opting to wallow in the mud of saṃsāra. Considering that the nature of the Buddha's mind and the nature of our mind is the same, what a pitiful situation we have allowed ourselves to remain in!

Meanwhile, the jewel of our buddha nature has been lying unnoticed in the mud too long. We must appreciate and respect this jewel, clean it, and put it on top of the canopy of awakening where its radiance will shine everywhere. Let's gather together the force of our joyous effort and do it! In the process, may we never denigrate or ignore our buddha nature and may we never be ungrateful for the Buddha's teachings. Unfolding the true beauty of our buddha nature involves aspiring for full awakening for the benefit of all sentient beings, so may we quickly give rise to this illustrious mind that is the cause of all happiness in saṃsāra and nirvāṇa.

8. Think of the Disadvantages of Nonvirtuous Karma, Confess, and Purify It

We boldly take monastic ethical restraints and the bodhisattva vow in our spiritual mentors' presence but are cowardly when it comes to keeping them. We much prefer seeking what we want when we want it to practicing the path to awakening, and in doing so, we blithely transgress our precepts and commit other nonvirtues without a second thought. But when it comes to confessing and purifying these transgressions, laziness sets in and we lack the time and energy to do it. If we take the time to consider it, we will see that the accumulation of destructive karma in each day is enormous and the accumulation of virtuous karma rather feeble. Faced with this distressing state of affairs and the suffering it will bring us and others, let's generate bodhicitta as the supreme method of confessing and purifying this mountain of destructive karma created by our self-centered mind and self-grasping ignorance.

9. Aspire to Be Born in the Pure Land

While practice in our polluted world is difficult—we are constantly buffeted here and there due to afflictions and karma—in a pure land all conditions are in place to be able to practice the Dharma with ease and to become a buddha. While many buddhas have pure lands, Amitābha Buddha's pure land is especially suited for us because we can be reborn there without having realized emptiness. Merit and virtue are needed to be born in Sukhāvatī, Amitābha Buddha's pure land, and there are no better methods to accumulate them than concentrating on Amitābha, his name, and his excellent qualities, and by generating bodhicitta. The root of gaining mindfulness and concentration on Amitābha is the aspiration to become a buddha. Without this indispensable ingredient of bodhicitta, we could practice mindfulness of Amitābha but it will not be successful. But once we have generated bodhicitta, mindfulness of Amitābha will prevent it from declining. Bodhicitta establishes the foundation for further realizations of the path. For those who have generated bodhicitta, dying will not be fearful and birth in the pure land will occur. However, if we aspire to be born in the pure land, but let the mind wander throughout the universe and do not cultivate bodhicitta even the slightest, even reciting Amitābha Buddha's name eon after eon will not bring about our desired goal.

If we generate bodhicitta, then even if we are not born in Amitābha's pure land, our future lives will be spent meaningfully aiding sentient beings in this world. In addition, completing the collections of merit and wisdom will occur without stress or obstacles.

10. Pray for the Buddha's Teachings to Remain in Our World Purely and Forever

The Buddha attained awakening for our benefit, yet we lacked the good fortune to be born while he was alive. Fortunately, the Buddha's liberating teachings still exist in our world. But despite this, the minds of human beings cling to wrong views and are addicted to the eight worldly concerns, even using the Dharma itself to bolster our prestige or bring us wealth. Nowadays, people are so enamored of worldly success that it is difficult to even hear the words *Buddha*, *Dharma*, and *Saṅgha*—our supreme refuge. Sheng'an Shixian writes (ERB 67):

> If, as a child of the Buddha, I am unable to repay such kindness—inwardly there shall be no benefit for myself and outwardly there shall be no benefit for others. It shall then be the case that, while alive, I provide no benefit to anyone, and after I die, I afford no benefit to those who come along afterward. In such a case, though the heavens may extend high above, still they remain unable to give me cover. Though the earth may be massive, it remains unable to support me. Then, if the phrase "a person possessed of

> the most extremely grave karmic crimes" does not apply to me, to whom could it even be applied at all?
>
> On account of this, I feel unbearable pain and discern that there is no way to escape [from this indictment]. Suddenly, I forget my inferior qualities and immediately generate the great resolve [for buddhahood]. Although I remain unable to turn back the Dharma-ending process dominating this era, I nonetheless will remain determined to strive to guard and maintain right Dharma throughout [this and all] my future lifetimes.

He then describes going to a bodhimaṇḍa—here referring to a temple or monastery—repenting and taking the forty-eight precepts,[61] "wherein each and every precept is devoted to bringing beings across to liberation." He calls on each of us to give rise to bodhicitta so that, thought after thought, our mind is focused on buddhahood. He urges us to practice the bodhisattva path and be reborn in Sukhāvatī, Amitābha's pure land. Having attained awakening there, we must return to this suffering world to spread the light of the Buddha's teachings, to purify the Saṅgha, and to liberate all beings. Pointing out that we have a precious human life with the eight freedoms and ten fortunes that provides the excellent conditions for generating bodhicitta, Sheng'an Shixian challenges us, "If you do not now on this very day proceed to generate this great resolve, then for which more suitable day [could you possibly] be waiting?" He encourages us to unite with like-minded people in generating bodhicitta (ERB 71):

> Those who have not generated it may now generate it. Those who have already generated it may now cause it to develop more fully. Those who have already caused it to develop more fully may now cause it to remain perpetually manifest.

Sheng'an Shixian continues by counseling us:

> Do not, fearing difficulty, shrink back in timidity. Do not, regarding this matter as easy, take it but lightly. Do not, seeking a swift conclusion, fail to make a long-enduring commitment. Do not, through indolence, remain bereft of heroic bravery. Do not, on account of being shiftless and spiritless, fail to incite yourself

> to bold action. Do not, drifting along in customary fashion, continue to put it off for another time. Do not, judging yourself to be foolish and dull-witted, continue depriving yourself of resolve. Do not, possessing only shallow roots [of virtue], judge yourself to be an inferior person with no share in this . . .
>
> Do not claim that a single thought is insignificant. Do not hold the opinion that "empty vows" are devoid of any benefit. If your mind abides in truths, then your endeavors will be genuine. If your vows are vast in their scope, then your practice will be profound . . .
>
> As for what we have vowed to achieve, it is for all of us together to gain rebirth in the Pureland, for all of us together to see Amitābha Buddha, for all of us together to engage in the teaching of beings, and for all of us together to perfect the right awakening.

Developing bodhicitta is not easy, but it is the most worthwhile thing we can do. We must be persistent and patient, practicing with enthusiasm and fortitude without allowing our mind to descend into despondency. Worrying about difficulties saps energy; remaining stuck in the past has no purpose. But if we have found a qualified Mahāyāna spiritual mentor, correct teachings, and virtuous Dharma friends, we must make use of this rare chance and do what will lead to the highest happiness for ourselves and all others. Having planted the seed of bodhicitta in our mind, it will sprout and its roots will grow deeper day by day. When we realize the nonarising (unborn, unproduced—emptiness) and attain the fortitude of the nonarising of phenomena, all concerns about the path being difficult will vanish.

The bodhicitta is so precious that we must do our utmost to generate, enhance, and protect it. The *Flower Ornament Sūtra* advises:

> Even if a wheel of fire about your head
> is wildly whirling and flaming,
> just do not abandon your bodhi mind,
> even amidst such strong suffering.

When we suffer, we give up what is not essential for our well-being in order to focus on what is important. The bodhicitta is tremendously important for the well-being of ourselves and all others; we must never relinquish it. To the contrary, if we reflect on bodhicitta at times of suffering, our mental suffering will decrease, and by generating compassion our physical suffering will be transformed so that it becomes meaningful on the path to awakening.

REFLECTION

Contemplating the ten factors will spur our generation of bodhicitta.

1. The first five concern mindfulness of the kindness that we have received from the Buddha, our parents, teachers, benefactors, and all sentient beings. Reflect on these until you recognize that you've been the recipient of tremendous kindness in this and previous lives.
2. Reflect on sentient beings' suffering of repeated birth and death in cyclic existence.
3. Generate respect for your own buddha nature.
4. Think of the disadvantages of nonvirtuous karma, confess, and purify it.
5. Aspire to be born in the pure land.
6. Pray for the Buddha's teachings to remain in our world purely and forever.
7. Generate bodhicitta and feel its importance for the happiness of sentient beings and for the continued existence of the Dharma in our world.

Vasubandhu on Cultivating Bodhicitta and the Bodhisattva Vow

Vasubandhu (c. 300), who is highly regarded in China, wrote the *Treatise on the "Generating the Bodhi Resolve Sūtra,"* in which he discusses the benefits of bodhicitta, the way to generate it in our mind, and the establishment of the bodhisattva vow. This is followed by chapters on each of the six perfections, two chapters on the view of reality—emptiness and signlessness—and dedication of merit.

Vasubandhu clarifies that bodhicitta is not for the faint-hearted (VTBV 23):

> Because empty space is endless, beings too are endless. Because beings are endless, the bodhisattva's generation of the resolve [to attain buddhahood] is equivalent in its vastness to the realms of [all] beings. As for the realms of beings, they are limitless.

Bodhisattvas who have generated bodhicitta but whose wisdom of contemplation is not yet moistened by deep samādhi in the dhyānas must set forth correct vows. Doing this will enable them to draw in followers and deepen their practice of bodhicitta and the perfections. This practitioner should proclaim, "I seek to realize the unsurpassed awakening and to rescue and liberate everyone without exception so that every one of them is caused to reach all the way to nirvāṇa without remainder." Vasubandhu continues (VTBV 39–43):

> "Therefore, in the initial generation of bodhicitta, it is the great compassion which is foremost. It is on account of the mind of compassion that one becomes able to generate ten ever more superior great right vows. What are those ten? They are:
>
> 1. Regarding those roots of virtue I have planted in previous lives and in this present body, I pray that all of these roots of virtue may be bestowed upon all of the boundlessly many beings and dedicated to the unsurpassed bodhi (full awakening). May it be that these vows of mine shall grow in each succeeding thought-moment, shall be produced again in each successive lifetime, shall always be bound to my mind, shall never be forgotten, and shall be guarded and retained by *dhāraṇīs*.[62]
> 2. Having already dedicated these roots of virtue to bodhi, I pray that on account of these roots of goodness, no matter where I may be reborn, I shall always be able to make offerings to all buddhas and shall definitely never be reborn in a land where there is no buddha.
> 3. Having already succeeded in being reborn in the lands of the buddhas, I pray that I shall always be able to draw personally close to them, shall follow along and serve them in every way, shall remain as close to them as a shadow to a body, and shall

never become distantly separated from the buddhas even for the briefest of moments.

4. Having already succeeded in drawing personally close to the buddhas, I pray that they will then speak Dharma for my sake in accordance with whatsoever is appropriate for me. May I then straightaway perfect the bodhisattva's five superknowledges.[63]
5. Having already perfected the bodhisattva's five superknowledges, I pray that I shall thereupon be able to reach a penetrating understanding of conventional truth together with its widespread artificial designations; that I shall also then completely comprehend, in accordance with its genuine nature, the foremost ultimate truth; and that I will gain right Dharma wisdom.
6. Having already realized the right Dharma wisdom, I pray that, free of any thoughts of aversion, I shall then explain it for the sake of beings, instructing them in the teachings, benefiting them, delighting them, and causing them all to develop an understanding of it.
7. Having already become able to create an understanding [of right Dharma] in beings, I pray that, availing myself of the spiritual power of the buddhas, I shall be able to go to all worlds without exception everywhere throughout the ten directions, making offerings to the buddhas, listening to and accepting right Dharma, and extensively drawing in beings [to the Dharma].
8. Having already received right Dharma in the abodes of the buddhas, I pray that I shall thereupon be able to turn the wheel of the pure Dharma in accordance with it. May it then be that all beings of the worlds in the ten directions who hear me proclaim the Dharma or who merely hear my name shall then straightaway succeed in abandoning all afflictions and in generating bodhicitta.
9. Having already become able to cause all beings to generate bodhicitta, I pray that I may constantly follow along with them, protecting them, ridding them of whatever is unbeneficial, bestowing on them countless sorts of happiness, relin-

quishing my life and wealth for their sakes, drawing in beings, and taking on the burden of right Dharma.

10. Having already become able to take on the burden of right Dharma, I pray that, even though I shall then practice in accordance with right Dharma, my mind shall nonetheless have nothing whatsoever that it practices. May it be that, in this, I shall conform with the way that the bodhisattvas themselves practice right Dharma and yet have nothing whatsoever that they either practice or do not practice.

For the sake of carrying on the transformative teaching of beings, one never relinquishes right vows. This is what is meant by the ten great right vows of the bodhisattva who has brought forth the resolve [to realize unsurpassed bodhi].

These ten great vows extend everywhere to all realms of beings and subsume all vows as numerous as the Ganges' sands. [Hence one reflects thus:] If beings were to come to an end, then and only then would my vows come to an end. However, beings are truly endless. Therefore these great vows of mine shall also never come to an end."

Vasubandhu then describes how each perfection acts as a cause of full awakening and comments that the four immeasurables, the thirty-seven harmonies with awakening, and all the many other excellent practices work together to bring perfect realization of full awakening.

REFLECTION

1. Slowly read and contemplate the ten superior great right vows that Vasubandhu articulated.
2. Be aware of how each vow builds on the power of the preceding one and empowers the subsequent one.
3. Take these vows into your heart and aspire to fulfill them.

Exhortation to Resolve on Buddhahood

Peixiu (797–870), a district magistrate at the time of writing *Exhortation to Resolve on Buddhahood*, later became the Chinese prime minister during the Tang dynasty. A layman, he was a devoted Buddhist and an educated literatus. His text on generating bodhicitta was so highly regarded that the Huayan and Chan patriarch Guifeng Zongmi (780–840) wrote a foreword to it, saying Peixiu was an emissary of the Buddha who carried out the Buddha's work in writing this essay.

In the foreword, Zongmi says that generating bodhicitta involves great virtue, vast merit, an understanding of emptiness, and the determination to treat our body as the vehicle for Dharma practice without being attached to it. Generating bodhicitta also entails a vast view, great empathy and compassion for others, and supremely strong determination. He cautions us against deviation, one-sided biases, laziness, and haste.

Deviation, for example, is seeking the Dharma outside of the mind and grasping at a self within this body. Comprehending the nature of our own mind and attaining excellent qualities equal to the Buddha's counteract the deviant view that awakening is somewhere apart from our own mind; understanding that form and consciousness are empty and like illusions counteracts the erroneous notion of self.

Looking only at the ultimate nature or only at cause and effect are examples of *biases*. Understanding the four truths and engaging in the six perfections counteract unbalanced focus on the ultimate nature and the wisdom aspect of the path; understanding true suchness (emptiness) and original awakening (buddha nature) remedy a disproportionate focus on conventional truth and the method aspect of the path.

Laziness is keeping the Dharma at an intellectual level only, without putting it into practice; laziness is also becoming so involved in emptiness and serenity that we forget sentient beings. Accumulating merit, generating wisdom and compassion, and making strong vows are the antidote to being too immersed in emptiness and serenity.

Making the body exhausted by pushing ourselves or depriving ourselves of a peaceful mind in an attempt to gain realizations according to a certain self-created schedule are examples of *haste*. Haste is remedied by making prostrations and offerings, praising the Three Jewels, reciting scriptures, and leading by being a good example when teaching others. It is important to keep our body and mind in balance when responding to life's circumstances. Resting when the time is right and practicing without impatiently waiting for results counteracts craving swift results. Following Zongmi's sage advice will enable our practice to flow more smoothly and consistently.

Peixiu begins by explaining the term "highest, perfect, and complete awakening" (*anuttara-samyaksaṃbodhi*). "Highest" refers to the unsurpassed or ultimate awakening, "perfect" means that it accords with the wisdom realizing emptiness, and "complete" indicates immeasurable wisdom that fully knows both the ultimate and conventional truths. This awakening is the magnificent path realized by all the buddhas, and it is what sentient beings are most obscured and deluded about. The initial resolve to attain highest, perfect, and complete awakening comes from admiring the Tathāgata's cessation of all duḥkha and obscurations, and feeling sad that so far we have neglected this opportunity ourselves.

Bodhicitta or bodhi mind must be generated from our "true mind"—from the pure aspect of our mind that is part of our buddha nature. It does not arise from identifying with our flesh-and-bones body composed of the four elements, which arises and disintegrates in each moment. It also does not arise from identifying with the false, obscured mind obsessed with sense pleasure and worldly success. Like the body, this mind is impermanent and unstable.

Our genuine body is "perfect and complete, empty and quiescent"; our genuine mind is vast in its scope and imbued with intelligence and awareness. The perfect and complete Dharma body is replete with countless virtuous qualities; it is empty and quiescent in that it goes beyond all forms and characteristics and is forever free of disturbance. The genuine mind is vast in that it coincides with the dharmadhātu—the sphere of reality (Dharma realm). It is imbued with intelligence and awareness in that it is a focused, penetrating, clear, investigating illumination. Encompassing great virtuous qualities, the genuine mind cuts through the fallacious thinking of the tetralemma—such as the distorted view that things arise from self, other, both, or causelessly—and the convoluted conceptual mind.

Like a full moon obscured by the clouds of afflictions so that we are unaware of it, the original purity of the genuine mind will manifest when the afflictions have been abandoned. As said in the *Flower Ornament Sūtra*,

"The mind, the Buddha, and beings as well—in these three, there are no distinctions." This genuine mind is the same as the essence of bodhi mind. When we do not see this, we become entwined with our false conceptualizations and engage in actions that bind us in continual rebirth. Having generated the resolve for the highest path, we should cultivate the three types of mind, establish the five vows (explained below), and engage in all the practices that lead to awakening. In addition, we should take the buddhas as our spiritual mentors and the bodhisattvas as our spiritual companions, regard sentient beings in the six realms as our followers, see cyclic existence with its afflictions as the field of practice, and vow in all future times to liberate sentient beings. This is the mind that has resolved to realize the highest, perfect, complete awakening.

Cultivating the Three Types of Mind and the Five Great Vows

The three types of mind are an essential support for bodhicitta. These are great compassion, great wisdom, and the mind established in great vows. Based on seeing that our mind is originally unborn and unceasing, we feel *great compassion* for sentient beings who are drowning in the duḥkha of cyclic existence. Although we have not yet attained awakening ourselves, we still want to liberate sentient beings by placing their liberation before our own. With such compassion, we engage in the four ways of gathering disciples, establishing them in refuge in the Three Jewels and in correct views so that they will practice the path to awakening.

Great wisdom is necessary to fulfill the aspiration of great compassion. Sentient beings have so many diverse faculties, dispositions, tendencies, and aspirations that wisdom and skill are needed to guide them. To gain such wisdom we must serve the Buddha and study the Dharma extensively. In this way we will know and will have practiced all the teachings and paths the Buddha taught. This will enable us to benefit others by teaching them the Dharma that is appropriate for their disposition and stage of the path at that particular time.

Although the fundamental nature of the mind is pure, it is obscured by afflictions and habitual tendencies that do not vanish quickly. To make ourselves suitable vessels for the Dharma, we contemplate the prospect of continual rebirth in saṃsāra without encountering the Buddhadharma. This frightful prospect inspires us to establish *great vows* and to wholeheartedly engage in the bodhisattva practices. The vows and practices mutually complement each other, and in this way we progress to awakening. As the *Flower Ornament Sūtra* says:

> The lamp of the bodhi mind takes great compassion as its oil, great vows as its wick, and great wisdom as its illumination.

Of these three—great compassion, great wisdom, and great vows—great vows is chief because it supports the compassion and wisdom that will enable us to liberate sentient beings. For this reason, the initial generation of bodhicitta entails making great vows. When we die, our body and wealth are abandoned, our relatives and friends cannot come with us, and all our power is lost. It is only these precious bodhisattva vows that will continue to lead and guide us until awakening. Therefore, we should not doubt their efficacy and importance but eagerly make them. The five vows are these:[64]

1. Sentient beings are countless, I vow to liberate them all.
2. Merit and wisdom are boundless, I vow to accumulate them.
3. The Buddhadharma is vast, I vow to study it.
4. The tathāgatas are countless, I vow to serve them.
5. Mahāyāna is unsurpassed and perfect, I vow to realize it.

Making these five great vows and maintaining them in our mind thought after thought, so that there is no time in which they are not present, is the meaning of implementing the great mind of awakening and upholding the precepts of the bodhi mind. This is the path that all the buddhas of the three times follow. The three types of mind and the five vows support each other.

A series of exhortations follows. If you are able to follow them and always maintain your bodhicitta, you will continually approach buddhahood until you succeed in attaining it.

Whether you are a monastic or lay follower, announce your vows to the buddhas, engage in attracting sentient beings to the Dharma, and constantly uphold the five vows whether you are sitting, standing, walking, or lying down. Never cheat or deceive sentient beings or neglect to uphold the trust of the Tathāgata. Maintaining the transmitted Dharma—the words and meanings of the Buddha's teachings in the scriptures—endeavor to gain the realized Dharma—the realizations of the teachings in the mind—especially the fortitude of the nonarising of phenomena. By serving as bright lights along the dark shore and as the rafts that carry sentient beings across the ocean of cyclic existence, cause sentient beings to realize the knowledge and vision of the buddhas. In this way, when the thousand buddhas of this fortunate eon appear, you will be a leader among the disciples and will attain full awakening.

Accumulate merit with sentient beings (the field of compassion) and with the buddhas and bodhisattva (the field of reverence). This is done by giving your external wealth—your possessions and body—and your internal wealth—your time, energy, and merit. When doing this, guard against the self-centered thought seeking reward in this life or even in future lives that would sabotage your generosity.

Make a strong determination to learn and master all the Buddha's teachings from now until attaining full awakening. To instruct others, endeavor to realize the four immeasurables, the six perfections, the provisional and definitive meanings of the Dharma, the law of cause and effect, the two teachings of sudden and gradual awakening, and the two doctrinal lineages that focus on the nature and on the dharmic characteristics. Schools focusing on the nature were the Madhyamaka, Tathāgatagarbha, Chan, and Perfect Teaching (Avataṃsaka), which emphasized the realization of emptiness. The school focusing on dharmic characteristics was primarily the Yogācāra.

Vow to encounter a wise and compassionate spiritual mentor, to serve him or her without fatigue or laziness, and to listen with eager interest to Dharma teachings. Happily accept instructions and guidance, and then put them into practice, as did Sudhana, the youth whose spiritual journey took him to fifty-three spiritual mentors, as related in the *Flower Ornament Sūtra*.

Furthermore, vow to always maintain the aspiration for full awakening, never letting it degenerate into a wish to become a śrāvaka or solitary-realizer arhat. Seeing yourself as interrelated with all sentient beings, dedicate all merit for full awakening and encourage others to do so as well.

In addition, never abandon monastics and lay followers who have the same resolve for awakening and the same great vows that you have. Rather, practice together with them, cultivating the meditative absorptions and wisdom. Toward some members of your "Dharma family" you serve as younger siblings and toward others you serve as older siblings. In this way, support and encourage one another, enabling everyone to succeed in their spiritual journey. If someone loses the path, everyone must come together to free him from his problems and bring him back to his purpose. When someone gains realizations of the path, take refuge with them. Having a good relationship with your fellow aspirants enables each person to benefit and the Dharma to remain long in the world.

Although you may have the resolve for awakening, until you fathom the nature of the mind, you will be stuck in the provisional perspective and not realize the ultimate nature. So strive to develop the correct cause of awakening by understanding (ERB 107):

> The perfect, bright, and pure awakening is originally devoid of any delusive ignorance. The illusional obscurations and "flowers floating in space" do not constitute the substance of reality. [This awakened mind] is distantly separate from any sort of attachment-based grasping and is as uniform in nature as empty space itself. Expansively great compassion and wisdom constantly flow forth from this quiescent and radiant mind.

The fundamental nature of the mind is pure. "Flowers floating in space" refers to floaters in the eyes—the vision of falling hairs that in fact do not exist. The appearance of inherent existence that ignorance projects on phenomena is not reality. The pure mind that realizes emptiness is unimpeded like space. In this still and luminous mind, great compassion can manifest to benefit sentient beings. Sūtras that speak of the means to cultivate this radiant mind are the Perfection of Wisdom sūtras, the *Perfect Mahāyāna Sūtra*, the *Flower Ornament Sūtra*, and the *Nirvāṇa Sūtra*.

The *Flower of Compassion Sūtra* (C. *Beihua jing*) instructs bodhisattvas to cultivate four inexhaustible treasuries: the treasuries of inexhaustible merit, inexhaustible knowledge, inexhaustible wisdom, and inexhaustible unified Dharma of the Buddha. To do this it is necessary to practice many factors that assist in the attainment of awakening:

- generosity, to attract others in order to teach them the Dharma
- ethical conduct, which is a support for accomplishing virtuous aspirations
- fortitude, through which the thirty-two signs and eighty marks of a buddha are perfected
- joyous effort, which leads to success in our endeavors
- meditative stability, to skillfully subdue and train the mind
- wisdom, to recognize and excise afflictions
- extensive study and learning, to gain unimpeded eloquence in teaching the Dharma
- the collection of merit, which is a necessity for progress
- thoughtful reflection, to destroy doubts
- love, to perfect a mind free from obstruction
- compassion, to teach and guide sentient beings without fatigue
- empathic joy, to increase affectionate happiness based on right Dharma
- equanimity, to eliminate attachment and animosity
- listening to the Dharma, to subdue the five hindrances (sensual desire, malice, lethargy and sleepiness, restlessness and regret, and doubt)
- transcending the world, to go beyond worldly existence
- dwelling in a solitary place, to abandon destructive karma
- joyfully according with the virtuous actions of others, to increase the roots of virtue
- the four establishments of mindfulness, to firmly comprehend the body as foul, the feelings as duḥkha in nature, the mind as impermanent, and all phenomena as selfless
- the four supreme strivings, to abandon nonvirtue and cultivate virtue
- the four bases of spiritual power, to perfect physical and mental pliancy
- the five faculties, to enhance and strengthen these five factors so that they can become the five powers
- the five powers, to demolish all afflictions
- the seven awakening factors, to gain an awareness of phenomena that accords with ultimate truth[65]

- the six harmonies of the monastic community (physical, verbal, and mental harmony, harmony in views, the sharing of resources, and the way to keep precepts), to restrain and train sentient beings while steering them toward purification

Cultivating these constitute the "accumulation of pure Dharma gateways through which we bring about liberation from cyclic existence." Thus motivated by bodhicitta, engage in these practices enthusiastically and with mindfulness. Then we should adorn and establish a pure land in accordance with our aspirations.

Four factors can make you lazy in Dharma practice and thereby create suffering. Avoid them:[66]

1. Inferior conduct is transgressing the prātimokṣa precepts that regulate your physical and verbal actions.
2. Inferior companions are śrāvakas and solitary realizers who could influence you to relinquish bodhicitta.
3. Inferior generosity is the inability to give everything, to choose certain recipients due to prejudice, or to give with the motivation to take rebirth in a celestial realm.
4. Inferior vows are the inability to single-pointedly vow to go to a buddha land. These are weak vows that render you unable to subdue and train sentient beings.

These are counteracted by the four swift factors of bodhisattvas:

1. Upholding your precepts and purifying your body, speech, and mind enable you to protect and maintain the Dharma teachings.
2. Becoming close to people who study and practice the Mahāyāna will naturally lead you to become involved in virtuous endeavors.
3. Releasing all miserliness and activating compassion leads to being able to give to everyone.
4. Single-pointedly vowing to go to and adorn Buddha lands aids you in training and taming sentient beings.

REFLECTION

1. Reflect on the four factors that can make you lazy in Dharma practice and create suffering. Which ones hinder you the most?
2. Reflect on the four swift factors of bodhisattvas that counteract them.
3. As you do this repeatedly, be aware of the positive changes in your mind.

The merit created by a bodhisattva when she first generates bodhicitta is beyond imagination. It dwarfs a trillionfold the merit of making huge and magnificent offerings to innumerable buddhas, the merit of encouraging a huge number of sentient beings to keep precepts and abide in the ten pathways of virtuous karma for eons, the merit of causing others to attain the various meditative absorptions of the upper realms and remain in them for eons, and the merit of instructing and guiding others to attain the stages of a stream-enterer, once-returner, nonreturner, or arhat. These virtuous deeds, while indisputably wonderful, are not the purpose for which buddhas first generated bodhicitta. Rather, their purpose was to continue the lineage of the Tathāgata and to prevent it from being cut off, to fill all world systems with the Dharma, to liberate the beings in all worlds, to know the creation and ceasing of all worlds, to know the defilement and purity of all worlds, to know the purity of the fundamental nature of all worlds, to know the happiness, afflictions, and latencies in sentient beings' minds, to know sentient beings' death in one life and birth in another, to know sentient beings' faculties and the skillful means to guide them, to know their thoughts and mental activity, to know the past, present, and future of all beings, and to know the uniformity in the minds of all buddhas.

Due to such intentions, these bodhisattvas are held in the minds of all the buddhas, who then bestow the magnificent Dharma on them. It is as if they had already actualized the entire path and attained the four fearlessnesses and the ten powers, and the merit, wisdom, and mind state of the buddhas, because they are bound to attain buddhahood. At this time of initially generating strong bodhicitta (that is, the time of attaining the first bodhisattva ground) they are praised by all the buddhas and become able to teach and subdue sentient beings in the various worlds. They can cause worlds to shake, illuminate all worlds, stop the anguish of unfortunate rebirths in all worlds, adorn and purify all worlds, manifest the attainment of buddhahood in all worlds, cause happiness in the minds of all beings, enter into the very nature of the entire dharmadhātu, maintain the lineage of all buddhas, and gain the wisdom light of all buddhas.

At the same time, bodhisattvas who have initially generated strong bodhicitta—first-ground bodhisattvas—find that there is nothing to attain in the past, present, or future. They seek only omniscience, and the mind is free from attachment to any aspect of the dharmadhātu.[67] Although these first-ground bodhisattvas are said to have initially generated bodhicitta, it is actually the perfection of the generation of the bodhi resolve. It is called "initial" because it is the first time they have perfected it by the direct realization of emptiness, thus becoming an ārya.

Should you wonder if it's actually possible to possess such incomparable faculties and qualities, recall that the ultimate nature of the mind of an ordinary person and of an ārya are the same. It is simply a matter of your thoughts—allowing afflictions and wrong views to take over the mind is the impediment. But if you awaken to the ultimate nature of the mind and its brilliance, you will be able to generate bodhicitta within the uniformly empty nature that is shared with all the buddhas.

In the meantime, as ordinary beings we can lessen the afflictions that interfere with our bodhicitta. Practicing generosity will lessen attachment and covetousness, whereas practicing the four ways of gathering disciples will decrease animosity. Cultivating serenity and insight will reduce our afflictions. This is true even if we are not able to cultivate these practices perfectly at this moment. In addition, we must continue to cultivate compassion. Generating both bodhicitta and the direct realization of emptiness is critically important; everything else is related to cyclic existence. It was in this manner that the Buddha himself progressed.

Peixiu concludes his *Exhortation* with final words of advice (ERB 127–29):

> It is essential to liberate all beings. It is essential to strive to gain the knowledge of all modes and plant roots of virtue throughout the auspicious eon during the reigns of the Thousand Buddhas.

> Thus one's merit and wisdom will naturally become vast and deep such that in the world, one will always be among the leaders of those who serve as guides [on the path] . . .
>
> After communicating one's generation [of bodhicitta], one should invoke that resolve in each and every thought. This will then constitute a correct cause for the realization of buddhahood. It is only appropriate that one should then feel profound sentiments of joyful felicitation. Neither monastics nor laity should allow themselves to become estranged from Dharma friends. How could even mountains and rivers [be allowed to] present an obstacle to [the realization of] genuine wisdom?

The Four Great Vows

The Mahāyāna Buddhist traditions throughout East Asia recite the Four Great Vows daily, making them the centerpiece of their Dharma practice. Containing the condensed meaning of all the bodhisattva precepts, the Four Great Vows are found in sūtras and commentaries such as *The Sixth Patriarch Platform Sūtra*, *Sūtra on the Practice of Prajñāpāramitā*, the *Lotus Sūtra*, the *Medallion Sūtra on the Bodhisattva Path*, and others.[68]

The Four Great Vows are as follows:

> Countless are sentient beings; I vow to liberate them.
> Endless are defilements; I vow to eradicate them.
> Measureless are Dharma doors; I vow to cultivate them.
> Supreme is the Buddha's Way; I vow to attain it.

The last of the four vows is the generation of bodhicitta; "the Buddha's Way" refers to bodhi, the awakening of the Buddha, and bodhicitta is the vow to complete the path to full awakening. To actualize this aspiration for full awakening, the support of the first three great vows is needed. The first great vow is to liberate each and every one of the countless sentient beings because we feel their suffering in saṃsāra as our own. This great compassion leads to the second great vow, to eradicate the numberless defilements of ourselves and all others. This shows that great compassion is neither sentimental pity nor a romantic idea of spirituality; it spurs the generation of wisdom that will eliminate the defilements completely. This leads to the third great vow, to cultivate the countless approaches that remove these defilements. Just as there are numberless defilements, there are measureless realizations and measureless skillful means to master to overcome them.

Although someone could protest that these four vows are too vast and may be impossible to actualize, such concerns do not plague a genuine Mahāyāna practitioner. Instead, her mind is focused on the awakening of all sentient beings, and thus she is willing to do everything possible to bring it about, such as eradicate the endless defilements that pollute her own and others' mindstreams, cultivate all the diverse remedies the Buddha has taught for overcoming defilements, actualize all awakened qualities, and attain the supreme awakening of a buddha.

REFLECTION

1. Compare the Four Great Vows with the Five Great Vows mentioned before.
2. Ponder each great vow and feel it in your heart. While doing this, let your mind and heart open. Don't let doubt interrupt your contemplation.

In his *Treatise on the Ten Grounds* (TTG 266), Nāgārjuna counsels us never to be lax in benefiting others:

> No matter where the bodhisattva abides,
> if he fails to initiate the transformative teaching of beings,
> thus allowing them to fall into the three wretched destinies,
> he then thereby richly deserves the censure of the buddhas.
>
> And so it is that the bodhisattva, no matter in what country he abides, and no matter whether he is in the city or village, in the mountains, or beneath a tree—wherever he has the power by which he is able to benefit and teach beings—if he instead withdraws from them in disgust, begrudging them their covetous attachment to the pleasures of the world and thus becomes

unable to initiate their transformative teaching, thereby allowing them to fall into the wretched destinies—this bodhisattva thereby becomes richly deserving of the censure of all buddhas now abiding throughout the ten directions and thereby becomes worthy of feeling shame and disgrace in their eyes, [worthy, too, of being rebuked by their asking], "Oh, how could you let such petty reasons occasion the abandonment of such a great endeavor?!"

Consequently, if the bodhisattva does not wish to become deserving of being rebuked by the buddhas, even when faced with all sorts of flattering, devious, and severely evil beings, he should not let his resolve degenerate. Rather he should benefit them in whatever way befits his powers to help them. He should resort to all manner of expedients and diligent resolve to initiate their transformative teaching.

The Bodhisattva Ethical Code in Chinese Buddhism

Two renditions of the bodhisattva ethical code exist in Chinese Buddhism. One is presented in the *Brahmā's Net Sūtra* (*Brahmajāla Sūtra*).[69] For monastics the bodhisattva ethical code comprises ten root precepts and forty-eight auxiliary precepts. The second version is presented in the *Treatise on the Grounds of Yogic Practice* (*Yogācārabhūmi Śāstra*) by Maitreya,[70] with four root precepts and forty-one auxiliary precepts. There is much overlap in the listing of the bodhisattva precepts in these two scriptures, and there is also much overlap with the bodhisattva precepts as found in Tibetan Buddhism.

In general, the bodhisattva precepts according to the *Brahmā's Net Sūtra* are considered more suitable for bodhisattvas who have attained some realization of emptiness, whereas those from the *Yogācārabhūmi Śāstra* are said to be more fitting for less experienced bodhisattvas. In the past, the set of precepts from the *Brahmā's Net Sūtra* (*Brahmajāla Sūtra*) was more popular in Taiwan, but in recent years many preceptors are following the version in the *Yogācārabhūmi Śāstra*. The *Brahmā's Net Sūtra* lists the bodhisattva precepts in a way similar to the *Prātimokṣa Sūtra*, in which the ten root precepts are referred to as defeats (*pārājika*). Here "pārājika" refers to a major transgression; it does not mean that a person who transgresses it will be expelled from the Saṅgha. The bodhisattva precepts are taken from now until full awakening, and all transgressions, no matter how serious, can be purified through confession and repentance. The bodhisattva precepts for lay followers have six major and twenty-eight auxiliary precepts. In many Chinese temples, monastics recite the bodhisattva precepts together twice a month. Chinese Buddhist monasteries also regularly hold day-long repentance ceremonies that lay followers may also participate in.

Bodhisattva Precepts according to the Yogācārabhūmi Śāstra

The four root bodhisattva precepts from the *Yogācārabhūmi Śāstra* are to abandon these activities:

1. Praising oneself and deprecating others—relinquishing great compassion, one is miserly and concerned with one's own name and fame and with receiving offerings.
2. Refusing to help those in need—losing one's great compassion, one makes no effort to share the Dharma or material goods with those who are in dire need.
3. Refusing to accept someone's sincere apology and not helping those who repent and wish to follow the correct path—giving in to anger, one forsakes one's great compassion and is not willing to teach or guide those who are repentant.
4. Deceiving others by teaching what appears to be the Buddhadharma but is not, teaching wrong views to others while telling them this is the pure Dharma.

The forty-one auxiliary precepts in the *Yogācārabhūmi Śāstra* are to abandon (unless extenuating circumstances are present) these activities:

1. Not making offerings such as bowing, chanting, or thinking of the excellent qualities of the Three Jewels and praising them.
2. Being greedy and discontent, and longing for material possessions.
3. Failing to greet or pay proper respect to elder or fellow bodhisattvas (those who have taken the bodhisattva vow before you).
4. Refusing to accept offerings (thereby depriving people of the opportunity to create merit by being generous).

5. Refusing to accept gold, silver, jewels, and so forth offered by the faithful (thereby denying the donor the opportunity to create merit).
6. Not teaching the faithful when requested.
7. Abandoning, making others abandon, or refusing to guide those who are evil and wrong.
8. Being restricted by the rules of the Fundamental Vehicle instead of working to benefit many beings.
9. Engaging in insincere deeds or speech for profit; engaging in unwholesome livelihood without integrity or regret.
10. Acting in an undisciplined manner, joking, and partying.
11. Thinking or saying that bodhisattvas should dislike and turn away from nirvāṇa or that bodhisattvas should not reject and dislike worldliness.
12. Not preventing or correcting slander.
13. Not teaching with sincerity and serious words because of seeking profit, fear of reprisal, or displeasure.
14. Returning insult for insult, anger for anger, beating for beating, or criticism for criticism.
15. Not apologizing; even if you are innocent, you should apologize to calm suspicions.
16. Refusing to confess and repent one's misdeeds or bad behavior.
17. Being motivated by hatred, unwilling to forgive someone.
18. Being attached to comfort, keeping pets and servants.
19. Being lazy, sloppy, and sleeping excessively or at improper times.
20. Engaging in idle talk about worldly matters.
21. Rejecting the guidance or advice of your teacher.
22. Failing to oppose the five hindrances to serenity: attachment to sensual pleasure, malice, lethargy and sleep, restlessness and regret, and doubt.
23. Being attached to states of meditative absorption.
24. Slandering the Fundamental Vehicle, not studying its teachings.
25. Refusing to learn the skillful means of the bodhisattva path and learning only the Fundamental Vehicle teachings.
26. Not learning the Buddha's teachings and only studying non-Buddhist teachings or worldly subjects.

27. Refusing to accept teachings on the profundity of the bodhisattva way, its ultimate meanings, and the immeasurable power of the buddhas and bodhisattvas, and slandering those teachings by saying they lack benefit, are not the Buddha's words, and cannot bring relief to sentient beings.
28. Motivated by greed or unhappiness, praising your own merits and virtues and slandering others.
29. Not attending a Dharma talk or discussion out of arrogance or displeasure.
30. Disrespecting or slighting a Buddhist teacher, laughing at or slandering them, and picking at a teacher's words without examining their meaning.
31. Not being supportive and benevolent by refusing to participate in road works, farming, arbitrating, and other beneficial public affairs.
32. Not visiting or caring for the sick.
33. Not correcting someone who is about to or who has created a misdeed.
34. Not repaying the kindness of those who have helped you.
35. Knowing someone has family or financial problems but not comforting him or attempting to alleviate his distress.
36. Refusing to help the poor who ask for food and clothing.
37. Accepting disciples but not giving them proper guidance and not providing sufficient food, clothing, shelter, or medicine.
38. Being disagreeable or uncooperative.
39. Not praising others who are worthy of praise.
40. Not scolding, correcting, or restraining someone who is acting harmfully.
41. Not using supernormal powers to teach or help sentient beings if you have them.

Here we see that the bodhisattva precepts in Chinese Buddhism and Tibetan Buddhism rely on similar textual sources and have much in common. By studying the bodhisattva precepts of all the Buddhist traditions we gain more knowledge about how bodhisattvas conduct themselves in daily life. This gives us much help when we encounter difficult situations and need guidance on how to act in beneficial ways. It also gives us a detailed map of how to steer our thoughts, words, and deeds so that they accord with bodhicitta. The benefit for self and others of doing this is immeasurable.

Bodhisattva Precepts according to the Brahmā's Net Sūtra

The ten root bodhisattva precepts according to the *Brahmā's Net Sūtra* are to abandon these activities:

1. Killing.
2. Stealing.
3. Sexual misconduct (for monastics, this means celibacy).
4. Lying.
5. Dealing in intoxicants.
6. Discussing offenses of members of the four assemblies.[71]
7. Praising oneself and disparaging others, and concealing others' good work so that they are blamed.
8. Being stingy regarding material possessions or the Dharma, humiliating and scolding a person who asks for something.
9. Holding a grudge, refusing to accept another's apology.
10. Slandering the Three Jewels.

The forty-eight auxiliary precepts in the *Brahmā's Net Sūtra* are these:[72]

1. Do not disrespect senior teachers.
2. Do not consume alcohol.
3. Do not eat meat.
4. Do not eat the five pungent roots (garlic, scallions, leeks, onions, and asafetida).
5. Do not fail to encourage others to repent.
6. Do not fail to request instruction in the Dharma from visiting teachers.
7. Do not miss the chance to attend Dharma lectures.
8. Do not turn your back on the Mahāyāna and adopt the Fundamental Vehicle.
9. Do not fail to care for the sick.
10. Do not amass weapons.

11. Do not serve as a negotiator for the military.
12. Do not get involved in trading that causes trouble for others—for example, selling human beings, slaves, or certain kinds of animals.
13. Do not make groundless accusations.
14. Do not harm the living by setting fires.
15. Do not teach non-Buddhist doctrines.
16. Do not be stingy with material wealth or the Dharma.
17. Do not seek to gain political influence.
18. Do not pretend to be an accomplished teacher.
19. Do not get involved in treachery.
20. Do not fail to help the living or the deceased.
21. Do not be intolerant of wrongs done.
22. Do not arrogantly despise your Dharma teacher.
23. Do not despise beginning practitioners.
24. Do not fear the superior [scriptures and views] and follow inferior ones.
25. Do not fail to properly fulfill administrative duties.
26. Do not receive guests improperly.
27. Do not accept personal invitations.
28. Do not offer personal invitations to monastics.
29. Do not earn your livelihood improperly.
30. Do not hurt people while feigning intimacy.
31. Do not be lax in rescuing holy articles or images and important persons (spiritual mentors, parents, and so forth) from danger.
32. Do not deviously confiscate the property of others.
33. Do not pass your time idly.
34. Do not retreat from bodhicitta.
35. Do not fail to make unshakable resolves.
36. Do not fail to initiate unshakable resolves on your own.
37. Do not intentionally go to dangerous places.
38. Do not sit out of ordination order.
39. Do not pursue personal gain.
40. Do not err in terms of who can be taught. Give teachings and precepts equally to those who request to receive them.
41. Do not seek disciples for the wrong reasons—for example, to receive respect, fame, or offerings.

42. Do not teach the precepts to the wrong persons—for example, those without fame or those with wrong views.
43. Do not intentionally break the precepts.
44. Do not fail to revere the sūtras and the Vinaya.
45. Do not fail to teach sentient beings.
46. Do not teach the Dharma using improper protocol.
47. Do not establish systems that undermine the Dharma.
48. Do not undermine the Dharma from within.

Whether or not we have formally received the root and auxiliary precepts, we can see that they contain good guidance for living a virtuous life that does not harm self or others and that benefits both self and others.

The bodhisattva precepts are called the "threefold pure precepts" because they are composed of (1) precepts of restraint, which include the basic prātimokṣa and Mahāyāna precepts to abandon destructive actions; (2) precepts to engage in virtuous actions; and (3) precepts to benefit sentient beings. In Tibetan Buddhism, these three constitute the perfection of ethical conduct.

Both monastics and lay followers can receive bodhisattva ordination. Laypeople who take the bodhisattva precepts according to the *Brahmā's Net Sūtra* do not need to already have the basis of the five lay precepts, whereas those who take the bodhisattva precepts from the *Treatise on the Grounds of Yogic Practice* must have received the five precepts first.[73]

Monastics who receive the bodhisattva precepts must do so on the basis of the bhikṣu or bhikṣuṇī ordination. The bodhisattva precepts are given as the final phase of the Three Platform Ordination, a retreat of at least a month, during which monastic candidates first receive the śrāmaṇera/śrāmaṇerī ordination, the śikṣamāṇā (for women only) ordination, the bhikṣu/bhikṣuṇī ordination, and the bodhisattva ordination. The preceptor and the temple where the ordination platform is held agree on which version of the bodhisattva precepts to give.

Preceding the ceremony to receive the bodhisattva precepts is a voluntary ceremony in which people offer their body to the Buddha. For lay practitioners, this is done by making three small burns on the inside of their arm, near the elbow joint. In the case of monastics, they kneel and a senior Saṅgha member places three cones of incense on their freshly shaven head. While the hall resonates with everyone chanting "Homage to our Fundamental Teacher, Śākyamuni Buddha," the incense is lit. It burns down, later forming three small circular scars on the head. This moving ceremony is performed with three purposes in mind. It symbolizes offering our body to the buddhas and bodhisattvas, being willing to endure suffering when working for the benefit of sentient beings and striving for full awakening, and being a validly ordained monastic "bodhisattva." In ancient China, monastics were exempt from arrest by civil officials and punishment by civil law because they were governed by the Vinaya precepts. To avoid arrest by the police, some criminals would don monastic robes. To discern who was a genuine monastic from imposters, the custom was instituted to burn three, six, nine, or even twelve incense cones on a monastic's head. The incense marks also serve as an important daily reminder of monastics' precepts. Every morning, monastics touch their heads where the burns are and remind themselves: as I have this minor burn, sentient beings are immersed in the burning sea of saṃsāra. I will never forget my vow to cultivate bodhicitta diligently and to liberate all beings. When lay followers take the bodhisattva vow, they may also participate in an incense-burning ceremony, in which case the incense cones are placed on their forearm.

REFLECTION

1. Contemplate each of the ten root precepts. In what way does each one help guide your life as well as your thoughts, words, and actions in a good direction?
2. Contemplate each of the forty-eight auxiliary precepts in the same way.
3. Think of the benefit you could derive by trying to live your life according to them.
4. Without formally taking them, divide them into groups and try paying special attention to one group for a week until you have practiced all the precepts.
5. How has doing this helped you and those around you?

The Bodhisattva Ethical Code in Japanese Buddhism

The lineage of the prātimokṣa ordination does not exist in Japan at present, although Zen priests and lay followers may take the bodhisattva precepts. This entails keeping sixteen precepts:

1. Do not kill, but cherish all life.
2. Do not take what is not freely given, but respect all things.
3. Do not lie, but speak the truth.
4. Do not engage in improper sexuality, but live a life of purity and self-restraint. (How this precept is kept depends on one's life circumstances.)
5. Do not take substances that confuse the mind, but keep the mind clear at all times.
6. Do not speak of the misdeeds of others, but be understanding and sympathetic.
7. Do not praise oneself and disparage others, but work on one's own shortcomings.
8. Do not withhold spiritual or material aid, but give them freely where needed.
9. Do not indulge in anger, but exercise restraint.
10. Do not revile the Three Treasures of the Buddha, Dharma, and Saṅgha, but cherish and uphold them.
11. Avoid evil.
12. Do good.
13. Liberate all sentient beings.
14. Take refuge in the Buddha and resolve that, together with all beings, I will understand the Great Way whereby the seed of buddhahood may forever thrive.
15. Take refuge in the Dharma and resolve that, together with all beings, I will enter deeply into the sūtra treasury, whereby my wisdom may grow as vast as the ocean.
16. Take refuge in the Saṅgha and in their wisdom, example, and never-failing help, and resolve to live in harmony with all beings.

While there are differences in the delineation of the bodhisattva precepts in the various Mahāyāna traditions, their essence and purpose are the same. Taking and living in the bodhisattva precepts brings only benefit.

Bodhicitta, True Suchness, and Buddha Nature

Pure mind and buddha nature refer to the same thing but approach it from different angles. "Pure mind" indicates that the nature of the mind is not and cannot be polluted by defilements. "Buddha nature" refers to the aspect of that mind that guarantees our potential and capability to become buddhas. When fully purified, this is called the "awakened mind" or actual bodhicitta, indicating that while ignorance was initially present and we did not know our pure nature, now with the removal of ignorance we see and understand it. From the perspective that unawakened beings do not yet recognize the pure nature of their mind, it is said that they do not have the bodhi mind, but from the perspective of the fundamental nature of the mind being pure of adventitious defilements, it is said that they have the bodhi mind.

In this latter sense, "bodhicitta" or "bodhi mind" refers to the pure mind that can never be tarnished. It is like a pearl that has been covered with mud for thousands of years. Even though it is hidden in mud and its luster cannot be seen, none of its shining beauty has been lost; it is just temporarily obscured. It can be removed from the mud and cleaned so that its beauty is visible to all. Its luster did not decrease even though it was covered in mud for millennia, and its luster did not increase once it was extracted from the mud. Similarly, our buddha nature is always pure. Its qualities do not decrease when it is covered with the mud of defilements and they do not increase when the defilements are eradicated.

Bodhicitta is buddha nature. In the Chan tradition the terms "true suchness," "buddha nature," "original nature," "ultimate reality," "pure nature," and so on have similar meanings. They are different terms that refer to what is indescribable. To realize the buddha nature or bodhicitta is to realize that it is uncreated; it does not disappear and it is originally pure. When it is covered by defilements, we experience saṃsāra; grasping saṃsāra as real is an affliction that must be overcome to attain buddhahood.

The Five Stages of Cultivating Bodhicitta

As taught in scriptures, the Chan and Tiantai traditions say bodhicitta is cultivated and expanded in five stages. The first is making the vow to become a buddha and liberate all the countless sentient beings. This aspiration for buddhahood is called "bringing forth the bodhi mind (bodhicitta)." Although it is necessary to attain the bodhi mind, it is not the fully developed bodhi mind. Rather it is an aspiration to attain genuine bodhicitta, the bodhi mind, the One Mind.

The second is to engage in many practices and meditations to overcome attachment, anger, and other afflictions and to work toward awakening.

The third stage is called "awakening of the bodhicitta." At this time practitioners have a taste of actual bodhicitta because for the first time they directly realize the ultimate nature. In Chan this realization is called "awakening," and it occurs when one realizes the pure mind, which is the actual bodhicitta. In other words, a practitioner deeply understands and has direct experience of his or her own bodhi mind. At the same time he realizes the emptiness of this pure mind. Here "bodhicitta" does not mean the aspiration to attain awakening in order to benefit all sentient beings; it refers to the direct realization of one's own buddha nature. When people say a Chan master is awakened, it means he or she has attained at least the third stage. This awakening, however, is not complete, perfect awakening in that not all the obscurations have been forever eradicated.

The fourth stage is continuing to cultivate the bodhisattva practice in order to become fully and perfectly awakened. It is like the new moon gradually growing until it becomes full. This involves completing and perfecting the six perfections, which may take eons. But bodhisattvas are not discouraged by the length of time it takes. Like the bodhisattva Sudhana in the *Flower Ornament Sūtra*, they are willing to do whatever is necessary for whatever length of time is required in order to become a buddha so that they have the qualities and abilities that enable them to be of the greatest benefit to sentient beings.

The final stage is called the "supreme, ultimate bodhicitta"; this is buddhahood.

These five stages are very similar to the five paths of a bodhisattva as explained in the Tibetan tradition: the paths of accumulation, preparation, seeing, meditation, and no-more-learning. Nevertheless the meaning of the word "bodhicitta" and the manner in which it is used in Chinese and Tibetan Buddhism are slightly different. In the Tibetan tradition, "bodhicitta" usually refers to the aspiration to become a buddha for the benefit of sentient beings, although "ultimate bodhicitta" refers to the realization of emptiness. This is the ultimate reality that is directly realized on the third stage above, the awakening of the bodhicitta, or what in the Tibetan tradition is called the "path of seeing." Is this a realization of the emptiness of the mind, or is it a realization of the mind that is empty? Buddhist traditions have different assertions regarding this issue.

Here too, "awakening" has different meanings. From the Tibetan perspective, for bodhisattvas it refers only to the last stage, buddhahood, the path of no-more-learning. Chinese Buddhism also uses "awakening" to refer to any direct, nonconceptual realization of selflessness, which occurs before buddhahood. Neither tradition says that this first experience of the ultimate nature is final awakening; they agree that this realization needs to be cultivated and developed over time to attain the final goal of buddhahood. In addition, bodhisattvas must continue to create vast merit to support that wisdom so that it becomes powerful enough to eradicate all defilements. "Awakening" can also refer to the arhatship attained by following the Śrāvaka and Solitary Realizer Vehicles; however, for Mahāyāna practitioners, this is not the full awakening of a buddha.

9 | Bodhicitta and Bodhisattvas in the Pāli Tradition

MANY PEOPLE associate the Śrāvaka Vehicle with Theravāda Buddhism and the Bodhisattva Vehicle with the Mahāyāna. They then think that Theravāda and Mahāyāna as well as the vehicles and practices they teach do not coincide. Historically, these misconceptions have manifested in Theravāda practitioners alleging that the Mahāyāna teachings are not the word of the Buddha, and Mahāyāna practitioners claiming that Theravādins are selfish and lack compassion. Such rigid concepts are erroneous, and the ill will they create among the Buddha's disciples would surely displease the Buddha.

If we were to learn more about one another's traditions, many of these misconceptions would evaporate. Please see chapters 4 and 5 in *Approaching the Buddhist Path* and chapter 1 in *Buddhism: One Teacher, Many Traditions*. As discussed in these chapters, there are reasons to believe that the Mahāyāna sūtras were the Buddha's word. In this and future chapters we will see that not only are love and compassion taught and practiced in Theravāda Buddhism but so is the bodhisattva path. While the majority of practitioners in one or the other tradition may favor the aim of arhatship or buddhahood, that does not mean that the other option, together with its teachings and practitioners, is not found in that tradition.

Compassion

The Pāli suttas emphasize compassion time and again as the motivating force for the Buddha's attainment of awakening (AN 1.170):

> There is one person who arises in the world for the welfare of many people, for the happiness of many people, out of compassion for the world, for the benefit, welfare, and happiness of devas and humans. Who is that one person? The Tathāgata, the Arahant, the Perfectly Awakened One.

Here the word translated as compassion is *anukampā*, which etymologically means to be moved in response to others.[74] We sentient beings are the beneficiaries of the Buddha's compassion. The commentary explains the passage above: "for the welfare of the multitude" indicates that the Buddha is endowed with wisdom and thus instructs sentient beings on how to obtain benefit now and in the future; "for the happiness of the multitude" means that with an open hand, he demonstrates the joy of serving others; "out of compassion for the world" indicates that the Buddha protects the world with love and compassion like those of a parent for their beloved child; "for the benefit, welfare, and happiness of devas and humans" shows that his primary audience consists of those suitable to realize the paths and fruits in this lifetime because they have the optimum rebirth and conditions to do so as gods and humans. Of course, the Buddha aims to benefit the beings born in unfortunate realms as well, first by helping them to attain rebirth as gods and humans. He works for the "benefit" or the ultimate aim of nirvāṇa, for the "welfare" of the path that leads to it, and for the "happiness" of the fruition-attainment (P. *phala samāpatti*)—the reexperiencing of nirvāṇa after initially attaining it—which is the supreme happiness.

The Buddha describes his compassion, which is totally unbiased and unlike our ordinary notion of compassion (SN 10.806–7):

> If, O Sakka, for some reason
> intimacy with anyone should arise,
> the wise person ought not to stir his mind
> with compassion (that is, attachment) toward such a person.
>
> But if, with a mind clear and pure,
> he gives instructions to others,
> he does not become fettered
> by his compassion and tender care.

These verses explain that a wise person does not instruct others or become close to them if there is danger that attachment (called "compassion" in the first verse) will arise between them. However, a wise person whose mind is clear and free from attachment teaches others for their benefit with compassion and tender care that are free from the stickiness of attachment.

Whereas ordinary people are compassionate toward relatives and friends because those people help them, the Buddha is compassionate simply because others are suffering, regardless of whether or not they benefit him. Whereas the compassion of ordinary beings is often mixed with attachment and expectations, which pull them into unhealthy relationships, the Buddha's mind is clear and his compassion and tender care are free from attachment, the need for approval, and other self-centered emotions. The Pāli Abhidharma explains that attachment is a mental state that sticks to its object as meat sticks to a hot frying pan. It is always accompanied by confusion, agitation, lack of integrity, and lack of consideration for others. Attachment is shrouded in unclarity, whereas true compassion is bright, clear, and without limits.

The Buddha's compassion is evident in the sūtras. Compassion was the force enabling him to speak to so many different kinds of people—the rich and the poor, the educated and the uneducated, those who respected him and those who scorned him. Motivated by compassion for others who are ensnared in cyclic existence by their ignorance and craving, he shared the teachings that brought temporal and ultimate happiness with whomever was interested. He did not ask for anything in return; there was no charge to attend his discourses.

Compassion also fueled the Buddha's choice of lifestyle. Because he was free from attachment, he could have lived in a comfortable setting without incurring any faults. However, out of compassion for future generations of practitioners, he continued to live a simple lifestyle as a monastic. He usually dwelled in the forest, wore patched robes, and went on alms round to receive food. In this way, he set an example for future practitioners to also live a simple lifestyle and practice sense restraint, and in this way to quickly attain nirvāṇa.

The Compassion of Arhats and Śrāvaka Learners

Accounts in the Pāli sūtras clearly show that arhats, as well as śrāvaka learners—practitioners who are on the path—have compassion. In fact, the Buddha encourages them to practice with the motivation of compassion (DN 16.3.50):

> Monastics, for this reason those matters which I have discovered and proclaimed should be thoroughly learnt by you, practiced, developed and cultivated, so that this holy life may endure for a long time, for the welfare of the multitude, for the happiness of the multitude, out of compassion for the world; for the benefit, welfare, and happiness of devas and humans.

That is, monastics engage in the path to liberation not only for their own benefit but also in order to preserve the Dharma so that future generations will have access to these liberating teachings. They practice to become exemplars who inspire others to practice the path and attain liberation, or full awakening. The Buddha stressed that out of concern and compassion for others, monastics must remain in harmony with regard to his teachings, without quarreling or dividing into factitious groups.

Speaking of Anuruddha, Nandiya, and Kimbila, three arhat monks, the Buddha commented that if people, devas, and even Brahmās thought of them with a confident heart, that would bring about their welfare and happiness for a long time. This would occur because rejoicing at others' virtue uplifts our mind and creates merit. The Buddha says (MN 31.22):

> See how those three clansmen are practicing for the welfare of the multitude, for the happiness of the multitude, out of compassion for the world, for the benefit, welfare, and happiness of gods and humans.

The Buddha also praises Mahākāśyapa for teaching the Dharma to others with compassion, and Mahākāśyapa himself says that he became a monastic and cultivated contentment with simple food, plain clothing, and rudimentary shelter in order to benefit others. His hope was that others would see value in this lifestyle, adopt it for themselves, and obtain liberation.

The Vinaya (monastic discipline) explains that monastics are to admonish one another with kindness. In this way, they will avoid negativity, correct bad behavior, and overcome complacency and laziness. They should admonish one another with compassion even if it temporarily brings aggravation, as long as there is the possibility of leading someone on the wholesome path.

Although we see a difference in the expression of compassion in the Pāli and Sanskrit traditions, all of the Buddha's disciples try to be of benefit to others. In the Sanskrit sūtras, bodhisattvas not only teach the Dharma but also actively engage with suffering people in society. They sacrifice their own comfort to directly relieve the misery of others. In the Pāli sūtras, śrāvaka learners and arhats teach the Dharma and live the simple lifestyle of a monastic out of compassion for others, wishing to set an example for others to follow on how to practice in order to attain liberation.

Compassion in Daily Life

Nowadays many people feel that they have to decide between benefiting themselves and benefiting others because doing both is either impossible or impractical. They see this as a black-and-white choice: because there is only a finite amount of various material resources and a limited amount of time, they must choose whom to benefit—self or others. Then, pushed by the self-centered attitude, they choose to benefit themselves.

Holding the view that benefiting self and benefiting others are mutually exclusive is restrictive. Seen from a broader perspective, intelligently benefiting others also aids us. When we help others, we immediately witness others experiencing the good results of our actions. Our actions cause the environment in which we live to be more pleasant. Similarly, wisely benefiting ourselves aids others. Maintaining good health and keeping ourselves well-balanced physically and mentally creates a better atmosphere for all those we encounter. It also gives us more energy to share with others and enables us to practice the Dharma more consistently for the benefit of all. Thus in the Pāli canon, the Buddha praises those who work for both their own welfare and the welfare of others. The two are mutually beneficial (AN 4.95).

> There are these four kinds of persons found existing in the world. What four? (1) One who practices neither for his own welfare nor for the welfare of others; (2) one who practices for the welfare of others but not for his own welfare; (3) one who practices for his own welfare but not for the welfare of others; and (4) one who practices for both his own welfare and the welfare of others . . .
>
> The person practicing both for his own welfare and for the welfare of others is the foremost, the best, the preeminent, the supreme, and the finest of these four persons. Just as from a cow comes milk, from milk curd, from curd butter, from butter ghee, and from ghee cream-of-ghee—which is reckoned the foremost of all these—so the person practicing for both his own welfare and the welfare of others is the foremost, the best, the preeminent, the supreme, and the finest of these four persons.[75]

The Buddha encouraged both his lay and monastic disciples to be kindhearted and compassionate and to express these emotions verbally and physically. In the *Advice to Sigāla* (*Sigālaka Sutta*, DN 31), the Buddha taught the householder Sigāla how to behave in a caring manner to people in a variety of relationships, such as friends, spouses, parent and child, employer and employee (master and servant), teacher and student, and monastic and lay follower. For example, friends should help one another, share one another's fortune and misfortune as if it were their own, and advance one another's prosperity and good qualities. Employers should assign tasks according to the employees' capabilities, pay them fairly, care for them when they are sick, and give them sufficient leisure time after they have worked diligently. Employees should respect their employers, carry out assignments with a pleasant attitude, complete their jobs, and be honest. Lay followers care for monastics with physical, verbal, and mental affection, supply the four requisites to facilitate their practice, and respect them for keeping precepts. Monastics reciprocate by living in pure ethical conduct, counseling lay followers to restrain from destructive actions and to be compassionate and engage in constructive actions, and showing them the path to fortunate rebirth and liberation. To the Buddha, kindness and compassion weren't simply to be developed on the meditation cushion; they were to be put into practice in daily life encounters in the various relationships we have with others.

In the Pāli canon monastics are separate from society in that they do not have a householder's lifestyle, but they are part of society in that they interact with all people. They are to be receptive to, accept offerings from, and counsel those from all socioeconomic, racial, ethnic, and educational classes. The monastics' duty is to show people how to live ethically and earn their livelihood in a nonharmful manner, to encourage them to practice mindfulness, to teach them the Dharma, and to be grateful recipients of their gifts so that the laity can accumulate merit from making offerings. Since there are always many people whom monastics can potentially benefit, it is recommended that they first serve those who have confidence in the Dharma and have a generous heart. The Buddha sent the monastics out to share and spread the Dharma, saying (SN 4.5):

> Monastics, go and travel around for the welfare of the multitude, for the happiness of the multitude, out of compassion for the world, for the benefit, welfare, and happiness of devas and humans. Let not two go the same way. Teach the Dharma that is good in the beginning, good in the middle, and good in the end with the right meaning and phrasing.

In traditional Theravāda societies and within some groups in the West, monastics' way of demonstrating compassion accords with the above description. However, in Asia and in the West there is also a call for monastics to become more involved in social welfare projects and for lay followers to become Dharma teachers. The ways in which monastics and lay followers live their compassion is changing as society changes.

Compassion may involve interceding when harm is occurring or when someone is behaving in an inappropriate manner. It is important to ensure our motivation is one of compassion, however, and not an urge to control others or to angrily correct them. In *What Do You Think about Me?* (*Kinti Sutta*, MN 103) the Buddha recommends not to rush to reprove someone who is behaving improperly. First, we should evaluate the situation. If our mind will not be disturbed, and if the other person is not prone to anger and is not attached to his views, speaking to him is suitable. If our mind won't be disturbed, and if the other person is prone to anger, but it appears in this situation that he is not firmly attached to his views, we should speak. Although he may be irritated, it will be a trifle and the benefit of helping him avoid nonvirtue is great. In a third situation, we may be troubled, but the other person will not be provoked because he is not easily angered even though he is attached to his view. Here, too, if we can help turn the person away from bad behavior, we should do so.

In the fourth situation, we will be disturbed and the other person provoked because they are prone to anger and attached to their opinion, yet we think we can still turn them away from committing a wrongdoing. Here, our discomfort and the other's sensitivity and hurt are seen as minor compared to the value of preventing them from engaging in a great misdeed. In this case, we should intervene.

However, equanimity and nonintervention are called for when we will be disturbed and the other will be provoked because they are easily angered and are strongly attached to their idea, and we don't think we can change their mind. If they are impolite, equanimity on our part is called for. If we correct someone over every small, bad-mannered action they do, both of us will get irritable and no good will result.

REFLECTION

Make examples of the following situations you have faced, heard about, or seen in the media. How did you or other people respond and what was the result of that response? If the result was not positive, what would have been a more appropriate course of action?

1. If our mind will not be disturbed, and if the other person is not prone to anger and is not attached to his views, speaking to him is suitable.

2. If our mind won't be disturbed, and if the other person is prone to anger, but it appears in this situation that he is not firmly attached to his views, we should speak.

3. If we may be troubled, but the other person will not be provoked because he is not easily angered although he is attached to his view, and if we can help turn the person away from bad behavior, we should do so.

4. If we will be disturbed and the other person provoked because they are prone to anger and attached to their opinion, yet we think we can still turn them away from committing a wrongdoing, we should intervene.
5. If we will be disturbed and the other will be provoked because they are easily angered and are strongly attached to their idea, and we don't think we can change their mind, we should not intervene but should practice equanimity.

A loving mind is needed when others criticize or strike us, our friends, or our relatives. It is also needed when we are tempted to criticize others. A loving mind, especially at the level of access concentration or actual dhyāna, dispels fear. Fear arises easily in a mind that is angry and self-absorbed, whereas a mind filled with love for all beings is not suspicious of others' behavior and does not dwell on their faults. By treating them kindly, someone with a loving mind does not become the object of others' hostility, jealousy, or resentment.

Love manifests in your physical, verbal, and mental activities. Physically refrain from harming others, protect them, be considerate of them when living and working together, give them gifts, and offer your help and service when they need it. Keeping your precepts, showing respect to those worthy of respect, and being considerate of others' property and possessions are also loving physical activities.

Verbally speak truthfully, kindly, at appropriate times, and with meaningful words. If you know the Dharma well, explain good conduct and meditation practices to others. Help to organize Dharma events and other activities that benefit others. These are expressions of loving speech because much communication is needed when planning events. Also point out others' good qualities, their talents, and specific actions that they have done well. Encouraging others to be generous and to refrain from harming others and explaining to them how to subdue their anger or overcome hurt are also loving physical activities.

By abandoning a judgmental, critical attitude, mentally focus your attention on others' good qualities and worthy accomplishments. Leaving aside arrogance, competition, and jealousy, wish them well. Cultivate loving actions of body, speech, and mind openly when you are in the presence of others and also privately in your own mind in their absence. Thinking and acting in this way requires practice and mental training, but it brings about better relationships and fosters a more peaceful, joyful mind in us. Cultivating single-pointed concentration on such love brings the spiritual benefits of higher stages of concentration and insight.

The monk Anuruddha spoke eloquently of loving actions when the Buddha questioned him about how the peaceful accord with his fellow companions came about (MN 31.7):

> I think thus: "It is a gain for me, it is a great gain for me that I am living with such companions in the holy life." I maintain physical acts of loving-kindness toward those venerable ones both openly and privately. I maintain verbal acts of loving-kindness toward them both openly and privately. I maintain mental acts of loving-kindness toward them both openly and privately. I consider, "Why shouldn't I set aside what I wish to do and do what these venerable ones wish to do?" Then I set aside what I wish to do and do what these venerable ones wish to do. We are different in body, but one in mind.

REFLECTION

1. Anuruddha's words above are wise advice. Think of times in your life when you could practice them.
2. Imagine maintaining acts of physical, verbal, and mental kindness in these situations. How would you feel acting in that way? What effects would your actions have on the situation and the other people in it?

Levels of Love and Compassion

The Buddha talked to all his disciples about the importance of love and compassion for others in daily life, and to those involved in cultivating states of samādhi, he recommended them as "objects" of meditation. Here love—and by implication compassion,[76] empathic joy, and equanimity as well—are deliberately cultivated through special meditation techniques and are spoken of in three levels, according to the level of samādhi attained: (1) Love cultivated at the level of *full concentration* (P. *appanā samādhi*) is a mental state of full meditative absorption at the level of at least the first dhyāna; this is the immeasurable love of the four immeasurables. (2) Love at the level of *access concentration* (P. *upacāra samādhi*) is in a mental state of the preparations for a dhyāna, just before full absorption. (3) The *preliminary level of love* (P. *mettāya pubbabhāga*) is love in a mind that is not in a state of concentration.

Love and compassion also lead to the liberation of mind (P. *cetovimutti*) when concentration is at the level of the first, second, or third dhyānas. They are called "liberation of mind" because the mind is free from the five hindrances, especially anger. This state of concentration is an excellent basis for cultivating the insight that leads to liberation by wisdom and the four states of āryas.

But even the rudimentary level of love is valuable. The Buddha said that a monastic who has this love—love that relates to sentient beings with the wish for their well-being—for even the length of a fingersnap can "breathe easy" and accept offerings without worry of not deserving them. However, this love isn't simply an ordinary positive feeling toward a few people. It is universal and extended to all beings.

The Bodhisattva Path

Bodhicitta and the bodhisattva path are presented in the Pāli tradition. The oldest sūtras in the Pāli canon talk of three types of beings who attain awakening or arhatship: (1) The śrāvaka (P. *sāvaka*) hears teachings from a fully awakened buddha, practices them, and teaches others according to his ability after attaining awakening. (2) The solitary realizer (P. *pacceka-buddha*) arhat attains awakening without the aid of a teacher in her last life, but does not establish a dispensation (P. *sāsana*)—that is, she does not turn the Dharma wheel. (3) A fully awakened buddha (P. *sammāsambuddha*) first becomes a bodhisattva, attains awakening without the aid of a teacher in his last life, and begins a dispensation, turning the Dharma wheel so that the Buddhadharma exists in the world. This is the awakening attained by Śākyamuni, and it is extolled as superior to the awakening of either the śrāvaka or the solitary realizer.

The *Nidhikaṇḍa Sutta* (in the Khuddaka Nikāya)[77] says that by practicing generosity, ethical conduct, self-restraint, and other virtues, a practitioner may attain the perfection of a śrāvaka (P. *sāvaka-pāramī*), the awakening of a solitary realizer (P. *paccekabodhi*), or the ground of the Buddha (P. *buddhabhūmi*).

The *Upāsaka-janālankāra*, a twelfth-century Pāli treatise written by Thera Ānanda in the Theravāda tradition of the Mahāvihāra, speaks of three types of awakening: the awakening of the śrāvaka, the awakening of the solitary realizer, and the complete and perfect awakening (P. *sammā-sambodhi*) of a buddha.[78]

While śrāvaka arhats, solitary-realizer arhats, and buddha arhats are equal in having realized nirvāṇa, there are some differences in their qualities, as noted above. All the paths leading to the goals of the three vehicles are presented in the Pāli canon, and the option of which one to follow is an individual choice. Nevertheless, the vast majority of people following the Theravāda tradition have chosen the path of the śrāvaka arhat because it is the prominent ideal presented in the Pāli scriptures. Even though the path of the bodhisattva is present, most Theravāda sages of ancient as well as modern times see that as a path for exceptional individuals. They thus encourage their disciples to follow the eightfold path of the āryas and attain nirvāṇa, as the overwhelming number of sūtras propound.

However, at present and in the past, some Theravādins practice the bodhisattva path.[79] It is incorrect to think that bodhisattvas exist only in countries with Mahāyāna practitioners. Some Theravāda students learn and practice the bodhisattva path, and ārya bodhisattvas may manifest among Theravāda practitioners.

Although the path of a bodhisattva is not the prominent path explained in the Pāli sūtras, many Theravāda practitioners throughout the centuries have found it appealing and have followed it. Many of the early kings of Ceylon were spoken of as having bodhisattva-like qualities of compassion and generosity similar to those of the Buddha in his penultimate worldly life as King Vessantara. These rulers included King Duṭṭagāmaṇī and King Sirisaṃghabodhi, as recorded in the Ceylonese historical text the

Mahāvaṃsa, and King Buddhadāsa, as recorded in the Ceylonese history text the *Cūḷavaṃsa*. By the eighth century some kings in what are now Sri Lanka, Myanmar, and Thailand were either referred to as bodhisattvas by others or declared themselves to be bodhisattvas or practitioners of the bodhisattva path.[80] In tenth-century Sri Lanka, King Mahinda IV (956–972) declared in an inscription that "none but the bodhisattvas would be kings of Ceylon."[81] The Thai King Lu T'ai of Sukhothai reputedly "wished to become a buddha to help all beings . . . leave behind the sufferings of transmigration." The twelfth-century King Alaungsithu of Pagan in present-day Myanmar had a Pāli inscription written after he sponsored the building of the Shwegugyi Temple. In this verse he declared his intention to become a fully awakened buddha, not a śrāvaka. Many other kings of ancient Myanmar also aspired for buddhahood.

While this connection between royal rule and the bodhisattva ideal may have been influenced by Mahāyāna ideas present in those countries at that time, Theravāda Buddhism was the prominent tradition in those areas. Clearly the kings as well as the populace found the bodhisattva ideal not only acceptable but also exemplary, and saw their leader as embodying bodhisattva aspirations and deeds.

Some Theravāda learned adepts and practitioners were also attracted to the Bodhisattva Vehicle. For example, at the end of the commentary to the *Jātaka*, its author vows to fulfill the ten bodhisattva perfections (*pāramīs*) in order to become a buddha and liberate all beings from saṃsāra and lead them to nirvāṇa. In addition, the twelfth-century author of the *Milinda-ṭikā*, Thera Mahā-Tipitaka Cūlabhava of the Mahāvihāra tradition in Sri Lanka, wrote of his bodhicitta motivation in the colophon of this book. Here he stated, "*Buddho Bhaveyyam*"—May I become a Buddha—implying he was a bodhisattva aspiring to become a buddha.[82] Furthermore, some of the scribes of Buddhist texts on palm leaves in Sri Lanka stated their aspiration to become buddhas and are consequently regarded as bodhisattvas.

In the Mahāvihāra Monastery in Anuradhapura, Buddhaghosa was seen as the incarnation of Metteyya (Maitreya) Buddha, although it is not said that Buddhaghosa took the bodhisattva precepts or practiced the bodhisattva perfections.

Some Theravāda monks have also sought full awakening. The Sri Lankan Bhikkhu Doratiyāveye (ca. 1900) was accepted by his teacher to receive special instructions. However, he did not practice them because, by doing so, he believed he would become a stream-enterer and he had previously made the bodhisattva vow to become a buddha. Nowadays, also, there are Theravāda monastics and lay followers in Myanmar, Thailand, Sri Lanka, Cambodia, and so forth who make the resolve to become buddhas for the benefit of all sentient beings.[83]

In short, while we usually think of bodhisattvas in connection with the Mahāyāna tradition, they are not unknown in Theravādin countries. Two Thai masters are regarded as incarnations of Maitreya Bodhisattva, and statues of Kuan Yin (Avalokiteśvara) have been unearthed in Thailand, especially in the south. In some areas, there is a festival in the autumn in honor of Kuan Yin and people maintain a vegetarian diet during that time. While this practice probably originated with Chinese immigrants to Thailand, it has been adopted by many Thais in those areas.

The Bodhisattva in Pāli Literature

The concept of the bodhisattva has been present in Pāli literature from the beginning. In the sūtras, the Buddha often referred to himself as a bodhisattva. For example, in the *Shorter Discourse on the Mass of Suffering*, the Buddha says (MN 14.5), "Before my awakening, while I was still only an unawakened bodhisattva . . . " In the *Wonderful and Marvelous Sutta* (*Acchariya-abbhūta Sutta*, MN 123), Ānanda recalls the Buddha calling himself "the bodhisattva" when he spoke of his previous time in Tuṣita and his early life before attaining awakening under the bodhi tree. In the *Great Discourse on the Lineage* (*Mahāpadāna Sutta*, DN 14), the Buddha speaks about previous buddhas and their lives as bodhisattvas.

Well before the Mahāyāna was spread publicly, bodhisattvas began to appear more often in Pāli literature and practice. Since the Buddha said he was a bodhisattva before he attained awakening under the bodhi tree, naturally people were interested in how he practiced and what motivated him. In addition, scriptures talked of other wheel-turning Buddhas—buddhas who teach the Buddhadharma in a place and at a time when it had not previously been taught. In doing so, these buddhas liberate many beings from saṃsāra and initiate the Buddhadharma in the world, where it will benefit countless beings. Metteyya (Maitreya) is said to be the next wheel-turning Buddha and six preceding buddhas were also mentioned.

The Buddha spoke the *Chronicle of Buddhas* (*Buddhavaṃsa*) at the request of Śāriputra. This comparatively late text in the Khuddaka Nikāya, tells the story of twenty-five buddhas, including Buddha Gotama (Śākyamuni Buddha) in a previous life, who generated bodhicitta and made the vow to become a fully awakened buddha.

It is said that many eons ago, in one of his previous lives, Śākyamuni Buddha was a young man who cared for his blind mother after his father's death. He thought to become a merchant in order to support her well. As she had no one to care for her otherwise, she came along on the boat for one of his trading expeditions. Encountering bad weather, the ship wrecked and the mother and son were set afloat in the sea. The other passengers had drowned, and when the young man saw his mother struggling to keep her head above water, he felt her suffering was unbearable and swam to rescue her. In the process he realized that all sentient beings were drowning in the ocean of saṃsāra. Filled with compassion, he thought to cross the ocean of misery that was saṃsāric existence in order to take others across. To do that, he aspired to become a fully awakened buddha. In this way he awakened the thought of awakening, becoming a bodhisattva.[84]

Some lifetimes after that, Śākyamuni was born as Sumedha, a matted-hair ascetic practicing the path to arhatship. Hearing that Dīpaṅkara Buddha[85] was in a nearby town and eager to meet a fully awakened one, he went there. Upon seeing the Buddha, Sumedha was deeply moved. Realizing that becoming a fully awakened buddha would be of much greater benefit to the world, Sumedha knelt down and, in the presence of Dīpaṅkara Buddha, made the aspiration-vow (P. *abhinīhāra*) to become a fully awakened buddha.

His faith and exuberance for full awakening were apparent that same day, when he learned that the Buddha Dīpaṅkara and his disciples were soon to come along the path. He began to clear the path for them to pass, but when he was unable to finish before they arrived, Sumedha prostrated to Dīpaṅkara Buddha and then laid down in the mud. Sumedha relates this moving event (BVA II A.52–54):

> Loosening my hair, spreading my bark-garments and piece of hide there in the mire, I lay down prone. "Let the Buddha tread on me with his disciples. Do not let him tread in the mire—it will

> be for my welfare." While I was lying on the earth it was thus in my mind: If I so wished I could burn up my defilements today.

When he initially invited the Buddha and his disciples to use him as a bridge to cross the mud, Sumedha was focused on his own welfare. He knew that if he wished, he could eradicate all defilements and become an arhat that very day. Nevertheless, he questioned this self-centered intention and made the following determination to become an omniscient buddha and to lead all other beings out of cyclic existence (BVA II A.55–58):

> What is the use while I [remain] ignorant of realizing Dharma here? Having reached omniscience, I will become a buddha in the world with the devas. What is the use of my crossing over alone, being a person aware of my strength? Having reached omniscience, I will cause the world together with the devas to cross over.
>
> By this act of merit of mine toward the supreme amongst human beings, I will reach omniscience; I will cause many people to cross over. Cutting through the stream of saṃsāra, shattering the three renewed existences (the desire, form, and formless realms), embarking in the ship of Dhamma (the eightfold path of the āryas), I will cause the world with the devas to cross over.

At that time, Dīpaṅkara Buddha gave Sumedha the prediction of his awakening: he would actualize his vow to attain full awakening, becoming a buddha with the name Gotama after four countless and a hundred thousand eons.[86] Had Sumedha not made that aspiration and vow to attain buddhahood, he would have realized an arhat's awakening that very day by listening to a discourse by Dīpaṅkara Buddha. Sumedha had no regret, however; he was joyfully determined to become a buddha no matter how long it took.

Sumedha then went into seclusion and contemplated how to fulfill his aim of full awakening. He saw that the main virtuous qualities he would have to develop were the ten perfections. The *Buddhavaṃsa* then briefly sets out the ten perfections (BVA 116–66), making known a full-fledged bodhisattva path to supreme awakening. It is complete with a firm aspiration to attain buddhahood, the bodhisattva vow, the path of practicing the ten perfections and fulfilling them to the highest degree, the view of selflessness, and so forth. The *Chronicle of Buddhas* also names the ten perfections and records the names of each buddha's chief male and female disciples, attendants, life span, parinirvāṇa, and other details.[87]

The *Basket of Conduct* (*Cariyāpiṭaka*) in the Khuddaka Nikāya contains thirty-five stories of the bodhisattva Gotama's dedicated efforts to complete the perfections during the times of previous buddhas. For example, the ten perfections can be practiced to a normal, higher, and ultimate degree. This is illustrated in the practice of generosity, the first perfection. Giving such things as food, drink, bedding, and sandals is normal generosity; giving his eyes and other body parts is higher generosity; and giving his own life is generosity at the ultimate level. The *Jātaka* contains about 550 stories of the bodhisattva in his previous lives while he was practicing the bodhisattva path and perfecting the perfections that would enable him to become a fully awakened buddha in our age.

In the *Great Discourse on the Lineage*, the Buddha spoke of six previous buddhas—Vipassin, Sikhī, Vessabhū, Kakusandha, Koṅāgamana, and Kassapa—after whom he arose as the seventh buddha. Each of these previous buddhas had also been a bodhisattva. He then describes Vipassin's bodhisattva activities from descending from Tuṣita to his awakening and teaching the Dharma and Vinaya. In the *Apadāna*,[88] thirty-five precious buddhas are mentioned, implying that all of them had generated bodhicitta and practiced the bodhisattva path.

In the *Lion's Roar on the Turning of the Wheel* (*Cakkavatti Sīhanāda Sutta*, DN 26), the Buddha predicted the future Buddha Metteyya, who also would follow the bodhisattva path prior to becoming a buddha. However the Buddha did not present the bodhisattva path and the full awakening of buddhahood as being limited to the previous six buddhas and to the future Metteyya Buddha. In the *Sutta on Serene Faith*, Sāriputta says (*Sampasādanīya Sutta*, DN 28.19):

> I have heard and received it from the Blessed One's own lips, "There have been in the past, and there will be in the future, Arahant Buddhas equal in awakening to myself."

In other words, the bodhisattva path and the attainment of full awakening through it are open to many others. As mentioned above, the *Nidhikaṇḍa Sutta* presents full awakening as one of three possible results that a spiritual seeker may aim for.[89]

> Discriminating knowledge, release of mind, the perfections of an ariya disciple (a śrāvaka ārya), the awakening of a solitary buddha (solitary realizer), and the requisites for (supreme) buddhahood—all these [qualities] can be obtained by this [treasure] . . . Therefore wise and educated men praise the acquisition of meritorious actions.

Here we see that buddhahood is not limited to people the Buddha specifically mentioned in other sutras but is open to all who may choose it.

The *Birth Stories of the Ten Bodhisattvas* (*Dasabodhisattuppattikathā*), a post-canonical Pāli composition, extolls the qualities of bodhisattvas and relates the stories of ten bodhisattvas, including Metteya, who in the future will generate bodhicitta, practice the perfections, and attain awakening. This work begins with Sāriputta asking the Buddha if there will be perfect buddhas in future eons, to which the Buddha responds (BD 1.1–2):

> Sāriputta, there have been limitless and countless ariya people in the world who have successively fulfilled the pāramīs, attained buddhahood, and, having completed a buddha's duty, passed away at the end of their life span. In the future, too, there will be limitless and countless ariya people who, having enjoyed the pleasures of the sensual world and the bliss of the Brahmā worlds, having successively fulfilled the pāramīs with courage and determination, will attain buddhahood and pass away having completed a buddha's duty.

Dhammapāla, a sixth-century commentator, composed the *Treatise on the Pāramīs,* which is included in his commentary on the *Basket of Conduct.* He draws on the *Jātaka*, *Chronicle of Buddhas*, and *Basket of Conduct*, which are Pāli canonical texts, as well as on the *Bodhisattva Grounds* (*Bodhisattvabhūmi*) by Asaṅga.

REFLECTION

1. Imagine and let your mind be inspired by the story of the Buddha in a previous life when he was a young man caring for his blind widowed mother, his insight into the nature of saṃsāra, and the awakening of his bodhicitta.
2. Contemplate Sumedha's encounter with Dīpaṅkara Buddha, his offering to Dīpaṅkara Buddha, and the way his mind transformed into bodhicitta. Imagine Dīpaṅkara Buddha prophesizing Sumedha becoming Śākyamuni Buddha. Recognize that you too have the potential to generate bodhicitta and attain full awakening.

For the Success of Bodhicitta

All twenty-four buddhas whose life stories are found in the *Buddhavaṃsa* traversed a similar path in becoming buddhas. First, they made an unshakable resolve (*praṇidhāna, pranidhāna*) to become a bodhisattva and then a buddha. This mental resolve is expressed repeatedly by making an aspiration-vow (P. *abhinīhāra*) to attain full awakening for the benefit of all sentient beings in the presence of many buddhas. This aspiration is concerned with both the short-term and long-term welfare of all beings, wanting them to have temporal happiness in saṃsāra and especially wanting to help them tame and purify their minds so that they can attain nirvāṇa and full awakening. Then bodhisattvas perform an act of merit (P. *adhikāra*) to demonstrate to each buddha their sincerity and dedication to fulfilling their aspiration. This is followed by each buddha making a prediction (*vyākaraṇa, veyyākaraṇa*) of when that bodhisattva will become a buddha and what that buddha's name will be.

For the aspiration to attain awakening to be successful and for buddhahood to be attained, it should be supported by eight conditions (BVA II A.59): The person who makes this altruistic aspiration (1) is a human being (*manussa*, or *manussatta*); (2) is a male (P. *liṅgasampatti*); (3) has the necessary supportive causes and conditions (P. *hetu*)—for example, a firm Dharma practice; (4) has generated the bodhicitta aspiration (P. *satthāradassana*) in the presence of a living buddha (not a spiritual mentor, statue, stūpa, bodhi tree, or śrāvaka or solitary-realizer arhat); (5) has gone forth as a monk (P. *pabbajjā*); (6) has achieved special qualities (P. *guṇasampatti*), such as the direct knowledges (P. *abhiññā*) and the higher states of meditative absorption; (7) has such deep dedication and devotion (P. *adhikāra*) for the Buddha that he is willing to give up his life and perform great acts of merit for the Three Jewels; and (8) has strong virtuous desire and determination to cultivate the qualities that bring about buddhahood (P. *chandatā*).

A bodhisattva's desire for full awakening should be so intense that "if he were to hear, 'buddhahood can only be attained after experiencing torture in hell for four countless and a hundred thousand eons,' he would not deem that difficult to do, but would be filled with desire for the task and would not shrink away" (TP 6).

At the time of generating bodhicitta when a person becomes a bodhisattva, his mind becomes completely fixed on and devoted to awakening; thereafter he investigates the perfections, trains in them, and fulfills them as Sumedha did.

In addition to generating the aspiration for awakening, great compassion (P. *mahākaruṇā*) and skillful means (P. *upāyakosalla*) are also conditions needed to practice the perfections. Skillful means is the wisdom that transforms the ten perfections into the collections necessary to attain awakening. Dhammapāla says (TP 6):

> These Great Beings devote themselves to working uninterruptedly for the welfare of others without any concern for their own happiness and without any fear . . . they are able to promote the welfare [of all sentient beings] and even on occasions when they are merely seen, heard of, or recollected inspire confidence [in others]. Through his wisdom a bodhisattva perfects within himself the character of a buddha; through his compassion, the ability to perform the work of a buddha. Through wisdom he brings himself across [the ocean of saṃsāra]; through compassion he leads others across. Through wisdom he understands the suffering of others, through compassion he strives to alleviate their suffering. Through wisdom he becomes disenchanted with suffering, through compassion he accepts suffering. Through wisdom he aspires for nirvāṇa, through compassion he remains in saṃsāra.

> Through compassion he enters saṃsāra, through wisdom he does not delight in it. Through wisdom he destroys all attachments, but because his wisdom is accompanied by compassion he never desists from activities that benefit others. Through compassion he trembles with sympathy for all, but because his compassion is accompanied by wisdom, his mind is unattached. Through wisdom he is free from "I-making" and "mine-making,"[90] through compassion he is free from lethargy and depression.
>
> So, too, through wisdom and compassion respectively, he becomes his own protector and the protector of others, a sage and a hero, one who does not torment himself or torment others, one who promotes his own welfare and the welfare of others, fearless and a giver of fearlessness, dominated by consideration for the Dhamma and by consideration for the world, grateful for favors done and active in doing favors for others, devoid of ignorance and craving, accomplished in knowledge and in conduct, possessed of the powers and of the grounds for self-confidence. Thus wisdom and compassion, as the means for attaining each of the specific fruits of the pāramīs, is the condition for the pāramīs. The same pair is a condition for the resolution as well.

Other qualities are also conditions to practice the perfections. These are zeal, competence, stability, and beneficent conduct. *Zeal* is energy in completing the collections, *competence* is wisdom in skillfully practicing the collections, *stability* is firm determination, and *beneficent conduct* is cultivating love and compassion. A bodhisattva also cultivates six inclinations—renunciation, solitude, nonattachment, nonhatred, nonconfusion, and release from saṃsāra—based on seeing the faults of their opposites. For example, seeing the disadvantages of lay life with its sense pleasures, he inclines toward renunciation, and seeing the disadvantages of a distracting social life, he inclines toward solitude. When the opposites of these six inclinations flourish in the mind, cultivating the bodhisattva practices becomes extremely difficult, if not impossible. Seeing the faults of the opposites of the perfections helps to create good conditions for us to train in them. For example, seeing the disadvantages of miserliness inclines us to practice generosity, and seeing the disadvantages of deceptive speech inclines us to practice truthfulness. Therefore, to actualize our deep admiration for the bodhisattva path and its results, it is wise to cultivate the conditions that enable us to practice the perfections and to abandon their interfering opposites.

In conclusion, although many people believe that the bodhisattva path as found in the Pāli scriptures is for only those who are destined to become wheel-turning buddhas, when we explore the Pāli literature more deeply, we find that Dhammapāla described a complete bodhisattva path that is open to all, should they aspire to follow it. In addition, we find that some Theravāda practitioners have followed that path and that historical texts in Theravāda areas refer to bodhisattvas subsequent to Śākyamuni Buddha.

10 | Mind Training

ALTHOUGH THE PURPOSE of all the Buddha's teachings is to train the mind, there arose in Tibet a special set of teachings called "mind training" or "thought training" (T. *blo sbyong*). It was developed by the Kadampa geshes, disciples of Atiśa and Dromtonpa, beginning around the twelfth century, but has its textual roots in Nāgārjuna's *Precious Garland* and Śāntideva's *Engaging in the Bodhisattvas' Deeds*, as well as in the *Ākāśagarbha Sūtra*, *Vimalakīrti Sūtra*, and *Akṣayamati Sūtra*, among others.

Taken up by all Tibetan Buddhist traditions, the mind-training texts center on the development of the two bodhicittas—conventional bodhicitta, which is the altruistic intention, and ultimate bodhicitta, the wisdom realizing emptiness. They especially emphasize cultivating bodhicitta by means of equalizing and exchanging self and others, and most are written in a pithy, straightforward style that aims directly at the self-centered attitude and self-grasping, the two principal enemies of bodhisattvas. The mind-training teachings eviscerate these hindrances and call out their ridiculous "logic" that leads to misery, replacing it with more realistic perspectives. The advice the mind-training texts give us is the opposite of what the self-centered attitude and self-grasping demand, and their recommended actions are the opposite of what our afflictive mind wants to do at that moment. Of course, that is what makes them so effective at quelling afflictions and protecting us from negativity.

The mind-training practices challenge us to reorient the framework through which we view the world, releasing the self-centered attitude and focusing instead on cherishing others more than self, and dedicating our lives to benefiting others temporally in saṃsāra and ultimately by showing them the way to full awakening. The practice of mind training helps us to remain balanced when we experience either happiness or suffering, without becoming giddy and overly optimistic when we are happy or discouraged and depressed when we face suffering. Whatever we encounter in life—wealth or poverty, success or failure, a multitude of friends or loneliness—we are steadfast in our pursuit of full awakening. In short, mind training shows us how to make all circumstances favorable to the path.

The Seven-Point Mind Training by Geshe Chekawa is perhaps the most well-known of the mind-training texts. I received the transmission and teachings on this text from my senior tutor, Ling Rinpoche, and have applied them throughout my life; this has brought great benefit to my mind and thus to all the beings I come in contact with. The seven points are (1) practicing the preliminaries, (2) training in the two types of bodhicitta, (3) taking adversity into the path to full awakening, (4) a summary of a lifetime's practice, (5) the measure of having trained the mind, (6) the commitment of mind training, and (7) the precepts of mind training.

The first point—the preliminaries of contemplating our precious human life, death and impermanence, karma and its effects, and the disadvantages of saṃsāra—were explained in previous volumes of the *Library of Wisdom and Compassion*. Regarding the second point on how to develop the two bodhicittas, the cultivation of conventional bodhicitta—what we commonly call simply "bodhicitta" or the altruistic intention—is the topic of the preceding chapters of this volume.

The third point comes below as we explore taking adversity into the path, referring to verses from several mind-training texts. The fourth point is a concise explanation of how to practice mind training throughout one's life and at death. This will be followed by the commitments and precepts of mind training—points six and seven—that give direction to our practice. To complete the chapter we'll look at some *gāthās*—short sentences or verses that apply to everyday actions, imbuing them with spiritual meaning and transforming them into the path.

Some mind-training texts dwell on how to transform adverse circumstances into the path. Such advice is applicable every day since, as we have all experienced, unwanted problems easily find their way into our lives. It's best to become familiar with this advice in our daily meditation when a strong affliction is not manifest in the mind. Recall a disturbing situation from the past and rerun it in your mind, but now think and imagine acting according to the mind-training instructions. At first this may seem unnatural, but as we become more familiar with a new, beneficial way of thinking, the easier it becomes. And when our perspective regarding difficulties begins to shift when we meditate, it will also change when we are in the midst of an actual situation.

Taking Adversity into the Path

Verses explaining how to take adversity into the path are dear to my heart. They have given me courage, compassion, and fortitude in difficult situations, such as when I fled Tibet and became a refugee, as well as in exile when I have done my best to help hundreds of thousands of Tibetans adapt to a new life without giving up hope of returning to our homeland.

In *The Seven-Point Mind Training*, the third point reads:

> When the vessel and its contents are filled with negativities, transform these unfavorable conditions into the path to awakening. Immediately apply whatever you encounter to meditation.

The "vessel" is our environment and "its contents" are the sentient beings who live in it. The degeneration of both is obvious: corruption, war, disharmony, and dispute are rampant between groups and nations and within them as well. Our environment is adversely affected by climate change, which will bring additional hardships to the sentient beings on planet Earth. In confronting this, we have four choices. The first is to hope it will go away and ignore it, which will only allow it to increase. The second is to become paranoid and aggressive, to yell and scream, and to accuse and threaten others, which only inflames a bad situation. The third is to despair and become depressed, which brings everyone down. The fourth is to get involved and try to help. Needless to say, this is the course we should choose. But it is important to maintain the proper mental attitude when doing so and to accept that our efforts may or may not produce the changes we seek. At the end, we are left with the state of our mind. How can we navigate living in these times and transform our experience into something valuable for what is most important for us as Dharma practitioners: attaining awakening so we can most effectively help in the long term?

Doing this begins with accepting the situation. Instead of becoming attached to hope, which here means magical thinking of success, or to fear that is based on imagining worst-case scenarios and living in dread of them, we ask ourselves how we can use these situations in our Dharma practice.

The answer depends on having a deep understanding of karma and its effects, knowing that whatever we experience is a result of our past actions. Try thinking: I'm experiencing difficulties now because of harmful actions done either earlier in this life or in previous lives. These actions were created under the influence of self-centeredness and ignorance. It's no use blaming others for my misery, and it's foolish to think that I deserve to suffer because I erred in the past. Rather, I will learn from my misdeeds. Since I don't like the result I'm experiencing, in the future I will avoid creating its cause.

If we're unsure what kind of causes we may have created in the past that bring this result, we can read about karma and its results. A mind-training text called *The Wheel of Sharp Weapons* discusses this, bringing in specific examples. In it are verses such as (WSW 9) this:[91]

> When my body falls prey to unbearable illnesses,
> it is the weapon of destructive karma returning on me
> for injuring the bodies of others;
> from now on I will take all sickness upon myself.

Accepting the reality of being ill eliminates the mental suffering—especially anxiety, worry, and fear—and makes being sick much more manageable. Think: This is a result of my physically injuring others in the past. What motivated such behavior? My self-centered attitude. Seeing the faults of self-preoccupation, I will now do my best to shun this attitude when it manifests in my mind; that will prevent my harming others in the future. In addition, I will do the taking and giving meditation, imagining taking all the illness of others on myself and giving them my happiness.

REFLECTION

1. In your meditation, think of a situation in which you experienced great mental suffering and contemplate this verse from *The Wheel of Sharp Weapons* (WSW 10):

When my mind falls prey to suffering,
it is the weapon of destructive karma turning upon me
for definitely causing turbulence in the hearts of others;
from now on I will take all suffering upon myself.

2. Accept your mental discomfort by linking it to the self-centered attitude and make a strong determination to not deliberately cause turmoil in others' minds and hearts.

3. Do the taking and giving meditation regarding this. At the conclusion, rest your mind in a peaceful state.

A similar approach is to meditate: "May my suffering suffice for all the suffering of others." Contemplate the various problems sentient beings are undergoing at this very moment: health problems, relationship problems, oppression, environmental hazards, and so forth. With a mind of compassion that cherishes all these beings and wants them to be free of suffering, think, "May the suffering I'm experiencing now be sufficient to eliminate all of their suffering." Imagine others being free of their pain. In doing this meditation, one surprising result is that we often realize that compared to what others are going through, our problem is not that bad. We can endure it. This gives us a lot of confidence and courage and alleviates our pain. However, we have to do this meditation with genuine compassion; if we do it just to get our own suffering to decrease, it won't work!

Another mind-training technique to use in difficult situations is to give all your suffering to the self-centered attitude, which is the real enemy responsible for this predicament. Here it is important to remember that the self-centeredness is not you; it is something apart from you, something that disturbs you and causes you problems. Feel that, having given the misery to the self-centered attitude, you are free of suffering.

The sincere practitioners of mind-training practice in a remarkable way, one that we have to build up to gradually. One prayer they make is this:

If it's better for me to be sick, may I be sick;
if it is better for me to get well, may I be well;
if it is better for me to die, may I die.

Their minds have shifted out of the self-centered perspective of ordinary beings that is anchored to "my happiness now" and they now look at life through the lens of "what will be best for all sentient beings in the long term?" With this new perspective, they feel completely comfortable in making the above wishes. Try thinking like this.

With this long-term perspective that not only understands karma but also knows what mental states are conducive to spiritual progress, a Kadampa master would think:

> If people despise me, I like it;
> if they praise me, my pride will grow.
> If they criticize me, I will clearly see my faults
> and have the opportunity to correct them.
> Suffering is fine. If I enjoy too much, I will exhaust my good karma.
> If I suffer, I exhaust my bad karma, and that is good.

When we are sincerely intent on generating bodhicitta and practicing the bodhisattvas' deeds, thoughts such as these make perfect sense. This way of thinking is not masochistic; in fact, it is beneficial. Self-centeredness brings us only pain. By relinquishing it and training the mind to cherish others even more than ourselves, our minds and hearts will be peaceful and content.

Maitrīyogi, one of Atiśa's principal teachers of mind training, thought in a similar way when he chanted "Melodies of an Adamantine Song":[92]

> Alas! To guide all beings who have been my parents,
> I'll extract without exception the five poisons of each being
> by means of the five poisonous afflictions present in me.
> Whatever virtue I may possess, such as an absence of attachment,
> I will distribute equally to all beings of the six classes [of sentient beings].
>
> Using the painful fruits [of my karma], such as sickness and so on,
> I will extract all similar sufferings of sentient beings.
> Whatever joy and benefit I may possess, such as absence of illness,
> I will distribute equally to all beings of the six classes.

If I do this, what occasion is there for me, even for a single instant,
to wander aimlessly in this ocean of cyclic existence?
Yet until I have attained [full] awakening,
whatever class of the five poisons and their fruits may lie in store,
I will exhaust entirely in this very lifetime.

I will extract them this very year and this very month;
I will exhaust them this very day and this very instant;
I will seek the means to cut even the thread of minor sufferings.
O Maitrīyogi, make sure that your mind becomes trained!

In the colophon Maitrīyogi says that he "regularly recites this song, wherein loving-kindness, compassion, and bodhicitta are sung as a diamond song," and that one time near the Ganges River, Maitreya Buddha, the future buddha who is the embodiment of great compassion, appeared to him in the form of a king.

Maitrīyogi brings up another important point in mind training: when experiencing happiness due to the ripening of virtuous karma created in the past, share the satisfaction with other sentient beings. Sometimes the happiness is such that we can give an object or share some kind words with others. Other times we mentally share our joy by dedicating it to others, as Maitrīyogi does when he mentally gives his joy and benefit to all the six classes of saṃsāric beings.

There is no reason to feel guilty when experiencing happiness, joy, or pleasure. We should be happy when we practice the Dharma! Rather, understand that it is a product of our own virtuous actions and make a strong determination to continue engaging in such actions. Rejoicing at our merit and virtuous actions is important. That increases the karma of doing them. Likewise, rejoicing in the merit and virtue of others makes our mind happy and we create karma similar to that of the person who did the action.

Specific Advice for Difficult Situations

Another mind-training text is *The Thirty-Seven Practices of Bodhisattvas* by the Tibetan sage Togmay Sangpo (1295–1369). This text is one of my favorites and I have taught it frequently at large Dharma gatherings both in

India and in the West. Like other writings in this genre, it is in the form of short, pithy verses or sentences and covers all the major topics on the stages of the path. Its verses on transforming adversity into the path are especially pointed, often giving advice that is hard to listen to when our mind is afflictive, because the advice is the opposite of our usual, worldly way of thinking, feeling, and behaving. But of course, that's why the advice is the remedy! One good way to approach this is to "play" with the advice—that is, to imagine following it. Investigate for yourself if the new perspective is more reasonable than following your habitual emotional patterns. Examine if the new strategies for dealing with difficulties work better than blindly doing what you have always done. Below are a few verses from *The Thirty-Seven Practices of Bodhisattvas* that will give you not only a taste of the entire text but also some practical advice you can apply immediately (12, 15, 16, 19, 36).

> Even if someone out of strong desire
> steals all your wealth or has it stolen,
> dedicate to him your body, possessions,
> and your virtue, past, present, and future—
> this is the practice of bodhisattvas.

Ordinary beings who do not know the Dharma usually become very angry when their possessions are stolen. They feel violated and want their things to be returned and the thief punished. But when we practice with awakening as our goal, we have already mentally given our possessions to others. In that case, this supposed thief already owns our former belongings and has now come to collect them. Not only is there no reason to be angry at him, but in addition we should dedicate to him our body, possessions, and merit of the past, present, and future. May he be free of suffering and have all the external riches he desires as well as the internal riches of nonattachment and generosity.

> Though someone may deride and speak bad words
> about you in a public gathering,
> looking on her as a spiritual teacher,
> bow to her with respect—
> this is the practice of bodhisattvas.

We don't at all like when people ruin our reputation or put us down in front of others. Our usual way of dealing with public criticism is to insult the person in return, embellishing his faults and humiliating him. In fact, those who point out our faults are our teachers. Just as we have to see the dirt in a room to clean it, only by seeing our misdeeds and character faults can we have the opportunity to correct them. If we are sincerely interested in transforming our minds rather than enhancing our egos, we will respectfully thank this person.

Have you ever seen a speaker criticized during a public talk? If the speaker thanks the other person, the issue is quickly settled and the talk can continue. Thanking the other person doesn't mean we necessarily agree with what he said; it means we appreciate his comment and will think about it.

> Even if a person for whom you've cared
> like your own child regards you as an enemy,
> cherish him specially, like a mother
> does her child who is stricken by sickness—
> this is the practice of bodhisattvas.

When someone we trust and care about deeply returns our kindness by treating us as an enemy, ordinary beings feel hurt and angry. This situation may be likened to that of a mother who cares for her child with love and even sacrifices her happiness for the benefit of the child, but then the child is delirious with fever and, not knowing what he is doing, attacks his mother. Here the mother understands that the illness is the source of the child's behavior; likewise, those practicing the bodhisattva path understand that their dear one is overcome by afflictions and karma, which are the actual source of their bad behavior. In short, rather than taking someone's bad behavior toward you personally, reflect that they are stricken with the sickness of afflictions and karma and have compassion for them.

Having a compassionate attitude doesn't mean we allow the person to continue with their poor behavior. We do what we can to protect ourselves and to help that person stop, but our actions are motivated by compassion, not antipathy. This is a difficult but essential practice.

> Though you become famous and many bow to you,
> and you gain riches to equal Vaiśravaṇa,

see that worldly fortune is without essence,
and be unconceited—
this is the practice of bodhisattvas.

This verse is the opposite of the previous three. Here we are well-known, respected, and even well-to-do financially. Many people know about our good qualities or Dharma knowledge, and we are widely admired. The self-centered tendency in this situation is to become smug and conceited, thinking that we are someone great and looking down on others. We could even start to think that we are above the law or that our negative karma will not ripen.

But in such situations, well-trained practitioners think that whenever others treat them like a guest of honor, it is in the nature of suffering. They see its impermanence and know that being attached to praise, reputation, or wealth is meaningless because with a small change in conditions they could lose everything. As Dromtonpa said, "Though others may rate us very highly, the most expedient course is to see ourselves in the lowest rank." I try to practice this, and do my best to put myself at the lowest level. This is in fact the most practical thing to do; otherwise considerations of hierarchy cause trouble and agitation.

I know some people who have little knowledge but act with great pretentiousness. I find their behavior so futile that inwardly I cannot help laughing. To be without pride is the practice of a bodhisattva. It makes our life much easier; otherwise our mind is continuously tormented by comparing ourselves with others, feeling jealous of those who are better and arrogant toward those whom we consider inferior.

In brief, whatever you are doing,
ask yourself, "What's the state of my mind?"
With constant mindfulness and introspective awareness
accomplish others' good—
this is the practice of bodhisattvas.

This verse sums up the bodhisattva practice. Though we may look like a great practitioner who is very holy and benevolent, we may harbor resentment, revenge, and envy in our hearts. This is not Dharma practice, even if others are fooled by it. For our own sake and for the sake of others, we must be mindful in all circumstances so that nothing in us is secret, pretentious, or deceptive. We must be straightforward and honest. Should we notice corrupt motivations or bad behavior of our body, speech, or mind, we must think, "I am a follower of the bodhisattva path, of the Mahāyāna Dharma. I have the opportunity to be guided by many precious spiritual mentors and to hear their teachings. With all these opportunities, if I still act badly I'm deceiving my spiritual mentors, the bodhisattvas, and the sentient beings who trust me and count on my help. This would be a horrible thing for me to do."

As Śāntideva says (BCA 2.27), "I beseech you with clasped hands to be mindful in all your activities." Therefore, we must practice for the benefit of others, dedicate all our qualities, happiness, and abilities of body, speech, and mind to the service of sentient beings. We should constantly see ourselves as the servant of others and do nothing else except work for their benefit. This means maintaining a sincere and compassionate attitude in all we do, even small daily activities. The gāthās presented below will show you how to do this.

REFLECTION

1. Remember a time when your wealth or possessions were stolen or someone deprived you of what was rightfully yours. How did you feel? What did you want to do?
2. To free yourself from the pain of anger and to meet the emotional or physical need of the other person, give up ownership of those items and mentally give them to the other person.
3. Think of a time when someone derided and criticized you in front of a group of people.
4. Watching your reaction to this event, what do you learn about yourself? Is there anger, attachment to reputation, self-righteousness, or self-pity? See this person as being like a spiritual teacher: because they pointed out your weaknesses, you can now see them clearly and go about remedying them.

5. Recall a time when someone you trusted turned on you and acted in ways that caused you pain.

6. See that the person was overwhelmed by the power of their afflictions, like your child who is stricken with delirium as a result of fever. Have compassion for them, just as you would for your sick child.

7. Make a determination to have mindfulness and introspective awareness and to be aware of the state of your mind as much as possible. With compassion, work to benefit others.

A Lifetime's Practice

Geshe Chekawa (1102–76), the Kadampa geshe who wrote the *Seven-Point Mind Training*, condenses a lifetime's Dharma practice into five forces: the motivation, seed of merit, destruction, prayers of aspiration, and familiarity.

The force of the *morning motivation* starts the day off well. Before getting out of bed we set our intention: "Today I will not harm others and will benefit them in whatever way I can. To make my life meaningful, I will cherish others and use my body, speech, and mind to cultivate bodhicitta. With mindfulness and introspective awareness I will be vigilant and notice afflictions and the self-centered attitude as soon as they arise and immediately apply the appropriate counterforce."

Establishing a positive and optimistic motivation at the beginning of the day affects everything we do. Even if we engage in one of the ten nonvirtues, due to the power of our initial intention in the morning, it won't be so strong. It's helpful throughout the day to recall your motivation and center yourself so you stay on course.

The force of the *seed of merit* involves purification and collection of merit. To generate and continually grow bodhicitta, purifying negativities—those created long ago and those created recently—and creating merit are very important. They are like the water and fertilizer that prepare the field of the mind so that when the seeds of the Dharma teachings are planted, a large harvest of realization will grow. The preliminary practices, such as the seven-limb prayer, taking refuge, reciting the names of the buddhas and prostrating to them, making offerings, reciting the mantra of Vajrasattva, and so on are excellent ways to purify and create merit. Do these practices when you feel blocked in your practice or your mind is dull and unreceptive. They will help to clear obstacles.

The force of *destruction* involves destroying the self-centered attitude and the self-grasping ignorance. To do this, begin by contemplating their disadvantages: self-centeredness is the source of all suffering; it prevents our generating bodhicitta, entering the Mahāyāna path, and attaining full awakening. Self-grasping ignorance is the root of saṃsāra; it gives rise to attachment, anger, and all other afflictions and is the source of all nonvirtuous actions. It prevents us from realizing the ultimate nature of phenomena, becoming an ārya, and attaining full awakening.

Understanding their faults, whenever they arise counteract them. Cherishing others as well as love and compassion banish self-centeredness, and the wisdom realizing emptiness overcomes self-grasping ignorance. Put on the armor of joyous effort and oppose these enemies and enhance their opposites.

The force of *prayers of aspiration* can be done throughout the day, but especially at the end of the day it's helpful to review your attitudes and actions. Rejoice at all virtuous actions you and others did. Regret whatever nonvirtues you were involved in and purify them with the four opponent powers. Then dedicate all the past, present, and future merit of yourself and others to your own and all beings' full awakening. Dedicate so that you will never be separated from the practice of bodhicitta in this and all future lives, that the bodhicitta you have generated will never decrease but always increase, and that the bodhicitta you have not yet generated will arise and grow. Recalling all the goodness in the world and the merit of sentient beings and holy beings delights and uplifts the mind. Be sure to do this every day.

The final force is that of *familiarity*. By continually being aware of the higher aims that are the purpose of your life, bring everything you encounter into the path to awakening. Through study and contemplation, familiarize yourself with all aspects of the path, especially the determination to be free from saṃsāra, bodhicitta, and the wisdom realizing emptiness. When you are well acquainted with those, enter the Vajrayāna and learn and meditate on deity yoga. As Śāntideva reminds us, there's nothing that doesn't become easier through familiarity.

Setting our motivation sets the foundation for the practice of mind training and the two bodhicittas. The seed of merit strengthens these and the force of destruction overcomes obstacles to them. Prayers of aspiration strengthen them even more, so that we will not stray from making the generation of the two bodhicittas the most important activity of our lives. Familiarity enables us to be successful in the cultivation of love, compassion, bodhicitta, and the six perfections, especially the wisdom that will free us from saṃsāra.

Practicing these five forces every day ensures that we have covered the most important factors of mind training. There are many levels in which these five are done—some briefer, others more extensive; some emphasizing one force, others emphasizing another—but however we do them, the result will definitely be beneficial for yourself and others.

The five forces are also practiced at the time of dying and were explained in *The Foundation of Buddhist Practice*, 226–27. Since the time of our death is uncertain, it behooves us to learn and become familiar with these. Then, like the great masters, our death will be peaceful and free from fear and regret.

The Commitments and Precepts of Mind Training

The sixth and seventh points of the Seven-Point Mind Training consist of short statements with great meanings. Learning and following these will prevent us from getting distracted by the allures of saṃsāra and prevent self-centeredness from sabotaging our Dharma practice. In this way, our Dharma practice will remain on track.

The Eighteen Commitments of Mind Training

The following commitments keep our mind rooted in the mind-training practice.

1–3. Always practice the three general points.

(1) Don't go against the mind-training instructions or transgress any of the ethical restraints you have taken. Don't think that because you practice mind training that you are above abandoning the ten nonvirtues. (2) Don't use mind training as a reason for taking unnecessary risks—for example, pridefully thinking that because you practice mind training, you are special

and won't get sick or injured. (3) Don't be partial—for example, practicing mind training with people you like but not with those you dislike, being generous with friends but miserly with enemies, being courteous to important people but not to those you consider inferior.

4. Change your attitude while remaining natural.

Don't be conspicuous or show off your Dharma training practice so that others will think you are an advanced practitioner. Externally act like other people, although internally you transform situations by practicing mind training.

5. Speak not of the shortcomings of others.

Don't belittle or disparage others or exaggerate others' faults and spread nasty stories about them. Avoid separating people who are harmonious by talking behind their backs. With a kind heart, offer advice to help others; your motivation is key.

6. Think not about whatever is seen in others.

Your mindfulness needs to be on your own actions, not on what others do or don't do. If you walk near a cliff, watch your own feet, not those of others. If you look critically at others, you will find faults, and once you are in the habit of judging others, eventually you will find fault with the Buddha. It's better to place our attention on others' good qualities, and if we do see faults, to recall that they are adventitious and are not in the nature of that person's mind.

7. Purify first whichever affliction is heaviest.

Whichever affliction is strongest in you, work on subduing that one first. If you have a problem with anger and often speak harshly, don't ignore that and instead focus on lessening your attachment to peanut butter. Learn the appropriate antidote for each affliction. For example, for anger, practice fortitude, forgiveness, and love. For lust, contemplate the unclean aspects of the body. For jealousy, practice rejoicing.

8. Give up all hope of reward.

Don't harbor corrupt motivations of getting something for yourself from practicing the Dharma. Instead, dedicate all the merit of your practice for the welfare of others and recognize that whatever personal benefit you receive from your practice is a side effect. Abandon the expectation to receive thanks, appreciation, acknowledgement, or status—for example, people commenting that you are for sure a bodhisattva.

9. Abandon poisonous food.

Self-centered attitude and self-grasping ignorance are poisonous food. Don't keep them close to you but throw them far away.

10. Do not serve the central object leniently.

Don't be lenient with your afflictions, thinking, for example: it's only a little belligerence and anyway it's justified because those other people really are domineering. Instead, see the disadvantages of the afflictions and apply the counterforces to them.

11. Be indifferent toward malicious comments.

If someone ridicules you, don't respond with sarcasm or slander on the one hand or hurt and self-pity on the other. Understand that others' comments tell you about their feelings and moods, and therefore don't take everything personally. In a month you won't remember it and in a year it will be far from your mind. So there's no sense in reifying it now and being miserable.

12. Do not lie in ambush.

Don't wait for an opportunity to take revenge on people for perceived attacks or inconsiderate behavior. Holding grudges and waiting for the perfect time to get back at someone only makes you miserable.

13. Never strike at the heart.

Don't hit others' sensitive points and abandon uttering spiteful words that you know will hurt someone. If you know someone's weakness, don't deliberately embarrass them in front of others in an attempt to make yourself look better.

14. Do not load an ox with the load of a dzo.

In Tibet a dzo, which is a hybrid of a cow and a yak, is a very large and strong animal, much larger than an ox. That is, don't give your responsibilities to others who aren't capable of bearing them. Don't try to get others to do your disagreeable tasks. This may happen in families where one of the parents is an alcoholic and the child takes on this parent's role. It may also happen in a school where the teacher gives a child an assignment that the child doesn't yet have the knowledge or skill to fulfill.

15. Do not compete by a last-minute sprint.
Don't stand back when others work hard on a project and then at the end step in and claim the credit for yourself. Don't try to get the biggest piece of pie, but share resources, knowledge, and prosperity. Practice putting down your self-importance.

16. Do not be treacherous.
This one is also called "Don't fill your belly in the wrong way." That is, don't deceive others, making them think you're doing one thing when you're actually doing another. Don't use people for self-gain under the pretense of benefiting them.

17. Do not bring a god down to a devil.
If we're supposedly generating bodhicitta but instead nourish our afflictions, then Dharma practice, which is like a god, has been brought down to the level of a devil.

18. Do not inflict misery for possession of happiness.
Don't wish your enemies suffering and feel good about it when they have problems. Don't harm others to get what you want. Such behavior is completely counter to the purpose of bodhicitta mind training.

The Twenty-Two Precepts of Mind Training
The following instructions are to strengthen our mind-training practice.

1. Perform all activities by one.
The "one" is bodhicitta. Whether you are meditating or engaged in daily activities, make sure that your motivation is bodhicitta. As the gāthās explained below illustrate, you can apply Dharma and train your mind in bodhicitta no matter what you are doing. Take advantage of every opportu-

nity to practice bodhicitta—even when you are eating, dressing, sleeping, or walking—and to abandon the eight worldly concerns. For example, before eating offer your food to the Three Jewels, and at the conclusion of your meal dedicate the merit to all the people who made your meal possible.[93]

2. Deal with all wrong and oppression in one way.

The "one way" is mind training. As you practice, external hindrances such as difficulties with other human beings or with animals may arise. Instead of succumbing to anger and revenge, generate love and compassion for them and do the taking and giving meditation, thinking: "May their suffering and negativity ripen on me and may I give them my happiness so that their lives can be peaceful and tranquil." When internal hindrances arise—such as strong attachment, self-pity, rage, and so forth—recall that these emotions have been following us since beginningless time. Since you care about other sentient beings and don't want to subject them to your foul moods and harmful actions, make a strong determination to apply the antidotes to these afflictions.

Remember that cherishing others and working for their welfare is the path to purify your mind and develop your excellent qualities and that nurturing resentment and refusing to forgive bring suffering to yourself. Nāgārjuna reminds us (SCP 26, 27, 30):

> Through relying on those [sentient beings] I attain the very great;
> through harming them I fall into distressing states.
> Even if I have to completely give up my life,
> it is fitting to be fond of them.

By interacting with sentient beings with a mind of love and compassion, we will attain the great awakening, whereas harming them leads to unfortunate rebirth and distressing events in our life. Although we may think we're getting even for a perceived wrong, harming others is actually an act of self-sabotage and in the long term the suffering results we experience are far greater than what we inflict on others. Understanding this, the wise see the great benefits that arise from sincerely cherishing others.

> It is those sentient beings that many
> relied on to attain siddhis.

> Among migrators there is no [merit] field for siddhis
> other than the great field of sentient beings.

"Siddhis" are spiritual accomplishments. Mundane siddhis are the first five superknowledges; the ultimate siddhi is the sixth—full awakening.

For someone who has firm confidence in karma and its effects, the greatest danger they face is that of creating nonvirtue, and there are many opportunities for this in our world. On the other hand, there are also many opportunities to create virtue and purify nonvirtuous actions by generating love and compassion, because we're continually encountering various living beings.

> This is the conduct of the great Sage;
> one should not be indecisive about its rationale,
> for as long as one does not actualize [such conduct]
> that long accomplishment is impossible.

The great Sage, our Teacher, the Buddha practiced in this way. The suitability of cherishing others and influencing them in a constructive manner in any way possible has been established by scripture and reasoning. After putting energy into understanding this, any doubt in its truth will vanish. However, spending our time in the eight worldly concerns and neglecting to transform our mind precludes all spiritual accomplishments. What we choose to do is up to us.

3. There are two duties: at the beginning and the end.

Every day we wake up and go to bed. When awaking in the morning, immediately generate a motivation of bodhicitta for the day: "As much as possible today I will not harm others. As much as possible today I will benefit them in whatever big or small way I can. Today I will be mindful of bodhicitta and enhance it." In the evening, review the day and rejoice at your virtuous actions and merit. Confess any negativities and purify any transgressions of precepts. Dedicate the merit from practicing like this all day: "May I never be separated from bodhicitta in all my lives. May all sentient beings quickly attain full awakening. May the pure Dharma exist in our world forever, and may all sincere spiritual mentors and practitioners have long lives."

4. Whichever of the two comes, accept it.

Whether you feel happy or sad, well or ill, whether you are successful or fail, are wealthy or impoverished, accept the situation. Don't get carried away emotionally by any impermanent situation. The economy goes up, it goes down. The politicians you favor are elected, they lose the election. You get married, your partner dies or you divorce. Whenever there is a change in your life, remain constant in your Dharma practice. Welcome difficulties or situations when your buttons are pushed; see them as challenges to cultivate good qualities and take them all into the path to awakening.

5. Hold both as dear as life.

Steadfastly adhere to general advice and commitments, such as to abandon the ten nonvirtuous paths of actions and practice the ten virtuous ones, and to keep your prātimokṣa, bodhisattva, and tantric precepts (if you have taken them). With dedication, follow the specific commitments of mind training to cherish others and abandon self-centeredness.

6. Train in three difficult things.

These three are as follows: (1) Prevent afflictions from arising. This entails recognizing them quickly by employing mindfulness and introspective awareness. (2) When afflictions arise, turn them away by employing the antidotes and returning your mind to a neutral or virtuous state. (3) Sever the continuity of the afflictions by realizing the emptiness of inherent existence. This is the ultimate antidote and will take some time to develop.

7. Adopt three main prerequisites.

These three are as follows: (1) Find a qualified Mahāyāna spiritual mentor who holds the pure lineage of the Buddha and make a strong connection with him or her. If you are new to the Dharma, this may take time; pray to meet a suitable spiritual mentor.[94] (2) Improve the state of your mind by receiving teachings, remembering them, and reflecting on them to gain a correct conceptual understanding. Then meditate on them to integrate them into your mind and your life. (3) Gather the physical and mental circumstances that are conducive to practice, such as confidence in the law of cause and effect, joy in practicing bodhicitta, and good Dharma friends who encourage and support your practice, as well as basic requisites such as food, clothing, and shelter. If you have all of these, rejoice and pray that others may enjoy these conducive circumstances. If you don't have them, consider the lives of others who don't enjoy the conditions to practice; generate compassion and imagine taking on the negativity that prevents them from having conducive circumstances and praying for them to have wonderful conditions for Dharma practice.

8. Meditate on the three undeclining attitudes.

These three are as follows: (1) Your relationship with your spiritual mentors should be without any disrespect. Be aware of the benefit you receive from your mentors and appreciate your relationships with them. It would be nearly impossible to progress on the path without their teachings and instructions. (2) Don't let your joy in cultivating bodhicitta or your faith in mind training decline. Rejoice at having encountered the mind-training teachings—especially those on bodhicitta and emptiness—which are the heart of the Buddha's teachings. (3) Don't let your mindfulness and introspective awareness of these points decline. Hold them firmly in your mind.

9. Never be separated from three things.

Don't allow your body, speech, and mind to be separated from virtue. Physical virtue is created by making prostrations, circumambulating holy objects, serving your spiritual mentors, and helping others with physical tasks. Verbal virtue is created by reciting prayers and mantras and using your speech to create harmony and encourage others in virtue. Mental virtue is created by cultivating the strong wish to properly practice the two bodhicittas and then making effort to practice them. The two bodhicittas are the conventional bodhicitta, which is the altruistic intention to become a buddha to benefit all sentient beings, and the ultimate bodhicitta, which is the wisdom realizing emptiness.

10. Always practice with pure impartiality to all objects.

Avoid bias with respect to people, places, and things. Bring them all into the scope of mind training.

11. Cherish the in-depth and broad application of all skills.

Apply your skill in mind training to all events. Reading or listening to the news becomes a teaching on karma and its effects; watching movies is an exercise in contemplating the illusory appearance of all phenomena; and documentaries are lessons on impermanence.

12. Always meditate on those closely related to you.

Although we practice equanimity toward all beings, it is important to care for those whom we encounter on a daily basis and with whom we have close connections—for example, our spiritual mentors, parents, colleagues, competitors, companions, roommates, and people who dislike us or whom we have aversion for on first sight. It's easy for afflictions to arise regarding these groups of people, so be especially alert when speaking or interacting with them.

13. Don't rely on other conditions.

Don't wait for perfect conditions before starting to practice: "Once I find a new job, I'll start attending teachings again." "When my children are older or my roommate's schedule changes so that it's silent in the house, I'll begin a daily meditation practice." Remember that your future life may come before perfect conditions, so make hay while the sun is out, as my American friends say. In addition, don't behave like a practitioner only when the sun is shining and your stomach is full, and then when problems arise get upset and blame others, like ordinary people do. Whenever problems arise—and they will, as this is the nature of saṃsāra—think of the situations of others who suffer from the same conditions and do the taking and giving meditation for them.

14. Exert yourself, especially at this time.

Many previous lives have been wasted in distraction, so don't let the rare opportunity of your precious human life slip by. The most important practice is not observing what others do and don't do, but to work on yourself. Value the Dharma, not worldly possessions and reputation. When you die your wealth, your friends and family, and your body will remain here. The karmic seeds on your mindstream and mental habits will go with you into future lives.

15. Do not follow inverted deeds.

There are six types of inverted deeds. (1) Inverted patience is being very patient and able to put up with many difficulties so that education, career, and worldly activities are done well, but having little fortitude when it comes to practicing the Dharma. (2) Inverted aspiration is having a strong aspiration and great determination to make money, get promoted, or win an argument, but a weak aspiration to subdue afflictions and counteract self-centeredness. (3) Inverted taste is taking pleasure in objects of the six senses, despite their being like "honey on a razorblade," but not seeking to taste the flavor of nirvāṇa by learning, thinking, and meditating on the Dharma. (4) Inverted compassion is feeling sorry for great practitioners who endure suffering while doing intense purification, who refrain from certain pleasures in order to follow their precepts, or who live simply without worldly clutter. On the other hand, we don't feel much compassion for people who engage in negative behavior in order to be famous, powerful, and envied by the public. Great practitioners don't need our pity because they have internal strength, but the people who continually create the causes for suffering are worthy of compassion. (5) Inverted loyalty is coaching our students, friends, and relatives to relax and have a good time engaging in worldly activities but neglecting to guide them in the Dharma. (6) Inverted rejoicing is rejoicing when our friends and relatives win the lottery, make some money under the table, or have an affair, but neglecting to rejoice at our own and others' virtue and diligence in subduing afflictions.

16. Don't be erratic.

Instead of meditating and doing some spiritual reading every day, you do it sporadically only when you need it to calm yourself. Or you practice diligently for many hours one or two days but after not having a spiritual experience, you get fed up and stop practicing. It's important to remember that all meditations that don't yield bliss or an "ah ha" moment are creating the cause for experiencing the beautiful results of practice later on.

17. Don't underestimate your ability.

Don't shirk responsibility, but with confidence enhance your abilities and then, without biting off more than you can chew, take on beneficial tasks.

Focus with firm resolve on accomplishing your goal and continue to create the causes for it until it comes to fruition.

18. Be liberated by two: investigation and analysis.

Investigation is a coarse examination of the object, whereas analysis is a deeper, more extensive examination. Investigation identifies the disturbing emotions that are stronger and more frequent; analysis identifies the distorted conceptualizations that lie behind their arising. With knowledge provided by both, prevent afflictions from arising by stopping the distorted conceptualization before it spins a false story about your being a victim, someone who is taken advantage of or not given a fair chance, and so forth. Allowing the mind to go around and around with these stories stifles our ability to grow. Instead, as Śāntideva recommended, if there is something you can do to remedy the situation, there's no need to be upset—do what needs to be done. If there is nothing you can do to change the situation, there's no need to be upset, so relax the mind and direct your energy where it can have a positive effect.

19. Don't boast.

Boasting is an activity sported by those who lack self-confidence. Working to benefit others and transforming your mind with the Dharma are simply the right things to do. There is no need to make a big deal about them in others' presence. Furthermore, if you boast, it makes others feel less important, and that is contrary to your aim of cherishing others.

20. Do not retaliate.

Don't keep track of harms you've experienced, waiting for the right time to seek revenge. Your human life is short, why spend it on holding grudges? What happened in the past is not happening now. Ruminating on past situations serves only to make you upset and angry. Why become aggravated and aggrieved over events that are not happening now? Open your eyes and see that at this moment you are in a safe environment and have the protection of the Dharma.

If someone says something nasty about you in front of many people, don't respond in kind. Remember that you created the principal cause to receive public rebuke because in the past you inflicted such behavior on others.

After many years of practicing the Dharma, if you are easily provoked to anger, that indicates that your practice is not very deep and the purpose of Dharma practice—to subdue the mind—has evaded you. Make a strong determination to renew your relationship with the Three Jewels.

One time when Geshe Langri Tangpa (1054–1123), a monk and the author of the "Eight Verses of Mind Training," was teaching, a woman holding an infant entered the hall. In front of the assembly she falsely accused him of fathering the child and gave him the child to raise. The monk didn't respond, but took the infant and raised him as if he were his own. Years later, the woman returned and demanded to have the child back. Again Geshe Langri Tangpa acquiesced without dispute.

In our time, there would have been a paternity test to quickly settle the matter and clear the monk from wrongdoing. But this story is told as an example of how a monk, having his purity challenged in front of an assembly, responded without anger or retaliation.

21. Do not be mercurial.

If things are going well, you get excited and tell many people about your success, but when your activities aren't going so well, you become very depressed and withdrawn. When people conform with your wishes, you think they are the greatest and become close to them, but as soon as they do something that doesn't accord with what you want, you dump them. When you hear a new teaching, you become excited and want to immediately do a long retreat, but after a week or so, you get tired of it. When your spiritual mentor praises you, you have deep faith in him or her, but when they point out your faults, you leave and look for another spiritual mentor who will tell you what you want to hear. Since such impulsiveness irritates others and prevents you from being consistent and accomplishing what you set out to do, make a conscious effort to be more stable and considerate.

22. Don't wish for gratitude.

When you help others, don't expect praise or thanks; this feeds the ego. Make the calm that arises from your heartfelt intention the reward. We cannot control how others respond to our kindness—sometimes they even reject it or become angry at us—so it's important to take pleasure in doing the action, not in receiving their gratitude or gifts afterward.

REFLECTION

1. One by one reflect on each of the commitments and precepts of mind training.
2. Think of specific situations in your life that each one applies to.
3. In your mind, imagine applying that commitment or precept to that situation and thinking in a different way.
4. Imagine the difference in outcome there would be from doing that.

Gāthās to Train the Mind

All countries in which the Mahāyāna is widespread share the special practice of enhancing bodhicitta through transforming common activities that are usually done with a neutral motivation—one that is neither virtuous nor nonvirtuous—into a bodhisattva's practice. *Gāthās*—short lines or verses extracted from sūtras or written by great masters—guide us to steer our mind to a virtuous state. When doing everyday activities, such as getting dressed, washing, brushing our teeth, or going up stairs, we recite a corresponding verse to broaden our perspective and imbue these ordinary actions with a compassionate motivation. Engaging in this mind-training practice is an excellent method for transforming neutral actions that we usually do without any particular motivation into virtuous activities done with love, compassion, and bodhicitta. Practicing bodhicitta in this way helps us to increase our collection of merit while continually familiarizing our mind with wholesome thoughts and aspirations. Washing the dishes is no longer a chore but a short meditation on cleansing defilements from the minds of sentient beings.

In some Chinese, Vietnamese, and Japanese monasteries, gāthās are written and placed near the area where a particular activity occurs. Other times monastics and lay devotees will memorize gāthās and bring them to mind when doing the corresponding activity. Sometimes mantras accompany these verses; if it is difficult to memorize the mantras, that's fine; reciting the verses and transforming your attitude is the purpose. Some of the gāthās are from the "Pure Conduct" chapter in the *Flower Ornament Sūtra*.

Waking up
Upon waking from slumber,
may each and every sentient being
awaken to omniscient wisdom
and regard sentient beings in the ten directions with compassion.

Getting out of bed
Unceasingly from dawn till dusk,
may all sentient beings protect themselves.
If they should lose their lives beneath my feet,
may they instantly be reborn in a pure land.
Om iddhiruni svaha (3x)

Using the toilet
As I relieve myself,
may each and every sentient being
abandon attachment, anger, and ignorance
and abandon all negative deeds.
Om laludaya svaha (3x)

Removing filth with toilet paper
As I cleanse filth from my body,
may each and every sentient being
be pure and gentle,
constantly in a state free from defilements.
Om garamirti svaha (3x)

Washing hands
As I wash my palms with water,
may each and every sentient being
have hands clean and pure
to receive and uphold the Buddhadharma.
Om shukalaya svaha (3x)

Washing the face
As I wash my face with water,
may each and every sentient being
access the doors to the pure Dharma
and be free from defilements at all times.
Om ram svaha (21x)

Holding toothbrush in hand
May each and every sentient being
attain the sublime Dharma
and be completely purified.
Om sarvashudda sarjbadalima sarvavashudali om ram svaha

Brushing teeth
When I brush my teeth,
may each and every sentient being
have harmonious and pure minds,
eating away all afflictions.
Om amoghamimali nivakala soyudani padmakumara
nivasayudaya daradarasu nimalisha svaha (3x)

Rinsing the mouth
When I rinse my mouth as well as my mind,
the water's touch brings the fragrance of hundreds of flowers.
With three doors of karma—body, speech, and mind—constantly clear and pure,
may I proceed to the pure land with the Buddha.
Om kam om gan svaha (3x)

Dressing (lay followers)
As I put on upper garments,
may each and every sentient being
reap excellent roots of virtue
and reach the other shore of nirvāṇa.

As I put on lower garments,
may each and every sentient being
gird their roots of virtue
by having integrity and consideration for others.

Smoothing my clothes and fastening my belt,
may each and every sentient being
examine and dedicate their roots of virtue
lest they get lost.

Dressing (monastics putting on antarvāsas)
How wonderful is this garment of liberation,
robe of an unsurpassable field of merit.
I now respectfully receive it above the crown of my head.
May I never be separated from it for life after life.

Dressing (monastics putting on uttarāsaṃga)
How wonderful is this garment of liberation,
robe of an unsurpassable field of merit.
I now respectfully receive it above the crown of my head.
May I wear it often for life after life.
Om dhupadhupa svaha (3x)

Dressing (monastics putting on saṃghāṭī)[95]
How wonderful is this garment of liberation,
robe of an unsurpassable field of merit.
Respectfully upholding the Tathāgata's instructions,
may I extensively liberate all sentient beings.
Om maha kapapata siddhi svaha (3x)

Joining Saṅgha assemblies
Hearing the sound of the bell reduces my afflictions;
wisdom grows and the awakening mind is born.
Leaving the hell realms and escaping the pits of fire,
may I attain buddhahood to liberate all sentient beings.
Om karatiye svaha (3x)

Ascending to the Dharma hall
When I have the opportunity to see the Buddha,
may each and every sentient being
attain unobstructed vision[96]
and behold all the buddhas.
Om amrte hum phat tat (3x)

Arranging the seat and sitting in meditation
When I arrange my seat,
may each and every sentient being
expand their practice of virtue
And see the ultimate nature of reality.

When I straighten my body and sit upright,
may each and every sentient being
sit on the seat of awakening
with minds free from attachment.
Om vasora anipanrani yutaya svaha (3x)

Leaving the room
When I leave my dwelling,
may each and every sentient being
gain deep insight into the Buddha's wisdom
and leave behind the three realms (desire, form, and formless) forever.

Walking without harming insects
As I lift my feet,
may each and every sentient being
emerge from the ocean of birth and death
equipped with a multitude of virtuous deeds.
Om tilivili svaha (3x)

Holding the (alms) bowl, before receiving food
When I see an empty alms bowl,
may each and every sentient being

attain the final state of purity
abiding in emptiness without afflictions.

Seeing an (alms) bowl filled with food
When I see a full alms bowl,
may each and every sentient being
be replete and abundantly filled
with all virtuous deeds

Concluding the meal
Those who practice making offerings
will certainly receive its benefits.
Those who take delight in giving
will certainly have peace and happiness later.

The meal is finished
May each and every sentient being
accomplish all their endeavors
and be fully endowed with the Buddhadharma.

Shaving hair
When I shave my hair and beard,
May each and every sentient being
Leave their afflictions far behind
And attain final cessation.
Om sidhanta mantara bhadaya svaha (3x)

Bathing
When I bathe my body,
may each and every sentient being
have bodies and minds free from defilements,
internally and externally brilliant and pure.
Om bajerona jacha svaha (3x)

Washing feet
When I wash my feet,

may each and every sentient being
be endowed with supernormal powers,
free from obstructions wherever we go.
Om ram svaha (3x)

Sleeping
When it is time to sleep and rest,
may each and every sentient being
have physical peace and security,
with minds free from disturbance.
Ah

Visiting someone who is ill
When I see a sick person,
may each and every sentient being
realize that their bodies are empty in reality
and abandon wrong and conflicting views.
Om srita srita kundali svaha (3x)

The gāthās below are from another source and are equally suitable to use.

Using the toilet
May all sentient beings discard their greed, hatred, and confusion and eliminate destructive conduct.

Washing the hands
May all sentient beings attain purified hands to uphold the Buddhadharma.

Bathing
May all sentient beings be pure and harmonious and ultimately without defilement.

Sitting cross-legged
May all sentient beings have firm and strong roots of goodness, and attain the state of immovability.

Sitting up straight

May all sentient beings sit on the seat of awakening, free from attachment.

Practicing contemplation

May all sentient beings see truth as it is and be forever free of opposition and contention.

Giving something

May all sentient beings be able to relinquish everything with hearts free from clinging.

In gatherings

May all sentient beings let go of conditioned things and attain total knowledge.

In danger and difficulty

May all sentient beings be free and unhindered wherever they go.

Traveling on a road

May all sentient beings tread the pure realm of reality, their minds free of obstructions.

Seeing a road uphill

May all sentient beings forever transcend saṃsāra, their minds free from doubt and confusion.

Seeing a road downhill

May all sentient beings be humble in mind and develop a strong base of awakened virtue.

Seeing a winding road

May all sentient beings abandon false paths and forever purge distorted views.

Seeing a straight road

May all sentient beings be straight and true in mind, without pretention or deceit.

Seeing blossoms on trees

May all sentient beings' features be like flowers with all marks of distinction.

Seeing fruit

May all sentient beings attain the supreme teaching and realize the way of awakening.

Seeing people attached to pleasure

May all sentient beings delight in truth and not abandon love for it.

Seeing people suffer

May all sentient beings attain fundamental knowledge and eliminate all misery.

Seeing or caring for a sick person

May all sentient beings, realizing that the body is but an empty shell, forsake opposition and conflict.

Seeing a monastic

May all sentient beings be harmonious and tranquil and ultimately conquer themselves.

Seeing handsome people

May all sentient beings aspire for all beings to have pure faith in the awakened ones.

Seeing ugly people

May all sentient beings not become attached to any nonvirtuous activities.

Seeing ungrateful people
May all sentient beings not increase the punishment of those who act harmfully.

Seeing grateful people
May all sentient beings know the blessings of the buddhas and bodhisattvas.

Washing dishes, clothes, etc.
I will cleanse the defilement from the minds of all sentient beings.

Walking down stairs
I will go to the lowest hell realm to rescue sentient beings there.

Walking up stairs
I will lead all sentient beings up through the bodhisattva grounds to the highest awakening.

The beauty about practicing the gāthās on a daily basis is that our mind is constantly steered toward love, compassion, and bodhicitta. With a wholesome motivation, doing even small tasks makes our life meaningful, so we experience happiness now and in the future.

REFLECTION

1. Memorize a few of the gāthās and practice thinking according to them as you go about your life.
2. For situations that you frequently experience that aren't mentioned above, make up your own gāthās and apply them. For example, every time you hear your child whine "Mommy" or "Daddy," think, "I will have patience and compassion for all sentient beings."

Notes

1. See, for example, http://www.youtube.com/watch?v=Nn46qZlU3To.
2. Charles Darwin, *The Descent of Man, and Selection in Relation to Sex*, rev. and augmented 2d ed. (New York: D. Appleton, 1901 [1871]), 124–25.
3. Alice Calaprice, *The New Quotable Einstein* (Princeton, NJ: Princeton University Press, 2005), 206.
4. Chapters 6–11 in *Following in the Buddha's Footsteps* discuss the cultivation of serenity, the dhyānas, and other meditative absorptions.
5. The first dhyāna of the form realm contains three Brahmā worlds: Retinue of Brahmā, Ministers of Brahmā, and Great Brahmā. See chapter 2 of *Saṃsāra, Nirvāṇa, and Buddha Nature.*
6. See AN 4:125, 4:126, 3:66.
7. A bodhisattva with unfabricated bodhicitta would be willing to sacrifice his or her life. However, only bodhisattvas who have attained the path of seeing are allowed to do so. Better yet, a bodhisattva would try to find a way to avoid such an atrocity occurring at all.
8. The five synonyms for "all beings" and the seven specific categories of beings mentioned above.
9. These are explained in Vism 9.60–76.
10. Invariable karma is an action that is the cause for rebirth in a specific meditative absorption and no other.
11. "Suppression" does not refer to psychological suppression, but to afflictions not appearing in manifest form due to the force of concentration.
12. These are qualities and practices that śrāvakas, solitary realizers, and bodhisattvas cultivate. See chapters 12–14 in *Following in the Buddha's Footsteps.*
13. Harvey Aronson, *Love and Sympathy in Theravāda Buddhism*, 85.
14. There are various types of liberation of mind; not all of them are merely states of serenity. For example, there is the "unshakable liberation of mind," which is the liberation of the fruit of arhatship, also called "the taintless liberation of mind, liberation by wisdom," in which concentration and wisdom are merged and the mind is completely released from all defilements.

15. According to Paramārtha, a sixth-century monk from central India, the *Avataṃsaka Sūtra* is also called the *Bodhisattva Piṭaka*.
16. Although Buddhaghosa says that meditation on each of the four divine abodes should be expanded to include all sentient beings, for some reason unknown to me (Chodron) Tibetan scholars say śrāvakas and solitary realizers cultivate them toward immeasurable sentient beings, but not all sentient beings.
17. See chapter 8 of *The Foundation of Buddhist Practice* for more on the eight worldly concerns.
18. See chapter 3 of *The Foundation of Buddhist Practice* to learn about primary consciousnesses and mental factors.
19. See chapters 12–14 in *Saṃsāra, Nirvāṇa, and Buddha Nature.*
20. To learn more about the qualities of the fully awakened ones, see chapters 1–2 in *Following in the Buddha's Footsteps.*
21. Patrul Rinpoche, *Advice to Kunzang Chogyal* (Brussels: Wisdom Treasury Publishing House, 2005).
22. Mañjuśrī embodies wisdom, Avalokiteśvara compassion, Vajrapāṇi power, and Kṣitigarbha increases the richness and fertility of the land. In Chinese Buddhism he is said to aid those born as hell beings. Sarvanivāraṇa-viṣkambhin purifies wrongdoings and obstacles, Maitreya embodies love, Samantabhadra is expert in making offerings, unshakable resolves, and aspirational prayers, and Ākāśagarbha purifies ethical transgressions. Drawing on stories in sūtras and tantras, Jamgon Ju Mipham Gyatso has written *Garland of Jewels: The Eight Great Bodhisattvas.*
23. Hopkins, *Compassion in Tibetan Buddhism*, 124.
24. This applies to bodhisattvas who are freshly entering the bodhisattva path; this wisdom is inferential and they generate direct insight into emptiness later, on the path of seeing. Bodhisattvas who first attained arhatship by following the Fundamental Vehicle and later enter the Bodhisattva Vehicle already have the wisdom that directly realizes emptiness.
25. The twelve links of dependent origination (*dvādaśāṅga-pratītyasamutpāda*) is a system of twelve factors that explains how we take rebirth in saṃsāra and how we can be liberated from it. See chapters 7 and 8 in *Saṃsāra, Nirvāṇa, and Buddha Nature.*
26. See Jeneen Interlandi, "The Brain's Empathy Gap," *New York Times Magazine*, March 19, 2015, http://www.nytimes.com/2015/03/22/magazine/the-brains-empathy-gap.html.
27. Dr. Sam Parnia at New York University discusses the possibility from a medical point of view: https://www.youtube.com/watch?v=WnoIf2NwaRY. This video speaks about the rebirth of Kyabje Ling Rinpoche, His Holiness's senior tutor: https://www.youtube.com/watch?v=tPNcwXVOQFM. Here is the account of the young Indian girl Shantidevi who remembered her previous life: https://www.youtube.com/watch?v=J7IK6OoU6SI. His Holiness has often spoken about her case. James Linegar is a young American boy who remembers being James Houston, a pilot shot down by the Japanese in World War II: https://www.youtube.com/watch?v=VnXxC-nVsJY&feature=youtu.be.

28. In the Pāli canon, the Buddha spoke of eight benefits of love. While there is overlap between the two lists, they are not exactly the same.
29. See chapter 2 of *Following in the Buddha's Footsteps*. The ten powers are knowing (1) what is possible and impossible, (2) the ripening result of all actions, (3) the paths leading to all destinations, (4) the world with its many different elements, (5) inclinations of sentient beings, (6) the dispositions of sentient beings, (7) meditative absorptions, (8) past lives, (9) sentient beings passing away and being reborn, and (10) liberation and full awakening.
30. See chapter 2 of *Following in the Buddha's Footsteps*. The Tathāgata is completely confident and lacks all fear in declaring that (1) he is fully awakened regarding all phenomena, (2) he has destroyed all pollutants, (3) he has correctly identified all obstructions to be eliminated on the path, and (4) when practiced, his teachings lead to the complete destruction of duḥkha.
31. See Marshall Rosenberg's work on nonviolent communication in Rosenberg, *Nonviolent Communication: A Language of Life*, 3d ed. (Encinatas, CA: PuddleDancer Press, 2015).
32. For more about developing concentration, see chapters 6–8 in *Following in the Buddha's Footsteps*.
33. See chapter 2 of *Saṃsāra, Nirvāṇa, and Buddha Nature* for more on these aspects of true duḥkha.
34. See chapter 3 of *Saṃsāra, Nirvāṇa, and Buddha Nature* for more on the true origins of duḥkha.
35. In his *Autocommentary to the Treasury of Knowledge*, Vasubandhu presents great compassion in another way, saying that it is possessed only by a buddha, not by bodhisattvas. He says the Buddha's compassion is great because it is produced by a great collection of merit and wisdom, it wishes sentient beings to be free from all three types of duḥkha, it focuses on all beings in the three realms of saṃsāra, it is concerned with the welfare of all these beings equally, and there is no other type of compassion that surpasses it. He goes on to differentiate it from ordinary compassion in eight ways: (1) ordinary compassion lacks hatred, whereas great compassion is free of ignorance; (2) ordinary compassion wishes to free beings from the duḥkha of pain, whereas great compassion wishes to free them from all three types of duḥkha; (3) ordinary compassion is concerned with beings in the desire realm, whereas great compassion focuses on beings of all three realms; (4) ordinary compassion is supported by the four dhyānas, whereas great compassion is supported by the fourth dhyāna; (5) ordinary compassion exists in the mindstreams of śrāvakas and solitary realizers, but great compassion is present in the mindstream of buddhas; (6) ordinary compassion is acquired through detaching from the desire realm, whereas great compassion is obtained by separating from attachment to the peak of existence; (7) ordinary compassion does not completely protect the welfare of beings, whereas great compassion completely protects their welfare; and (8) ordinary compassion is unequal because it feels only for suffering beings, whereas great compassion extends to all beings equally. See the *Abhidharmakośabhāṣyam of Vasubandhu*, vol. 4, English translation by Leo M.

Pruden, from the French translation by Louis de La Vallée Poussin (Berkeley, CA: Asian Humanities Press, 1991), 1143–44.

36. Hopkins, *Compassion in Tibetan Buddhism*, 111.
37. Four points to purify destructive karma. These are regret, generating bodhicitta and taking refuge, engaging in a remedial action, and making a determination not to do the harmful action again.
38. Goodman, *The Training Anthology of Śāntideva*, 25.
39. Goodman, *The Training Anthology of Śāntideva*, 126.
40. In Tibetan the practice is known as giving-and-taking. We changed the order of the words to correspond to the order in which they are practiced.
41. See Geshe Jampa Tegchok. *Transforming Adversity into Joy and Courage*, chapter 11, for an excellent and expansive explanation of the taking-and-giving meditation.
42. Jamyang Shepa (1648–1721) was a learned and well-respected scholar and practitioner from Labrang Tashikhyil Monastery. His textbooks are followed in Drepung Gomang Monastery. *Tulku* indicates his reincarnation.
43. Since there are no solitary realizers in our world at present, in the *Library of Wisdom and Compassion* they have often been included with the śrāvakas, unless the two diverge on a major point.
44. Some scholars say the fortitude of the nonarising of phenomena is attained on the bodhisattva path of seeing or the eighth ground, not on the bodhisattva path of preparation. Others say it is attained only on the eighth ground. Because this fortitude involves realization of emptiness, it is sometimes applied to those Fundamental Vehicle practitioners who have realized emptiness directly.
45. Some scholars assert that śrāvakas and solitary realizers have ordinary great compassion in the sense that they think, "How wonderful it would be if sentient beings were free from duḥkha and its causes" and "May they be free of them." However, they lack special great compassion that is the great compassion Candrakīrti says is one of the causes of a bodhisattva. That compassion is willing to shoulder the responsibility to protect all sentient beings from saṃsāric duḥkha.
46. Candrakīrti's verse makes clear that the inferential understanding of emptiness is essential for sharp-faculty practitioners to generate bodhicitta and enter the Mahāyāna path of accumulation. But what about modest-faculty disciples who accept the emptiness of inherent existence and the existence of nirvāṇa because of their faith in the Buddha or in their spiritual mentor? Some scholars say they generate bodhicitta, become bodhisattvas by entering the Mahāyāna path, and then gain the inferential understanding of emptiness. Other scholars say that although such people are called "bodhisattvas," they are not full-fledged bodhisattvas and have not yet entered the Mahāyāna path because they lack the conviction that liberation is possible, which comes from realizing emptiness. Only when they gain this inferential realization do they become actual bodhisattvas. Similarly, there may be practitioners who hold the Yogācāra view, meditate on great compassion, and want to become buddhas. Although they may be called "bodhisattvas," they too are not actual bodhisattvas because they lack the correct nondual understanding.

    These scholars say having the correct conceptual view of emptiness according to the Prāsaṅgika system is also necessary for practitioners to enter the path of accumulation of the Śrāvaka and Solitary Realizer Vehicles. That is, feeling disgust with saṃsāra leads to renunciation, but they must also know that another state—nirvāṇa—exists and can be attained. They obtain that confidence in the existence of nirvāṇa by gaining the inferential realization of the emptiness of inherent existence. For example, to find safety, someone on a sinking ship must not only want to exit the ship, they must also see land in the distance and know that they can reach it.

47. For more on the view of a personal identity, see chapters 3 and 7 in *Saṃsāra, Nirvāṇa, and Buddha Nature.*
48. Some translations say it is a waterwheel in motion. The idea is the same.
49. "And the like" includes the sources and constituents.
50. As cited in Gyaltsap (on Āryadeva's *Four Hundred*), in *Yogic Deeds of Bodhisattvas*, 200.
51. See *Pearl of Wisdom, Book 1*, 58–64, for the text of this practice. Instructions on how to do it can be found at https://thubtenchodron.org/2000/01/purification-visualization-prostration-thirty-five-buddhas/.
52. This line is not in the root Tantra but is added when reciting the verse to take the bodhisattva vow.
53. In English, see Dagpo Lama Rinpoche, *The Bodhisattva Vows*; Geshe Sonam Rinchen and Ruth Sonam, *The Bodhisattva Vow*; and Sakya Drakpa Gyaltsen, *Chandragomin's Twenty Verses on the Bodhisattva Vow* in the Recommended Reading section. In Tibetan, see Ngulchu Dharmabhadra's (1772–1851) brief but detailed text *The Essence of "The Main Path of Bodhisattvas' Training": Notes on the Bodhisattva's Precepts* (*Byang-sems kyi bslab-bya'i zin-bris byang-chub gzhung-lam snying-po*). "The Main Path of Bodhisattvas' Training" is Tsongkhapa's commentary on the "Ethical Conduct" chapter of Asaṅga's *Bodhisattva Ground.*
54. We may wonder why it is not as negative to know that the action is negative but to go ahead and do it anyway. Knowledge that the action is destructive will inspire a sincere practitioner to do purification, thus lessening the heaviness of the negative karma.
55. For more on the four opponent powers, see chapter 12 in *The Foundation of Buddhist Practice.*
56. If bodhisattvas engage in actions that appear unethical, although as ordinary beings we don't know their motivation, their compassion is so strong that they are willing to accept the criticism, legal action, and ostracism that results from their actions.
57. See Thubten Chodron, *Working with Anger*, and His Holiness the Dalai Lama, *Healing Anger*, in the Recommended Reading.
58. These hindrances and the methods to overcome them are described extensively in chapter 7 of *Following in the Buddha's Footsteps.*
59. The source is chapter 8, "Analysis/Elaboration on Samādhi," verses 29–31, of the *Abhidharmakośa-bhāṣyam of Vasubandhu*, vol. 4. In Chinese, this text was divided into thirty scrolls, and this chapter is in scroll 29.
60. Some, but not all, of these seven are mentioned in Tsongkhapa's *Great Treatise*

(LC 2:22–24), but they are found in more than one list. Some of them are also mentioned in Gyaltsab's commentary to the *Ornament of Clear Realizations*, and Śāntideva's *Compendium of Trainings* (*Śikṣāsamuccaya*) explains the four modes of generating bodhicitta: (1) having seen the exalted body of a buddha, one wonders, "What if I were to attain such [a body]?" (2) seeing and hearing about the inconceivable strength of buddhas and bodhisattvas, and so forth; (3) not being able to bear the decline of the Mahāyāna teachings; and (4) not being able to bear that sentient beings are tormented by suffering.

61. These could refer to the forty-eight auxiliary bodhisattva precepts in the *Brahmā's Net Sūtra* or the forty-eight unshakable resolves of Amitābha.
62. Dhāraṇīs are verbal formulas that encapsulate the meaning of a lengthy text and serve as mnemonic devices. Dhāraṇīs are also similar to mantras that provide protection and overcome adversity.
63. For more on the superknowledges, see chapter 8 of *Following in the Buddha's Footsteps*.
64. The import of these five great vows is the same as that of the four great vows that are traditionally explained below.
65. The English text did not include the eightfold path of the āryas. I don't know if this was an accidental omission or if it was absent in the Chinese text.
66. These four factors and their antidotes, the four swift factors of bodhisattvas, are from the *Flower Ornament Sūtra*.
67. See chapter 17, "The Merit Associated with Generating the (Bodhi) Resolve," in the *Flower Ornament Sūtra* for more details.
68. See Master Hsing Yun, *From the Four Noble Truths to the Four Universal Vows*, trans. Ching Tay and Mu-Tzen Hsu (Hacienda Heights, CA: Buddha's Light Publishing, 2002), 58–62.
69. Traditionally this text is said to have been translated from Sanskrit into Chinese by Kumarajiva in 406. However, some modern scholars believe it was composed in China in the mid-fifth century. See Ann Heirman, "Vinaya from India to China," in *The Spread of Buddhism*, ed. Ann Heirman and Stephan Peter Bumbacher (Leiden, Netherlands: Brill, 2007), 175.
70. Tibetans ascribe this treatise to Asaṅga, Maitreya's student.
71. The four assemblies are bhikṣus, bhikṣuṇīs, upāsakas, and upāsikās. The last two are lay followers who have taken refuge in the Three Jewels and the five lay precepts.
72. For an explanation about the meaning of the auxiliary precepts, see *Exposition of the Sutra of Brahma's Net*, trans. A. Charles Muller (Seoul: Jogye Order of Korean Buddhism, 2012), 318–424.
73. This paragraph is from private correspondence with Bhikṣuṇī Tzushin (Kind Star), July 22, 2009.
74. The word is the same in Sanskrit and Pāli. It is formed from the prefix *anu*, meaning alongside or along with, and the verb *kamp*, to tremble. We tremble along with or alongside another and feel their pain. In the *Bodhisattvabhūmi*, *anukampā* is translated into Tibetan as *rjes su snying rtse ba*.

75. Perhaps this sūtra is a precursor to the Mahāyāna idea of the Buddha's truth body and form body fulfilling the purposes of self and others, respectively.
76. Above, *anukampā* was the Pāli term translated as "compassion." Anukampā is a more general type of compassion that is described in the commentaries as "the state of having a tender mind." It is a sense of goodwill toward others that everyone has to some extent. When speaking of compassion as one of the four immeasurables that can be cultivated to a state of dhyāna, the Pāli term is *karuṇā*.
77. The Khuddaka Nikāya (Minor Collection) is the last of the five nikāyas, or collections, in the Sūtra Basket of the canon.
78. Ven. Dr. W. Rahula, "Theravāda–Mahāyāna Buddhism," in *Gems of Buddhist Wisdom* (Kuala Lumpur, Malaysia: Buddhist Missionary Society, 1996), http://www.budsas.org/ebud/ebdha125.htm.
79. Guy Armstrong, "The Pāramīs: A Historical Background," https://www.crab.rutgers.edu/~adelson/Paramis_intro.pdf. I [Chodron] also heard this from Theravāda monks during my stay at a Thai wat in 2007. In addition, when I described meditation on a buddha as it is done in Mahāyāna traditions to the abbot of a Theravāda monastery in Thailand, he commented that visualizing a bodhisattva above your head and holding that visualization in mind with faith and reciting that bodhisattva's mantra are ways to cultivate certain types of samādhi.
80. See Jeffrey Samuels, "The Bodhisattva Ideal in Theravāda Theory and Practice," *Philosophy East and West* 47, no. 3 (1997): 399–415. This article may also be found at https://info-buddhism.com/Bodhisattva-Ideal-Theravada_JeffreySamuels.html. Samuels gives more detailed examples as well as historical references for many of these kings.
81. Ven. Dr. W. Rahula, "Bodhisattva Ideal in Buddhism," in *Gems of Buddhist Wisdom*, http://www.budsas.org/ebud/ebdha126.htm.
82. Ven. Rahula, "Bodhisattva Ideal in Buddhism."
83. Ven. Rahula, "Theravāda–Mahāyāna Buddhism."
84. Some say that this was the first time the bodhisattva who was to become Śākyamuni Buddha generated bodhicitta. I (Chodron) don't know the origin of this account but have read it more than once. See https://dharmanet.org/DellaBodhisattva.htm.
85. Dīpaṅkara is the fourth buddha whose story is told in the *Buddhavaṃsa*. He is said to have lived four incalculable world-periods and a hundred thousand eons ago. It is said that countless other buddhas had appeared in the world before him.
86. "Four countless and a hundred thousand eons" means four countless eons plus a hundred thousand regular eons.
87. These twenty-five buddhas are Dīpaṅkara, Kakusandha (Kondañña), Maṅgala, Sumana, Revata, Sobhita, Anomadassin, Paduma, Nārada, Padumuttara, Sumedha, Sujāta, Piyadassin, Atthadassin, Dhammadassin, Siddhattha, Tissa, Phussa, Vipassin, Sikhī, Vessabhū, Kakusandha, Koṇāgamana, Kassapa, and Gotama.
88. The *Apadāna* is a collection of autobiographical accounts and poems of Buddhist sages and senior monks and nuns. It is located in the Khuddaka Nikāya.

89. *Khuddakapāṭha* 8:15–16.
90. This is the view of a personal identity that grasps an independent I and mine.
91. For commentaries on *The Wheel of Sharp Weapons*, see Thubten Chodron, *Good Karma*, and Geshe Lhundub Sopa, *Peacock in the Poison Grove*, in the Recommended Reading section.
92. Thupten Jinpa, trans., *Mind Training: The Great Collection* (Boston: Wisdom Publications, 2006), 171.
93. The verses and an explanation of how to offer your meal and dedicate the merit can be found in Thubten Chodron, *The Compassionate Kitchen: Buddhist Practices for Eating with Mindfulness and Gratitude* (Boulder, CO: Shambhala Publications, 2018).
94. See chapters 4 and 5 in *The Foundation of Buddhist Practice* for the qualifications of a good spiritual mentor and how to rely on them in a way that furthers your spiritual development.
95. The antarvāsas is the *shamdup*, or lower robe; the uttarāsaṃga is the *chogu*, or seven-strip robe; the saṃghāṭī is the *namjar* made of many patches.
96. This refers to the five sublime eyes: (1) the physical eye limited to the range of sight of the being that possesses it, (2) the divine eye that sees the death and rebirth of all beings, (3) the wisdom eye that knows all conditioned and unconditioned phenomena, (4) the Dharma eye that knows the attainments of all āryas, and (5) the Buddha eye that views all phenomena from the state of full awakening.

Glossary

Abhidharma. A field of study and its texts that contain detailed reworkings of material in the Buddhist sūtras according to schematic classifications.

access. See *preparatory stages for a dhyāna*.

access concentration (P. *upacāra samādhi*). A level of concentration that prepares the mind to enter the next actual dhyāna.

actual dhyāna (T. *bsam gten gyi dngos gzhi*). A more refined dhyānic concentration attained upon completing its preparatory stages.

afflictions (*kleśa*). Mental factors that disturb the tranquility of the mind. These include disturbing emotions and wrong views.

afflictive obscurations (*kleśāvaraṇa*). Obscurations that mainly prevent liberation; afflictions and their seeds.

aggregates (*skandha*). The four or five components that make up a living being: form (except for beings born in the formless realm), feelings, discriminations, miscellaneous factors, and consciousnesses.

arhat. Someone who has eliminated all afflictive obscurations and attained liberation.

ārya (P. *ariya*). Someone who has directly and nonconceptually realized the emptiness of inherent existence; someone who is on the path of seeing, meditation, or no-more-learning.

basis of designation. The collection of parts or factors in dependence on which an object is designated.

bodhicitta. A main mental consciousness induced by an aspiration to bring about others' welfare and accompanied by an aspiration to attain full awakening oneself. It marks entry into the Mahāyāna.

bodhisattva. Someone who has genuine bodhicitta.

bodhisattva ground. A consciousness in the continuum of an ārya bodhisattva characterized by wisdom and compassion. It is the basis for the development of good qualities and the basis for the eradication of ignorance and mistaken appearances.

buddha. All aspects of a buddha. It includes the four buddha bodies.

Buddhadharma. The teachings of the Buddha.

cognitive obscurations (*jñeyāvaraṇa*). Obscurations that mainly prevent full awakening; the latencies of ignorance and the subtle dualistic view that they give rise to.

collection of merit (*puṇyasaṃbhāra*). A bodhisattva's practice of the method aspect of the path that accumulates merit and is the main cause for a buddha's form body.

collection of wisdom (*jñānasaṃbhāra*). In the wisdom aspect of the path, a Mahāyāna exalted knower that focuses on the ultimate truth, emptiness, and is the main cause for a buddha's truth body.

collections (requisites, *sambhāra*, T. *tshogs*). A bodhisattva's practice of method and wisdom that leads to full awakening.

concentration (*samādhi*). A mental factor that dwells single-pointedly for a sustained period of time on one object; a state of deep meditative absorption; single-pointed concentration that is free from discursive thought.

concomitant (T. *mtshungs ldan*). Accompanying or occurring together in the same mental state.

consciousness (*jñāna*). That which is clear and cognizant.

conventional existence (*saṃvṛtisat*). Existence.

conventional truths (*saṃvṛtisatya*). That which is true only from the perspective of grasping true existence. It includes all phenomena except ultimate truths. Syn. *veiled truths*.

counterpart sign (P. *paṭibhāga-nimitta*). The meditation object of a dhyāna consciousness; a conceptual object that arises on the basis of a visible object.

cyclic existence (*saṃsāra*). The cycle of rebirth that occurs under the control of afflictions and karma.

death (*maraṇabhava*). The last moment of a lifetime when the subtlest clear-light mind manifests.

defilement (*mala*, T. *dri ma*). Either an afflictive obscuration or a cognitive obscuration.

deity (*iṣṭadevatā*, T. *yi dam*). A manifestation of the awakened mind that is meditated on in Tantra.

deity yoga. A meditation practice that involves uniting one's mind with the realizations of a meditation deity.

dependent arising (*pratītyasamutpāda*). This is of three types: (1) causal dependence—things arising due to causes and conditions, (2) mutual dependence—phenomena existing in relation to other phenomena, and (3) dependent designation—phenomena existing by being merely designated by terms and concepts.

desire realm (*kāmadhātu*). One of the three realms of cyclic existence; the realm where sentient beings are overwhelmed by attraction to and desire for sense objects.

deva. A being born as a heavenly being in the desire realm or a being born in the form or formless realm.

dhyāna (P. *jhāna*). A meditative absorption of the form realm.

dualistic appearance. The appearance of subject and object as separate, the appearance of inherent existence, the appearance of conventional phenomena (to a sentient being).

duḥkha (P. *dukkha*). Unsatisfactory experiences of cyclic existence.

duḥkha of change. The unsatisfactory situation of the instability and changing nature of what is pleasant.

duḥkha of pain. Evident physical and mental pain.

Dzogchen. A tantric practice emphasizing meditation on the nature of mind, practiced primarily in the Nyingma tradition.

eight worldly concerns (*aṣṭalokadharma*). Attachment or aversion regarding material gain and loss, fame and disrepute, praise and blame, pleasure and pain.

emanation body (*nirmāṇakāya*). The buddha body that appears to ordinary sentient beings in order to benefit others.

emptiness (*śūnyatā*). The lack of inherent existence, lack of independent existence.

enjoyment body (*saṃbhogakāya*). The buddha body that appears in the highest pure lands to teach ārya bodhisattvas.

establishments of mindfulness (*smṛtyupasthāna*, *satipaṭṭhāna*, T. *dran pa nyer bzhag*). One of the seven sets of practices comprising the thirty-seven harmonies with awakening. It focuses mindfulness on the body, feelings, mind, and phenomena.

exalted knower (*jñāna*, T. *mkhyen pa*). A realization of someone who has entered a path. It exists from the path of accumulation to the buddha ground. Exalted knower, path, ground, and clear realization are mutually inclusive terms.

extreme of absolutism (eternalism or permanence, *śāśvatānta*). The belief that phenomena inherently exist.

extreme of nihilism (*ucchedānta*). The belief that our actions have no ethical dimension; the belief that nothing exists.

fetters (*saṃyojana*). Factors that keep us bound to cyclic existence and impede the attainment of liberation. The five lower fetters—view of a personal identity, deluded doubt, view of rules and practices, sensual desire, and malice—bind us to rebirth in the desire realm. The five higher fetters—desire for existence in the form realm, desire for existence in the formless realm, arrogance, restlessness, and ignorance—prevent a nonreturner from becoming an arhat.

five dhyānic factors. Investigation (*vitarka*, *vitakka*), analysis (*vicāra*), joy (*prīti*, *pīti*), bliss (*sukha*), and one-pointedness of mind (*ekāgratā*, *ekaggatā*).

five heinous crimes (*ānantārya*). Killing one's mother, father, or an arhat, wounding a buddha, and causing schism in the saṅgha.

five hindrances (*āvaraṇa*, T. *sgrib pa lnga*). Hindrances that interfere with attaining serenity: sensual desire (*kāmacchanda*), malice (*vyāpāda, byāpāda*), lethargy and sleepiness (*styāna-middha, thīna-middha*), restlessness and regret (*auddhatya-kaukṛtya, uddhacca-kukkucca*), and deluded doubt (*vicikitsā, vicikicchā*).

form body (*rūpakāya*). The buddha body in which a buddha appears to sentient beings; it includes the emanation and enjoyment bodies.

form realm (*rūpadhātu*). A realm in saṃsāra in which the beings have subtle bodies; they are born there by having attained various states of concentration.

formless realm (*ārūpyadhātu*). The realm in saṃsāra in which sentient beings do not have a material body and abide in deep states of concentration.

fortitude of the nonarising of phenomena (*anutpattika-dharma-kṣānti*, T. *mi skye ba'i chos la bzod pa*). A special realization of emptiness and nonduality by bodhisattvas that makes them irreversible on the path to full awakening.

four fearlessnesses. The Tathāgata is completely confident and lacks all fear in declaring that (1) he is fully awakened regarding all phenomena, (2) he has destroyed all pollutants, (3) he has correctly identified all obstructions to be eliminated on the path, and (4) when practiced, his teachings lead to the complete destruction of duḥkha.

four opponent powers. Four points to purify destructive karma. These are regret, generating bodhicitta and taking refuge, engaging in a remedial action, and making a determination not to do the harmful action again. See chapter 10 of *The Foundation of Buddhist Practice*.

four truths of the āryas (*catvāry āryasatyāni*). The truth of duḥkha, its origin, its cessation, and the path to that cessation.

four ways of gathering or assembling (*saṃgrahavastu, saṅgahavatthu*, T. *bsdu ba'i dngos po bzhi*). (1) being generous and giving material aid, (2) speaking pleasantly, (3) encouraging disciples to practice, and (4) acting congruently and living the teachings through example.

full awakening (*samyaksaṃbodhi*). Buddhahood; the state where all obscurations have been abandoned and all good qualities developed limitlessly.

fundamental innate mind of clear light (T. *gnyug ma lhan cig skyes pa'i 'od gsal gyi sems*). The subtlest level of mind.

Fundamental Vehicle. The vehicle leading to the liberation of śrāvakas and solitary realizers.

gāthās. Short verses or lines extracted from sūtras or written by great masters that steer our mind to a virtuous state.

god (*deva*). A being born as a heavenly being in the desire realm or in the form or formless realms.

grasping inherent existence (*svabhāvagraha*). Grasping persons and phenomena to exist truly or inherently; syn. *grasping true existence*.

grasping true existence (*satyagrāha*). See *grasping inherent existence*.

ground (bhūmi). A path. Ten bodhisattva grounds span the bodhisattva paths of seeing and meditation.

harmonies with awakening (*bodhipākṣya-dharma, bodhipakkhiya-dhamma*). Thirty-seven practices condensed into seven sets that lead to liberation and awakening.

hell being (*nāraka*). A being born in an unfortunate realm of intense physical pain due to strong destructive karma.

highest yoga tantra (*anuttarayogatantra*). The most advanced of the four classes of tantra.

hungry ghost (*preta*). A being born in one of the unfortunate realms who suffers from intense hunger and thirst.

ignorance (*avidyā*). A mental factor that is obscured and grasps the opposite of what exists. There are two types: ignorance regarding ultimate truth and ignorance regarding karma and its effects.

impermanent (*anitya, anicca*). Momentary; not remaining unchanged in the next moment.

inferential cognizer (*anumāna*). A mind that ascertains its object by means of a correct reason.

inherent existence (*svabhāva*). Existence without depending on any other factors; independent existence.

insight (*vipaśyanā*, *vipassanā*, T. *lhag mthong*). A wisdom of thorough discrimination of phenomena conjoined with special pliancy induced by the power of analysis.

introspective awareness (*saṃprajanya*, *sampajañña*). An intelligence that causes one to engage in activities of body, speech, or mind heedfully.

invariable karma. Propelling karma that is the cause for rebirth in a specific level in the form or formless realm and no other.

karma. Intentional (volitional) action; it includes intention karma (mental action) and intended karma (physical and verbal actions motivated by intention).

karmic seeds. The potencies from previously created actions that will bring their results.

latencies (*vāsanā*). Predispositions, imprints, or tendencies.

liberation (*mokṣa*, T. *thar pa*). A true cessation that is the abandonment of afflictive obscurations; nirvāṇa, the state of freedom from cyclic existence.

liberation (*vimukti*, *vimutti*, T. *rnam grol*). Sanskrit tradition: complete freedom from saṃsāra; Pāli tradition: a conditioned event that brings nirvāṇa.

liberation of mind by love (P. *mettā cetovimutti*). A mind genuinely wishing all beings to be happy that has temporarily abandoned the five hindrances, especially anger and malice, through the force of concentration.

Madhyamaka. A Mahāyāna tenet system that refutes true existence.

Mahāmudrā. A type of meditation that focuses on the conventional and ultimate natures of the mind.

meditative equipoise on emptiness. An ārya's mind focused directly and single-pointedly on the emptiness of inherent existence.

mental consciousness (*mano-vijñāna*, *mano-viññāṇa*). A primary consciousness that knows mental phenomena in contradistinction to sense primary consciousnesses that know physical objects.

mental contemplation (*manaskāra, manasikāra*, T. *yid la byed pa*). A mind that meditates on either grossness and subtleness or on the four truths in order to attain either the dhyānas or the union of serenity and insight on emptiness.

mental factor (*caitta, cetasika*). An aspect of mind that accompanies a primary consciousness and fills out the cognition, apprehending particular attributes of the object or performing a specific function.

mind (*citta*, T. *sems*). That which is clear and cognizant; the part of living beings that cognizes, experiences, thinks, feels, and so on. In some contexts it is equivalent to primary consciousness.

mindfulness (*smṛti, sati*). A mental factor that brings to mind a phenomenon of previous acquaintance without forgetting it and prevents distraction to other objects.

mindstream (*cittasaṃtāna, cittasantāna*). The continuity of mind.

momentary (*kṣaṇika*). Not enduring to the next moment.

monastic. Someone who has received monastic ordination; a monk or nun.

nature truth body (*svabhāvika dharmakāya*). The buddha body that is the emptiness of a buddha's mind and that buddha's true cessations.

nimitta. The sign or mental image that is the object for cultivating serenity. It is of three types: the preliminary, learning, and counterpart nimittas.

nine stages of sustained attention (*navākārā cittasthiti*, T. *sems gnas dgu*). Stages of concentration on the way to attaining serenity.

nirvāṇa. The state of liberation of an arhat; the purified aspect of a mind that is free from afflictions.

nirvāṇa without remainder (*anupadhiśeṣa-nirvāṇa, anupādisesa-nibbāna*). (1) The state of liberation when an arhat has passed away and no longer has the remainder of the polluted aggregates. (2) An ārya's meditative equipoise on emptiness when there is no appearance of true existence.

nonabiding nirvāṇa (*apratiṣṭha-nirvāṇa*). The nirvāṇa of a buddha that does not abide in either the extreme of saṃsāra or the extreme of personal peace of a śrāvaka's nirvāṇa.

nondeceptive (*avisaṃvādi*). Incontrovertible, correct.

nonexistent (*asat*). That which is not perceivable by mind.

object (*viṣaya*, *visaya*, T. *yul*). That which is known by an awareness.

object of negation (*pratiṣedhya,* T. *dgag bya*). Something that appears to our mind, which in fact is nonexistent and is to be negated or refuted.

observed object (*ālambana*, *ārammaṇa*, T. *dmigs pa*). The basic object that the mind refers to or focuses on while apprehending certain aspects of that object.

one final vehicle. The belief that all beings—even śrāvakas who have become arhats—will eventually enter the Mahāyāna and become buddhas.

ordinary being (*pṛthagjana*, *puthujjana*, T. *so so skye bo*). Someone who is not an ārya.

path (*mārga*, *magga*, T. *lam*). An exalted knower that is conjoined with uncontrived renunciation.

path of accumulation (*sambhāramārga*, T. *tshogs lam*). First of the five paths. It begins when one aspires for liberation day and night for a śrāvaka path, or when one has spontaneous bodhicitta for the Mahāyāna path.

path of meditation (*bhāvanāmārga*, T. *sgom lam*). Fourth of the five paths. It begins when a meditator begins to eradicate innate afflictions from the root.

path of no-more-learning (*aśaikṣamārga*, T. *mi slob lam*). The last of the five paths; arhatship or buddhahood.

path of preparation (*prayogamārga*, T. *sbyor lam*). Second of the five paths. It begins when a meditator attains the union of serenity and insight on emptiness.

path of seeing (*darśanamārga*, T. *mthong lam*). Third of the five paths. It begins when a meditator first has direct, nonconceptual realization of the emptiness of inherent existence.

permanent (*nitya*, *nicca*, T. *rtag pa*). Unchanging, static in nature. It does not mean eternal.

permanent, unitary, independent self. A soul or self (*ātman*) asserted by non-Buddhists.

permission (T. *jenang).* A meditative ceremony in which the recipient receives the inspiration of an awakened deity's body, speech, and mind.

person (*pudgala, puggala*, T. *gang zag*). A being designated in dependence on the four or five aggregates.

pervasive duḥkha of conditioning. Taking the five aggregates under the influence of afflictions and polluted karma. This is the basis of the duḥkha of pain and the duḥkha of change.

pliancy (tranquility, *praśrabdhi, passaddhi*). A mental factor that enables the mind to apply itself to a constructive object in whatever manner it wishes and dissipates mental or physical rigidity.

polluted (contaminated, *āsrava*, *āsava*, T. *zag pa*). Under the influence of ignorance or its latencies.

Prāsaṅgika. The Buddhist philosophical tenet system that asserts that all phenomena lack inherent existence both conventionally and ultimately.

prātimokṣa. The different sets of ethical precepts for monastics and lay followers that assist in attaining liberation.

preliminary practices. (1) Meditating on important initial stages of the path, such as precious human life, death and impermanence, karma and its effects, and the defects of saṃsāra. (2) In the context of tantra, practices that purify negativities and collect merit, such as taking refuge, reciting the names of the buddhas and prostrating to them, making offerings, reciting the mantra of Vajrasattva, guru yoga, and so on.

preparatory stages for a dhyāna (access, preparations, *sāmantaka*, T. *bsam gtan gyi nyer bsdogs*). Stages of meditation that prepare the mind to enter an actual dhyāna.

primary consciousness (*vijñāna*). A consciousness that apprehends the presence or basic entity of an object. There are six types of primary consciousness: visual, auditory, olfactory, gustatory, tactile, and mental.

probing awareness (reasoning consciousness, *yuktijñāna*, T. *rigs shes*). A consciousness using or having used reasoning to analyze the ultimate nature of an object. It can be either conceptual or nonconceptual.

pure lands. Places created by the unshakable resolve and merit of buddhas where all external conditions are conducive for Dharma practice.

realized Dharma. The realizations in a person's mindstream.

sādhana. The means of achievement expressed in a tantric text or manual that details the steps of visualization and meditation in the practice of a deity.

samādhi. See *concentration*.

saṃsāra. (1) Constantly recurring rebirth under the control of afflictions and polluted karma. (2) The five aggregates of a person who has taken rebirth in this way.

Sautrāntika. A Fundamental Vehicle tenet system that asserts that functional things are ultimate truths and phenomena that exist by being imputed by thought are conventional truths.

self (*ātman*, *attan*, T. *bdag*). (1) Conventional I, the person, (2) independent I that does not exist, (3) inherent existence.

self-grasping (*ātmagrāha*, *attagaha*, T. *bdag 'dzin*). Grasping inherent existence.

self-sufficient substantially existent person (T. *gang zag rang rkya thub pa'i rdzas yod*). A person that can be identified independent of the aggregates. Such a self does not exist.

sentient being (*sattva*, *satta*, T. *sems can*). Any being that has a mind and is not a buddha.

serenity (*śamatha*, *śamatha*, T. *zhi gnas*). Sanskrit tradition: concentration arisen from meditation that is accompanied by the bliss of mental and physical pliancy in which the mind abides effortlessly without fluctuation for as long as we wish on whatever virtuous or neutral object it has been placed. Pāli tradition: one-pointedness of mind; the eight attainments (meditative absorptions) that are the basis for insight.

six perfections (*ṣaḍpāramitā*, T. *phar phyin drug*). The practices of generosity, ethical conduct, fortitude, joyous effort, meditative stability, and wisdom that are motivated by bodhicitta.

solitary realizer (*pratyekabuddha*, *paccekabuddha*, T. *rang sangs rgyas*). A person following the Fundamental Vehicle who seeks liberation, emphasizes understanding the twelve links of dependent arising, and pursues their practice without teachings from a master in their last lifetime before becoming an arhat.

sphere of three. The agent, object, and action.

śrāvaka (hearer, P. *sāvaka*, T. *nyan thos*). Someone practicing the Fundamental Vehicle path leading to arhatship who emphasizes meditation on the four truths.

stabilizing meditation (*sthāpyabhāvanā*, T. *'jog sgom*). Meditation to focus and concentrate the mind on an object.

stages of the path to awakening (T. *lam rim*). A systematic presentation or sequential practice of the steps of the path to awakening found in Tibetan Buddhism.

subjective aspect (*ākāra*, T. *rnam pa*). The way that a mind engages with its object.

substantial cause (*upādāna-kāraṇa*, T. *nyer len gyi rgyu*). The cause that becomes the result, as opposed to cooperative causes that aid the substantial cause in becoming the result.

subtle latencies. Latencies of ignorance and other afflictions that are cognitive obscurations that prevent simultaneous cognition of the two truths.

superknowledge (*abhijñā*, *abhiññā*, T. *mngon shes*). Direct, experiential knowledge, of six types: (1) supernormal powers, (2) divine ear, (3) knowledge of others' minds, (4) recollection of past lives, (5) divine eye (includes knowledge of the passing away and re-arising of beings and knowledge of the future), and (6) the destruction of the pollutants. The sixth is attained only by liberated beings.

supernormal powers (*ṛddhi*, *iddhi*, T. *rdzu 'phrul*). The first of the six superknowledges, gained in deep samādhi: to replicate one's body, appear and disappear, pass through solid objects, go under the earth, walk on water, fly, touch the sun and moon with one's hand, go to the Brahmā world, and so forth.

supramundane (transcendental, *lokottara*, *lokottara*, T. *'jig rten las 'das pa*). Pertaining to the elimination of fetters and afflictions; pertaining to āryas.

taking and giving (literally giving and taking, T. *gtong len*). A meditation practice for cultivating compassion and love that involves visualizing taking others' suffering, using it to destroy our self-centered attitude, and giving our body, possessions, and merit to others.

tathāgata. A buddha.

ten powers. Qualities found only in a buddha. The ten powers are knowing (1) what is possible and impossible, (2) the ripening result of all actions, (3) the paths leading to all destinations, (4) the world with its many different elements, (5) the inclinations of sentient beings, (6) the faculties of sentient beings, (7) the meditative stabilizations and absorptions, (8) past lives, (9) sentient beings passing away and being reborn, and (10) liberation and full awakening.

tenet (*siddhānta*, T. *grub mtha'*). A philosophical principle or belief.

thirty-seven harmonies with awakening. Thirty-seven qualities and practices that śrāvakas, solitary realizers, and bodhisattvas cultivate. See chapters 12–14 in *Following in the Buddha's Footsteps*.

thought (*kalpanā*, T. *rtog pa*). Conceptual consciousness.

three characteristics. Impermanence, duḥkha, and no-self.

three realms (*tridhātuka*, *tedhātuka*, T. *khams gsum*). Desire, form, and formless realms.

transmitted (scriptural) Dharma. The words and meanings of the Buddha's teachings in the form of speech and scriptures.

true cessation (*nirodhasatya*). The cessation of a portion of afflictions or a portion of cognitive obscurations.

true existence (*satyasat*). Existence having its own mode of being; existence having its own reality.

truth body (*dharmakāya*, T. *chos sku*). The buddha body that includes the nature truth body and the wisdom truth body.

twelve links of dependent origination (*dvādaśāṅga-pratītyasamutpāda*). A system of twelve factors that explains how we take rebirth in saṃsāra and how we can be liberated from it.

two truths (*satyadvaya*). Ultimate truths and veiled (conventional) truths.

ultimate nature. The ultimate or deepest mode of existence of persons and phenomena; emptiness.

ultimate truth (*paramārthasatya*). The ultimate mode of existence of all persons and phenomena; emptiness.

unfortunate realm (*apāya*). Unfortunate state of rebirth as a hell being, hungry ghost, or animal.

union of serenity and insight. Absorption in which the bliss of mental and physical pliancy has been induced by analysis.

unpolluted (*anāsrava*). Not under the influence of ignorance.

Vajrasattva. A meditation deity whose practice is especially powerful to purify destructive karmic seeds and other defilements.

veiled truths (*saṃvṛtisatya*). Objects that appear true to ignorance, which is a veiling consciousness; objects that appear to exist inherently to their main cognizer, although they do not; syn. *conventional truths.*

view of a personal identity (view of a [distorted] personal identity based on the transitory collection, *satkāyadṛṣṭi, sakkāyadiṭṭh,* T. *'jig lta*). Grasping an inherently existent I or mine (according to the Prāsaṅgika system).

Vinaya. Monastic discipline; a body of texts about monastic life, discipline, and conduct.

wind (*prāṇa*, T. *rlung*). One of the four elements; energy in the body that influences bodily functions; subtle energy on which levels of consciousness ride.

wisdom truth body (*jñāna dharmakāya*). The buddha body that is a buddha's omniscient mind.

Yogācāra (*Cittamātra*). A Buddhist philosophical tenet system asserting that objects and the consciousnesses perceiving them arise from the same substantial cause, a seed on the foundation consciousness, and that the mind is truly existent.

Recommended Reading

Aronson, Harvey B. *Love and Sympathy in Theravāda Buddhism*. Delhi: Motilal Banarsidass, 1996.

Chang, Garma C. C., ed. *A Treasury of Mahāyāna Sūtras: Selections from the Mahāratnakūta Sūtra*. University Park: The Pennsylvania State University Press, 1983.

Chodron, Thubten. *Don't Believe Everything You Think*. Boston: Snow Lion Publications, 2012.

———. *Good Karma: How to Create the Causes for Happiness and Avoid the Causes of Suffering*. Boston: Shambhala Publications, 2016.

———. *Working with Anger*. Ithaca, NY: Snow Lion Publications, 2001.

Dagpo Lama Rinpoche. *The Bodhisattva Vows: A Practical Guide to the Sublime Ethics of the Mahāyāna*. Seri Kembangan, Malaysia: E Publication Sdn. Bhd., 2007.

Dharmamitra, Bhikṣu, trans. *On Generating the Resolve to Become a Buddha*. Seattle: Kalavinka Press, 2009.

Dudjom Rinpoche. *Perfect Conduct: Ascertaining the Three Vows*. Ithaca, NY: Snow Lion Publications, 1999.

Goodman, Charles. *The Training Anthology of Śāntideva: A Translation of the Śikṣā-samuccaya*. New York: Oxford University Press, 2016.

Gyaltsap. *The Yogic Deeds of Bodhisattvas: Gyal-tsap on Āryadeva's "Four Hundred."* Commentary by Geshe Sonam Rinchen. Translated and edited by Ruth Sonam. Ithaca, NY: Snow Lion Publications, 1994.

Gyaltsen, Sakya Drakpa. *Chandragomin's Twenty Verses on the Bodhisattva Vow*. Dharamsala: Library of Tibetan Works and Archives, 2002.

Gyatso, Tenzin (Fourteenth Dalai Lama). *An Open Heart: Practicing Com-*

passion in Everyday Life. Edited by Nicholas Vreeland. New York: Little, Brown and Company, 2011.

———. *Beyond Religion: Ethics for a Whole World*. New York: Houghton Mifflin Harcourt, 2011.

———. *The Four Noble Truths*. Translated by Geshe Thupten Jinpa. Edited by Dominique Side. London: Thorsons, 1997.

———. *The Good Heart: A Buddhist Perspective on the Teachings of Jesus*. Boston: Wisdom Publications, 1996, 2016.

———. *Healing Anger: The Power of Patience from a Buddhist Perspective*. Ithaca, NY: Snow Lion Publications, 1997.

———. *How to Expand Love: Widening the Circle of Loving Relationships*. Translated and edited by Jeffrey Hopkins. New York: Atria Books, 2005.

———. *How to See Yourself As You Really Are*. Translated and edited by Jeffrey Hopkins. New York: Atria Books, 2007.

———. *Transforming the Mind: Teachings on Generating Compassion*. London: Thorsons, 2000.

Gyatso, Tenzin (Fourteenth Dalai Lama), and Howard C. Cutler, M.D. *The Art of Happiness: A Handbook for Living*. New York: Riverhead Books, 1998.

Gyatso, Tenzin (Fourteenth Dalai Lama), and Thubten Chodron. *Buddhism: One Teacher, Many Traditions*. Somerville, MA: Wisdom Publications, 2014.

Gyeltsen, Jaydzun Chögyi, and Guy Newland. *Compassion: A Tibetan Analysis*. Boston: Wisdom Publications, 1984.

Hopkins, Jeffrey, trans. *Compassion in Tibetan Buddhism*. By Tsong-ka-pa. Ithaca, NY: Snow Lion Publications, 1980.

———. *Cultivating Compassion*. New York: Broadway Books, 2001.

———. *Meditation on Emptiness*. Boston: Wisdom Publications, 1996.

Horner, I. B., trans. *Chronicle of Buddhas (Buddhavaṃsa) and Basket of Conduct (Cariyāpiṭaka)*. In *The Minor Anthologies of the Pāli Canon*, vol. 3. London: Pāli Text Society, 2007 [1975].

Jinpa, Thupten, trans. *Essential Mind Training*. Boston: Wisdom Publications, 2011.

———. *Mind Training: The Great Collection*. The Library of Tibetan Classics 1. Boston: Wisdom Publications, 2006.

Kolts, Russell, and Thubten Chodron. *An Open-Hearted Life: Transformative Methods for Compassionate Living from a Clinical Psychologist and a Buddhist Nun*. Boston: Shambhala Publications, 2015.

Pabongka Rinpoche. *Liberation in the Palm of Your Hand.* Translated by Michael Richards. Edited by Trijang Rinpoche. Boston: Wisdom Publications, 2006.

Rinchen, Geshe Sonam, and Ruth Sonam. *Eight Verses for Training the Mind.* Ithaca, NY: Snow Lion Publications, 2001.

———. *The Bodhisattva Vow.* Ithaca, NY: Snow Lion Publications, 2000.

Sharma, Parmananda, trans. *Bhāvanākrama of Kamalaśila.* Delhi: Pradeep Kumar Goel for Aditya Prakashan, 1997.

Sopa, Geshe Lhundub, with Michael Sweet and Leonard Zwilling. *Peacock in the Poison Grove: Two Buddhist Texts on Training the Mind.* Boston: Wisdom Publications, 1996.

Tegchok, Geshe Jampa. *Transforming Adversity into Joy and Courage.* Ithaca, NY: Snow Lion Publications, 2005.

Yeshe, Lama. *Life, Death, and After Death.* Boston: Lama Yeshe Wisdom Archive, 2011.

Index

R

T

U

V

W

Y

Z

About the Authors

The Dalai Lama is the spiritual leader of the Tibetan people, a Nobel Peace Prize recipient, and an advocate for compassion and peace throughout the world. He promotes harmony among the world's religions and engages in dialogue with leading scientists. Ordained as a Buddhist monk when he was a child, he completed the traditional monastic studies and earned his geshe degree (equivalent to a PhD). Renowned for his erudite and open-minded scholarship, his meditative attainments, and his humility, Bhikṣu Tenzin Gyatso says, "I am a simple Buddhist monk."

Peter Aronson

Bhikṣuṇī Thubten Chodron has been a Buddhist nun since 1977. Growing up in Los Angeles, she graduated with honors in history from the University of California at Los Angeles and did graduate work in education at the University of Southern California. After years studying and teaching Buddhism in Asia, Europe, and the United States, she became the founder and abbess of Sravasti Abbey in Washington State. A popular speaker for her practical explanations of how to apply Buddhist teachings in daily life, she is the author of several books on Buddhism, including *Buddhism for Beginners*. She is the editor of Khensur Jampa Tegchok's *Insight into Emptiness*. For more information, visit sravastiabbey.org and thubtenchodron.org.

Also Available from the Dalai Lama and Wisdom Publications

Buddhism
One Teacher, Many Traditions

The Compassionate Life

Ecology, Ethics, and Interdependence
The Dalai Lama in Conversation with Leading Thinkers on Climate Change

Essence of the Heart Sutra
The Dalai Lama's Heart of Wisdom Teachings

The Essence of Tsongkhapa's Teachings
The Dalai Lama on the Three Principal Aspects of the Path

The Good Heart
A Buddhist Perspective on the Teachings of Jesus

Imagine All the People
A Conversation with the Dalai Lama on Money, Politics, and Life as It Could Be

Kalachakra Tantra
Rite of Initiation

The Life of My Teacher
A Biography of Kyabjé Ling Rinpoche

Meditation on the Nature of Mind

The Middle Way
Faith Grounded in Reason

Mind in Comfort and Ease
The Vision of Enlightenment in the Great Perfection

MindScience
An East-West Dialogue

Opening the Eye of New Awareness

Practicing Wisdom
The Perfection of Shantideva's Bodhisattva Way

Science and Philosophy in the Indian Buddhist Classics, vol. 1
The Physical World

Sleeping, Dreaming, and Dying
An Exploration of Consciousness

The Wheel of Life
Buddhist Perspectives on Cause and Effect

The World of Tibetan Buddhism
An Overview of Its Philosophy and Practice

Also Available from Thubten Chodron

Insight into Emptiness
Khensur Jampa Tegchok
Edited and introduced by Thubten Chodron

"One of the best introductions to the philosophy of emptiness I have ever read."—José Ignacio Cabezón

Practical Ethics and Profound Emptines
A Commentary on Nagarjuna's Precious Garland
Khensur Jampa Tegchok
Edited by Thubten Chodron

"A beautifully clear translation and systematic explanation of Nagarjuna's most accessible and wide-ranging work. Dharma students everywhere will benefit from careful attention to its pages."
—Guy Newland, author of *Introduction to Emptiness*

Awakening Every Day
365 Buddhist Reflections to Invite Mindfulness and Joy

Buddhism for Beginners

The Compassionate Kitchen

Cultivating a Compassionate Heart
The Yoga Method of Chenrezig

Don't Believe Everything You Think
Living with Wisdom and Compassion

Guided Meditations on the Stages of the Path

How to Free Your Mind
Tara the Liberator

Living with an Open Heart
How to Cultivate Compassion in Daily Life

Open Heart, Clear Mind

Taming the Mind

Working with Anger

About Wisdom Publications